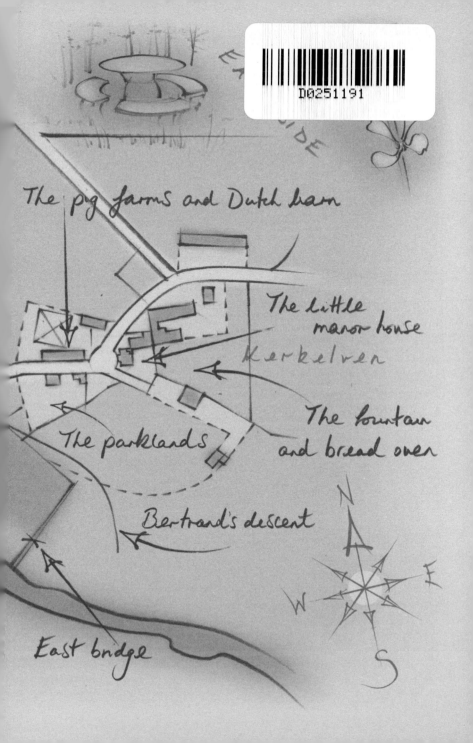

the
Field
by the
River

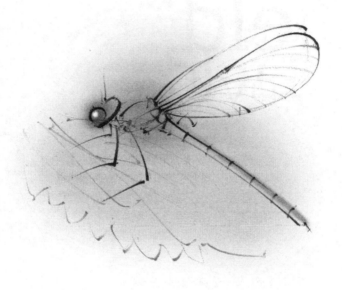

'Vision is the art of seeing the invisible'
Jonathan Swift

the
Field
by the
River

Uncovering the nature of
country life

Ken Burnett

PORTICO

First published in the United Kingdom in 2008 by
Portico Books
10 Southcombe Street
London
W14 0RA

An imprint of Anova Books Company Ltd

ISBN 9781906032326

A CIP catalogue for this book is available from the British Library.

10 9 8 7 6 5 4 3 2 1

Reproduction by SX Composing DTP, Rayleigh, Essex
Printed and bound by CPI Mackays, Chatham, ME5 8TD

This book can be ordered direct from the publisher.
Contact the marketing department, but try your bookshop first.

www.anovabooks.com

Contents

Introduction

Prepare to enter the field by the river

From certain perspectives it's not much, this field. Viewed from a satellite out in space it would barely register. It doesn't appear on any but a few maps of the area and looks unappealing on those where it does. In the totality of the French landscape it is a mere speck, not significant in any way. There are thousands of other fields like it. Maybe millions.

At first glance – usually all it gets – it's just an ordinary, apparently empty field like any other among all the empty, or near empty, fields around here and across France and the rest of the world. Prone to flooding where it's flat, and unproductively hilly and overgrown everywhere else, a farmer would dismiss it out of hand. You may think it undeniably picturesque, even pretty, as you drive past, but not worth stopping for more than a toilet break, or perhaps a picnic lunch if you can find a way to get in. 'Thank God for fields,' you might silently proclaim if you were particularly sensitive, or desperately in need of the loo, or feeling more than usually generous and observant as you drive by. But you miss a lot when you pass a field like this in casual haste because, as you will see, despite contrary appearances this field is far from empty, far from ordinary.

What kind of a story is this?

It's perhaps easier to say what it's not. It's not a nature story, although nature is everywhere throughout it. It's not really about the countryside, that's just where it's set, though it is, in a way, a countryside companion. It's not about rural living, farming or hunting, though country folk, farmers and hunters all appear in it. It's not (much) about expatriates living in France and it isn't a lifestyle guide, though it does feature thousands, even millions, of real lives. It's not a voyage of discovery because although I've made lots of discoveries in and around the field, my voyages here have been tiny and most of my discoveries have already been made, often and by others, long before me. It's not a story of exploration, because throughout the year in question I've been lucky enough, most of the time, to stay at home. And while at times I've strayed into new, unknown territories, such explorations as there have been were more about exploring myself than anything.

It is though, I hope, a tale laced with adventure, a narrative chock-full of surprises. It aspires to do nothing more than to delight, entertain and inform you. For surely those three count among the most useful and valuable of all things and, hopefully, the most enjoyable. For more than a decade the field by the river has been a constant source of new experiences, insights, enchantments and delights for me, so I hope that through this book I can share these delights with you without, it has to be said, actually inviting you round for tea. It's not just you, of course; I hope also to share this field with as many other people as I possibly can, even if your and their tastes and interests are wildly different from mine.

But there are already quite enough sober and serious writings on most of the themes covered in this story. So most of the time I've taken a more oblique, even at times irreverent and tongue-in-cheek, stance. Serious and profound though my love of this field is, I wouldn't want anyone to experience and absorb its delights with too straight a face, for that would surely diminish the enjoyment and defeat the point.

The art of really seeing

On its journey this observation of what goes on in one large(ish) field asks and seeks to answer many questions, some significant, some trivial, hopefully all intriguing; Who lives here, and why? What do they do with their time and what does that have to do with the rest of us? Why do frogs and toads migrate when newts and salamanders don't? Are the birds we see territorial residents or passing visitors? Where do robins go in summertime? How do trees work? Are ants clever, or just pre-programmed? What do ducks and herons get up to when they think they're not being watched? What are moles, moths and mushrooms all about? What are we looking at when we gaze up at the stars? What changes might be coming to fields like these and how will those who live here adapt? And what else might we find in our forest if we choose the best time to lift and look under the mosses, part the leaves and overturn some stones?

It pays to be observant here. Most of the other creatures that live in and around this field and its neighbouring hamlet, Kerkelven, from which it takes its name, are only too aware of and watchful of me whenever I am about. Humans may be the top species of all that's yet been found in nature (there may of course be superior beings clever enough to have remained hidden) but our apparent superiority inclines us at times to be complacent, even short-sighted. Too often we of the people species don't really look at what's in front of or around us. So we can too easily overlook the really interesting stuff that is right before our eyes.

That a place of such interest and enjoyment should also be streaked with blood, infused with history, alive with intrigue, complicit in dastardly cover-ups, riddled with secrets and veiled in several unsolved mysteries will not come as much surprise to you, once you have got to know it better.

Both field and forest are just bursting with life. Apart from the human inhabitants countless thousands of other creatures live here, all dependent on a complex, fragile, interconnected ecosystem to survive and thrive. This is no exaggeration or colourful embroidery; the range of residents is extraordinary. Thieves live here, and murderers, fools, dimwits, scolds, misers, noisy and silent types, crawlers, slitherers, scamperers, gliders and flappers, itchers and biters, dribblers and spitters, sociable as well as solitary beings, shy and nervous sorts, geniuses alongside dolts, high achievers and failures, the industrious alongside the lazy, the workers with the wasters, the passive cohabiting with the hyperactive, the meek mingling with the mild, the friendly and the fiercely aggressive all bundled in together . . . They and more all live here together in this field in a delicate, shifting balance, in what for the most part passes for harmony but is often anything but.

This land has been here for centuries, since time began. There are parts of the woodland now where the foliage is so thick even the wildlife can't easily get access, so no human foot has trod there for generations, or longer. What lies hidden there? Who lives there and how do they spend their time?

As one who walks across and around it almost every day the field and the forest by the river are sources of constant mystery and unanswered questions and . . . well . . . equally, who gives a poop? Sometimes the field is just so gorgeous, natural and uncomplicated that it seems plain stupid to be worrying about anything beyond simply revelling in it. After all, life is too short to worry for long. My constant companions as I tour the field, our three dogs Max, Syrus and Mortimer, don't ever ask such questions, for they would simply never occur to them. I don't imagine any of the other creatures who share the field, who live in the woods, grass and river, would ever bother with such things either, even if they could think of them. To the woodpeckers, owls or herons who've made their homes here, or the buzzards, such concerns don't register. Just conceivably a fox might pause to ponder upon it on a particularly bad hunt one night, or a jumpy deer between flights. But the moorhens? Or the ducks? Naaah.

The idea of recording what goes on in this field came to me quite suddenly one day after a surprise encounter with a kingfisher. I bumped into the startled bird while enjoying my daily (well, thrice daily) constitutional, with the dogs tagging along as usual.

Even before I saw him he took off like an arrow from the riverbank, a streak of blue following the course of the river about a metre above its shimmering surface. Then he was gone, almost before I'd realised what I'd seen.

I thought, on meeting that glorious kingfisher, that I would like to share the privilege of such a sight with as many other people as possible. Our encounter lasted no more than six short seconds but I realised then, beyond doubt, that the brief glimpse of perfection that I'd been lucky enough to catch contained all that I knew about this shy, mysterious creature. I was barely aware of the tip of what I should know about such a strikingly beautiful thing.

And I share this place with it!

So I started to wonder why that should be. It dawned on me that, despite living here a full thirteen years, there were hundreds of wonders in my field that I bumped into on a regular basis, yet I knew next to nothing about most of them.

So, a project started to unfold, and quickly grew. You're reading the results of it now. It wasn't an original idea, of course. The seventeenth-century so-called father of modern ecology, the Reverend Gilbert White, had more or less the same idea 250 years before me – or a version of it, at least, which he immortalised in his classic *Natural History of Selbourne*. I did have the idea independently, though, some months before I came across Gilbert in the course of trying to learn a bit more about what goes on in this field.

On glimpsing the kingfisher – and you have to be really quick, believe me – I was stunned. It stopped me where I stood not just because this tiny bird is so beautiful, so delicate, so mysterious, so shy, but because its natural, instinctive action when it saw me was to flee in terror. As soon as it had realised my existence the kingfisher had upped and flown off, so quickly it was little more than a blur.

This upset me, as I'm sure you'll understand.

The encounter took me back to my very first visit to Kerkelven many years earlier, when with family in tow I came to look at a house that we might buy in the middle of tranquil rural Brittany, in the northwest corner of France.

It was about noon on a very hot, high-summer day. I'd already more or less decided that the near ruin we'd just looked over wasn't at all suitable (too much work, endlessly expensive, right next to a pig farm, too big, etc.) when, dragging my two small children reluctantly in my wake, I decided to take a look around down by the nearby river. Being bigger and better equipped than sons Joe and Charlie for wading through long grass, I was comfortably in the lead as I mounted the overgrown riverbank and . . . stopped dead in my tracks. I stood motionless, transfixed, with my flapping hand reaching behind me to silence the kids as one after the other they piled noisily into me. But the object of my fixation, a male otter standing fully upright on his hind legs in mid-river, just stayed motionless where he was, looking inquisitively but fearlessly at me. It was the first time I'd ever seen an otter in the wild and I've only seen them once since, playing and swimming under the big bridge downstream. I think it was the otter's first experience of its kind too, but I doubt if he treasures the moment as I do.

I've never forgotten the magic of that encounter. I think it played a major part in the backtracking I was to do later, as we reversed our first decision on the house.

So, I've mentioned a couple of the surprising creatures with whom I share this field. There are many others. Like the kingfisher and the otter, they're also mostly very shy and quite hard even to see, far less to get to know.

The experience with the kingfisher woke in me the realisation that, though I'd made my home in the countryside some years before, I really didn't know it well at all. I saw that, quite apart from integrating successfully (well, partially at least) with the local human community, there was a whole natural community on my doorstep that I'd barely encountered, far less learned to understand and appreciate. So, during the year covered by this project, I've set out by various means to change that. It has been an amazing, illuminating, delightful experience.

There are other delights here too, in the abundance of produce that comes along each year in this field – the annual harvest of apples and pears, the chestnuts, hazelnuts and the extraordinary variety of mushrooms that grow spontaneously here. I might have a hard time living off this land, at least at first, but many other species both survive and thrive here, the field catering for their every need.

I've learned a lot in this field, more perhaps in the last year than in the preceding thirteen. My view of it is quite different now. I confess there was a time, not very long ago, when I was so wrapped up in myself and what I was doing that I wouldn't have noticed half of the things that I now see in this field, that have become so important to me. When, if I'd seen a hoopoe at Kerkelven, it probably wouldn't have registered. When, if I'd stumbled upon a nettle mite, I'd have viewed it just as one more bug in my bug-infested field. When I'd have missed the snake hiding in my wall, when I'd have overlooked the signs I now see that show something significant happened in the field overnight. I would have missed a lot back then because I wasn't in tune with this field, so even if I'd looked as hard as I could, I wouldn't have been able to see much.

It is of course supreme arrogance for me to refer to this field as mine in any way more proprietarily than I might say this town is mine, or this football team is mine. When they're not fleeing from me in fear most of the creatures that live here pay scant regard to me. The things that go on here, both exciting and routine, would happen with or without me in total indifference. My presence is all but incidental. It may even be detrimental. I think about that a lot, as I ponder upon my field.

But ten years after we bought the house I did indeed buy this field, and paid money for it. It is still the biggest thing I possess. In truth I paid probably quite a lot more for it than it's worth, at least in open-market terms. But I rate it the best value of anything I have ever bought, by far.

I take great pride in telling visitors such as hunters, fishermen, campers and the like that '*je suis propriétaire ici*'. Yet it seems amazing to me that one human being is stupid enough to imagine he owns something as big and full of life as this and feels he really has some sense of control over it . . . that's plain daft, bordering on offensive. But what I do have is the privilege of living by it. Even though with that comes some measure of responsibility for its upkeep and protection. Again, how silly is this? The field has got on just fine for centuries without any protection from me or my kind. Rather than upkeep it we're much more likely to destroy it.

That's why I'd like to share some of the beauties and wonders of the field with you now. I want to show you the life, the colours, the vibrancy and the excitement that's everywhere in this brilliant field. I think these things specially well worth sharing for I fear they may not be with us for long.

Then, there's the unknown

Though I've already learned a lot from this project, I still have much more to learn about the field and its occupants. For one thing, there are creatures here that I can't identify, even with the help of all the field guides and nature books that over the past year I've surrounded myself with as part of my bid to become more familiar with the field and everything in it. And things turn up here that frankly no guidebook could ever have prepared me for, such as locusts, praying mantis and, once, five pure white young bulls. So much of what I think or might assume that I know about this place is not quite what it seems. Kerkelven is a good cure for the curse of assumptions, a good training ground for the open mind. It's taught me to always expect the unexpected.

The valley of the Sarre

The field is in deep country. It could be part of the set for *Emmerdale* or *The Archers*, from *Jean de Florette*, or *le Grand Meaulnes* (not quite the French equivalent of these two English soaps, but near enough). Our side of the river is pristine, there's no construction of any kind anywhere in sight. On the far bank, however, you'll see four houses studding the valley side that slopes steeply down from the Guern/St Barthélémy road. Viewed from this road, which passes directly in front of them, these houses are mere cottages but because they've been built into the slope they're surprisingly large when seen from the river view, their backside. Tall fir trees form the wood to the right of the cottages, above the meadowland where our far-bank neighbour, farmer le Beller, grazes his herd of fine Friesian cows.

I love meeting his cows as I stroll by the river. They are so placid and relaxed, but always take a lively interest in me, often rushing up to greet me and trotting along their side of the river to accompany me for as long as they can, as I pass by, huffing and puffing and blowing hot steam into the morning air (them, not me) while giving me queer looks with their big cow eyes.

A simple low bridge carrying the road from Quistinic to Plouay across the river forms our boundary, signalling the furthest point of our stretch of the valley. A mere two kilometres further downstream our little river joins the deep, wide river *le Blavet*, which flows from the centre of Brittany all the way to its estuary near the port of Lorient, about fifty kilometres from us.

Our river is *la Sarre*. It meanders from its source somewhere in the hinterland, taking a winding, convoluted path to join the Blavet, just down the road from us. The Sarre's valley is low and fertile with good farming land along its entire length. Tall trees densely line its route, crowding together to get the best place, at times falling over each other in an endless jostling for position. Every so often someone has to trawl these tree-crowded banks and cull the most untidy. A painful necessity, but for the greater, common good.

Many beasts of the field and fowls of the air choose to have their homes by the river, living here come rain or shine, wind, heat or cold. Often the riverbank is quiet and can seem deserted. At times, though, particularly in summer, it's a hive of industry as busy as the busiest thoroughfare in the world. Then it reminds me of those scenes from innumerable sci-fi films with three-dimensional traffic from all corners of the galaxy coming and going up, down and sideways in profusion and seeming abandon but each on a determined mission to somewhere. It's an insect traffic cop's nightmare, but the traffic here flows pretty smoothly, all the same.

So, what kind of a field and forest is this?

Superficially, the field by the river is easily described. You'll find our field at minus 3.12 degrees longitude, 47.98 degrees latitude. Its surface area is 1.4 hectares (about 3.5 acres, roughly 20,000 square metres) with a further hectare of woodland attached. Our wood is a remnant of ancient forest, Brocéliande, so we often refer to it as such, for 'forest' sounds more exotic and magical, which of course it is. The forest has life and character. It has history, legends and secrets. It has depth, mystery and hidden places. Compact it may be, but ours is truly a forest, not merely a wood.

It isn't big. I don't really know how many trees we have, as whenever I've tried to count them I get quickly confused as they stand so close together and all look so alike. I'm not saying they move, but for sure I wouldn't be able to spot if they did. I reckon we must have around five hundred properly grown trees, with countless bushes, shrubs, plants, undergrowths and sundry other scrubby stuff. Many of these trees are oak, beech and chestnut but there are also birch, alder, ash and several others. Although identifying tree species is far from easy, I'm a lot better at it now. Some are apple trees (about thirty, I reckon), there's at least one pear tree and other fruit bushes too, bearing blackcurrants and blackberries. Some of our trees are thin and tightly packed, some are weedy and spindly, some are great sprawling giants, some are magnificent specimens that would grace any royal park. All are important. This is their home too.

The field slopes gently from the west to the river, but by the time it reaches the second cataract it's completely level, flat and lying quite low. That's why it floods so readily in winter and early spring. The forest, however, is much more steep. The downside of this is that it's less comfortable when walking through our wood, unless steep woodland paths are your thing. The upside is that our house, Kerkelven, is securely installed high above its valley, safe from floods, damp and any other uninvited intruders that might rise up from the valley below.

The river was always central

As the Nile is to Egypt, so is our river, the Sarre, to Kerkelven. The scale, of course, is a bit more modest.

Not so long ago this river may have been a thoroughfare of

some kind. The sturdy flat stones of what look like landing places can still be seen on both sides of the banks, though I doubt it was ever deep enough to allow commercial traffic. More probably these were washing areas, where in times gone by the womenfolk of Kerkelven would come down with their laundry to scrub and beat clean in the waters and on the rocks of the Sarre.

The Sarre is still a source of life and movement. Fish swim in it, cows drink from it, herons catch fish in it, pond-skaters do their weird dance on its surface, damselflies show off upon it, birds sing along it and rats do the unspeakable things that rats do, in it and all around it. And I sit by it and think how lucky I am.

As it floods each year the Sarre brings its silt to nourish the fields by the water's edge. But it's a bit too much of a flood plain where our field is, so it's not great for crops and for that I am eternally thankful. This means my field has been left uncropped for decades or more; it's not so much gone to seed as been put out to grass, so it's just done its own thing, gone its own way, which is to say it hasn't changed, it's stayed pretty much as it always was and, if I have my way, always will be.

Neighbours and neighbouring lands

Where we are the sides of the valley are quite steep, though upriver it quickly levels out (to the right of our field, looking from the field towards the river) into flat and comparatively featureless meadowland, called *la prairie* (the prairie) by locals. I won't say much about our neighbours or their farms, at least not yet, though, because there's only three housefuls of them actually in Kerkelven. I'll just quickly introduce you to a few of the main characters.

The Field by the River

From the moment we arrived here, my great buddy both socially and on walks around our hamlet has been Mathurin le Belligo. Mathurin is the perfect neighbour sent from wherever it is that they make perfect neighbours to make our lives here not just tolerable, but good. Kindly Mathurin used to be a farm worker on neighbouring farms until he retired, but that was a long time ago. Now in his late eighties and in failing health, Mathurin has been married to Angèle for more than sixty years, most of which they've lived at Kerkelven. They've always risen early and are usually in bed by 9 p.m. though they make exceptions when any of their large extended family visit, which is often.

Most of the land hereabouts was owned and farmed since before Napoleon's time by Bertrand's family, the Jouannos. Then the year before we arrived Bertrand, last surviving member of the Jouanno family, a bachelor with no children, retired and sold up. He too is now getting on a bit, and must be nudging eighty. Some years before he retired, Bertrand had built a new house for himself and his mother. She died and after a decent passage of time Marie-Thérèse, a widow from the village, moved in and Bertrand was bachelor no longer. Like Mathurin, Bertrand used to come with me on occasions for long walks in the environs.

When Bertrand retired his farm and buildings were all bought up by the farmer, the recently deceased Emile, except for our house, which was so old and ramshackle that no one wanted it. It lay empty for thirty years, awaiting our occupation. Emile lived with his family at Petit Kerkelven, about a kilometre from us. His daughter Lucie and her husband Jerome still live there today.

Emile's son Loïc now farms his father's land as a tenant to his brothers and sisters, who with him inherited all the farm buildings and land, equally. He lives at Pleumelin, a nearby town. The old pig-farm buildings, though ruined now and deteriorating daily, are for sale and have been for some time, with no buyer in sight.

Raymonde and Elodie, with their three children, complete the Kerkelven roll call. We see little enough of them though, for if they're not out at work they'll be away on their boat, staying with Raymonde's parents in the Alsace or borrowing their pretty cottage at Concarneau, a spectacularly beautiful part of the north Brittany coast.

Sadly for us, after spending all his long life so far in Kerkelven, our great friend and close neighbour Bertrand with his partner Marie-Thérèse has recently packed his bags and sold his birthright, to move to the nearby village of Guern, citing the onset of age and a declining inclination to constantly drive everywhere. So we have new neighbours from Paris to get used to. Kerkelven is always changing. They seem OK on first encounter, do Patrice and Anne-Claire. Time will tell, for sure.

A minimum about this region

To be honest there's a lot to recommend close study of this quirky, colourful and charming part of France, for there's just about something of everything here. Brittany is a land soaked in history, culture and tradition going back beyond even the ancient Druids and their legacy of mysterious standing stones. Its myths and legends are captivating and its people warm, hospitable and friendly. Its scenery is grand, its cliff-lined coast thrillingly dramatic with sweeping craggy bays and inlets, quaint fishing villages and beautiful sandy shores. Ancient, largely unspoiled, traditional hamlets dot the landscape amid tranquil rural vistas that are charmingly reminiscent of pastoral scenes from a bygone age. Although Kerkelven is one of these, history of the conventional sort is not what this tale is about, so you'll find only a little of it here.

The daily grind of a country squire

It's not a life that would appeal to everyone. Of course Kerkelven is at its best in the summer. In winter, this place can easily seem quiet, even dreary. At times it's dull, lonesome, overwhelming, drab, even sad. Our house here can be cold and draughty. Cleaning it is a never-ending chore and dust, like the insects, becomes just something else you live with. Walking the dogs can seem a drudgy routine.

But overall life here is pretty good. I don't commute. While others struggle in to their daily work on cramped commuter trains to Waterloo or Euston I walk around the field by the river.

Kerkelven is a healthy place to live, no traffic fumes or traffic wardens, no terrorists, few time pressures, or troubles of any kind. It's a good place to come if you're looking for peace.

Living among the Breton people is itself a calming experience. They are a quiet, undemonstrative, very distinctive and appealing race. Life is simpler; priorities are different. For the most part people here are judged not by their wealth or their influence but by their sociability. They're friendly people, the Bretons, if you make an effort to be friendly to them. They have a well-developed sense of fairness and almost invariably are as honest as the day is long. You can leave your house unlocked and open all day, no worries. People leave their cars unlocked too, without a thought. (Or at least the English do. As Bretons are always expecting disaster to fall they tend to lock and shutter everything.) It is, though, a different way of living, at a different pace. And along with their history and culture, the cuisine of the Bretons is as wholesome, varied and colourful as you'll find anywhere. If a bit fattening and alcoholic.

Buying the field

The idea of buying this field came to us when we discovered that the field that we called 'long grass' wasn't in fact owned by neighbouring farmer Jean-Michel Lévesque, who farms it. Instead it belonged to a rich landowner from a distant village. Our poor neighbour was merely a tenant. Although he would cut the grass a couple of times each year and his dad would collect the apples in the autumn, Jean-Michel had just one main use for the field: he needed it to keep up his acreage so he could claim the maximum subsidy under France's over-generous participation in the European Union's Common Agricultural Policy.

I saw no reason to disturb that. If we were to buy the field Jean-Michel could continue as tenant so would have no reason or interest to oppose the deal.

Bertrand and Marie-Thérèse thought we were mad. 'Why buy,' they exclaimed, 'when you can go there any time you want and do in it whatever it is that you might want to do? No one else uses it, or hardly at all. You can enjoy it all you could ever wish, without paying a sou.'

They also reminded me that even as owner I would be powerless to keep other undesirables out, should I want to, such as hunters, fishermen or day-trippers and their likes, on account of France's odd laws on trespass.

Their logic seemed unarguable. But I really wanted that field. One day some workmen from the local council had come and chopped down trees along the riverbank and I'd felt powerless to stop them. (Though I would have stopped them then if I could, in hindsight what they do is brilliant steward-ship of the riverbank. They just don't do it often enough.) Anyway at that time I had some spare cash and couldn't think of anything better to do with it than to buy that field.

The Field by the River

Along with much of the agricultural land and woodland around us, the long-grass field was owned by a certain Madame Séverine le Gendre (née Taillec). Her husband Sebastian, who had clearly married very well, appeared to manage for her the property side of her affairs. Friends in the village spoke of him in hushed, disparaging tones, for he had no proper job other than to collect rents and buy and sell from the likes of us. They evidently viewed him as a sort of kept man.

Sebastian le Gendre is a wizened old fox with a reputation for tough if not slippery negotiation. He lives in Cléguérec, the other side of Malguènac, an inconveniently long way to go just to buy a bit of land. But he has three of the loveliest daughters, all in their twenties and all, mysteriously, living at home with their parents. Madame le Gendre is a nice enough if somewhat harassed-looking woman, but she has that strange knack of seeming almost invisible and being instantly forgettable. Even now I can barely call her to mind. But her daughters . . . that's another story.

Mégane, the middle daughter, is the businesslike one of the three and she helps her father with matters financial. Charming and lovely, I sense she's also even tougher than he is. She has the dark hair, flashing eyes and pale, creamy skin of a Celtic beauty; with little hints of roses in her cheeks, hot passions and fiery temper lie thinly veiled behind those deep emerald eyes. Truth is I'd have paid twice the asking price just to prolong the deal-making.

But again, that is another story.

The deal-making begins. The coffee and cakes come and go. Voices are raised and heels are dug in. Then, compromise, we shake hands and I get a smile from Mégane, though I can't tell whether it's contempt or approval.

In the end I officially paid £3,000 for the field. It's a

common practice to pay a further sum in cash under the table but I'm not admitting to that here.

Scandalised, my neighbours told me I had paid twice what it is worth. For me, this has never seemed a problem. My attitude, indeed my only guideline in any negotiation, is to ask 'What is whatever I'm buying worth to me?' Though of course I'll pay less than that if I can, that's what I'll pay up to, to secure the deal. I'm like this when haggling for souvenirs and stuff in parts foreign. I judge I've got a bargain if it's worth to me just a little more than what I paid for it. That way, I'm usually happy with my purchases, however much the vendor makes (and I rarely begrudge him or her a living).

So what would have been the right price for this field? Well, mathematics was never my strong suit but I couldn't ever work that out, however numerate I might become. It's something beyond price, something that has shown me what value really is. In exchange for this place, I gave just money. Wow! Who's the fool, in the transaction over this field? Well, no one really, I suppose, though you might wonder at M. le Gendre, who clearly didn't want it. Whatever, I'm convinced it wasn't me. I got what I wanted at a price that now seems to me foolishly low.

Our year starts in September

It's pure chance that I'm starting here, but a year is a circle, so September is as good a time to start as any. We've just survived a particularly wet and rather disappointing August. The tourists have all gone. The weather is still great. There's a lot happening here, now.

Yes. September will do as well as any other time. It's a good time and place to start.

September

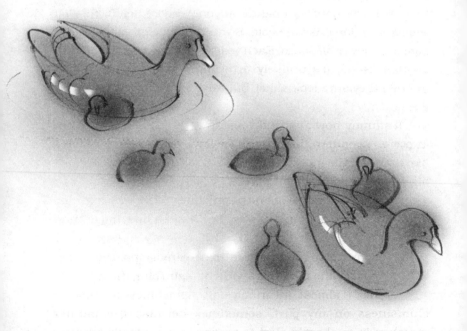

And it looks like the summer is over

Suddenly, rather too early, the moorhen family has gone.

I take their departure as the first irrevocable sign that summer also will all too soon be leaving us. It will return, of course, and so will the moorhens, but it seems a long dark time till then. Perhaps merely a product of global climate changes, the fine weather meanwhile is holding well so, whatever price the planet might pay later, we in Kerkelven can enjoy the Indian summer that lingers here and over the rest of Brittany, seemingly for several very agreeable weeks.

The moorhens, though, have surely seen signs already of winter's approach and have gone. They've nested and raised their families here as long as anyone can remember but it seems they don't like the cold. So at the first sign of summer's passing, they're off south. Each year two of them return to raise another brood. It's unlikely to be the same pair each time (though they sure look alike), but must be their descendants I guess.

It's funny how attached you can get to creatures that flee at every encounter, the instant they detect your presence. It's like that with the moorhen family that lives on our neighbour's big pond. I'm so proud and protective of them I worry for their welfare daily. They care about me not one whit. Every morning for the last five or six months as they've been busying around getting on with their lives I've either gingerly tiptoed by, or patiently crept along our path to some vantage point or other where I can see the moorhens without disturbing them.

In this I almost invariably fail, sometimes because of clumsiness on my part, sometimes because the mother moorhen is so sharply alert to predators, but mostly because either Syrus, Max or Mortimer, or some combination thereof, blunders past me setting all the moorhens to squawking.

When this happens Ma Moorhen's first instinct is always for her babies. Wherever she is she'll beetle from the undergrowth, wings a-flapping, to gather up her brood and usher them off to safety. Ironically if she'd only tell them to stay where they are, she and her clutch would be secure from all dangers, perfectly safe on the stout, sturdy nest which she and hubby have built in the middle of the pond. He's a shy, almost reclusive sort, the father. Both parents seem to share the manual chores equally, but I've always assumed it is the mother who so conscientiously brings up the kids. Mind you, as moorhen sexes are notoriously hard to tell apart I may have sexed them the wrong way round and it may be the father who is the good mother. In practice they take it in turns to share the parenting, which is just as well because, to be honest, I'm not sure if even the chicks would know which is which.

Whatever, at the first sign of alarm she/he is always quick to escort the brood from the safety of the nest to hide them rather obviously in the bushes by the water's edge. Perhaps there's an illusion of safety in the thick scrubby undergrowth. But, of course, that's also where all the predators hide, such as foxes or a neighbour's cat. For such impressively industrious and effective creatures, the moorhens seem at times dangerously slow on the uptake. It can be a fatal mistake and too often we find a tiny carcass, or bits of it, strewn across our path.

They're queer birds, though. And they walk funny. When the mother moorhen walks, her leg and neck jerk in unison as if linked by some taut invisible wire. Her other leg appears similarly attached, so as she moves her head darts from side to side in rhythmic mechanical precision like a robot bird. Behind her the children just wobble untidily. When startled they all accelerate giddily hither and thither giving the whole procession an absurdly comic aspect.

The moorhen pairs have two clutches of chicks each year with, normally, four or five babies at a time. They all hatch out within about a day of each other and look very sweet as, little black dots, they waddle from their twiggy nest to paddle ferociously behind their brisk and businesslike parent, struggling to form a line. If they're lucky maybe two or three from each clutch will survive each season and make it to fledge and their first flight. Soon after, they decide to quit Kerkelven and just up sticks and go (usually, they even leave the sticks). I've always assumed that this was natural migration to escape the approach of winter. For some reason, until quite recently, I imagined they'd go to Spain, but this was pure fancy on my part; I really had no idea, it just grew in my mind to become assumed reality. Spain is where I would go, if I were a moorhen.

But moorhens, so the Royal Society for the Protection of Birds (RSPB) tells me, are usually year-round residents and seldom travel far. Mostly, they don't migrate. So, once nesting and chick-rearing are out of the way they may just go down the road a bit, to get some peace and quiet from our dogs and to evade the fat bloke in short trousers who keeps gawping at them whenever he passes and imagines he hasn't been seen.

This would explain why, at times, I've stumbled upon a moorhen or two down by the river in wintertime. And why each time they've flapped off in embarrassed haste.

Alarmed to find my prior assumptions about moorhen migration so wildly off beam I've done some further investigating and some sources do claim that moorhens can travel after nesting. But I can't find a good explanation as to why our annual visitors leave us each year. It's a mystery and is also, to be honest, a bit upsetting. If they stayed here, by now we'd have a substantial and thriving moorhen population. I'd rather like that.

Evidently, they wouldn't.

But, mustn't grumble, we should be glad for what we get. When they are here I delight in the moorhens and show them off proudly to all my friends who all oooh and cluck as if they mean it, but I'm sure most secretly think I'm bonkers. My charmingly down-to-earth old school pal Robert from Scotland, who visits Kerkelven most every year, confirmed this. Once when I eulogised at him about our delightful summer visitor he replied, 'What's so great about a wee fat black duck skittering across your pond? For goodness sake, just eat him!'

I think he was joking. But I'm not sure.

Meet the residents

In addition to the four humans that live in the house called Kerkelven, there are numerous others who reside here too. Thousands of them, in fact.

It's a cliché to say that if all the insect inhabitants of an old French farmhouse were to flap their wings at the same time the roof would fly off in a single piece. Well it wouldn't be true in Kerkelven because we have a big, heavy, thatched roof. And because most of our residents are spidery (i.e., they can't fly, however much they flap). But if all of them were to hop at the same time it is likely that our house, which has stood resolutely here for more than 350 years and must weigh many hundreds of tons, would in fact skip down the road good style.

Countless as the sands of the seas may be the residents of our house but we share our lands, and particularly our big field by the river, with many, many more equally interesting creatures. Not only are they uncountable, there are rather a lot of different types. Aside from the house insects, swallows, bats, dogs, cats (recently) and domesticated tropical fish, there are herons, buzzards, hawks, most common European birds and a few rare ones too, mice, coypu, rats, voles, moles (actually all of Toad's friends are here), weasels, stoats, owls, spiders, ants and other creepy-crawlies too numerous to mention. Plus hornets, wasps, three types of snake, frogs, toads, newts, several types of lizard (including the legless kind), bees, beetles, butterflies, moths, flies and even salamanders. Oh and mosquitoes. We have them too, by the bucketful. And at times we've been joined by badgers and hedgehogs, not to mention the kingfishers, otters, bulls, locusts and praying mantis I mentioned earlier. Then there's the swifts, jays, wood pigeons, Barbary doves, tree creepers, woodcocks, tits, greenfinches and most other colours of finch too, even the shy and, in these parts, rare roe deer. And I should mention our neighbours' sheep, pigs, chickens, guinea fowl (well, we've no pigs in Kerkelven now, and a lot fewer chickens, since old Emile the farmer passed on). And of course I mustn't forget all the other unknown, unidentified creatures who I know are there because from time to time they cry out in the middle of the night.

A late lunch in the sun

This event is a Kerkelven speciality, a highlight of our summer, an occasion far from rare yet of singular specialness. As the days for savouring them are now few, those that remain are particularly treasured.

There's no summer pastime so fine, I find, as a long leisurely lunch in shade or sunshine, outdoors. This is when we serve our hand-picked guests only our favourite fare, copious quantities of big juicy Breton prawns (probably from Mexico or Thailand though everyone, including the locals, assumes they've just been netted offshore, on the morning of purchase) with lashings of home-made garlic mayonnaise washed down liberally with that superb-value summer wine, rosé de Provence. Other wines will do on such occasions (a fino sherry makes a nice change) but bizarrely this particular cheap plonk is best. Sometimes langoustines (Dublin Bay prawns, a small lobster also known as scampi) will appear also, even accompanied by smaller seafoods when in season, such as whelks and winkles, though I generally consider these two too small or tasteless to justify the effort of wheedling them from their shells. This feast of seafood can be followed by any variation from France's wildly excessive yet indispensable range of cheeses, hams and pâtés accompanied by a selection of colourful salads perhaps involving rocket leaves, shavings of Parmesan, or old Gouda and quail's eggs. Yummy.

This treat is usually appropriately honoured by over-indulgence, then almost invariably followed by a snooze on the sunbeds and eventually, for those still capable of movement, a short constitutional down to the field before returning for yet more eating and drinking. Lunch can be drawn out to four or even six hours in this way and it's always time well spent. Great conversation helps of course, though after a few rosés the debate invariably improves, irrespective of the company. Or at least it appears to improve, though really, who cares if it does or not?

Summer may be on the wane but we can still squeeze in many more such lunches before it's too cool to eat outside. This means much sky-watching through September, but disappointments are few, even well into October. Then, it really does begin to look and feel like the summer is over. Though the climate here is cooler and less reliable than down south, most years if we are hardy we could easily eat outside into November.

September though is a sad month for lots of people. Holidays are at an end. It's back to school for anyone under eighteen and back to work for most other people.

The end of August comes down like a shutter all over France. This is the season known as *la rentrée*, the unavoidable nationwide return to work after a summer of ease. Like a bad hangover it inevitably brings with it an oppressive, depressing feeling that seems to hang almost everywhere throughout France at this time, leaving everyone feeling flat that the summer is over.

This is odd. Because really it isn't, far from it. Though even if it were, something equally fine – autumn – will soon be coming to take its place.

Life beneath the flagstones

There is a curious underworld even here beneath our feet. The thick heavy flagstones that cover our front garden are roof and shelter to a wild profusion and variety of life including several families of lizards, some worms, slugs, snails, plus ants in their millions and countless other insects that all wiggle and slither and squirm their way around below us, usually without our ever appreciating their presence. From time to time they pop their heads up from their subterranean homes and intrude into our world above, where we sit dining and drinking.

Most numerous, most industrious and most impressive of these are the ants. They live under the flagstones in armies and sally forth in platoons throughout the day and night fetching this and carrying that, patrolling near and far and generally going to no end of trouble to keep their comrades and their colony living in the style to which they've become accustomed. Such industry impresses us so much that we'd have to have a lie down, even if we weren't there already.

Growing through the cracks between the flagstones there's also a profusion of plant life that just can't be persuaded to move elsewhere however often and however efficiently we apparently eradicate their traces.

Lurking in the corner

Like quite a few Breton hamlets, the ancient village of Kerkelven boasts in its centre a huge mound that largely conceals a communal stone bread oven. This domed granite structure, about three metres high by five across, was built not long after our house and is now covered in by the earth of ages, with only its huge entrance still clearly visible, sealed by a large single stone that needs two strong men to move. Inside is a perfect vaulted space with large stones that radiate up from the earthen floor to be held in place as if by magic by a central keystone. We still use this oven, not for its original purpose, which was to bake the village's daily bread, but for cooking a suckling pig or similar on feast days.

Just in front of this vast oven, in the furthest part of our small courtyard, are the remnants of an ancient well, all that's now left of an ornate stone fountain of religious significance that probably, in its time, looked rather splendid. These shrines were once widespread in this region in the gardens of the well-to-do. Ours is ruined now with little of its former grandeur left standing, the old mini-chapel that once stood here having long since been knocked over, probably by some farmer's tractor in the days when such artefacts were despised rather than valued, and the fine, now rare carved stones that topped it will have been carried away and dumped indiscriminately somewhere. I keep hoping I'll find them so I can rebuild that shrine. The actual spring is still there, cold and clear, though in this season it's barely half its full winter depth.

So nothing is draining from it now. The hamlet of Kerkelven though is actually on a gentle slope, so when it rains the surface water drains from the spongelike fields above our neighbour Elodie's place and from there flows under her land into our well. Then, via a carefully carved channel in the huge stones, it exits into a less than lovely large pipe that goes beneath our road and carries the flow into Fox Creek, the (mostly dry) burn that runs along the eastern edge of our big garden. From there, for most of spring, autumn and winter, this water flows, again by pipe, under Bertrand's descent into the burns below. Toads, newts and a family of salamanders live and breed in and around the well's effluence, presumably surviving by feasting on whatever washes past their homes and on anything foolish enough to wander curiously into the pipe thinking, 'Hullo, what's in here then?'

They're a bit like the deranged cannibal Alexander 'Sawney' Bean and his family, who in sixteenth-century Scotland captured and – eventually – ate anyone who passed by their cave.

Toads, newts and salamanders are probably no less frightening than the Bean family to those residents of Kerkelven who constitute their prey, but I find them really rather appealing creatures, well worth getting to know.

Noises off

Like similar events all summer long before them, these feasts in the end days of the season are invariably accompanied by the constant chirping, clucking, singing and continual comings and goings of the bird population of Kerkelven, or at least the more domesticated segment of it that lives in the bushes and trees around our houses and flits back and forth above and around us as we dine. They become an unceasing background for us locals, like wallpaper, though visitors often remark upon it and in truth it is extraordinary. Equally enchanting are the brightly coloured butterflies that flutter among the buddleia with their dinner-mates, the startlingly birdlike hummingbird hawk moths. Their feast I'm sure is every bit as fine as ours.

In the skies above us, somewhat detached from the riffraff beneath and soon to be off to warmer climes, soaring squadrons of swallows dip and dive and zoom in careful formation, clearly enjoying the time of their lives. Like their less fortunate, more terrestrial fellows below, they too ignore us, but more easily and totally.

There are so many birds of Kerkelven, they seem so tireless and so wrapped up in their own comings and goings, that whatever we do appears utterly irrelevant to them. Every so often a squabble will erupt between a small gang of them, feathers will fly and much clucking and squawking will resound, then we all slip back into doing what we all do best and like doing most; us to our slow inebriating self-indulgence and them to their eternal gibbering, bickering and occasional swooping.

Chacun à son métier, as they say here.

I suppose, you have to take the long view

The temptation to spend every afternoon at home is nigh overwhelming here but given the wealth of dramatic coastline that's just down the road, it has to be resisted, at least on occasions. That most of the tourist throngs have now headed homewards means there's more room for the rest of us, so visits to the coast become possible again because now there's somewhere nearer than five kilometres inland to park the car.

Curiously, as if at a signal, many of the beaches in Brittany (one third of all France's coastline is to be found in this region, the most beautiful and dramatic third too) transform into the preserve of completely naked people. Early September is the short season in the sun of the naturist. Overnight all but the most public seashores become nudist beaches and although no signs go up, at least that I have seen, anyone wearing a cossie, however skimpy, can expect to be frowned upon.

Now I'm no prude, believe me. Neither am I averse to ogling firm French female flesh as it bounces across the local dunes and estuaries. And Breton women are as much a feast for the eyes as you'll find anywhere in this land of spectacularly gorgeous people.

But it has to be said, naturists here, whatever their motivations, are usually not exposing their charms for the benefit of other people. There are honourable exceptions of course, but many if not most of the bodies that go on show at this time of year should by rights be kept well covered up. The European parliament should do something about it, should create a law to compel it. Some, it has to be said, are not fit for viewing by anyone, even those condemned to live in them, far less those of a nervous disposition. One wonders what on earth their owners can be thinking of?

Not surprisingly the menfolk here are even less appealing than their women and for some unfathomable reason seem even less inhibited about flaunting the fact.

So no, despite the greatly thinner crowds, I think I'll stick at Kerkelven this September and give the coast a miss for a few more weeks at least.

Screaming blobs of fat

This isn't a description of the startled nudists mentioned above. Rather it applies to something even scarier that's found hereabouts at this time.

Mostly the creatures that inhabit the neighbourhoods of Kerkelven will be broadly familiar to those who live in the UK or most of Europe, at least to those that live in the countryside.

But *frelons* are something different. Though they are native to the sceptred isle, I've never seen them there and I believe they're quite rare. In fact I've never seen their likes anywhere other than Kerkelven. If you are scared of flying insects with attitude, these little mothers could be your worst nightmare.

Having reluctantly tolerated the appearance of these beasts for more Septembers than I care to remember, this year I determined to find out a bit about them. I reckoned that if I could learn to get along with, if not actually love, the *frelons* I could pretty much get along with anything (except, perhaps, cleg flies and mosquitoes).

With the sociable common wasp, the *frelon* (known as the hornet in the UK and yellow jacket in North America) is part of the family *Vespidae* and belongs to the order of insects called *Hymenoptera*, which also includes the bumblebee, honeybees, ants, sawflies and the ichneumon wasp (sometimes inaccurately called the ichneumon fly), the scientific name of which rather aptly means 'persistent burglar'.

But though we have ichneumon wasps at Kerkelven too, for now it's their cousins, the hornets, that interest me. They are more visibly intrusive, and for years we've had a nest of them at the back of our house. This is the month in which they come out to play.

They are traitorous buggers. From inside the rafters of our own roof they sally forth to plague us as we sup a last glass of wine or get ready to give the dogs their final walk of the day. Invariably a few sneak round to gather at our front door, mesmerised, or at least blinded, by the light. Then one or two of their number are detailed off to slip unnoticed in among us, and wreak havoc upon the end of our evening.

While, as more than a few mozzies and clegs have learned

to their cost, I couldn't quite claim that I 'wouldn't hurt a fly', my attitude to the wildlife that's around and among us has always been very benign. It's actually improved from 'live and let live' to almost universal positive encouragement and welcome. But one has to draw a line when it comes to sharing the end of the day with a houseful of hornets.

Yet despite whatever we might do to deter them – which, in the past, has ranged from coaxing and cajoling them outside through organically based supposed deterrents to, I'm ashamed to admit, attempts at bombing and smoking them out and even at times calling out the fire brigade (not cheap, I can tell you, and they rarely wipe their feet) – each year, or maybe after a gap year, the hornets come back. Once we had a nest of them under the eaves above our front door. Neighbour Mathurin (who, unusually for a Breton, is very sentimental about killing wildlife) had to don his broad beekeeper's helmet complete with face net and, swaying perilously, climb a long ladder, borrowed from old Emile, and blast the blighters with something nasty and chemical. No easy task at any age, I suspect, far less at his. But he wouldn't hear of me doing it.

My son Joe, when describing an encounter with a particularly persistent pair that attacked him in our kitchen, said, 'They come at you like screaming blobs of fat.' I thought this a particularly sharp depiction for they are indeed just like that: globules of boiling fluid, large and vicious, propelled at great speed to indiscriminately inflict terror and pain on anything unfortunate enough to get in their way.

Or so it seems. Now I'm adept at trapping hornets, usually with an upturned whisky tumbler and an old postcard. When they're thus secured I take them outside and with a single sharp movement set them free. I do this very gingerly, with great care and not a little reluctance, yet I've never known them to actually attack me, or indeed, anyone. I wonder if we're not a tad harsh on the hornet. After all, he lives here too.

Walking the dogs, September

My experiences of and in the field by the river are formed largely from my daily perambulations around it, accompanied in very loose formation by all three of the dogs. Max, Syrus, me and Mortimer, usually in that order, take the first of our daily constitutionals for about an hour around nine in the morning then again just after lunch (when my wife Marie comes too) and finally at the end of the evening (also with Marie, particularly for the stargazing), before the dogs are fed and head off to their beds in one or other of the two large sturdy kennels we have built for them in their enclosure.

They don't actually have beds. We've tried supplying them with various sorts of bedding but invariably they eat it or shred it. They don't choose a particular kennel and stick to it. Instead they sleep around, pretty much with abandon. Imprisoned though they may be for most of the day, their enclosure is far from a Guantánamo Bay for dogs. It's more like an austere training camp for frugal aesthetes. Piped music and soft furnishings are not wanted here. The only thing they might wish for, I guess, would be more food. But then they'd just get fat.

Except in emergencies (upset tummies or when we've slept in) our three canines neither wee nor poo in their own enclosure. Just because you're an outside dog doesn't mean you've been badly brought up.

So of a morning I feel obliged not to lie abed overlong, imagining three tense pooches with crossed legs awaiting me anxiously. We're forever hurrying back from outings or visits to friends saying, 'We'd better get back for the dogs', and of course over the years at dull dinner parties they've provided us with many an invaluable excuse for leaving early.

Pen portraits of the pooches

Each of our dogs has its own distinct personality with both plus points and shortcomings, delights and detriments. To understand their different characters you have to grasp the differing levels of their emotional attachment to me.

Syrus – the wild rover. Syrus is the leader of the pack, the strong character, irrepressible, the most persistent and the most tireless. He'll chase anything and everything and is always instantly up for any action. He's also the only one that bites. Syrus is a biter by nature, not through nastiness but just because that's what he does. He's highly strung, excitable and too friendly for his own good. So when he runs up to visitors and they respond by getting overexcited too (a surprising number of French country folk are afraid of dogs), that's when he'll nip, particularly if the human lashes out. Curiously though, Syrus only ever bites French people, and then only men. Being a biter, however, can be fatal for a dog here, so he has to be muzzled. Most probably he'll never be cured of it, so when out and about he will always have to wear his muzzle (except on night walks; I reckon anyone daft enough to be wandering unannounced round our place at night deserves at least a little nibble).

Unlike the other two, who are both getting on now in doggie years, old age simply hasn't occurred to Syrus. He's an eternal teenager, independent, the most self-sufficient of the three. He's most likely to do his own thing, to wander off on his own agenda. And least likely to worry if he runs off for a while, most likely to get up to bad things when he does. But he craves affection and seeks approval whenever he can find it, particularly from me.

But though he's the cocky dog of the walk, all strut and bravado, deep down Syrus is a big pussy. Sometimes when chasing rabbits he'll crawl into a tiny thicket where there's no room for him to turn round. Then, to the tune of much distressed yelping, for a few glorious minutes the rabbits make mincemeat out of him.

Max – the busybody witch. Max is the female. She's mostly indifferent to me and shares her affections freely and equally with pretty much anyone else at any time. She's the most uninvolved, most dismissive and most shallow of the three. She has no need for the rest of us, at all. Apart that is for food and other material comforts, or when she's unwell. If we were all to be annihilated in a freak camping accident Max would cope, no bother. Max is always scratching, sticks her nose in everything, is most friendly with small children (who will always regard her as favourite) and is most likely to get muddy head to toe or to run off and get genuinely lost for hours (Syrus runs off, but he never gets lost). I treat Max with the same politeness and affection as the other two, but somehow it isn't the same. My feelings for her don't run so deep and she knows it, of course. So every so often I try to compensate.

Mortimer – the plodding devoted servant. Mortimer, biggest and most solid of the three, is my dog from nose to tail. His loyalty to me is total, his world revolves around his affection, gratitude and love for me (at least this is what I like to think; my family may say different). And the feeling is reciprocated, if neither absolutely nor consistently then at least warmly. He's a great lug, but I do love him.

Mortimer resembles nothing so much as a gigantic shaggy blanket on legs. While I assume that he's my dog through and through I often think he'd be just as likely to bestow his loyalty and affection on a potato, if the potato would take him for his daily walks. Mortimer doesn't run off, or run anywhere (he seldom breaks even into a brisk walk), nor will he ever lag behind, at least not deliberately. Mortimer's tail seldom stops wagging, everything pleases him, he's constantly happy just to be alive. His greatest pleasure, though, is in eating. He lives to eat. Mortimer is always happy to see me, is never judgemental, is totally supportive and enthusiastic. Whatever we talk about (well, I talk; he, I hope, listens) is great by him. Sometimes we sneak off for walks on our own, just the two of us, which gives him special delight. Whatever we do, Mortimer loves it and literally laps it up. We never disagree, Mortimer and me, never squabble, are always right there for each other. It can only be love, this thing between us, and it's unconditional at that.

All three dogs are friendly beyond any definition of

reasonableness and have no capacity for discernment whatsoever. Given the nigh total hostility towards or indifference to mankind from almost all other species in Kerkelven the unquestioning affection of these dogs is a bit hard to fathom. I suppose we do feed and walk them, which means we satisfy their every whim.

Now at nearly fourteen years of age Marie and I can say with satisfaction that our dogs have all had a good life. Syrus, particularly, has had a good life and managed to get some bites in too, so were he to be put down for it now he may well think that fair enough. But I reckon he has another three to five years left in him yet and I intend to see he enjoys them. I'm less optimistic about the prospects for the other two, particularly big Mort.

Max, Syrus and Mortimer all love each and every walk unreservedly but most specifically, they enjoy the first of the day. I don't think Marie should take offence at this, I just feel early mornings are particularly splendid, we go further afield at this time and generally there's more going on in the animal kingdom in the early hours. Though I have no certain knowledge of this, from my observations most of the creatures of woods and hedgerow and almost all birds of the air seem to sleep a lot, often in the form of afternoon naps. Who can blame them? So it's in the early hours of the morning that you'll see most action from them.

The downside of dogs

* They scare away the wildlife. There used to be all sorts of vibrant life hereabouts – otters, owls, coypu . . . Now as I walk my acres these obnoxious beasts surround me like guardian orcs from Middle Earth, smugly over-muscled minders intent on scaring off anyone or anything that might cross my path. They particularly scare the birds.

- They depend on me, utterly. They eat a lot, they cost a lot and I have to be there for them always or put them in kennels, which costs even more, or pay our friend Angie to walk them (which isn't much of a saving).
- They're badly behaved and seldom do what they're told.
- They have to be walked at least three times each day (not such a hardship, actually, but I wouldn't let them know that).
- They scare the neighbours' children yet wouldn't impress for even an instant any burglar worth his salt.
- They never help me with anything, even though there's always lots to do.
- They cost money at the vet's.
- They bark, so are annoying to all within earshot.
- They fart.
- They poo *a lot!*
- They eat poo too. Disgusting.

The upside of dogs

Of course I love my dogs. They have at least as many upsides, too. Well, most of the time. Let's see. I love them because:

- They treat me like an equal.
- They always come for walks with me, whatever the weather.
- They are gentle, supportive, faithful, true, undemanding and consistent. They trust me.
- They never disagree with me.
- They neither criticise my appearance nor choice of apparel. Nor do they whinge when I wander off somewhere unexpected.

- They don't complain even when they have cause. That includes when I leave them for weeks on end in the care of some infinitely less tolerant minder, so I can nip back to London for a break.
- They're easily pleased. It takes just a look or a kind word to set all three tails wagging.
- They provide an invaluable and very versatile excuse, adaptable for almost any occasion.

Our dogs are all rescuees from old Emile's farm. We inherited the first two, the siblings Max and Syrus, when Emile was about to dispose of a litter from one of his guard dogs (a lovely creature called Lassie, who led an unhappy life). I asked my young son Joe, who was about eleven at the time, to pick two males from the litter, stressing that, because I didn't fancy puppies, on no account was he to saddle us with a female. Thus I learned that you can't leave your children's sex education solely to the boys and girls of the playground. He still claims it was a mistake anyone could make.

The arrival of Mortimer six months later was an altogether more shocking tale.

With several siblings Mortimer was born on a stormy, very wet winter's night to his wonderful mother Galgarin, a Belgian shepherd, one of the most beautiful dogs I've ever known, certainly the dog with the nicest nature. She was permanently chained at the back of the pig farm, in the open air, and I used to go and see her a lot and talk to her. I even fed her at times and rigged up a little shelter for her, though I wish I'd done more.

It was a dog's life, particularly in the rain and the mud. But when she had her litter old Emile thoughtfully allowed her inside to a corner of the pigshed where, good mother that she was, she made a nest of sorts. A few days later he chanced to show the new litter to Bertrand, but Bertrand got a mite too close and Galgarin snapped at him. She can have meant no harm, it was merely a natural reaction, but old Emile was so incensed he waited until Bertrand had gone then took the puppies – there were about six of them – and fed them, living, to the pigs. This provoked a furious argument between Emile and Bertrand but he, like us, only found out what Emile had done when it was already too late.

The night I heard this gruesome tale I visited Galgarin in the dark of her bare earth shed. She was touchingly happy to see me, but seemed on edge and excited, perhaps not surprisingly. I tried to calm her, but she would not settle. Then I saw that she was trying to shield something. In the gloom I shone my torch upon it. My God! It was a rat!

Or so I thought. For the mud-splattered bedraggled creature that I beheld had the colour and the appearance of a rodent and a badly used one at that. I washed him down and realised that it was indeed a dog, a puppy just a few days old, frightened but not badly injured.

With some determination I saw Bertrand and Bertrand saw Emile, strong words passed between them and the pup was guaranteed no harm.

Mortimer was a fine young puppy and he grew up healthy. His father was a collie that also belonged to Emile and with Galgarin he had bred handsomely. Emile was so struck with the survivor of his barbarity he promised him to his granddaughter, though in truth the as yet unnamed Mortimer seemed to prefer to spend his time with us.

Then the pup was run over by a car that he'd greeted overenthusiastically and both his back legs were broken. These were greenstick fractures, not serious in themselves (again we only found out about them afterwards) but this was enough for

Emile and his family to lose interest in him, and so, by proxy, Mortimer became ours.

In a weak moment I agreed that Joe, who was dually obsessed by science-fiction comics and stand-up comedians at the time, could give them names. He called the twins after two comic-book heroes and Mortimer after a real-life comedian. He could have just as easily been called Reeves.

And that is how they came to be.

A shock for a night visitor

Don't think they're all sweetness and light, though, these dogs. You wouldn't be the first visitor to Kerkelven to err in that assumption, and I'm sure you won't be the last.

Far from it. One night a polecat inadvertently wandered into the dog's enclosure. At least, I think it was a polecat. It had a polecatty-type head and polecatty-type fur, though by the time I happened along there really wasn't more of it that was identifiable as anything very much. We slept through the entire incident, although from the debris one can deduce that there would have been a fair amount of noise for a few minutes at least.

I feel considerable sympathy for that polecat, if that is what he was. He must have been distracted, sick or demented to make such a basic error. I presume it was dark. He may have looked at the chicken wire that encases their enclosure and thought, 'Hullo, chickens!' He may have been distracted by smells wafting from the dogs' dinner, which that night may well have been chicken-flavoured Pedigree Chum. Though in truth there would as usual have been little enough of that left, except perhaps some residual gas. He must have wormed his way in through that wire with some difficulty. And as he padded furtively round the gable end of one of the two doggie sheds (which from a distance could look to a dim polecat a tad like chicken coops) he must have got the shock of his short but eventful life.

I can only imagine what, in that split second, must have flashed through his tiny polecat mind. There would have been nowhere to run to. Negotiation would not have been an option. It must have been quick.

It's not a mistake that he could expect to learn from. Perhaps this incident goes some way to explaining why polecats are not very common hereabouts.

King of the nuts

The river, for so long at low ebb and so denied its full force and weight, is now starting to pick up pace having slowed to little more than a trickle through the summer heat. On half speed at first, momentum builds through September and soon it's powering along like a sprinter. The river is our focal point, our hub.

Insect, bird and animal life is particularly abundant this month, so it might be a good time to introduce you to some of the plant life of Kerkelven. A walk around the field at this time is an education, if you have eyes to see.

Just this morning I found a pile of hazelnuts on a boulder by the east burn, obviously deliberately collected there by some creature or other for some purpose or other, presumably involving eating. But who made this neat pile, why, and when will they return? It's an unsolved mystery among many here.

We have four hazel trees, just bushes really, that mark our eastern boundary with Bertrand's field. The fact that they're on the far bank and were obviously planted at some time lends me to think they must belong to him rather than me, though I can't see that knowledge makes even a little difference here. The hazelnut of course is the king of all nuts, though the weedy specimens our (or rather Bertrand's) trees produce are hardly deserving of the name.

The ancient Celts, who surely lived in these woods and fields long before we did, revered the hazel tree and its fruit, according it magical properties to do with wisdom, poetic inspiration and increasing the milk yield of cows. Salmon also eat hazel nuts – the number of bright spots on their skins is said to equal the number of nuts they've eaten. When first I heard of this I wondered how on earth salmon could gather hazelnuts. But the answer is easy, as I realised when, one day, I sat by the river's edge while acorns were falling. A light went on. If salmon like nuts, maybe they get hazelnuts in the same way.

Since days of yore the hazel has been seen as cool. Legend tells us that Ireland's ancient King Fionn MacCumhail (Finn the Cool) imbibed the salmon's wisdom accidentally by licking his fingers while preparing a meal of sacred salmon that he was forbidden to eat. Druids made their staffs out of hazel branches, so they might appear cool and wise. And because they're good for hitting people with.

There is magic in the things we see around us these fine days. As I forage for hazelnuts swarms of butterflies rise up like fairies to float gracefully if unsteadily around me. Short their lives might be but it seems these tiny brightly coloured wisps get their share of the good things in life, including rampantly energetic sex. Butterflies appear to enjoy their brief time among us rather exuberantly, as if they at least believe that they've truly won first prize in the lottery of short lives.

Every now and then our dogs see or sense something, which may be a fox or pheasant, or something less pleasant. Or maybe something made a foul smell on this spot in the recent past. Whenever this happens the dogs spring instantly alert, tails stiffen and are raised skyward, noses are pressed to the ground. A lot of serious sniffing about begins.

A flash along the riverbank

I've seen it again, but still this time, as last, it was just a blur, more an impression than a sighting. For sure, it's the smallest bird I've ever seen, and to be honest I've no idea what kind of bird it is. Maybe it's a wren, but it doesn't bob genteelly like they do, it darts. Plus, fleeting though my glimpse was, I'd swear its tail was horizontal, not pert and upright as is the wren's. So I gallop off to find my reference book, to see what bird is smaller than the diminutive wren.

Only, apparently, the goldcrest and its rarer, even more colourful cousin, the firecrest. And it wasn't one of these, I don't think. Though I can't be sure, this creature seemed all dark brown or black. It lives at the very water margins, where river and bank are fused and seeing is hard. It's so tiny and it flies so low and quick, it would be scarcely surprising if it has eluded naturalists up until now.

It's a mystery, and no mistake.

The strange phenomenon of flight distance

As I've wandered around the highways and byways, nooks, crannies and corners of Kerkelven I've observed something strange and a bit wonderful about the different species of birds. Equally marvellously, it appears to apply to animals too and probably also to insects, though the distances there may be harder to estimate.

I now know this phenomenon to be called the 'flight distance' of each animal, because Yann Martell refers to it as such in his lovely book, *Life of Pi*. It seems that each different species will allow humans to get within a certain distance before flying (or galloping, shambling, scurrying or scuttling) off. According to Yann, this is the minimum distance at which an animal wants to keep a perceived enemy. For a flamingo, he says, it's 300 yards, for a giraffe it's 150 yards if you're on foot and 30 yards if you're in a car (this is hard to explain as it's much easier to suddenly rush up to them and knock them over if you're in a car). Whatever, if you are outside a creature's flight distance it will most probably ignore you. Get even a teensy bit inside it and the creature becomes tense. Very quickly thereafter, unless you back off, it will turn and flee.

Zookeepers, apparently, are quite familiar with this concept, indeed a thorough understanding of it is essential in their work.

Though we don't have giraffes or flamingos in Kerkelven, the phenomenon seems to apply here just the same. Robins have a flight distance of only a few feet. Kingfishers have a flight distance of whenever they see you (which is mostly before or about the same instant that you see them). Herons too have a very long flight distance, maybe two to three hundred yards. Thrushes and blackbirds less so, maybe fifty to a hundred yards. Rabbits are about the same. Wood pigeons, just a few feet. Seagulls, twenty yards. Sheep, about the same. Lizards and snakes (if they spot you), five feet. Snails, toads and frogs . . .

OK, the argument does break down a bit. None of the above distances are corroborated. And clearly it doesn't always apply, e.g. with dogs. As soon as you broach their flight distance they run up to you and lick you all over.

I confess I was somewhat miffed at reading this part of Martell's book because until then, I thought I'd stumbled upon this realisation all on my own and was about to develop Ken's theory of flight distance, or something similar. But the theory

Yann sets out of the same name is just as interesting and just as valid. And on reflection I'm tickled pink to discover that it's a science in itself, with serious studies devoted to it.

In zoos and wildlife parks animals get used to humans and so their flight distance dramatically reduces. In an environment like Kerkelven, where our lackeys, the dogs, are constantly interfering nuisances and where hunters and their likes continually remind animals of how dangerous and untrustworthy is anything that walks on two legs, animals increase their flight distances in the interests of their own safety. But it's undeniable that some species are much more shy, or jittery and untrusting than others. Perhaps their confidence in their own abilities is a key factor; how fast they can run or how high they can fly. Or how many other creatures want to eat them.

Harvesting mice

The tiny harvest mouse is one of the smallest mammals in Europe (only the aptly named lesser shrew is smaller) and we find quite a lot of them in our field, along with their somewhat larger first cousin, the field mouse.

The harvest mouse's minuteness combines with a perhaps understandably shy disposition to make him one of nature's hardest finds and least offensive beasts. If you're lucky you'll see him scampering rapidly through the lush grass like the weft of a very fast loom weaving through the delicate grassy tapestry of green and gold. So small, gentle and fragile is the harvest mouse, yet our dogs pursue him and his family with utter ruthlessness, combing the field like a search party on the trail of a felon, going over each clump and blade minutely with paw-tip precision, upturning every stone, sniffing out every twist and tangle, even burrowing nose-deep to root out any desperate little diggers they can find. On the rare occasions when they catch one there's no pause for thought, no time for appeals for mercy as the poor wee beast is grabbed in slathering jaws, tossed in the air like a Breton pancake and golloped down in one before you can say, 'Now stop that, you horrible bastard!' The terrified little harvest mouse doesn't even touch the sides on his way down to suffer what must be a dismal, lingering death in the gut of whichever of our three was quick enough that morning.

The dogs are not fussy, of course, field mice are just as favoured and get the same summary treatment, as will any small rodent unlucky enough to cross their path. Indeed there may be a bit more nourishment in a field mouse, but they're just as hard to catch.

Our only consolation in contemplating this horror is that being generally keen but useless, the dogs don't succeed in mouse harvesting all that often.

Seventeenth-century naturalist Gilbert White, who I mentioned in the introduction, can claim to have first identified and classified the harvest mouse. Because it's so great, I want to share with you his description of finding a nest just like those that my dogs search for so eagerly. (Note though that Gilbert's love of nature didn't deter him from employing fairly drastic ways of preserving it for future enjoyment.)

I have procured some of the mice that I mention in previous letters, a young one and a female with young, both of which I have preserved in brandy . . . One of these nests I procured this autumn which is most artificially platted, and composed of the blades of wheat; perfectly round, and about the size of a cricket-ball; with the aperture so ingeniously closed that there was no discovering to what part it belonged. It was so compact and well filled, that it would roll across the table without being discomposed, though it contained eight little mice that were naked and blind. As this nest was perfectly full, how could the dam come at her litter respectively so as to administer a teat to each? Perhaps she opens different places for that purpose, adjusting them again when the business is over: but she could not possibly be contained herself in the ball with her young, which moreover would be daily increasing in bulk. This wonderful procreant cradle, an elegant instance of the efforts of instinct, was found in a wheat-field suspended in the head of a thistle.

Such language! Doesn't it paint a perfect picture? I particularly like 'This wonderful procreant cradle, an elegant instance of the efforts of instinct . . .' though I worry at the nonchalant way he rolls those poor blind babies back and forth across the table. That I come across such nests fairly frequently as I stroll in my field is ample proof of the simple but exquisite delights of the countryside.

On the splendid quality of the light and air

If you could bottle the Breton light you would make a fortune from it. People when they see it just stop and stare, no other response is worthy. Artists came here for it, from all over. Most famous of these was Paul Gauguin, who set up a studio in the area in the late nineteenth century and built a school for artists around him at nearby Pouldu on the spectacularly jagged south Finistère coast, before buggering off to Tahiti where even if the air and light were not so sweet at least it was warmer and there were plentiful rather lovely and very friendly Tahitian women.

Gauguin's charmingly atmospheric painting *Breton Girls Dancing* alone makes this an important period and place for art, though he painted many others here. Lured by the curious unearthly combination of air and light others came here at the end of that century, to paint and sculpt and do similar stuff. Among them were artists such as Serusier, Bernard, Vlaminck, Claudel and Maxine Maufret (no, I've never heard of most of them either). They called themselves the Symbolist school and did as best as mortals can to capture the effects of Brittany's light on canvas. They succeeded only in part. Others I'm sure will keep trying.

No one in Kerkelven could fail to rejoice in the quality of light and air here. The best time to see its effects is just before sunset; the best place is down by the *étang*, our neighbour's pond, where the view across the prairie is sheer magic.

This is the only place I've ever experienced the changing colour of light. It's not a single colour, more a subtle multiple graduation of hues as the sun slowly goes down, transferring its light onto everything in turn, each different surface reflecting that light in subtly different ways. The predominant colours here are blue, purple, red ochre, orange, silver and gold. You can actually see the changing light as it travels across the land. These colours don't merely spread around you, they wash over and around you in a radiant glow. You have to remind yourself to keep breathing.

Attempts to describe these September sunsets, though, are largely futile. You just have to watch. Come when the sky is not overcast but there's scattered cloud about. Take field glasses but leave the dogs behind, for they show no prospect of ever appreciating such things. By all means bring a camera but unless you really know how to use it you'll just be disappointed later and it will surely distract you from what you should be doing, just revelling in the wonder of things.

So be content to look and marvel. Imprint the scene that's before you on your memory by whatever means you can, to make sure you'll never forget.

Me and my tractor

Kerkelven isn't all about walking. About once each week in spring and summer I cut the grass in a wide perimeter around our field. The purpose of this is to make walking easier, though it soon came to be a justifiable activity of its own. I used to attempt cutting the grass along the riverbank with an ordinary domestic sit-upon lawnmower, but the undergrowth got the better of this machine so many times (replacing the long rubber and steel big elastic-band-type thing that drives the blades costs €120 on each occasion) that eventually I splashed out and bought a three-quarter-sized tractor.

OK, maybe it's only half-sized when compared to today's biggies but despite what Loïc the farmer says, it is a real tractor. Honest.

And it gives me such pleasure.

When you've lived for twenty years in a big city the most mundane of countryside events can seem absurdly thrilling. Cutting the field's long grass by tractor is an unremarkable activity, you might suppose, but you'd be very wide of the mark.

We have a lot of grass and normally I would dismiss mowing the lawn as a tedious, rather tiring chore but my trimming by tractor is a high spot, a privilege for this townie that I can't possibly classify as work and therefore not enjoy.

I managed to afford and justify the purchase of my tractor by buying it at or around the same time as I was selling my motorbike. After many happy years together this was a painful parting, but a super-fast racing bike and an ageing fat bloke past middle years don't seem ideally made for each other, in several ways. I still miss my bike, but the tractor compensates quite a bit.

Which is strange. The transition from a 150mph 1,200cc BMW motorcycle to a diesel-driven tractor that bowls along at just 6km per hour takes quite some adjusting to, both mentally and physically.

But I just love the tractor and the way it does what it does. Where the bike roared, it throbs. Where the bike purred, it clanks. Where the bike zoomed, it dawdles. Where the bike was all about travelling quickly in style, the tractor is about style at its slowest. Both are much more about the journey than the getting there.

Instead of revving it up on country lanes I now plough a lonely furrow down by the river's edge. Actually, I don't plough at all, never have. I pull behind my tractor a grass-cutter specially designed for long grass. It's a flat-bed platen, a great horizontal plate housing a heavy, huge, ugly, revolving blade. As the tractor moves forward the big blade turns rapidly and everything beneath is finely chopped. It's a bit untidy with the grass it leaves behind but, hey, you can't have everything.

After a few faltering starts with much clanking and wheezing I set off. It's a crisp, cold late September afternoon, more winter than autumn. Low in the sky the setting sun turns the river to burnished copper. Suddenly God (at least it looks like it ought to be God, the God of Michelangelo and the saints and angels) seems to be rearranging the clouds above. Then the sun bursts forth, showering broad golden shafts of sunlight from the now silver, amber and gold-fringed clouds onto the grateful ground beneath.

Forget your Jacuzzis and your crack-cocaine, this is

perhaps the most relaxing sensation you'll find anywhere. I can't call it ploughing but equally grass-cutting doesn't do it justice. So, tractoring it is, tractoring in the fields of gold. I apologise, reader, for the soppy rhetoric. My excuse is it's quite overwhelmingly beautiful. It reassures me and I'm sure all the other creatures of Kerkelven that, truly, all is as it should be in our world.

Things that fall on your head

The moment I saw our pear tree I realised that it might topple over at any time. From that first sighting I've had a premonition that one day it will fall on my head; that this will be how things will end for me.

Please don't imagine that this is a piddly little George Washington-type fruit tree. Far from it. The thing is, this huge pear tree – it's about seven metres tall, the size of a full-grown oak – is growing directly out of the low wall on the left side of our path down to Bertrand's field. It's truly massive and unbelievably old (the wall, as well as the tree). Neither look very sturdy, or permanent. At some time in its distant past, perhaps when it was quite young, the tree must have keeled over and it now rests (apparently firmly, but can you trust a tree?) at a bizarre and dangerous-looking 45-degree angle from the perpendicular.

The first time we came here I remember gathering our children close to me like chickens and quickly shepherding them across the likely falling place of this great tree as it dangled threateningly above us like Damocles' sword. Marie, I reckoned, was insured and could look out for herself.

As time goes by I worry about it more and more. Surely the soil around it must weaken, over time. And the old tree itself must get heavier and heavier. Is it just my imagination that even the parasitic ivy is loosening up and getting ready for flight? My nightmare is of hearing a loud and telltale creak then turning to run up the hill but slipping and sliding and slithering on the mushy soil – too slow, too slow, says the wind as the great tree comes crashing down . . .

I envisage something like the almost weekly catastrophe that struck that persistently optimistic character Wile E. Coyote in the *Roadrunner* cartoon, when a huge tree or a ginormous boulder would fall from a great height onto him, bounce a bit off his bewildered bonce and then, bouncing again with rather unlikely precise vertical alignment, would hammer, hammer, hammer him firmly into the ground.

This hasn't happened to me yet with our pear tree, even after more than a dozen years. But that doesn't mean it isn't going to.

This pear tree is perhaps the largest pear tree there's ever been. So why, I wonder, does it give such small pears? They're tiny, not much bigger than a big grape, or a small plum. But what it lacks in size it makes up for in quantity. Each year, just as all the abundance from this great tree appears, they start to fall. In a mere day or two, thousands of these tiny fruit fall like hailstones onto the path beneath. Before long there's a veritable carpet. In time, they begin to rot and a not unpleasant rather alcoholic odour of mashed fruit begins to pervade the forest.

But nothing in the forest stays as it is for long. Soon the whole area smells like Paddy's Bar in Kilburn early on a Saturday morning, just after closing time, when all the noisy customers have finally left and the bartender is wondering whether to clean up a wee bit now or leave it until later, in the hope that it'll smell better, or go away, or good fairies will visit and do it for him. It's a powerful, serious odour, but quite a comforting one.

Bees, wasps and small birds come along to feast on the decomposing fruit and before long become quite drunk. Butterflies get blotto. Damselflies binge-drink in it. The bumblebees particularly become more bumbly than usual. Soon it gets a bit sticky underfoot and we just wish that the whole horrid mess would go away. Like many of nature's messes, clearing it up would be beyond contemplation. But leave it and in time it'll go away by itself. The soil here must be worth a fortune. Just the smell knocks the legs from under you.

Like the light, we should bottle it.

Blackbirds, song thrushes and other birds are partial to fruit during autumn and winter. Apples are a particular favourite, when insects are hard to find. Our windfall fruit or berries from our hedges will provide food for the thrushes and their relatives, the redwing, mistle thrush and fieldfare.

Suddenly we have a profusion of apples, thousands and thousands and they've started falling, big time. It's not surprising that our apple crop is impressive as, not counting the trees in the small field (and there are eight of them), we have thirty apple trees on the slopes of the hill next to the forest. But we have only one pear tree.

Sidling up to some slitherers

Though most people never encounter them and even those that think of it assume they must be very rare, there are three types of snake found in surprising abundance around Kerkelven. These, in descending order of size and reverse order of dangerousness, are the grass snake, the smooth snake and the viper, also called adder. We also have the slowworm, which looks like a snake but is actually a legless lizard, with eyelids, different scales and jaws that don't dislocate to swallow animals larger than its mouth. But despite appearances the slowworm is neither snake nor worm, it is a lizard, so we'll leave it for now.

Grass snakes usually gather in groups for hibernation, hiding wherever they'll be safe and sheltered, such as under a woodpile, in a hollow tree or among tree roots or decaying vegetation. Then, usually, they'll entwine together to pass the cold months in intricate knots, presumably asleep, cosy and warm. Here they remain until March or April, when the frogs, toads and newts emerge from a similar seasonal slumber so are available for dinner. About this time the males will grab the females in their jaws as a prelude to mating (consent, apparently, is an irrelevance). Then, some time between June and August, the female will find a convenient mass of moist and mouldy vegetation amidst which to burrow and deposit her eggs. She will prefer horse or cow manure, though, if it's available, as the heat speeds up incubation. Her eggs may number anywhere between a dozen and fifty.

The smooth snake is quite easy to catch and, like the grass snake, when caught it may emit a horrid smell and try to bite, but this unfriendly phase passes and it quickly becomes tame. Some say smooth snakes particularly show a considerable amount of intelligence.

Vipers hibernate in autumn in a hollow under dry moss, among heather, under woodpiles or, apparently, in the discarded and leaf-covered ground nests of birds. They reappear about April and may then be seen coiled on a sunny bank apparently more concerned to enjoy the sunshine than to find food. They pair in the spring and the young (varying from five to twenty) are born in August or September.

Adders resist a life of captivity more than grass or smooth snakes. Short-tempered and sulky, individuals will often refuse food to the point of dying from starvation, this 'hunger strike' being its effective protest on being deprived of liberty. Try catching a viper and it is highly likely to bite you, but in its natural state the viper is neither aggressive nor hostile. To escape being seen it will stay very still, but as soon as it realises it's been discovered it immediately heads for cover.

Sex with snakes

I still feel badly about this. It was about a year ago, the tail end of last summer and as usual Mortimer, Max, Syrus and I were rummaging around in the underbrush unearthing all sorts of fascinating goings-on. Last year seemed to be a season unusually enriched by snakes because we'd found more than a few, usually curled up contentedly in some quiet corner, or else flopped inconveniently in the middle of one or other of our paths. Invariably we'd leave them undisturbed where they lay, silently envying their moments in the sun.

On this occasion though I wasn't so considerate. Between two clumps of grass on the slope of the woods where the undergrowth was more than usually penetrable I found what looked like the biggest or at least longest adder I'd ever seen. And it seemed to be sleeping. But my goodness it was big, with coils and coils of it going round and round ad infinitum.

I just couldn't resist trying to see the full extent of this monster so cautiously, with the use of a long forked stick, I gave it a gentle poke. It stirred but didn't move. I of course prodded a bit harder. Slowly a snake's head unfolded from the coils and looked witheringly at me. Thankfully looks can't kill, at least not quickly, so I selfishly prodded again the coiled folds of serpent flesh. At that instant a second snake's head appeared from further down in the tangled coils and it too fixed and held me with a baleful, accusing eye. In a split second I realised what I'd done. I'd disturbed two snakes, presumably a male and a female, in their biennial ritual of sexual congress. They weren't sleeping, they were shagging. Just as they were thinking that, for them, 'tonight's the night', I'd come along a-poking with my forked stick and so had put the kibosh on their poking for probably another two years. (It's the female snakes that have sex only every second year. The males may be up for it more often, but with whom is an open question.)

As the full weight of the awfulness of my actions flooded in upon me they slowly and deliberately uncoiled from their serpently embrace, extracting themselves gradually and (well, this is one time you wouldn't want a love bite, is it not?) very carefully from their entanglement to slither off in quite different directions.

I felt so, so, so bad.

I sat squatted upon my haunches with head in hands as Mortimer, who had seen nothing of either snakish lover, slobbered gently and comfortingly in my ear. Needless to say this didn't assuage my guilt or ease my regret, it just gave me an earful of dribble.

But as I've thought more about this I've convinced myself that really I must have disturbed the pair after the deed, in post-coital slumber, unwinding perhaps following a frantic, fulfilling and most likely successful sexual act. I do hope so. Not just because this thought makes me feel better, but also because it suggests that snake shagging may not after all be a sedentary and tranquil affair, that there may have been some fairly vigorous one-on-one action from these two sexy slitherers just minutes before my dogs and I arrived, to spoil the moment.

I later learned that adders, as with other European snakes, usually mate in the spring and deliver their offspring in the high summer. So, a further pointer to what I think I can now safely assume: these two were just having a quick cuddle.

Despite the fear they engender in others I find snakes more than a little fascinating and seek their company whenever I can. Once when my scary sister-in-law was staying I found a large grass snake out by the parked cars (I think it must have been dropped there by a buzzard, which I believe in ancient times would have been considered a good omen) and took it into her bedroom where she was (until then) enjoying a holiday treat of full French breakfast in bed.

Ah, happy days! The thing I remember above her screams though was the awful pungent smell of the beast (the snake, not her). My new-found pal Gilbert White writes of this in one of his rambling letters. He says to his naturalist friend:

> . . , I wish I had not forgot to mention the faculty that snakes have of stinking *se defendo*. [It means in defence of themselves. Gilbert was a bit of a smart-arse and was forever lapsing into Latin.] I knew a gentleman who kept a tame snake, which was in its person as sweet as any animal while in good humour and unalarmed; but as soon as a stranger, or a dog or cat, came in, it fell to hissing, and filled the room with such nauseous effluvia as rendered it hardly supportable. This is an innocuous and sweet animal; but, when pressed hard by dogs and men it can eject a most pestilent and fetid smell and excrement, that nothing can be more horrible.

That just about sums up sister-in-law Lynne's bedroom that sunny, late summer's morning.

A spider's tsunami
In our field a hundred thousand sparkly spiders' webs appear

as if by magic overnight. Each of the field's countless shoots and plants is festooned with an overnight creation, all hung with pearls, bejewelled with silver strings of dripping dew.

Our neighbouring field is freshly ploughed. At every welly-booted step across this newly turned sod tiny black spiders rush for cover. These can't be the spider workers from our field come to see what's going on. No, it seems each field has its own vast population of spiders. But unlike Ken and Marie's spiders, now presumably enjoying well-earned respite from their labours, some time late yesterday the spiders in neighbour Loïc's field must have literally had their world turned upside down when crash, that cruel plough of his smashed through their homes and habitats. Though not perhaps as devastating as this, I suppose my tractor-mower does its own mischief too, as it does its work.

For them, the simple act of a human's ploughing must seem as cataclysmic as a cyclone, destroying not just their homes and their handiwork but also their means of catching supper. What's just happened must have instantly reshaped their world much as a giant tidal wave or a Richter Scale 10 earthquake would reshape ours. Yet these unnatural disasters strike the insect world daily and the Disasters Emergency Committee launches no appeal for the spidery survivors.

But they don't seem in the least put out. Perhaps there are different ways of finding food if you're a spider. I can find no piles of spider dead bodies and I see no streams of spidery refugees making their way with only what they can carry to the comparative sanctuary of our field, which never gets ploughed.

Perhaps when your life and way of living are regularly turned upside down, you learn to cope.

Jonathan and Eric

We are often accompanied on our evening walk by two of the many residents of our house at Kerkelven, Jonathan and Eric. These are common pipistrelle bats who have made their home in our thatch. They are hard to tell apart and from other bats, so we can't always be sure it's them and can't ever be sure which is which. But the bats that so often come with us on our last walk of the day have since time long past invariably been referred to as Jonathan and Eric.

At least we're as sure as can be that they're pipistrelles. Bats move so quickly through the twilight with their dark-grey colouring that even when they swoop up close they're surprisingly hard to identify for sure. I know, because Marie and I have not just sat hunched over opened textbooks, we've even taken these open texts with us on our night walks. These haven't helped much though, as they're not too easy to read standing up, at twilight. But later, over cocoa, they have taught us quite a lot about bats.

Bats are very special creatures – they are the only back-boned animal that can truly fly – and sharing our house and walks with them is a real treat. Marie might disagree with this. They figure high in several of her many phobias, particularly the one where as they swoop very low – which unquestionably they do – both Jonathan and Eric simultaneously get caught in her flowing curls. They also have very sharp claws, of course.

In fact this is a largely groundless fear (at least, it hasn't happened yet). Bats actually see very well and are rarely wrong-footed in their aerial acrobatics. In part this is because, particularly at night, their sharp vision is aided by their well-developed facility for echolocation. Every schoolboy and girl knows that bats have their own radar. This may not function well indoors though. Recently a very large bat of unknown type got into our house and flapped around alarmingly for a while. On its way out it did indeed bump Marie quite hard on the head, proving me wrong yet again and probably giving itself something of a headache, as well as Marie.

Finding fish

Occasionally on walks around Kerkelven Bertrand would regale me with his childhood memories, one of which included fishing for trout in the river. He was convinced the river was no longer home to any fish of a reasonable size as he hadn't seen any for many a year. We would shake our heads at the memory of happier, 'fish-a-jumpin' days, sadly concurring that the modern-day dominance of fertilisers in farming and the inevitable chemical pollution that ensues mean that nowadays any fish bigger than a moderately plump minnow is, for our beloved Sarre, a thing of the past.

We would walk on in silence, again with much shaking of heads. It didn't occur to us on these occasions that quite often on our walks we'd meet and spend a cordial moment with a fisherman or two. They must have put on their strange garb and come to Kerkelven for a reason, but it never dawned on us, as we enjoyed our harping upon better days gone by, to ask their views. I suppose we thought they were after the minnows. Or perhaps, just used fishing as an excuse to get out of the house.

Then a keen fisherman friend came to lunch with us one September day and he, when strolling along the river, pronounced with absolute certainty that this water, our river, must hold big fish.

I assured him this had once been the case, but was no longer so.

'Then what,' he exclaimed, 'is that?'

I followed his pointed finger towards the big pool in front of the first cataract. The sun shone obliquely on the water and, sure enough, three big submarine-shapes swam serenely and silently into view. Blimey! Fish! And big ones. Trout, he said, rainbow trout. You might see salmon too, he ventured. But seeing living healthy swimming trout that day was thrill enough for me.

Often enough since I've seen trout singly and in shoals of three, five or seven (always odd numbers – what's that about?) but I've yet to see a salmon. I think I would know the difference . . . And I've never seen them jump.

But oh what a difference those fish have made, to me.

This I suppose explains why we also have fishermen. Each season, down by the river, bloody big ones too. As with the hunters I can't prohibit their access (they need a permit from the local town hall but that's no sweat) for though I claim the river and actually own right up to its banks, technically the riverbanks and the river itself are owned by the local council and held for the common good of all.

Not that I would willingly confess this to anyone except you, of course. I prefer people to assume it is my river.

In truth the fishermen don't bother me much and I suppose, grudgingly, that it's nice to see other folk enjoying the river. As long as its stocks are stable and capable of renewal, which I'm assured they are. And that the fish they catch have had a happy life here and didn't suffer. If you have to be a fish and end up on a plate, better I think that you come from Kerkelven than many other places we could name.

Anyway, they rarely catch anything, these big fisher folk, and are civil enough so I'm polite in return, though with my unruly band of dogs I have more than once disturbed the tranquillity of their day.

I never saw anything

Something big happened in the forest overnight. Something unusual was on the move, something substantial, something very unsettling. Whatever it was skirted around the edges of the forest, along the paths, by the round table down where the rivers meet.

All three of the dogs went bananas. I first realised something was up when we crossed old Emile's field and suddenly, as if at a call, all three dogs sped off together towards the middle distance, racing as if the devil himself was after them, to disappear as one into the undergrowth along the river's edge.

Then . . . silence.

They seemed to be gone a while. Even the birds stopped what they were doing and watched the place where their tails had disappeared. For a long time the air seemed heavy with the silence. Then one by one, more cautious now, tense, sniffing and searching, darting here and there, edgy and pawing, all three emerged. They seemed to consult, silently agree, then raced off again, this time to the stone table.

Well, they went over that stone circle like a forensic search team. Each and every day they pass this table several times and normally wouldn't even acknowledge it. Now it was the centre of their attentions as they clambered over it and all around it, noses hoovering over every centimetre. Something had been here, something they sensed but I couldn't, something that raised hackles on the back of each dog. It wasn't something insignificant, or minor.

But I saw nothing.

It took me a while to drag all three away. But whatever had so excited them clearly wasn't there now and wasn't about to reappear. So the incident, like many others, was forgotten.

Rats as big as dogs

Apparently there's one for every human in New York and in London you are never more than two metres from the nearest rat. Here rats are in the ascendancy, outnumbering humans by several to one. But country rats are much nicer, cleaner and better behaved than city rats, viz Ratty in *Wind of the Willows*, who actually was a water vole and not a rat at all. (Though you still wouldn't want one running up your trouser leg, believe me.)

And we do have rats, and aplenty, at Kerkelven. But mainly they're water-based and stick to their world as long at least as we stick to ours.

It's quite possible that the thing that caused such a commotion down by the river was a *ragondin*, what English people call coypu, a large ratlike rodent as big as a small dog. Literally, as big as Syrus.

That's a big rat.

Coypu come originally from South America. Though they've now been almost eradicated there, some years ago they almost overran the fenlands of southern England and they're endemic in the Marais, the large, formerly swampy area well to the south of here. We used to see a lot of them here at Kerkelven, hanging about at the river's edge just at the waterline in family groups of three, four or more. From a distance, particularly as they swim, they can look like otters or muskrats, but closer up they just look like huge, fat and rather unpleasant rats.

Coypu have bright orange incisor teeth, are herbivores and the female has her nipples on her back, so that she can feed her little ones when she's in the water. Once we saw a pure white one, surrounded by several others. He was a genuine albino, with small pink piggy eyes. But he was also an adult. How he'd lived for so long with that colouring is impossible to say. But large though they are, coypu (I prefer the French name *ragondin*, which sounds more like the animal) are shy and secretive. Farmers hate them, probably with good reason.

So the coypu live low in rivers or drainage canals and forage silently in small groups in the early mornings when they can slip safely unseen along the rivers, ditches and other watery passageways wherein they live. People rarely see them or know they are there. If they did, they'd persecute them for sure, rooting them out one by one, burning their nests and killing their babies. Universally hated by all, the coypu knows without doubt that everyone is his enemy.

We haven't seen any coypu around here for quite some time now. After a few early morning encounters like the one described below, the dogs have scared them off.

This saddens me though. I know I shouldn't, because they are a pest, but I miss them. They are one of that rare and vanishing kind, a truly savage beast living wild and free in the heart of our land.

Bristles at dawn

The most dangerous time for a meeting with a coypu is the eerie half-light before the dawn, when everything is indistinct shadow and walks by the river's edge assume a dangerous aspect, merely because of the gloom.

One late September morning Mortimer, Max, Syrus and I were trudging over the fields at a particularly early hour as I had a plane to catch, to attend some meeting or other in London. The contrast of surroundings was not lost on me and my mind was most probably elsewhere as in the gloomy still-dark of early morning we stepped out boldly across our neighbour's newly ploughed field. If I was concentrating on anything it was probably where to put my next footstep as I couldn't really see clearly beyond my knees.

Then all hell broke out.

In the half of a half-light that was all there was at that hour I could barely distinguish anything. The noise was clear but so loud and coming from so many throats at once that it was hard to distinguish. It was a snarling, snapping, keep-away sound, not quite a full rip-yer-throat-out fight but very near it. Then in a circle one by one I managed to pick out the three dogs. They were actually slowly spinning. Max and Syrus, being white, weren't too difficult to discern but Mortimer's rusty brown meant he was little more than a vague, bear-shaped blur. But what it was they were fighting – and there was something else in there with them, at least one – was impossible to see (on account, I learned later, of its deep dark fur). I just knew that it was big, big enough and ferocious enough to be making at least half of all the noise and keeping my three furry friends – now snapping, snarling fiends – at bay.

The din was terrific. The swirling shapes in the gloom made it near impossible to see what was going on, but it didn't sound pretty. At times as they circled they seemed almost to be standing up. Their shapes and colours merged into one demented dervish-like blur.

Then suddenly, the dogs stopped. Mortimer yelped a bit then fell silent, like the others. I think then that I spoke for the first time, saying, 'What the bloody hell . . .?' or something similar. With a final ferocious guttural snarl the coypu – there was indeed only one – backed defiantly into the river and with a mighty splash was off.

We four were left looking at each other, or what remained of each other, in what was now a clearing, proper but still gloomy half-light. Given what we'd just been through I half expected to see serious wounds, a severed limb or two and more than a few tears and tatters.

There was blood, quite a lot of it. Poor Mortimer's nose was in shreds. His foam-flecked muzzle had two deep wet red gashes across it. The other two were excited but unscratched. I suspect in the mêlée they'd had the sense to push Mortimer forward, so he'd take the brunt. Fair enough. After all, he is the biggest.

From that moment, I believe, Mortimer learned one of life's most valuable lessons – cowards live longer. From that morning on, in fights he is most hesitant, the first to hold back.

Moonlight in the forest

In dead of night an owl screeches across the valley, reminding us that there is another world out there and this, the night, is its time.

While others are drifting off to slumber you have to be ready, to grab the chance to enjoy the true dark night the instant it presents itself. As the moon approaches full, and if the cloud cover leaves off long enough for you to enjoy it, this is the time to go night walking around Kerkelven. In dead of night the paths and byways become spookily reminiscent of a horror-movie set. But much grander, more real and scarier and you are immersed within it, it's all around.

Imagine it's very, very dark. This dark is Africa dark, the kind of dark that you only get deep in the countryside, or in the very heart of the forest. When the cloud is thick there's no ambient light, nor moon or starlight, whatsoever. The only light anywhere comes from your weedy little torch, which allows you to see just a little of what's ahead and around you but of course all the while enabling each and every one of the creatures that are certainly out there, watching and waiting, to see you, clearly and with ease. They can already hear you, you know only too well. Now it dawns on you that you are the easiest prey ever.

On an instant the clouds break up and scatter and the big, bulging moon breaks through, flooding the night with its reflected light, creating a weird, eerie world of shadow and light. Moonbeams filter through the topmost branches of the forest, slanting down upon the rocks and paths, trees and undergrowth beneath. Dust and the debris of the night rise up to meet the light. It's still, a stillness disturbed only by muffled rustles and the perhaps imagined scrapes, sighs and murmurs of night denizens on the prowl. Did you really hear that sound back there, see that movement in the corner of your eye, feel that fleeting waft of passing wind? In the background the river rumbles on, murmuring unceasingly.

The face of the man in the moon seems to be scowling down at you more hostile than ever. An owl calls, and from the 'twit-twoo' sound you know it must be a tawny. Other owls screech and scream from various corners of the field. But there are also different, unearthly calls and cries that punctuate the night air, more frightening because they can't be identified.

Pools of darkness and light alternate to create a swirl of dancing shadows. The moonlit air appears to glow, everything around seems luminous and unreal. Dark shapes become fantastic creatures. Rocks become beasts, trees seem to move in ways they shouldn't. Of course, trees shouldn't be moving at all. As you hurry along, anxious to get home now, what seemed solid becomes insubstantial. You can depend on nothing but the dangerous dark. Leaves and branches sway when there is no wind. The light gets lighter and the dark gets darker, deepening to solid black. As you quicken your pace the whole forest seems to move behind and around you to contain and keep you. Now would be a likely time for that werewolf to appear, if it's coming.

At the forest's edge you stop, feeling foolish, and step back but the moment is gone. It will return, and so you toddle off happily to bed, reflecting upon the oddness of the moon and its queer effect upon the earth below. It isn't a perfect sphere, this moon, more like an oversized potato. This may not seem romantic, but there it is.

Just being here at such a time is spellbinding. Realising that the woods around you are full of bustling life takes your wonder to a new dimension.

Something making a feeble, throaty, croaking noise struggles past in the darkness, about tree height. I've no idea what it is but it might be a duck or a goose that's got lost or is returning home from an evening on the tiles. The night closes in around with pools of light glimmering through the groaning trees.

Suddenly the house appears before me looming out of a gathering mist, its floodlights bristling with rays that radiate into the void of night.

That front door seems more than just appealing now. If, that is, I can make it without being rushed from behind . . .

Welcome to a walk in the woods of Kerkelven, by moonlight.

Today is the last Sunday in September, and the first day of the hunt

A rifle shot rings out in the cold morning air signalling the attempted murder of another woodland creature. The commencement of the hunting season always seems a particularly glum time to me. For a minimum of twelve long winter weeks Kerkelven and its environs come to resemble the suburbs of Baghdad. It's particularly noticeable on the weekends. (At other times gainful employment tends to keep the active male Breton otherwise occupied.)

Please don't misunderstand me. I can sympathise with, even support, those who hunt for food, for I too am a meat eater. And as with Kerkelven's fish, I feel that food that's lived its life in and around my field by the river is many times more fortunate than food raised more artificially elsewhere.

Also, there's an argument put forward that claims much of the wild land in this area remains uncultivated only because hunters have lobbied for it to stay that way. There may be some truth in this, though land here is plentiful and most rough land is unfarmable. The farmers rather than the hunters would be the more powerful lobby here, even if, often, they are the same people. If there's even a smidge of truth in the claim though, I'm grateful for it, even if I could find several better reasons for preserving the countryside. I know that in some countries hunters are increasingly expected to pay for the creatures they kill and the money thus raised is reinvested in conservation. I do see some value in this, though I find the basic premise – killing for pleasure – deeply flawed.

In days gone by, the forefathers of today's hunters depended on the hunt to eat, as well as to reduce vermin. Both of these functions still pertain and I have no problem with that. But even though much of whatever hunters kill might still end up in the pot, for the most part, the hunt here has evolved from functional necessity to pure sport. It's become, more than anything, a social outing, a chance to dress up in combat garb and have fun with the boys. Hunting is mainly a man-thing, it seems. Not many women seem to want to gang together on cold mornings armed to the teeth with lethal weapons and to maraud in Rambo-style khaki fatigues across the countryside killing small animals.

But hunting is a strong tradition here. So of a Sunday morning you will find a high commotion outside the home of our lovely neighbour Bertrand, who is only slightly wedded to the hunt for social reasons. But these social reasons (and perhaps the proximity of our bits of the forest) dictate that all his chums come calling early at his place, or at least they did, until he shacked up with his girlfriend Marie-Thérèse, who likes a lie-in of a Sunday, so they moved down the road to gather outside ours. Which is why at eight o'clock on a Sunday morning now you will find Bertrand's ruddy-faced fat friend Obelix (so called for his striking resemblance to Asterix's buddy of that name in that wonderful cartoon by Uderzo and Goscinny), plus Moon-face from Lann-Vraz, the butcher, the local mechanic and a dingy assortment of local ne'er-do-wells assembled outside our window to get the hunt off to a flying start. My tirades of verbal abuse about the inappropriate earliness of the hour scarcely dents their ardour. Well, I did once shout at them from the safety of our window but mostly it's Marie's ear that gets bent, or the dogs'. These guys have guns!

Despite the early hour it's quite usual for the hunters to have already had a good drink before they set off. I suppose there has to be some other attraction, it can't just be tramping over muddy fields and through brambles in the pouring rain at an ungodly hour trying to get a glimpse of something living and shootable.

We shouldn't mock. It takes a heroic effort of will to walk across a ploughed field in wellies when eight parts pissed, carrying a heavy shotgun.

Before long it's like a rifle range outside our house and anything that moves is likely to be blasted. Like the dogs, I jump every time I hear a ricochet. And so it will be for the next three months. I feel like crawling from the front door waving a white flag, though no one would cease firing I'm sure, even for a second.

When the boys were young, Marie, Joe and Charlie would at times meet the hunters in the woods and all three would instantly raise their hands above their heads in automatic submission and make to go quietly. This tactic much discomforted the hunters, seeming to trouble them almost as much as the boys' loud and seriously untuneful whistling of *Colonel Bogey* as they walked through their woods.

In small ways we might ape *le Maquis*, the Resistance, but we do surrender in reality, burying our heads under the pillows and hoping it'll go away. It will, in February.

Am I being too harsh? Perhaps. I exaggerate, if only slightly, to make a point. But there are better ways, I'm sure, to enjoy our countryside, which is already facing too many threats. If we don't start to show it serious respect we won't have it for much longer.

And we'll only have ourselves to blame for that.

So what, the summer is over?

The moorhens are all gone now. So are the swallows, and quite a few other birds too, or at least they won't be far behind. The frogs and toads will soon be getting ready to hibernate, the bats will be toddling off to their beds, the coypu have probably already stored up their potatoes in their little crannies and crevices by the water's edge (apparently, potatoes are what they like) and soon will be blissfully snoring away. Or at least, hoping to survive their long fast and the winter cold. Whatever, there's a definite end-of-season air about.

But there are others here, who will stay, who throughout the impending autumn and winter won't be going anywhere, instead for various reasons of their own will continue on in Kerkelven. In their way, they are just as interesting, as mysterious, as scary and as fascinating as all those who have left, or will be off soon. Though they may be a bit more difficult to see and to understand.

So though the summer is over, that's no sadness for Kerkelven, because a new season is beginning, its signs are all around and they promise as much fun and fulfilment as the summer just passed.

October

Now it's time you visited our house

The council's signpost at the bottom of our road has us as living in Grand Kerkelven, but we don't use that because it sounds poncey. To the people who live here this place is just known as Kerkelven. There are two Kerkelvens in the immediate vicinity, however, and the other one is undeniably known as Petit Kerkelven. Apart from its chicken sheds Petit Kerkelven has just one house, and therein until recently lived our farmer and *bête noire*, Loïc's dad, old Emile.

Kerkelven the village gives its name to our house also, because our house is *le petit manoir*, the little manor house, originally home to the big noises hereabouts. Sometimes it is spelled Kerquelven or Kerkelvin. Our house was built in 1655 and some of its outbuildings (sadly not all owned by us and our descendants) even date two or three years earlier. Kerkelven means at the house of Kelven. Though its origins are lost in the mists of time, it's safe to assume that someone important of that name lived here in times long past.

A bit more about the inhabitants

As you probably know by now, I'm called Ken, father in this family. That's really enough about me. My wife is called Marie. She's gorgeous. We've known each other for the best part of four decades, have been together 35 years or more, married for 31 of them. Sometimes I struggle to resist the nigh-over-whelming urge to rush up behind her and smite her over the head with a shovel, but otherwise we are pretty happy, all in all.

Our sons are Joe and Charlie, fine, strapping youths of 25 and 21 respectively. They've both now left home to make their way in life independent of their parents' rule and supervision, though they come home on a fairly regular basis, i.e. when hungry.

Since our twin felines, Pearl and Ruby, passed away earlier this year, for the first time in ages we have no living cats, at least none that we're feeding (this is an oblique reference to the appalling Lazarus, our neighbour's cast-off tom, who despite all discouragements has stuck to us like a limpet). Then there's Ebb, our tropical fish. All the other fish died years ago but Ebb lives on, indestructible. Flo, his last surviving partner from the original tank-full, died at least two years ago, but Ebb hangs on in there like he's immortal. With these and the four humans above, that appears to be all the residents of our house covered. But it isn't, far from it.

Our household also includes the three dogs, Syrus, Max and Mortimer, whom you met earlier. But they don't actually live here, not in the house. They are not allowed indoors for in the Breton tradition they are outside dogs, living winter and summer in a large kennel located behind where we park our cars.

Why we came here

We moved here from London in 1993. It wasn't that life in the big city was an empty shell, an abyss of dark despair, or anything like that. To be honest we were very content with the life we lived then. But equally, we were always open to something new.

We'd bought our house in France back in 1989 as a summer retreat. For thirty years before then it had been neglected and unloved and that seemed a shame. But such a span of time is nothing to our house, which if left moderately alone will probably last another 350 years at least. This, as I've said, is the manor house and in those days they built their posher houses to last. Even modest accommodation back then was more solidly built, but our house of Breton granite throughout will surely, for the foreseeable future, stand whatever tests time can throw at it. If some evil warlord were to drop a nuclear bomb on Paris or London, or even nearby Pontivy, when the dust settles Kerkelven will still be standing, minus perhaps its roof and maybe a few of its inhabitants. But the house and, I suspect, most of the bugs will survive, no doubt. The sturdy stones that have held up our house these past three and a half centuries will have moved not a millimetre.

There were several reasons for our coming to live in France and back in 1993 they all seemed to coincide. More than anything it just seemed my life then was back to front, and I had the power, the freedom and the means to turn it completely upside down and so get it the right way round again. Life was the wrong way round because I was spending just six weeks of it each year at our holiday home in Kerkelven and loving every minute of it whereas for the other forty-six weeks I was back in London, tired of that crowded city and the pressures of its life and, to be honest, wishing I were in France. And I could go anywhere. I'm lucky enough to be able to work wherever there's a telephone connection and somewhere to plug in a computer.

So, almost without any expectation of success, one day in conversation with Marie I just ventured the suggestion, 'Why don't we turn everything around and move to France?'

She was obviously ill-prepared for this question and on the spot couldn't think of any of the 53 perfectly good reasons against my plainly daft idea. So she said yes.

Kerkelven the house

We may be an ordinary enough family but our house is distinctly out of the ordinary, so I will tell you a bit about it.

It's old. Recently we rather noisily and flamboyantly celebrated its 350th birthday.

The stone walls of our house are a metre thick, more in places. As you come in the low front door with its typical Breton semi-circular domed stone top you are greeted by three massive beams, whole trees in fact, oaks from somewhere around here that have been propping up the first floor of this house ever since it was built. The phrase 'they don't make 'em like this any more' springs to mind. Dozens of crossbeams quite unnecessarily assist these three stalwarts in their supporting role. Now facing you there's a stone spiral staircase (from outside it looks like a turret) that leads to the floor above. Halfway up this you'll find a slit window, through which you can fire arrows at your neighbours. At the top is an alcove, originally conceived as a medieval long-drop toilet that opened directly onto the ground behind the house. We don't use it for that any more. It's now a store cupboard.

To your right as you come in at ground level there's a huge fireplace beneath a massive carved oak beam that acts as a not very efficient deflector, channelling smoke and flames up into the vast chimney above. The façade of this fireplace has various nooks, ingles and domed arches wherein in ages past Breton housewives presumably did various cooking and householdy-type things, like drying salt and making the soup. There's a smaller but similar, slightly more ornate stone fireplace upstairs and an unused but even bigger one next door in the converted barn. This fireplace and the four-sectioned niche that's next to it have both been ascertained by experts from *Le Département de Patrimoine* (the French equivalent of English Heritage) to be at least a hundred years older than the house. These pieces were probably brought here by the gentleman farmer who built this place, as acquisitions from a larger house, perhaps one being demolished at the time, somewhere in the south. This can be said with some certainty because both fireplace and niche are rather more ornate than the traditional plain Breton decorative style, which in its simplicity sometimes borders on the severe.

Two large niches (for your madonnas, saints, or perhaps a bowl of flowers) break up the severity of the exposed stone walls. We've filled in around the hundreds and hundreds of exposed stones with a sandstone-coloured pointing, a massive job I have to say, all done painstakingly by hand. (Well, when I say we've done it, workmen actually did the work. So I suppose it wasn't painstaking after all. But we paid them, which is a bit painful, at best pretty tiresome.)

So, it's a curious relic of a bygone age, our house, odd, but in itself a bit special, not grand but a very spacious and solid one-off. However, it enjoys a less than perfect aspect. To be honest if I could I'd turn it round, to turn its back on our neighbours and face the sunset. But shifting this pile of big, chunky granite cubes even a few centimetres would be quite a job.

Meet the other humans

The total population of the hamlet of Kerkelven is just nine people. Quite recently it was as high as thirteen, which still isn't many although just before we came here it was only three, Bertrand, then a bachelor (quaintly named *célibataire* in the local language, a possibly misleading term for the English) and Mathurin and Angèle, whom you met in the introduction. Kerkelven enjoys a rare but far from unique distinction for a rural Breton village – its population in recent years has grown. There's something of a regeneration going on here, in the countryside, and it seems set to continue.

What really goes on inside our house?

As we share our old rambling farmhouse with a large, richly diverse array of other creatures, we have to accept it is their home too.

Let me tell you just a bit about one of these.

Recently we were treated to an unusual display of insect enterprise. Our kitchen window that overlooks the fields and river isn't large or fancy. The simple wooden frame is hinged at the left side and opens inwards. Its wooden ledge, though firmly set into the deep stone window space, is modest and narrow. The frame is attached by two little holes to the window, within each of which holes, one imagines, a simple screw fixes the simple wooden ledge to the frame. Well, on the day of my tale my attention had been drawn to an ant who appeared to be fighting with a very large spider (I mean big – the spider was about fifteen times the ant's bulk) right in front of us, on our window ledge. The fight was brutal and short and despite the size difference the ant had killed the spider all the same. Now, it just had to get it into the house.

This was far from easy. Most humans would just have given up and moved on. But not this ant. And for sure this was no itsy-bitsy spider. This was the giant Shebob of *Lord of the Rings* fame. It was gargantuan, the Godzilla of the spider world – big, black and hairy.

Quite oblivious to the appalled gaze of its landlord (really, I'd rather the ant hadn't dragged the corpse into our house even if it is also its house), this enterprising ant grabbed the vast spider by its rear end and proceeded to drag it, backwards, into one of the screw holes. 'Never,' I thought, and called the wife. 'Impossible,' she exclaimed. But without a pause and herself disappearing rear end first into the hole the Herculean ant tugged and tugged at that spider and slowly but surely, bit by bit, its huge abdomen squeezed into that hole, then in unison its eight legs followed. After that the head was easy, and soon ant, spider and all were inside. But where? In the house, or inside the wooden window frame? And what unspeakable things where happening in there, as we watched?

We just shrugged and left them to it. Such is life – and death – in Kerkelven.

The significance of signs

Country people constantly make knowledgeable-sounding observations such as, 'It's been a very good year for wild flowers.' Or, 'There's a lot of lapwings around just now.' Or they ask seemingly sensible questions, like 'Where have all the owls gone?' 'How come there's such a plague of horseflies this year?' 'What's happened to all the dragonflies?' 'Why are there so many robins?' Or, 'How is it that sometimes hares seem abundant, yet at other times they're almost entirely absent?'

The natural world is subject to constant variations and fluctuations, but what do they mean? What is the country newcomer to make of them? Are they signs of climate change, or something else equally sinister? Are they portents of dire things to come? Last year we had a bumper fall of acorns from the many oaks that are in our forest. Some of our neighbours said this indicates there's a very cold winter coming.

Could they be right? As we'd sit contemplatively at the stone table in the western corner of the field acorns by the dozen would fall noisily on our heads, zinging like bullets into the river, scaring the dogs and I've no doubt frightening the fish. If this is nature's weather forecast it may be something we humans do rather better, for this is dangerous, painful and not particularly efficient or reliable.

Bumper apples, scarce apples, more mushrooms, fewer

mushrooms – what does it all mean? And what inference should we draw from a crop exactly identical to last year's? This could be the most ominous portent of all. What's the night sky all about, sometimes fiery red, then clear, then cloudy? And what of morning mists and sunny starts? In fact there's so much chopping and changing going on, it sometimes seems very difficult really to get it quite right, for nature.

Undeniably, nothing around here is constant. One year foxes are regularly sighted, the next, hardly at all. Last year there were no swallows around our house, but plenty above the field. This year, the air above the house is swarming with them. Some years I'll not see a kingfisher. Then, if not thronging, I'll see one or two every day for a week or so. The winter before last a flock of fifty or more herons seemed to have made Kerkelven their home. Last year there was just one.

What can we tell from such events? Perhaps nothing. Perhaps a lot.

Faced with such questions I recall once turning to our sage and elderly neighbour, old Bertrand, to seek his insight into this issue. He's a salt of the earth, Bertrand, a true child of the countryside, raised in these rural landscapes who – up till then – had lived all his life here, a farmer all his working days, now venerable and pushing eighty, a unique storehouse of country wisdom and local ways. If central casting were to search for the ideal (OK, apart from the language thing) candidate to play say, old Walter in *The Archers,* or the oracle in some similar country soap story, they'd pick our wizened, wrinkled old pal Bertrand, for he so looks and seems the part.

On that particular day an unusually high wind was blowing in from the east, the dogs were running around dementedly and weird cloud formations streaked the sky, wildly lit by a more than usually erratic, polluted-looking sunset. I turned to old Bertrand to seek the comfort of his life experience, to ask his wise insights, saying, 'Tell me, old buddy, what does it all mean?'

Bertrand sucked contemplatively upon a straw then spat significantly and said, without any lack of confidence or even a hint of shame, 'Don't ask me, neighbour, I have absolutely no idea.' Then he told me what he'd just heard, on the weather forecast.

Yes, it would be a tragedy to lose the old ways.

Stormy, wet and warm

The first days of October are as changeable as the weather. I can stroll round my field comfortable in T-shirt and shorts while around me it's blowing a gale. Clear sky and bright sunshine give way moments later to black clouds, showers and even occasional thunderclaps, each alternating with the other every few minutes. It's very *Wuthering Heights*. Fallen leaves and bits of broken boughs strew the paths and roadways but it's exciting rather than uncomfortable, not at all unpleasant.

This is the time when those fiercely territorial birds the tawny owls appear at dawn and dusk with many a screech and squawk, indicating that somewhere in the deep forest a pair of them are fighting, one to maintain control on his tiny patch of territory, the other hoping to usurp ownership from the self-same owl who may recently have dispossessed him. We think of these serene birds as wise and sedentary schoolmasters, but such sudden life-or-death struggles are not uncommon among tawny owls. For the loser, death by starvation is in prospect, for the winner, the right to eke a meagre survival chasing small rodents who, thanks in part at least to my three dogs, may by now be rather thin on the ground.

Still, for the winner it's a result, I suppose. Tawny owls, by the way, are the ones who sit bolt upright on their branches (usually with a full moon behind them, slightly to the right) and go 'twit-twoo'. Other owls just screech, apparently. Marie, who knows more than I do about such things (for the moment, at least), tells me that this twit-twooing, if that's the verb, is a duet between male and female tawny owls. The male, she says, does the 'twit' and the female the 'twoo'. You can tell the females because they're less hoarse and slightly higher pitched. (Twitchers – bird enthusiasts – come out with such amazing things.)

Neither Marie nor I would qualify as twitchers, even if we should want to. But we're learning a lot about the birds here through a combination of observing the exceptionally profuse local birdlife, frequent referral to at least four well-used reference books and an online link to the RSPB. As chores go, this learning is really rather fun.

Then the weather changes yet again. The truth is early October here isn't quite autumn yet; it's still late, late summer, which can be a time of considerable delight. Crispy misty mornings (just the remnants of mist by the time I get up) giving way to clear blue summer-like skies and surprising warmth, the loveliness of these days making up not a little for all the wet and windy days that will follow. A heavy dew is all around so the field is wet and wellies are a must. As I promenade, a jetfighter screams low over Loïc's field behind a deep-brown lady blackbird perched tranquilly on the handle of an upturned roller that Loïc abandoned where it stopped some months, or even years, ago. The bird chirrups throatily, paying no attention to the appalling noise or to me.

Down in the field there's an uncanny radiance, an ethereal glow has spread everywhere on account of the angle of the morning sun upon the soaking landscape. Briefly our world is bathed in golden light. The foam on the river, the dew-soaked grass, the gently gurgling waters and again that eerie stillness. The sun on the dew clearly illuminates the spider canopies and platforms that appear to spring up overnight but probably have been there, unseen, for yonks. I find this jaw-droppingly wonderful but seem to be alone in noticing anything out of the usual. These splendid end-of-summer days are hard to believe and impossible to beat.

Walking the dogs, October: the beauty of still

The wind drops and we get the still, for days on end. There is so much quiet here. But when you stop to listen you realise the air is filled with birdsong. It isn't constant; it moves up and down in volume, near and farther away and there are gaps separating it. Birds sing with greater gusto in the early morning and late in the day. At times it resembles a conversation, the exchange taken up first along the edge of the river then answered from deep in the wood. Then real silence. The river seems to stop, its flow is imperceptible.

Is this just idle daily chitter-chatter or is it about something more substantial? It seems impossible to know. Mortimer flops at my feet, entirely uninterested. In the distance Max and Syrus, oblivious too, enjoy their year-round passion of rooting for mice in the long grass.

The island that formed in the middle of the river below the third cataract is a lot smaller now and soon will disappear altogether as the river gathers weight and pace. There are many butterflies still about, fewer of the very vivid brightly coloured sort but lots of yellows and browns and quite a number of the pretty little miniature ones. Occasionally a cabbage white will fly high over the woods.

During these long morning walks the twins, Max and

Syrus, range far and wide, revelling in their freedom and forgetting about everything but themselves as they search for anything edible. Mortimer follows faithfully at my heel, in part through devotion but mainly I suspect because he can't be bothered to do anything else. Compared with the feverish excitement of his kennel-mates he drags himself around the field rather than gallops, but I know he loves these walks more than anything (except mealtimes) and is never happier than when he's following me on our circuit.

'Come on, Old Sunshine,' I exhort in my most encouraging tone, but he still plods along at constant pace, tail a-wagging, mouth lolling, head upturned to look for approval. Infirm and unhurried he may be, yet Mortimer is perfectly content to progress in this way. He fails to observe most of what I see though, and seems interested in nothing at all except the back view of me.

Each to his own.

Wasps
Just above the biggest uplighter mushroom on the great pollarded willow tree a colony of wasps have made their home in a crevice which, if I could get close enough to see it, which I can't because they swarm rather angrily around intruders, I would note they have built into and around the crack in the bark to create a rather fantastic sweeping, many-roomed structure. This big nest was started towards the end of spring by a queen wasp who chewed up small bits of wood in her tiny jaws, mixing it with her saliva to make a kind of papier-mâché that she then used to build a small nest into which she could start laying her eggs. The first of these eggs then hatch out as sterile females, the workers, who take over the job of feeding the larvae that emerge from the eggs that the queen is laying all the

time. As if in payment for this kindness the larvae produce a sweet liquid that the workers love.

In mid-October though, the nest is empty of the larvae which the workers have been feeding throughout the summer. So there's no more sweet stuff, which sends the workers flying around, looking for something sugary. This is why in autumn you may be bothered by wasps when you're sitting outside eating your jam sandwich. Now the worker wasps (sterile females) and drones (the males) constantly come and go from their exits in the bark singly and in convoys like scrambled fighter pilots purposely going about their flying business. Though both drones and workers are about to die, they keep working to secure the future of their species, which I suppose many people wish they wouldn't. But, there's much to be admired in the common wasp.

Wasp queens are bigger than the workers, so I think those big lassies that I see each morning might be the new queens who should by now be with child and looking for somewhere to hibernate. Marie has read that they may now be suffering from a shortage of sugar so wants me to spread jam around the outsides of their bike (it's bees that have hives, wasps live in bikes). She thinks a portion or two of jam might sweeten their final hours. After risking life and limb to do this, the little devils studiously ignore what I've so carefully spread before them, which may indicate the futility of tampering with nature, or perhaps they just don't like Marie's jam.

Sitting in the sun

I've just seen two flies fighting ferociously. This was more than a minor squabble, they were really going at each other. Now one of them has landed on my arm, just near my spider friend (who settled on me as soon as I sat down and seems quite at home on my shoulder). I can see that one of the fly's legs, the middle leg on its left side, is damaged, it's holding it out stiffly at an odd angle, it seems broken and dead.

Presumably that's bad news for a fly, the beginning of a sticky end. But my spider, who might be expected to consider this a dinner opportunity, shows no interest whatsoever.

My, but this pale October sun can be warm too, so I've paused by one of my benches to enjoy a sit. Now there's lots of life around – butterflies, dragonflies, daddy-longlegs, and numerous other flies, brightly coloured and drab as ditchwater too. The activity level seems unusually high, if not frantic. Then a tiny butterfly drifts into the picture, a wonder of miniaturisation no bigger than a sixpence, black and orange wings perfect in every detail. In time he too drifts off but not before he's lifted my spirits, as have all my neighbours today.

Having so enjoyed the company of butterflies I feel a bit ashamed that I know so little about them. Are they thriving in our field, or are they under threat? I resolve to find out.

Given their limited life expectancy there's a surprising amount of literature about butterflies. Short, colourful and even brutal their lives may be, but people certainly find a lot to say about them. There are, I find, long lists of good books on butterflies, plus numerous illustrated guides and an endless variety of Internet sites.

Dog bites fly
Oops! Mortimer's just caught one in his teeth. He can move when he chooses.

The devil is in the detail
I've just found something interesting on the path by the old oak. He's an occasional visitor to Kerkelven at this season (or

perhaps a very shy and secretive resident), a large, long, black insect called the devil's coach-horse beetle (*Staphylinus olens*). I'd found one just once before, not long after we came here. He seemed such an odd and interesting character that I've never forgotten him and was quite thrilled to stumble across one of his kind again. Then, he was just a big and scary beetle. Now I can see that there's much more to him than that. So, again, I fall upon my trusty reference sources for enlightenment.

One of the larger European beetles, the devil's coach-horse beetle can give a painful bite with his strong pincer-like jaws and he also emits a foul-smelling odour as a defensive secretion from a pair of white glands at the end of his abdomen. Long, with big jaws and a thick, juicy body in several scaly segments, he really is something of a gruesome sight, it has to be said, with his head bent forwards embodying as he does all the horrific attributes that make women and small children scream and run at the sight of big beetles.

The devil's coach-horse is a type of beetle called a rove, so called because he's constantly on the move (order *Coleoptera*; family *Staphylinidae*). Rove beetles prey upon (as well as live on) disabled or dead animals. Some actually inhabit the fur of living mammals where, helpfully, they will eat their fleas and ticks (though upon reflection I think I'd rather have the fleas and ticks). The devil's coach-horse is a fast mover and can fly, though he usually chooses to stay on the ground (which seems a tad silly to me). Rove beetles are close relatives of the unpleasant-sounding burying beetles. These horrors are very strong (for beetles). Two adults can move an animal as big as a rat to a suitable location, where they will bury it. They normally excavate beneath the corpse, causing it to sink into the ground. What they do with it thereafter can be left to your imagination.

So now you know why I treat this singular beetle with

respect whenever I meet him. In reality, though, I find he's not as frightening as his name or his looks imply. But as he eats mainly insects, spiders and worms, many of the other residents of Kerkelven may not agree with me.

Sunsets on fire

As these clear sunny days draw to an end we get treated to two of the world's finest natural displays – the setting of the sun and the rising of the moon. At this time of year they come together within minutes of each other. In Brittany's clear air the light is exceptional, ultra-sharp and clean, every colour and tone precisely defined. First the pale full moon rises in the east as the process of sunset begins. It takes maybe forty minutes, perhaps an hour in its fullness for the sky to transform from bright blue through scarlet and deep crimson to fiery red and then to reddish gold. At times it's all these shades at once and everything in between. It's awesome. The silence in which this all happens seem to confirm that every other living thing too finds all this utterly overwhelming and like me can do nothing other than watch in wonder.

Killers are really not nice people

I've just found five dead baby rabbits on the path. From the look of them they've been beaten to death, but more likely they've been pulled by dogs from where they were sleeping and mauled. This seems to be the work of the hunters and their hounds.

Though these dead rabbits seem too small to eat, I'm not sure that even if they had been killed for food I'd feel much better about it. As it is, they've just been left where they lie.

Who are these killers? What kind of people do these things?

Hunters here often appear to be quite nice people and,

actually, may well be so at other times. Which makes dealing with them doubly difficult. It's most often quite ordinary guys who go hunting. I wish I could claim otherwise, that it is only the dim or antisocial elements that maintain the hunt, but it isn't so. Here all levels of society partake. Hunting flourishes because it's vigorously, enthusiastically pursued not by the few but by the many, not by the elite but by all and sundry. Garage owners and shopkeepers, firemen and postmen, aristos and bourgeois, peasants and, of course, farmers. They're all at it, whenever they can get the chance.

Put a gun in the hand of any man, whoever he is, and he will change, inevitably and almost always for the worst.

Some of these hunters may well be nice, reasonable people but equally some that I meet do appear to need to justify themselves and their sport. They swagger and strut, parading their artillery and their power. When you meet them on your path or in your woods they know full well they have an unchallengeable right under French law to be there, but they still look ill at ease, staring at their boots, shifting their body weight nervously from one bechained leg to the other. They clearly hate meeting me and my three dogs for we must disturb their hunt no end, tipping as we do this unequal contest a tiny bit more towards the hunted, increasing by just a bit their quarry's slender chance of escaping the guns.

So Syrus, Mortimer, Max and I make as much noise as we can. I shout at the dogs and curse their sniffing and snuffling around the packs of surprisingly small and meek hunting dogs, which always seem so friendly and starved of affection from their single-minded, half-pissed owners. I issue loud *bonjours* and *ça va biens* and hang around longer than I need to, just to annoy them. I know its childish and I dislike it probably as much as they do. It's just that when we see wrongs around us, the feeling that we should put up resistance is itself hard to resist.

It's been a day for encounters. This morning by the river I met the heron. I saw him the moment he became aware of me and took to instant flight. I wish he wouldn't fly off like that, just because he's had a glimpse of me.

This evening Marie and I also ran into two rare but very welcome and somewhat more sociable visitors to our part of the forest, Marie-Thérèse and Bertrand, our former neighbours. They'd come to our woods (or so they said) to collect chestnuts, which of course are much too small just now to eat, for it's a little too early. Tellingly, their bucket was empty. I suspect their motive instead was a romantic assignation in the woods, once more for old time's sake, the saucy pair. But Marie thinks I need help.

Still, it was nice to see them.

Spiders

In these early mornings the field is spread with spiders' canopies, each hung with dew like glistening tambourines or Red Indian (Native American) dream catchers. Their threads are so fine, apparently just one teaspoonful could contain a million webs, though how they might be counted is beyond me. I'm told these little spiders have a brain no bigger than a grain of salt yet they create such delicate, intricate beauty and constantly adapt their webs to catch the most flies. So it seems to me there has to be something compelling the spider to do what he does, more than just genetic inheritance and blind instinct.

In fact many spiders see rather well. Some spiders have 360-degree vision. They can leap the equivalent of the length of a football pitch. Maybe there's much we could learn from the humble spider.

Even those spiders that are blind, and there are some, can compensate for their lack of vision with superb development of their other senses, such as smell and touch, perhaps even intuition.

Nature's master builders

Tempting though it is to imagine that some divine hand has wrought the wonders that greet me these days on my early morning walks, it is tiny spiders and no one else that are entirely responsible for it. It's the sweat and toil of these minute fellows all on their own that create this beautiful, almost invisible wall of death that I find refreshed, renewed and even more impressive each time I see it.

Mortimer trots beside me unthinkingly and inevitably blunders into several of them. Instantly these masterworks are destroyed forever. Great lumbering brute, I think, and my cogitations on the universe and its ultimate mysteries are put on hold until a future time as I try to steer the insensate beast away to where he can do less damage.

Spiders build their webs with threads up to three metres long at times. The craft of web building, say scientists, is inherited. But . . . where did they get it from in the first place? Seems to me it must have been learned at some time.

At this season some spiders' egg sacs appear as small globules of white attached to long blades of grass. They're easily mistaken for pieces of chewing gum chucked carelessly by a passing visitor but, in fact, inside you'll find thousands of tiny spider eggs and, presumably, in the fullness of time they'll overflow with thousands of little spiders. Though if you find what you think is one but instead it sticks your fingers and thumb together, it probably is chewing gum.

Other spider egg sacs look like small tents or parcels, stuck to slender grasses, often swaying perilously in the wind. Presumably being born in such a place is a normal, natural start to life for baby spiders, or spiderlings, though it seems to us likely to be something of a scary awakening, like coming round in a mobile maternity ward attached by invisible bungee ropes.

Several different species of spider create sacs like these for their offspring, but I think the ones I see mostly belong to the nursery web spiders. Isn't that a lovely name? The female nursery web spider can be seen in June and July carrying her egg sac around in her mouth until they are almost ready to hatch. Then she builds the nursery web and will stay to protect her little ones from predators. The spiderlings stay in their tent until they change their skin for the first time. Called the moult, this phenomenon happens several times for most spiders, mostly pre-maturity, but can occur throughout their lives. (Birds also moult, changing their plumage from summer to winter as necessary, usually when it wears out.) Nursery web spiders sound like great parents, but the male disappears as soon as his job as inseminator is done. The mother does live up to her name for a while at least, but not long after her massive brood has hatched out, she too leaves the tiny babies to fend for themselves. Only a few survive.

Other close relations of the nursery web spiders are the aptly named fishing spiders and raft spiders. They get up to lots of things, do spiders. Signature spiders get their name because each individual spider spins a pattern in a part of his or her web and this pattern is as unique as a fingerprint. How cool is that?

The deaf, dumb and blind kid

Like some great ringmaster, our spider hangs in the centre of her web, reacting by touch to the minutest sensation coming from the intricate web of fibres that radiates from the outer fringes of it right to the centre, right to the spider's feet. Suspended upon the bull's eye, the spider perches like the Who's legendary deaf, dumb and blind kid, senses razor-sharp, playing by intuition, never missing a fall. The tiny creature's web is football-field huge to her, the size of a soup plate for us. It is literally a dinner plate for the spider. Her varied, nutritious menu never stops being served.

Her body is apparently covered with tiny hairs, her skeleton is on the outside and her heart is to be found halfway up her back. Thanks to these minute sensory hairs on her body and legs she can detect the movement of her potential prey from the slightest change in the air currents around it. She also has chemo-sensitive hair (literally, hairs that smell), which informs her what kind of dinner has just landed on her sticky plate. Combine this with her lightning-fast reactions and who needs sight to hunt?

She can stay motionless for ages. You blink. That instant something tiny disturbs the tranquillity of her web, perhaps a small fly or even a big juicy grasshopper. She is upon it so quickly that the unlucky would-be passer-by can be killed, trussed, bound, packaged and suspended in the spidery larder almost before you have finished your blink. She paralyses her prey by injecting a venom that liquefies its insides. At this, understandably, the surprised victim stops struggling and submits to its new status, as dinner.

Then for our spider it's back to the centre of the web and the anticipation of waiting again, suspended upside down, the perfect dining machine. Or, perhaps, the perfect food packer.

But they are short, their lives, and harsh. The smallest ones live but a few months while for the biggest and most robust it's mostly only a year or two at best, though spiders in captivity can live a lot longer and some species, such as tarantulas, live up to twenty years.

Yet surveys of spider populations claim up to two million spiders in an acre of meadow. OK, there may be a tad fewer in the woods, but that's still between twelve and sixteen million spiders in Kerkelven, about the human population of Cairo.

Wow! But how do they count them? I've always marvelled at whoever it is that can count the people of Cairo, but spiders in a field . . .?

Spiders of course can't fly, but they are very light so when they cling to a short line of silk the slightest breeze is enough to lift them aloft and carry them considerable distances. According to spider enthusiast Stuart Bennett, some spiders have put these conditions to spectacularly good use. He calls this 'aerial dispersal', or 'ballooning'. If I were a spider I think I'd call it bloody good fun.

Soft and pliable a spider's web might be, yet it has the equivalent breaking strain of iron. Spider silk is only about 1/200th of a millimetre in diameter and is so light that if a spider could spin a strand around the world it would weigh less than six ounces. I bet there are some that could.

Ballooning, so says Mr Bennett, is most noticeable in the autumn when large numbers of spiders can be spotted ballooning together. A spider intent on ballooning climbs to a high point and turns to face the wind. Several strands of silk are expelled and these are carried up into the air. The spider then, according to Stuart, stands on tiptoe (I didn't even know spiders had toes) and, when the force of the air currents is sufficient, they release the grip of their leg claws and awaaaaay they go.

This, of course, is hang-gliding, only they probably invented it long before we did. Now who says these little chaps don't know how to have fun?

Name that spider

Of the more than 70,000 different species of spider found worldwide there are at least many hundreds of different species found readily in Europe, including the common (or garden) spider, the crab spider, the daddy-longlegs spider and the tiger (or wasp) spider – we'll meet her in her season, the summer – and I suspect we'll meet several other types of spider in their time too. There's certainly many dozens of different varieties to be encountered in the field at Kerkelven.

Spiders are near relatives of the scorpion, which I've not seen here, and of the harvestman, ticks and mites, which I see in several varieties including the velvet mite, that microscopic red spider-like creature that scuttles so apparently aimlessly yet in such numbers on our garden walls in the summer.

Spiders evidently do catch and eat each other. As, apparently, do quite a lot of insects and many birds and beasts. I make no observations on human behaviour in this regard. What my neighbours do when they close their doors at night is their business. Though humans generally frown on cannibalism, except perhaps for survival, it seems quite commonplace and natural for many other creatures.

Cannibalism can, in fact, be quite beneficial. Obviously, a voracious cannibalistic species would quickly eat itself out of existence. But when cannibalism occurs in response to overcrowding it can increase the species' chances for survival. If it is too successful its growth can threaten its own food supply. Clearly it is to a species' advantage when food is scarce for at least some of the population to remain well fed and healthy even at the expense of others. Among those species that produce many offspring, such as frogs, cannibalism of siblings helps ensure that at least some young have a chance of surviving into adults, thus continuing the species.

Spiders, of course, are not insects, they're arachnids. You can tell the difference easily because whereas insects have only three pairs of legs, spiders have four. And spiders don't have antennae.

Mushrooms are us

It's mushroom season again and we've just driven past a truly impressive array of the big parasol variety down by the riverside in the field next but one to ours, downstream, farmed by Loïc but belonging to the landlord M. le Gendre. Intrigued but already behind schedule we decide to lunch as planned and to return later with the dogs and the camera, to have a good look.

Imagine our distress when we returned a mere hour and a half later to find that they were all gone! As we were blathering on over our lager, someone was half-inching those lovely mush.

What's the connection between the hundreds of species of fascinating and exotic fungi that sprout up suddenly all over Kerkelven around this time of year and athlete's foot, dandruff, ringworm and the like? They all like damp, moist places. All are particular in choosing conditions in which they can thrive (so now you can boast about your dandruff – at least you know it wanted you). And all make great subjects for conversation at dinner parties.

Athlete's foot, dandruff and the multitudes of types of mushrooms are in fact close relatives. But generally the woodland varieties are much the more pleasant, in fact they can be utterly delightful, delicious even. If you give them to a friend, generally the friend will be grateful, which might not always be the case with athlete's foot, dandruff and a range of other fungal infections. Mushrooms are not just good to eat, mushrooming can be a compulsive and richly rewarding hobby. Searching them out in all their variety and splendour can become an entrancing passion. At least, it can round our way. And as the mushroom season is short it's a dedication you can cast aside well before it becomes boring, to pick it up afresh next year.

Actually that's not quite the whole story. Mushrooms are found here all year round and some varieties, such as the puffball, seem to prefer the summer to the autumn. But in October their range and numbers positively explode.

There are three main types of mushroom; those that form

a symbiotic relationship with a plant or tree, those that live on decaying plant matter and help with its decomposition, and those that parasitically attack plants and trees and can sometimes kill them. As far as I'm concerned, though, there are basically two types of mushroom, those that are found in and around Kerkelven, and the rest. I'm not sure which is the greatest, numerically.

I love the way mushrooms just pop up in the most unexpected places. There are beautiful colours, rich, dark and autumnal, not just those shades of browny-yellowy-red that you only seem able to find in nature but also greys, black, white, purple, rust, greens and blues. Some are sharply conical, others are flat-tops, some are like umbrellas turned inside out. They don't last for long, it's true. Aside from their fragility and susceptibility to even tiny knocks they seem to enjoy only the shortest of lives, even though they are apparently all around in spore form, just waiting to sprout. Life for your typical mushroom is short, beautiful and moist, which suits them down to the ground.

But there's much more to your mushroom than you might at first imagine. Alongside other life forms the fungus is something of an oddball, it doesn't quite fit in the world of animals and plants. Mushrooms, or rather their parent group fungi, are neither. They are all of their own, something original in themselves, quite different from everything else.

According to mushroom expert John Wright in his book *The River Cottage Mushroom Handbook*, fungi are not organisms, they are actually organs. This may explain why so many of them look so rude. The organism, called the mycelium, stays underground, invisible or otherwise hidden, for example inside wood. Mycelium is a bundle of microscopically thin hair-like filaments, like a clump of cotton wool or, perhaps, like candy floss. It's the mycelium that's the real business; the mushrooms and toadstools we see above ground are just its naughty bits.

Mushrooms and toadstools function as reproductive organs only. They pop up each year in the same place, seemingly without roots, because that's where the mycelium is and they grow so quickly because they have the mycelium to nourish them.

Think of this the next time you shop for mushrooms at your supermarket.

Monster mushrooms

Today we found a mushroom (*Leccinum versipelle* I think it was, the orange birch bolete described below, or it might even have been a lurid bolete) measuring just over twenty centimetres across and thick with it, weighing nearly half a kilo. Not far from it we found the stump and decaying remains of a monster mushroom about three times its circumference and therefore many times its size. These extreme mushrooms grow quickly in the very damp weather and don't seem to live long. Then, equally quickly, they decay into a putrescent pile of gunk like something from the film *Alien*, which might leap up and cling to your face but instead just hangs around the field for ages, being disgusting.

Fungi reproduce by producing spores, tiny cells inside a protective coating. These then are spread by the elements and can travel considerable distances. Wherever they land, they grow.

The uplighter fungus (a.k.a. hoof fungus, willow bracket or tinder bracket)

This charming fungus looks like an uplighting wall-lamp, or like a great white bowl filled with black and orange cream. It's only seen on the trunks or large branches of trees, growing horizontally outwards in big, flat semicircular protuberances the shape and size of a pudding plate. I've only ever found them here on trees down by the river's edge. White and orange when new and springy to the touch, they quickly solidify and dull down in colour, becoming almost black, hard as stone and firmly fixed like grim death to the trunk of their tree. At first I thought they must live a long time, either that or they die really quickly but, unlike most other mushrooms, don't decay. However, I've found they add a new layer each year – rather like when a tree makes rings – and this bit, the white bit, is the only part of the fungus that is still growing.

I suppose the uplighter does also look a bit like an upturned hoof, but I think my name's better. Not nice to eat (they look a bit chewy and would probably break your teeth).

We have a true world champion uplighter growing happily on the west-facing side of one of the great pollarded willow trees down by the river. It is huge, the nonpareil of hoof mushrooms but grown so large it couldn't be anything that a horse would have on its foot. No, uplighter is a much better name. This one is about fifty per cent new growth, quite recent growth too I think.

The woodman's knob (a.k.a. the parasol or shaggy parasol)

Forgive my indelicacy, please, but there really is no polite way to describe this chap. This huge, elegant, sensuous growth is my favourite of all the woodland mushrooms. It's the mushroom every other mushroom must envy for its sheer style and beauty (only surpassed, perhaps, by the rare Enid Blyton red, the large fairy toadstool with milky-white spots).

Doyen of fungi, the woodman's knob is truly splendiferous

and not at all plentiful. To discover a perfect specimen is a singular treat that will have you skipping and jumping, even singing, for the remainder of your day.

From late September the woodman's knob (*Macrolepiota procera*) is found by roads and pathsides, on tracks and under hedges, often tucked away discreetly, but equally, often shamelessly displaying itself in the open, standing firm and proud even though such exposure surely reduces its already short life expectancy to near negligibility. The woodman's knob seems to appear overnight almost fully grown, at a length, or height, of about six to eight inches (though it may well be we just haven't noticed it when it was little). The bulb, or knob end, can grow to the size of a tennis ball. The stem, or shaft, is creamy white and greyish of colour and slightly curved, while the top of the bulb is whitish-brown, marked with perhaps six to eight large round white spots. When new the bulb is closed, giving the woodman's knob its decidedly phallic appearance (hence the quaint, traditional name), but within days it opens out to a much more respectable umbrella, the top of which becomes quite flat, extending to about eight inches across. Pixies could picnic at it, very comfortably. One we saw at the foot of the 45-degree path was so big and bulbous with a huge brown nipple in the middle of it that Marie felt 'Madonna's boob' would be a better name for it. But it was a woodman's knob. Next day we found another, even bigger. Had the top been pizza, Pizza Hut would have been more than proud and could have charged handsomely for it, by the slice. Measured across when fully opened out its diameter reached a good 31 cm (over a foot). I'd say that's medium large, if not family-sized.

So why is the woodman's knob so rare and almost always solitary?

I've no idea, except perhaps that, as its ultimate destiny is to fall over and by then it's a pretty bulky thing, other fungi may shun its vicinity rather than risk being squashed in the process. I suspect the truth is, woodman's knobs are their own worst enemy. They grow so large and bulbous at the top that within a few days of their seemingly miraculous appearance they become top heavy and fall over, wrenching their fine, delicate roots from the earth and tumbling to die ignominiously on their sides.

Isn't nature mysterious? Oh yes.

But sadly it's also possible that these lovely fungi don't last long because they are 100 per cent edible and quite delicious too, so that greedy Frenchies grab them as soon as they appear. To prevent this calumny Marie and I have at times resorted to gathering a few of the more dramatic specimens ourselves. Fried gently in olive oil with a generous measure of finely chopped garlic it's easy to see why so many people consider the woodman's knob to be the truly delicious wild taste of the woods.

The big orange mushie (a.k.a. orange birch bolete) and the jack-o'-lantern

The big orange is just as its name (given by me) suggests. The colour is quite vivid, not at all dull. They are plentiful and can be eaten. Apart from this and that their tops get quite sticky after it rains, they're unremarkable. Another strikingly orange but largely tree-dwelling mushroom is the jack-o'-lantern (*Omphalotus olearius*). It's found for only a few short weeks around the time of Hallowe'en, it looks like the chanterelle and is bioluminescent, so it glows in the dark. Magic! Scientific names apparently include *Omphalotus illudens* and *Olitocybe illudens*, both of which sound rude to me. Although it looks and smells tasty, the jack-o'-lantern, unlike the chanterelle, is very poisonous. It probably won't kill you, but according to various sources that I've consulted, it will give you very unpleasant cramps, vomiting and diarrhoea. But it must look as if it tastes really good for there are reports of repeat poisonings of individuals who were tempted to try them a second time.

The bioluminescence is generally only observable in low light conditions and only, apparently, when your eyes are acclimatised. The whole mushroom doesn't glow, only the gills (the frilly bits under the cap), and they glow a ghostly greenish colour. This is due to luciferase, the same type of chemical that makes fireflies glow. However, in jack-o'-lantern's case the luciferase is a waste product and is transported to the gills to get it out of the mushroom.

Unlike the chanterelle, the jack-o'-lantern has true, sharp, non-forking gills; this is the only 'simple' way of distinguishing between the two.

I'm not sure how helpful this advice will be if you aren't quite sure what non-forking gills are and your chums are already huddled round a campfire with the scrambled eggs at the ready.

The jack-o'-lantern is asexual, I'm told. Unlike presumably the woodman's knob and more than a few others.

The death cap

This one killed Pope Clement VII in 1534, somewhat denting his reputation for infallibility. Over the years it has dispatched lots of other people too, killing more than all other mushrooms put together. In fact eating the death cap is almost invariably fatal: half a cap is enough to kill you, it destroys your liver and there's no known cure. Even more scary, it looks just like some other mushies that are perfectly safe and delicious to eat. And the death cap is likely to be found just about anywhere.

So, this nasty little freak of nature needs to be avoided at all costs. You can recognise the death cap (scientific name *Amanita phalloides*, also known as deadly white cap) by its white cap (not much help that, I appreciate) and by the fact that your husband, who ate one first, has just fallen over.

As neither of these tips is particularly helpful, you'd perhaps be better advised to check rather carefully before tucking in to the fry-up you have planned for your next social gathering.

Kerkelven doesn't support these little bastards, at least not as far as I'm aware.

The magpie ink cap and others

Black-topped, beautiful but deadly and to be avoided. There are lots more poisonous sorts that I could mention, like the puffball (some varieties), the earth ball and the brain mushroom. I've not seen the others on my travels, as far as I know, but the reddish-brown, golf-ball-sized puffball is a regular on our pathways in August, September and into October too.

Dartboards, hats, umbrellas and golf balls

The sheer variety of our fungi is astounding. There are mushrooms that look like all sorts of things, there's even one that looks for all the world like a piece of calves' liver that's gone off a bit. I can't give them all names, for goodness' sake. But though there are plenty of good books to help both the amateur and the real enthusiast, in case you're wondering this isn't a book about mushrooms, so I'm going to move on. But before I do there is one more species of the fungus family that I just must visit. An occasional if elusive Kerkelven resident it is too, quite the most impressive fungus to be seen anywhere, outclassing even the fabled woodman's knob.

The Enid Blyton red, or pixie toadstool (a.k.a. fly agaric)

Deep under the mulch, deep in a thicket, deep in the forest grows the most desirable, rarest mushroom of them all, the Enid Blyton red or fly agaric (*Amanita muscaria*), also known as the pixie toadstool. (My names are so much more exotic than the traditional labels, don't you think?)

Slightly smaller than the woodman's knob and a great deal more demure, the Enid Blyton red – red but with big white spots, and featured in all good children's fairy stories, particularly those that grew in the fertile imagination of the master storyteller, Enid Blyton – is a sturdy conical toadstool of a particularly vivid colour and interesting pointy shape suggestive of all the good things of childhood. Though they are the same thing merely at a different stage, the flat-topped red spotty ones are interesting in a mild way but are pale shadows of the steeply sloping conical kind, the true EBR at its best. I have seen one but once, in the forest depths. Marie also found one down by the bus shelter once. But they are exceedingly rare and quite lucky, it is said, for the finder. Unless he or she eats her discovery, for despite their loveliness these beauties are quite poisonous.

A toadstool really isn't any different from a mushroom except toadstools are usually poisonous and are often a pretty red colour with a round top and a slender stalk.

There's even mushrooms on Poo Mountain

Mushroom varieties do flourish in the most unexpected places, including all over the repellent pile that we've come to know as Poo Mountain, the enormous pile of pig manure deposited a while back by Loïc at the corner where his field joins ours. As you would expect, these mushrooms are of a sickly indistinct variety, not surprising perhaps, being raised as they are on effluent. They're bleached blackish grey, stunted and stumpy, weedy, small and with Chinese hats. Other mushrooms don't seem to last more than a few days while these are around for barely 24 hours, so I've formed a theory about them, as follows. Mushrooms, we know, thrive in damp and moist places. As we've seen earlier, their spores seek these out and that's where they take root. The damper, moister and danker the better, for mushrooms. So when they land and take root on our pile of poop, Poo Mountain, they imagine, 'What could be better than a steaming soggy seemingly permanent pile of poo?' Then . . . the smell. It's no wonder, if you think about it, that they survive mere hours. Indeed it's a miracle they survive so long.

A recipe for disaster

Take care, though, if you would collect and enjoy the fungal fruits of the forest. The blue-green stuff that gives Stilton and Roquefort cheeses their distinctive taste (yes, this stuff is a fungus too) may be benign, but as you'll have seen many mushrooms are poisonous, or at least unwholesome. Some of these species have adapted to look very like those of the more digestible species. They can make you very, very sick. And each year several people die from eating bad mushrooms.

Not us though. We take ours along to the local chemist who, for free, will tell you whether or not what you've so painstakingly collected will kill you. Tonight we are tucking into a lovely steak dinner with – you've guessed it – mushrooms. And from our forest too, sautéed woodman's knobs, no less, neatly sliced to disguise their origins and protect the sensibilities of our guests. We will explain this tasty treat of course, over the coffee.

Goodbye to the mountain

Poo mountains, thankfully, are not really permanent features of Kerkelven and this one was ploughed into the soil, mushroom spores and all, just as October was drawing to its sunny close.

At least most of it was. In typical Loïc fashion, he missed a substantial blob of it, about thirty per cent, just at the point where I pass on my morning walk. Maybe he didn't need it. Still, each day I'm left with this very tangible, festering reminder of my charming but sometimes thoughtless and often untidy neighbour, Loïc, who, like many farmers hereabouts, thinks nothing of littering the beautiful countryside he's inherited. (Not just with biodegradables or emptying the ashtray from his tractor onto the middle of our path. I get a bit tired collecting up his discarded fertiliser sacks and suchlike.)

Poo mountains come about here because Loïc has on his little farm at nearby Pleumelin a large number of pigs and very little space in which to dispose of their numerous and continuous outpourings. Pigs may come and go, and certainly do, but the flow of poo from their little bacony back ends never ceases. Loïc deals with this endless flood of piggy poop by dropping it unceremoniously on us. Well, to be fair, right next door. I suppose I can't complain because he does deposit it on his land and he does use it, eventually, as a fertiliser. And I have to accept that, though his land is pretty close to mine, it's always a long way from the house. I just wish that when he misses a bit it wouldn't always be the bit that's closest to me.

It could be worse. I haven't slipped on it and fallen in. Not yet.

Cutting a path through the forest

Cutting a proper path through a long stretch of dense ancient undergrowth requires considerable resources of grit, tenacity, perseverance and sheer hard work. A full-size tractor would probably help, in fact would probably do the job leisurely in a couple of hours or so, rather than the two and a half weeks of sweat and tears that it took when Marie and I gave ourselves the project of reopening a path in the forest that had been neglected and overgrown for at least a decade or two.

Still, it's amazing what you can achieve with clippers, saws and the good old chainsaw. And a wife who works head down while you're looking around, enjoying the fine autumnal day.

This time last year, mid-October, Marie and I commenced and completed this marathon, gargantuan task down in our forest. For more than a decade the great path that dissects our orchards from the rest of the forest had become densely overgrown. Tough trees and tangled briars had multiplied in profusion across it. We residents had neglected it completely and even, in time, had come to forget it was ever there.

Then, as with the advent of winter the undergrowth had naturally thinned, we had remembered it and the project had formed in our minds.

Without our little tractor we could not even have begun it. Even with this sturdy machine it was to prove a challenge to our determination and endurance. But we worked at it morning and evening. We drove at it and churned it up, we dragged at roots and hacked at boughs and branches and slowly by centimetres we won back the pathway from the clinging woods.

Now as we daily enjoy this path and the improved access it affords we are glad of our industry and perseverance. The country has many simple pleasures and clearing a path – a small and insignificant chore perhaps – is one of them, one we take delight from, every day.

A huge buzzard sweeps out of the line of trees to my right over the dogs' heads and wings off towards the river. The light again is extraordinary, the sun low in the sky, the river's surface shimmering and dappled, glowing silver and gold. Now we can begin to get access to parts of the forest previously off limits because they have been much too overgrown. Access still is difficult though, because of the long lines of lethal brambles that spring up and spread out low and tangled in every direction. A stout pair of clippers is obligatory for such enterprises. The paths we clear here are more transient, for left alone they can disappear almost as quickly as they arrive. It reminds us that nothing in the forest is ever permanent.

Now we can also go mushrooming in Bertrand's forest. The slope in his part of the woods is less steep than in ours and the forest has many nooks, glades, dells and bowers, little hidden secret corners that are really beyond delightful. Titania and Oberon would be at home here. Merlin too, I think.

And all around, in every corner and crevice are mushrooms of all kinds, colours and sizes. Fungus, the Bogeyman, would love this place as well. But there's still no sign of the elusive, alluring Enid Blyton red.

Foreign visitors

At times we can come across strange and exotic creatures right here in our forest. Recently we found some locusts, full grown and bright green, about ten centimetres long and thick to boot. Having eaten tiny grasshoppers by the plateful in China, these by comparison would be king prawn size, and the average appetite (if appetite there was) could manage about five at the most.

But we didn't eat them.

And we've just found a solitary praying mantis. Big (compared with those I've seen in Africa) and quite fat, Marie reckons it's a female and, in her words, up the duff. So we can perhaps expect hordes of little praying mantises to swarm over us any time soon. That's if the cold doesn't get them first. We'll see.

We think these foreign invaders must have blown in from north Africa, but if so they've come a mighty long way. Perhaps a less thrilling explanation could be they've flown from the back of a passing Intermarché lorry delivering fruit and veg from Africa to the local supermarket. Well, they're welcome here and I'm sure they'll fare better in our field than most anywhere else they might end up, though sadly I suspect we won't see their likes again, at least until the next supermarket lorry passes.

But Kerkelven is full of surprises. I find, upon further enquiry, that what I've been calling locusts aren't locusts at all; they're large great green bush crickets, a kind of grasshopper. Locusts are brown, not green, and are certainly found round my way even if I've never spotted them. And, although they are rare, praying mantises are indeed found living wild in northern France. Well, knock me down all over the place.

The dripping forest

October is traditionally rather wet in our part of South Brittany (a bit like September, November and about seven or eight other months). You wouldn't stay here if you don't like it wet. But October wet where we are can be really damp and soggy, wetter than other wets. It's wet that gets in everywhere, including your bones. Wet is in the air. It gets behind your ears and even into your underwear. Seeping, penetrating wet. Wall-to-wall wet. Wet that soaks through stones. Wet that seems unlikely ever to dry.

In the morning the drip, drip, drip of the forest can be a spooky sound, the only sound, irregular, persistent, all-pervasive, but strangely comforting for all that. The dripping forest is a good place to come if you need stillness, a place to think.

There's no shortage of water in Brittany, or so it seems. Last night it rained and rained, coming down in stair rods. Today, the world is soggy. It feels like perfect conditions for growing mushrooms, or even seaweed. As I walk with the three rather damp dogs the mist is still hanging in the air, so the atmosphere, while breathable, feels like water only partially diluted with air. The field resembles nothing so much as a huge, dripping sponge.

Drip, drip, drip, drip, drip, drip, drip.

It's freezing-cold rain too. 'Lovely weather for ducks,' we may say, but even ducks aren't stupid enough to come out on a day like today. The dogs cling around my legs like limpets, every so often looking up at me as if to say 'What the f*** are we doing here?' I have no valid answer, but still we trudge on. Walks are a religion here.

The birds are too soggy to come out, the nooks and crannies where they shelter must be long since waterlogged. I can't imagine they'll feel there's anything much to sing about on a day like today. Insects will be sheltering under the uplighter fungus. Only the fish are in their element. And maybe the frogs.

Every leaf, every blade of grass is forming a droplet ready for its next drip. Steam rises from the river and from the dogs' backs as we squelch along. It's probably billowing from my bowed head too. The mist surrounding us gives a confined, closed-in feeling as if overnight someone's put up walls, real solid walls but which stay tantalisingly indistinct and out of view. There's steam also billowing from the last remnants of the near-permanent pile of pig poo (showing, for you physicists out there, the not inconsiderable latent heat of slowly composting slurry).

A minute leak in my right welly boot doesn't help as I gingerly enter the river just east of the third cataract to photograph a bizarre mushroom growing horizontally out of the bank. I discovered it yesterday and it may be gone tomorrow. The light was poor and it's arguable if it was worth it. Still, you have to try. Wading calf-high in the river with a gently flooding right boot adds to the bizarre feeling that I have drifted off to sleep and woken in a not unpleasant but strange and eerie waterworld.

Just as I'm thinking it's lovely weather for ducks, suddenly I disturb a moorhen, hiding under the banks. Though he or she must be loving this, he still flaps indignantly and noisily off. I would have wondered why he hadn't left last month with his fellows from the big pond, but such was my fright I nearly wet myself there and then, which would only have completed my sense of submersion in this strange wetscape I now call home.

Here in Kerkelven the weather changes much more often than the weather really should, or has any right to. The last few days of October are sunny and mild. Yet on the pathways, woodland tracks and gullies all around Kerkelven you'll find ample evidence of the record fall of acorns, alleged sign of a harsh, severe winter ahead. This one is forecast to be the coldest in living memory, or so the locals tell us. I'd better fix my leaking welly boot.

Starry, starry night

Isn't the Internet wonderful? From the comfort of our home or office we can search the world for anything we want, at any time. In just seconds, we can have dates, pictures, charts and diagrams from anywhere on our screens for easy printing, if not always for easy reading.

I wanted to find out about the stars, particularly those that shine above Kerkelven. I'd heard that light pollution is increasing and that streetlamps now outshine the Milky Way. This is the colloquial name given to the side-on, from-its-outer-edge view of our galaxy that people on our planet can enjoy, if conditions are right. On a clear night the Milky Way is what we see spread like a band across the night sky, it's the creamy swathe of stars that is our galaxy, that little swirl of space debris wherein we, and all other life so far discovered, live. Whereas thirty years ago skywatchers above Manchester, England could count up to seven thousand stars in the Milky Way, now they're lucky to see two hundred. Yet from Kerkelven, when I look up on a clear moonless night, I see a display of stars beyond counting.

I'm not sure what we can do about growing light pollution, but if it's the price of progress then we don't want to pay it here.

There's a website where all you need to do is key in your latitude and longitude and up comes a map of the heavens from your vantage point, that very night. How useful is that?

Well, it's rather a congested map and a bit difficult to read, but that's nitpicking.

We are so lucky. Technology is such a boon.

Imagine in the olden days, our ancestors had no such benefits. They lived ignorant, short, deprived lives, mostly out of doors.

They didn't have television, the Internet, DVDs, email, home pizza deliveries or iPods. And they didn't have central heating.

All they could do was go outside, look up and marvel at the scene above them, the wondrous glory of the everlasting stars.

Which they could see much more clearly than we can, because back then, even here, the stars they saw would be less obscured by pollution and artificial ambient light.

Perhaps people then, denied the Internet, didn't know what they were looking at, couldn't tell planets from stars, didn't know any of the stars' magnitudes, their constellations, how they move relative to each other, didn't even know their names, or how near or far away they are.

I suppose they could only look at them in even greater splendour than we do now and wonder.

And thanks to their much less complicated lives they could spend more time actually out there, looking up.

We might be better informed, but I'm sure they were more enchanted.

Dead James

James died alone at dead of night, victim of a hit-and-run. We found him next morning lying in a ditch, terribly mutilated, quite dead. This was just after we'd moved here, our two boys were young and impressionable, very taken with country life and a bit shaken by the suddenness and brutality of country death.

'We must bury him,' said Joe, looking very glum and fighting back his tears. Though he'd only known and named him post mortem, the permanence of James' condition had rather frightened him. He wanted to keep James where he could see him, in the hope that something might change. But it didn't. Still, he didn't cry. Charlie, being younger, was inconsolable. Poor, dead James.

Repeating this mantra the two boys carefully picked up the remaining bits of this sticky, squashed baby snake and gently, reverently carried him to our small field where, clearing some weeds under a spreading apple tree, they dug the first hole in what was to become a long and disconsolate tradition, the burying in our small field of now hallowed ground of all our expired pets and sundry deceased fauna from the field and forest.

This was all some years back, of course. Poor dead James, as he was always referred to, became an icon in our family. He was soon to be joined in his repose by the mortal remains of owls, rabbits, foxes, assorted birds, several hamsters and more than a few cats. We have still got room for three dogs though. Their plots are reserved. I surmise that Marie may also have marked out a suitable place for me to occupy, in the fullness of time.

Our former neighbours, the pigs

Kerkelven, in recent times, was a working pig farm. Even when the old house fell into disuse, the former outbuildings that now belong to the immediate descendants of our recently deceased neighbour Emile, formed part of a large and complex pig factory that was the mainstay of Emile's fragile business.

The pigs have all gone now, but their smell remains. The pong of pig's urine is one of nature's most distinctive, persistent and pervasive odours. When we first came here there were upward of three hundred pigs kept in a variety of sties, tumbledown sheds and other enclosures around the farm, mostly in the buildings directly behind our house. Kerkelven was what's known as a '*Hotel des Cochons*', a hotel for pigs. They'd come here (not through choice, but were delivered in a big black prison truck) at about a month or two old and they'd stay for about three more months of intensive fattening, before being sold off to the butcher. The sole exception to this rule was that from time to time Emile would pick one of these beasts out for his and his family's personal consumption.

Despite Emile's general indifference to animal welfare the pigs were not treated or kept badly during their stay here. There may be economic reasons for this, I don't know. But they weren't overcrowded or neglected and generally seemed content enough here, except of course on those days when the butcher from the village would come round and one of their number would be selected for the chop.

I liked the pigs and would often pause to talk to them of a morning, an activity in which I was discovered more than once by old Emile or one of his offspring, to their obvious alarm.

But the pigs were nice, and always happy to greet a visitor. From time to time they would escape and I'd find myself obliged to round them up and escort them home. As they'd scurry homeward obligingly ahead of me they, with their pert, wobbly pink bottoms, looked from behind more than a bit like bare-naked ladies and walked like they were in high-heeled shoes.

Perhaps I've been sitting in the sun too long, or am going native. Of course I don't mean I was ever attracted to them. Well, perhaps just slightly, particularly to the one I called Emerald, the one with the green teeth.

Chestnuts for *gouter*

Marie decided that, like all the mothers in the region, she too should roast Spanish chestnuts for young Charlie to take to school with him, to eat during his morning or afternoon break. This ritual time is known in France as *gouter*. It means to taste, and is applied to anything the children bring with them to eat at break time.

Marie gathered her chestnuts from the profusion just lying around on our land. She even bought a special chestnut frying pan, or griddle, or skillet, with holes in it, designed for use over a blazing open log fire.

She experimented, tested, roasted, tossed. It's a heavy implement, not easy to use. An open fire is preferred and in those days we did frequently gather round a roaring log fire and toss a chestnut or two. It was quite fun.

And then Charlie decided he didn't like them.

To be honest, try as I might, I don't like them either. But I love the idea of them. Chestnut gathering and roasting is such a quintessentially autumnal, rural activity. It's charming to think that somewhere it's still a part of country life, even if it's not for us.

November

Winter's coming

Despite the unseasonable mildness of the last several weeks there are indeed signs around now that winter is on its way. It's not just that our neighbours give us odd looks when we persist in still eating out of doors. In truth autumn winds have blown, leaves are beginning to fall and as if to usher in November chills the weather changed abruptly overnight: this morning the first frost was on the cars. (It was also, of course, just about everywhere else.)

It's only the love of summer that makes us dread the winter so. For Kerkelven in winter can be heaps of fun and interesting too. I rummage about the attic to find our heavy-duty winter duvet, discarded up there in abandon months earlier, the instant the first swallow appeared. Fleeces, anoraks and woolly jumpers all make their way downstairs too, in readiness for the coming cold.

A French fireworks night

The French don't traditionally celebrate bonfire night. Our Guy Fawkes parties were an annual feature at Kerkelven as the boys were growing up. I remember them fondly for their sheer good fun, alcoholic excess and the pleasure of yet again seeming quaintly idiosyncratic to our bemused neighbours as we danced around the bonfire letting off squibs and generally being badly behaved.

Sudden changes of colour

Somehow it's escaped me all these years. I must have seen it, must even have been among it, I've perhaps remarked upon it but I've never really noticed it. This is the season of gold. It's everywhere, not overall, because there are other colours too, but all around. It's undeniable and extraordinary. No superlatives do it justice. Right now, in our field on a crisp sunny early morning, a walk by the river and forest is like a stroll through Montezuma's palace gardens.

I've been away for just the past three nights but in that time the yellow-green of the forest has turned to gold flecked with rust. From the river the forest has become a wall of gold. It's blooming impressive, so I drag visitors down to see it. Some clearly think me bonkers, particularly Joe, Charlie and their friends.

Despite the lateness of the season and their sudden changes of colour the trees are mostly still laden with leaves, but I'm guessing the fall can't be far off now. The trees seem to have a secret system which ensures that, rather than falling all at once, their leaves drop in a steady, ordered flow with, as it were, some preordained sequence. The gentle whispering of their slow but continual falling is a pleasant accompaniment on a riverside walk whatever the time of day. Why they don't all fall at once and how the fall takes place so evenly, with such order and disciplined regularity, I've really no idea. Nor can I fathom, over the strong milky coffee that restores me after each walk, why it should be that nature can drop so much debris, yet everywhere still looks lovely, while whenever we humans drop even a few bits of litter it all seems so untidy and wrong.

Along the wood's frontage on our field a massive metamorphosis has begun, starting with the subtle but accelerating change in colour. Gradually and very dramatically the trees will all change their apparel in the coming days and weeks. Not simultaneously, and in a very varied range of hues and colours, the effect will be as spectacular as any *son et lumière* show.

On the fall and the fog

Different species of trees lose their leaves at different times. The fruit trees seem to go first. The oaks hold on to their leaves well into winter, except for the old oaks, bless them, whose leaves start falling quite soon after the fruit trees. After several dry days the carpet of leaves is crisp and crinkly underfoot. When Syrus runs through them they rustle and crackle under his feet.

It is possible to stand under a riverside tree early in November and be rained upon by softly falling leaves. This is a nice feeling. Equally relaxing is to sit on the bench by the river, lean your head slowly back and watch as the leaves fall gently down towards you from the overhanging branches. Both are a bit soppy I suppose and really I should have better things to do with my time, but I can't think what. A sudden flurry of wind will come along and, hey presto, you're enveloped in swirling leaves, a sensation that's both refreshing and cheering. In my field, not for the first time, I give thanks that no one can see me as I overindulge my sensual side.

I do sometimes wonder at the simple delights I take in this field. If anyone were watching I'd show more decorum, for sure.

Max, Syrus and Mortimer sniff around for rodents as usual, oblivious to all this. They are a metaphor for humanity generally, which misses most of what's happening because it's always sniffing around looking for something else.

There's a lot of fog about these days, particularly in the early mornings. At times it's just a light, eerie, wispy mist that hangs insubstantially around the valley, once again giving everywhere and everything the spooky air of a Hammer Horror movie. Some days it's thick, cold, clammy and penetrating, a real horror, most unlovely. As we walk around, dogs and me, we strain to glimpse characters from *Night of the Living Dead* who,

I imagine, are all hanging around the fringes of this chilly, ghostly fog, just out of view.

Then all of a sudden it clears and we're again bathed in soft autumnal sunshine. The grass is long and soggy, slumped and fallen, the ground wet, springy, soft. To the west where wet weather is clearly coming we can see, so clear and sharp you feel you could touch it, the rainbow's lovely form, as Burns put it, 'evanishing amid the storm'. These days are quite extraordinary, nights too. Autumn sometimes has a bad press with tourists and the like but a fine autumn here takes some beating.

How the weather here changes. It's been raining solidly now for 24 hours. The river is flowing at twice the speed it was yesterday. The slope hasn't increased, so it can only be the combined weight of new water from the rains all rushing together down gullies, crevices, cracks, brooks and rivulets joining in to swell the river in tumultuous throng. But the river seems to be coping very well. Why doesn't it all come at once and overwhelm us in a flood? Sometimes, of course, it does. Nature here seems very powerful, but generally quite ordered, sure of itself, restrained even. This is probably just as well, for us. We walk in the drizzle by the riverbank, heads bowed against the elements. Poor vulnerable things, if nature were to decide to flex her powers, to show us what she can do, we'd have no chance. Just what she can do is in the air, a breath away. But we are safe, for now at least.

Perhaps not for long. The rain has continued, backed by high winds that quickly turned to tempest. Last night was such a night! It's thrilling to be abroad in the battering storm, the noise cataclysmic as every tree groans and growls as though run through with wind and rain. Throughout the long storm Kerkelven seemed like nothing as much as a vast celestial toilet stuck on flushing. Then, after a seemingly endless pummelling comes the hush, a tangible, visible quiet, a strange calm that lasts perhaps just seconds, like the eye of a storm, before again the vast cacophony of shifting air pressures dashes across the skies or falls from the heavens to break just above our heads. The dogs cling around our feet, frightened by the howling winds and the straining of the tormented trees but, like us, lulled into false security by the short silence of the hush.

The riverbank looks like its been wrung through a mangle and then beaten with sticks for hours. Everything has been flattened by the sudden weight of water that burst upon it. There's a sense of shock in the air, as if the severity and completeness of the tempest were utterly unexpected.

Why do leaves fall?

Chlorophyll is a molecule in plants that absorbs sunlight then uses this energy to synthesise carbohydrates from carbon dioxide and water. This process is known as photosynthesis, the basis for sustaining the life processes of all plants. Since animals and humans obtain their food supply by eating plants, photosynthesis can be said to be the source of our life force too.

During spring and summer, leaves attract the sunlight and house the chlorophyll that are essential to photosynthesis. When it is difficult for a tree's roots to obtain enough moisture from the cold soil, during winter, it can't afford to lose too much water through transpiration, so the leaves have to go.

It's the decreasing length of our winter day that causes the rich leaf colours of autumn. Less daylight triggers the plant cells to produce a hormone called abscisic acid, which in turn forms a corklike layer of cells at the base of the leaf, where it joins the twig. This acts as a seal across the vascular tissue that normally carries water and nutrients into the leaf and takes waste products away. As a result, the leaf effectively starves, the stem that holds it to the plant weakens until eventually it is carried away by a gust of wind.

At this point the leaf is not making chlorophyll (which makes it green) because it isn't getting the nourishment it needs. Chlorophyll is actually an unstable substance that breaks down and needs to be replaced all year round, but cooling autumn temperatures speed up the decomposition, replacement chlorophyll isn't produced and the green of the tree fades away.

In its place appear more stable pigments than chlorophyll – carotenes, which can be further divided into the xanthophylls and the carotenoids (just in case you wanted to know). These chemicals are responsible for the reds, yellows and oranges. Another group of chemicals, the xanthocyanins, which produce the rich crimsons and purples, are created by the last end-of-season gasps of photosynthesis, which are trapped in the leaf by the abscission layer as it firms up. The production of xanthocyanins is encouraged by dry sunny days and cool crisp nights, so we enjoy the most spectacular autumn colours when we have this weather.

Hot summers also contribute to autumn colours, as does a lack of high winds in autumn – presumably because the leaves don't blow away.

Tractoring in the fields of gold

Just as the trees are turning colour now from multiple shades of green to auburns, amber, bronze and gold, the river in the early morning is a steamy vale of gold.

These days it's a pale full moon that rises over Kerkelven. The large equally pale sun is striking seen through the haze of early morning mist. At night the sunsets are on fire, with clouds that Michelangelo would envy and that God Himself might choose to sit upon, if He were coming.

Far above me as I take my turn around the field on my tractor the sky suddenly fills with gliding, circling gulls. Where have they come from and why are they here? Have they spotted me from their aerial travels, and do they think my tractor and I signal the chance of a meal for them? They must have the most fantastic warning or lookout system. And eyes that miss nothing that moves on the earth beneath.

Closer in, just around my head, are swarms of a quite different kind, a small mosquito-like insect, though not an easy one to catch for closer examination. But I do, and find they're a kind of midge. According to my book these are most likely to be the non-biting kind of midge, though they seem unaware of this. They're also not supposed to tolerate wind and sunshine and though their sheer numbers can be a nuisance, apparently they seldom hang around for long.

Again, I'm not so sure. Somehow the little chaps appear to have survived frost, storms and floods and now seem to be thriving on mouthfuls of me. These tiny flying insects infest the air at the river's edge in their millions. They can be quite pretty to watch as they swarm and swoop, but sit among them long enough and you'll find they are feasting on you in total disregard for what the books say. It's a bit more annoying than just ticklish. In the absence of a proper name I call them the trouser-gnat, after their propensity to invade intimate clothing to wreak their havoc. We seem able to tolerate the taking of tiny chunks from our bodies for only a short while, which perhaps is just as well for, I imagine, in their combined attack they would soon weaken me to slumber and as I dozed they would feast and finish me off, leaving nothing but my wellies.

The whump-whump of the motor and the whirring sound

of the horizontally slicing blade become quite calming, like background music. So I sit circling my field in solitary slow contemplation. I get round the whole field in thirty minutes, or even a tad less. But this, sadly, may be the last mowing I can justifiably give this field until the grass starts growing again in the spring. Doing it merely for pleasure would, I suppose, be just too weird.

Early birds

I've noticed that birds get up early and are often not around in the afternoon. Perhaps that's their preferred time to have a rest, for which, given the early hour of their rising, I can hardly blame them. They sleep at night, perched on branches.

But do these early birds actually get the worms? Not, I suspect, if they're all up and about before dawn, which seems to be the case. For the early hours are not the best time for birds to feed, because the light is poor and insects are not around (they, possibly, are true slug-a-beds as, presumably, are the slugs).

But birds do consider the early morning good for singing because sound transmission tends to be good then. Perhaps the worms come out to listen, are off their guard and that's when they get caught. But search as I might, I find no evidence to prove that early birds do actually get the worms.

Maybe they just get up early because, once you are up and about, you find it's the nicest time of the day.

Apart from a few hardy souls like robins, most other birds, even those that winter here, don't come out at all when it's really cold, preferring to stay in the trees or huddle together in the underbrush. Next day when the sun comes out they're back, for the mornings at least. I think they must have some-where quite warm to hide and spend rather a lot of time there, frankly, when they should be out singing, or catching insects, or crapping on cars. They may even have little beds hidden in the lower branches of the trees and dry dark holes underground for when it gets stormy.

Winter singing is interesting because generally birds don't sing when the weather is bad. But the trend towards milder winters means birds are singing more at this time. Because they think it's daytime birds also sing more in brightly lit areas such as towns or where there's high light pollution, but it has to be quite mild too.

On the odd sunny days, of course, we all sing. Other than then, gloom is the overriding aspect of these late autumn days at Kerkelven. Gloom spreads its foulness over all, so before long everyone is depressed, even the squirrels and the robins.

It can be alarmingly quiet. At times through the clean autumn air all you can hear is the steady dropping of leaves. Still, there is never-ending industry in the field, though not much of what's going would be evident to the unobservant, except perhaps for the buzzing of flies and mumblings from the river.

But lift a stone or shake a bush and you're sure to find some woodland resident chasing or being chased, something hiding itself, or hiding something it wants to keep from others.

Mushrooms are pushing up from the mouldy undergrowth, ducks are silently paddling in the river, tree creepers are shinning quietly up barks, leaves are loosening, squirrels are secreting their nuts to see them through the winter and the young queen wasps have found a corner somewhere to hibernate, maybe in one of our sheds.

You might see any or all of these under a Kerkelven shrub these days and hear them too if you listen hard enough.

An ugly brown raised scar across the surface of my smooth-as-a-billiard-table path to Bertrand's field betrays the antisocial wanderings of that cuddly-looking but actually rather disruptive little character, the mole. Their cheeky little holes pop up all over the place, particularly in nice flat recently mowed places, playing havoc with tidy lawns, which, fortunately, are not often found here. In Kerkelven these blighters appear to have no natural enemies except me (and to be honest I really rather like them). For sure I wouldn't harm them, but they avoid me all the same, as they do most surface life. Moles aren't nocturnal, as I've always supposed. In fact they are busy day and night, seeming to work in four-hour shifts. Moles aren't actually blind but have small piggy eyes that are pretty much useless except for registering light. They are carnivores, so won't eat your garden plants though they may kill them accidentally, when they pop up somewhere uninvited. Moles are not rodents, they're insectivores, from the same family as anteaters.

There's a fallen tree in the river and its floating branches trap all sorts of interesting detritus, whatever flotsam and jetsam that passes with the flow. Today's catch includes a plastic water bottle, a dead owl, some interesting bits of wood, a gob of scum and something else that is floating just below the surface and out of reach so I can't quite see what it is.

The river though is dangerous now and races around the tree at breakneck speed to keep up with the rest of its swollen, fast-flowing waters. It's icy cold too, so unless the council is coming along to do its duty and clear the debris (which seems unlikely) it may be better for me to leave the tree where it is until the summer.

Winter may be coming and the trees may be changing but the jays still squawk and squabble, the wood pigeons noisily break out from their shelters as before. If swallows are like Messerschmitts, say, and chaffinches are like Cessna twinseaters and buzzards are like Stealth bombers, then wood pigeons are like the Sunderland flying boats of the bird world. By the look of them it's inconceivable they could possibly fly. On take-off they seem unlikely to make it, taking an inordinately, heart-stoppingly long time to achieve lift-off, skimming the tops of the trees with their massive under-carriage and carrying away a few twigs and leaves in the process. In the air they have the grace and fluidity of a Covent Garden prima donna, resembling, more than a little, a hippopotamus with wings. But they thrive around here all the same. Kerkelven's wood pigeons are among the chubbiest you'll see anywhere. (OK, that's an understatement. They're fat!)

In one of our trees I notice a visiting flock of maybe a dozen long-tailed tits. They remind me of the flock of waxwings that a school chum and I spotted when I was a youngster. We reported the arrival of these not exactly rare but still infrequent visitors to our part of Britain to our local paper, the *Nairnshire Telegraph*, and our account appeared in their 'Noted in Passing' column. It was the first time I ever saw my name in print. Like the waxwings, these long-tailed tits are crested, and their colourful crests wave regally like bright, tiny parakeets as they bob from bough to bough, brightening up the newly leafless tree. But they are not so rare here and I've seen them, usually in pairs, quite a few times. They are a very charming and dainty bird, quite a delight to watch for fifteen minutes or so.

A raucous pair of crows fly noisily from the woods behind. Seconds later a shrew of a jay flaps irritably away, scolding her partner as she goes. The gentle long-tailed tits seem affronted by these ruffians and flitter off in a posse.

Cold snap

On account of the clear skies and full moon it was really cold last night so we've awoken this morning to a deep frost. This isn't helped by our central heating still not working, on account of a banjaxed boiler. Expensive though such repairs always are, they also take an inordinately long time and, of course, breakdowns only occur in seriously cold weather.

It's already warm in the very bright sunshine but everywhere else is bitter cold. Steam rises in clouds from ponds and river and also from Poo Mountain, the anticipated removal of which didn't quite happen. In Kerkelven it's best not to speak too soon, or to count your chickens before they've hatched.

On odd occasions when the sun shines on the water big fish, trout, can be seen drifting silently through the shallows, but you have to be sharp-eyed to spot them. What moves them, I wonder, apart from the waggling of their tails?

Though they were continuing back and forth on their foraging business just a day or two ago, seemingly as normal, there's now no activity from the wasps' nest by the river. Death seems to have come quickly to them in the cold of the night. I come back in the evening, just to check. There are no telltale bodies by the tree, just stillness and an eerie quiet. They must have all died as they slept.

While the river's high water subsides, even if not for long, the island makes a valiant comeback. In the first steamy light of dawn it looks just great, like the legendary Avalon, the flow of the river crystal clear and silver, the rich rust-brown bed and the banks overhung with vegetation that is, like the leaves on the trees, still green but on the turn, transforming to browns, reds and golds. The island appears and disappears almost at whim, itself a victim of the ever-changing weather.

Out walking, I disturb a feeding frenzy of small birds,

mainly chaffinches it seems, but I think I see some bluetits and also a woodlark or two. Different bird species appear to get on well together, mixing in perfect harmony, sharing the same trees and the food they somehow find from all around. If ever there's a dispute it's usually between the constantly argumentative jays or one robin roughing up another because of some territorial insult. Mostly, though, the different species seem to get on with each other just fine.

An odd little dragonfly has just begun to appear in the forest. It's a new kind to me, about two to three centimetres long, coloured reddish-grey with the characteristic double wings of the species jutting out at right angles. It doesn't seem at all shy. Despite recent frosts lizards are still running about on the walls of Kerkelven with even very young ones coming in view, surely rather strange for November?

It's night, and now there's no moon, but it's not dark at all because there isn't a cloud in the sky, nor even any haze. I don't think I've ever seen the night sky brighter or more filled with stars. They look really great when seen through the bare branches of a newly naked tree, particularly when it's hung with mistletoe.

As you look up, awestruck, think on this. Not so long ago we believed that our galaxy, the one we see so splendidly from our vantage point at Kerkelven, edge on, was the only galaxy there was. Now, thanks to developments like the Hubble telescope, we can see that there are millions, even billions of other galaxies like ours. Someone has calculated, and I can't dispute this, that there are more stars in the heavens than there have been human heartbeats since the dawn of time.

And the beautiful chain was broken . . .

The hunter turned and shot the fox full in the face, killing it instantly. It was a lucky shot (though not for the fox), but messy. Pieces of the dead fox splattered on the surrounding trees. Not wishing to soil his hands the hunter cut off the fox's tail, for he had to bring back a trophy to prove his worth. In other circumstances he would have taken the whole carcass but he realised that was impractical now.

It was a chance killing, though this time chance didn't favour the fox. Moments before, one of the hunter's three dogs had accidentally stumbled on where the fox was hiding. It could just as easily have passed half a metre or so on either side as it had often before, but today the dog walked right on top of him and the startled, unlucky fox instinctively turned to run, straight at the hunter. He didn't have a chance. Cover is thin now. 'Cover' is a bit of a euphemism really. It's an unequal hunt at best, but here more unequal than elsewhere.

The hunter has no thought for anyone else who might chance along at this time. Leaving the remnants of the fox spread around he stuffs its once-proud brush into an inside pocket and, nervous dogs in tow, turns to trudge silently away. If he's thinking of anything he doesn't share it with anyone, even his dogs. When he meets his fellow hunters twenty minutes later he shows them the tail and tells them of his kill, but it's very low key, very matter of fact.

'Well done, Claude,' they will say, 'it's a good kill.'

The incident with the fox will then be forgotten. Even though with that act of thoughtless barbarity a compact has been made that forever marks the human from all other creatures of the forest. This one kills for pleasure and for not much pleasure at that. Even the fox eats what he kills, usually.

But foxes are considered vermin here, pests, so most people will think that whatever happens to them is fine. But when I meet these hunters my intended open hostility goes out the window (OK, I know a field hasn't got windows), for the formal politeness of the French ensures it's hard to be cold, even with these guys. So I usually ask if they have had any luck, hoping all the while that they won't tell me even if they have. Even then Claude declines to mention the fox he's just killed and they all look a bit furtive, shifting from foot to foot before mumbling *bonne continuation* and shuffling on.

Beating about the bush

Do hunters crap in the woods? Alongside bears and popes, it seems quite likely. They certainly do some shitty things.

Worst among these is their despicable practice of releasing into the wild as shotgun-fodder tame pheasants they've raised themselves and whose tails they've clipped so they can't fly more than fifty metres. This makes the hunt doubly diabolical by affording for the hunters even easier kills than usual. That they have to do this speaks eloquently of how thoroughly they have already denuded our forests, stripping them in their greed of all living things.

You might imagine that this would be enough to satisfy anyone's blood-lust. But no. Clipping the tail feathers of these bewildered, terrified creatures ensures that they can do little more than leap maybe three metres in the air, thus providing the brave hunters with a plainly easy-peasy shot.

Early in our time here Marie had to suffer a Basil Fawlty moment in the woods when our three eager canines, Max, Syrus and Mortimer, stumbled for the first time upon a pheasant thus released into what they'd come to consider as their wild wood. For them it must have been a bit like all their birthdays arriving at once.

As easy a prey it is for the hunter, so too is the clipped pheasant easy prey for dogs, even dogs as dim as ours. Marie found and grabbed a stick and tried to beat them off as they pursued the frightened bird round and round in the underbrush. Dogs and pheasant alike would have been invisible to anyone watching from the road at that time, but not our Marie, beating about the bush. Marie must have looked more like a whirling dervish or an Armenian sabre dancer than someone trying to save an already condemned pheasant from its latest torment, the dogs.

The Breton head butt

Much ado is made in this region of its people's distinctive and individual approach to greeting friends and acquaintances. Men meeting other men invariably shake hands firmly and purposefully, a civilised *bonjour* that breeds goodwill and *bonhomie*. I like it very much, for it conveys camaraderie, manliness and civilised behaviour in one warm gesture. But when women are involved (woman on man and woman on woman), the practice throughout France is to kiss. In many areas a single quick and dry peck on the proffered cheek is quite sufficient, but a kiss on each cheek is more customary in most regions. Air-kissing would be frowned upon and of course its opposite, actual slobbering, is not permitted anywhere. In some regions the custom extends to three discreet kisses.

But in Brittany they just have to go a little bit further. Here, to the consternation and annoyance of natives and incomers alike, the custom on greeting with kisses is four. Though some people consider this utterly excessive and attempt to get away with fewer (which can in large gatherings lead to total confusion), four kisses, two on either cheek, is the norm here, though if you meet someone you've already met and kissed that day, further kissings are usually dispensed with.

Thus meetings involving above ten people (Bretons have

large families so such gatherings are commonplace) can lead to much head-bobbing, dribbling and general confusion.

In every such group, of course, there is always someone who can't quite get the timing or the sequence right. Oftentimes this will be a foreign male (women tend to be much better at these things), perhaps of early-adolescent awkwardness, prone to blushing in female company at even the best of times. For him, meeting the women of his adoptive land is far from his favourite time. His greeting, no doubt well intended, often doesn't quite come off and sometimes can lead to what might be termed 'the Breton head butt'. It doesn't need much describing, for I'm sure you can readily imagine what happens on such an encounter. So please spare a thought for the prepubescent male who knows he has eighteen female friends or relatives coming round this lunchtime, for the traditional dinner at *Toussaints* (All Saints' Day).

As an incomer (therefore foreign, ill-bred and capable of any degree of inappropriate behaviour) I've often been tempted to pretend that I think the actual number of expected kisses is six, or eight, or to just keep on going until stopped, to see what might happen.

But Breton women are just too intimidating. Maybe one day . . .

Into the river

The season of gold being a time when the river is running slow I decide to seize the moment to go in and lop off some low-hanging branches and, while I'm at it, to get to know this river a bit better. So snug in my thigh-high waders and wrapped around with woolly jumper and scarf I descend the riverbank at the confluence of the Sarre and the west burn, by the round stone table, then slip noiselessly into the river, instantly sinking almost crotch-deep into soft sticky mud. My God, it's cold! The slumbering river is not more than a millimetre from spilling over the tops of my waders, thus filling my beautiful boots with its freezing waters at which point, frozen to the crotch, I would probably convulse, lose my footing and so be gently swept away to a watery grave in slow motion, unable to do anything to save myself because I'd be weighed down by massive oversize welly boots filled to their brims with the icy flow. In this part of the Sarre there's no one to hear you scream.

As I struggle to free my feet from the mud the red and amber bodies of dead leaves drift sedately by me in a steady, gentle flow, accumulating in piles at every obstacle however minor, till enough of them have gathered so they can spill over to join the throng again, eventually to gather en masse in the almost dead water between cataracts three and three and a half, Kerkelven's equivalent of the Sargasso Sea.

I haven't worn my waders for ages, I'm not sure why, for I love them beyond what's reasonable. Their sturdy green rubber leggings cling seductively to the tops of my thighs and hold me firmly all the way down, forcing me to walk like a jackbooted Mussolini. Which I find secretly thrilling. But in the water these boots are so effective. As they've been hanging forlornly in our shed since about this time last year, I first wipe the webs and debris from their topmost edges then upend each boot and give them a sharp knock to dislodge any spidery nests or creeping crawlies that might be clinging to the sides, or lurking down at the bottom. In a hurry I slide them on, but it occurs that I've not been as thorough as I should have in checking the toe areas. It's too late to go back now so, though fearful of squelching a foot-load of spiders or something worse, I slide my sock-clad foot and leg down as quickly as the tight rubber will allow. Very briefly it reminds me of my old wet suit, but that's probably more than enough about the appeal of rubber, for now.

In the river I realise that, in all this mud, progress is far from easy. More than once I again come dangerously close to being swamped. But once balance is asserted I can't fail to see how nice and peaceful it is here and to appreciate that, from this perspective, the field and the forest look quite different. It's late afternoon and there's a gentle mist rising from the surface. The yellow haze of the sun mingles with this to bathe the landscape in a warm autumnal glow. To curb my enjoyment three anxious faces all present themselves above the bank, looking down upon me as if I've finally gone insane. To be honest I have no idea what my dogs think of me. Assuming they think of me at all, I suspect they see me as somewhere between mystic deity and provider of the next meal, but whatever their opinion I'm sure it's not enhanced by discovering me in this position, particularly as I'm continually getting stuck in really deep mud and must look as if I could be sucked under at any time.

I trim some branches (my original purpose in being here) before finally accepting that it is easier to climb out and move along on dry land to the next branch that needs lopping. Maybe after the winter floods there'll be less mud and I can do this again, for it is fun. I climb out, but not before I have a good chance to rummage around among the stones, roots and branches that decorate the water's edge. Again I can see that many of these big stones have been placed there, perhaps in the golden age of the Sarre, when it was used for, well, who knows what? Commerce, perhaps, or travel. More likely, just doing the laundry.

As tired but happy dogs and I wend our way homeward a pure black pheasant rises up from the field and flies slowly towards the distant line of the forest, where he instantly disappears. Though he seems to fly quite well I doubt if he's a native. More likely his feathers have been clipped and he'll be shot in the morning. We leave him be.

Fine malts and evenings by the fire

When it's cold outside, Kerkelven has its compensations. Log fires are a bit of a ritual here, piled high and burning brightly. A ready supply of firewood is no problem of course. Our vast fireplaces lend themselves in every way to evenings snugly spent bathed in the warm comforting glow of blazing log fires. In every way, that is, except that these splendid vast fireplaces of ours *don't sodding work.* Smoke is the problem, uncomfortable

billows of it that get in the eyes, in the clothes, in the food, everywhere. To create an effective through draught that will reduce the smoke to tolerable levels we have to sit with the barn door open, which to a very large extent defeats the point.

This is where I feel fine malt whiskies come into their own. I keep a rich selection of the best and the oldest from the western isles of my native shores. A few generous sips of the sixteen-year-old Lagavulin and all seems well again with the world. What's a bit of wood smoke anyway? Why bother with a wee bit of a draught? Heap the fire higher. Now lassie, where's my book . . .?

Planting a palm tree

We already had a palm tree in our front garden when Marie gave me another one, a big one, for my birthday. I decided that the new one, being just that bit bigger than the old one, would look best growing through the gravel in the corner by the remnants of the ancient ruined stone fountain, which itself sits looking rather less than splendid in the corner of our front yard.

But of course that's where the original palm tree then sat and, if the new one were to replace it, the old would first have to be dug up and moved elsewhere.

So one rainy cold late-November day, helped somewhat reluctantly by number-two son, Charlie, I dug up the old palm tree. Its roots were huge, thick, sinewy, deep and tangled, and none of the assortment of tools we had brought for the task proved of much use, as the trunk of the palm had grown hard against the stones. Digging it out took forever, on both pairs of knees with slippery wet and frozen fingers, scraping and scrabbling with our bare hands in the freezing cold to lift each half-handful of earth, roots and gravel. It wasn't really possible to save most of the roots, which presumably it needed to survive. By the time we could lift it to safety it seemed rather obvious that we'd killed it. It was an ex-palm. Extinct.

We respectfully moved it aside, for later disposal.

So in its place we planted the new palm tree, itself not an inconsiderable operation, and stood back to admire our handiwork. It was, to a gnat's whisker, the exact same size as the one we'd so painstakingly dug out. We'd forgotten to take account of the extra height given to it by the pot in which it came. Or at least, Charlie rather unhelpfully claimed he had realised the position from the start, but just didn't like to say anything as I'd seemed so keen.

After some deliberation I decided not to bury him there and then next to the new palm tree. Again, the decision was as close as a gnat's whisker.

I just couldn't face any more digging.

Our septic tank runneth over

'You'll have to come, you absolutely must. It's really important and could cost us all lots of money . . .'

Our neighbour Elodie was most insistent that when residents of the nearby village gathered to discuss new rules for septic tanks, we should be there. As we always do what she says, we complied.

To appreciate the reverence with which I and my neighbours approach all things to do with septic tanks, you have to have the kind of mind that can conceive of a life without mains drainage. Imagining such a thing is almost impossible for townies, indeed for anyone who through the force of oft-repeated habit can simply flush and forget.

That's a dignity and convenience denied to most country dwellers.

The myth and the magic of *les fosses septiques*

Strictly speaking ours is a *fosse toutes eaux* rather than a *fosse septique*, meaning it takes all effluent, not just the really nasty stuff. Not that that is, particularly, a commendation in any way. It just sounds nicer.

Before we moved here, when we were looking for somewhere, Marie said to me, 'I don't care where we live as long as it's somewhere where we can be connected to the mains drainage. I don't want our bodily waste to be sitting in a big tin can outside the back door, for all to see and poke their noses into.'

I nodded good-humouredly at her and the subject passed to other things. This (with hindsight rather sensible) requirement was forgotten until it was way, way too late. I have to say the whole sorry business has been thrown in my face many times since.

When our team of local artisans was restoring Kerkelven, they buried the house's first-ever septic tank in the garden about a hundred metres from our back door. We promptly forgot about it and went about our business as normal. (What the inhabitants of Kerkelven did for the more than three hundred years before then scarcely bears thinking about, but I suppose the answer might have been found piled up under our quaint long-drop, which you may recall I mentioned a few pages back.)

Septic tanks work, basically, on the simple principle that however disgusting and awful something is, as long as it's out of sight it doesn't matter. Those of a nervous disposition should perhaps skip this section but if you are still with me, dear reader, you need to know that everything that drains from anywhere within our house (excepting kitchen waste, which has its own system that I will describe later) – solids and liquids from baths, showers and WCs – all drain through a mysterious series of pipes (assisted by flushing as necessary) into that septic tank buried deep below. There in the inky blackness it swirls and lurks until the whole thing is quite full to the brim, which takes only a month or two of average usage. Its capacity is about 3,000 litres, that's quite a few flushes. Thereafter for whatever comes in, an equivalent volume is forced out to soak away into the good mother earth and then by filtration through rocks and gravel whence it emerges pure and sweet into the fields and river beyond. The tank requires emptying and cleaning every few years or so, some say after four is best, some claim you can leave it for ten.

So our splendid ancient pile, Kerkelven, is built upon a base composed of whatever it is in that poo, soapsuds and water mix that is left behind when the soapy, scummy water drains away.

Urrrgggh!

I know what you're thinking.

This sounds utterly disgusting, does it not? And so it would be too were it not for those wonderful saviours of our species, those microscopic allies, mankind's best buddies, the bacteria, who lurk within that septic tank in their hundreds of billions and just love it when they hear the flush above because for them it signals – dinner!

Yes, our benign and numerous friends the microbes digest and break down all that waste matter so that the whole sorry morass is rendered sweet, clear, clean and inoffensive. The beauty is this system works in a renewable, sustainable (if admittedly still pretty disgusting) way.

The perfect product

The French have a lovely and very useful word – *propre*.

It means 'just so'. Right. Proper. Clean. They apply it to all sorts of things, even to septic tanks, which, you can imagine, one wants to be just as *propre* as it's possible to be.

So some entrepreneurial French manufacturer has come up with a product called *Propercyl* that claims to do just this: with regular usage to keep your septic tank properly *propre*.

But what it actually does, if anything, is a mystery.

Propercyl is a nondescript greyish powder of rather mysterious composition that comes in handy sachets for individual use. Priced by the box of twenty, each sachet works out to cost around half a euro. Not cheap, even if you were to eat it, keep it, or brush your teeth with it. But the instructions on the box advise you, on a weekly basis, to tear open a single sachet and deposit it down your toilet, then flush.

Why, I thought, this *Propercyl* must be the very most perfect product. No middleman, no evident action or obvious efficacy, no waiting or waste. You just buy it and flush it straight down the loo. And everything is as it ever was. *Propre.*

How I wish I'd thought of that. I wonder if they need a UK agent?

Now here's weird

I was standing on the oxbow by the bench, looking downstream in wonder at the recently reborn island, marvelling at how splendidly unearthly it appears, shrouded in mist with the streaming sun reflecting on the water.

Suddenly I became aware that Mortimer was digging vigorously at my feet. Not a dog noted for his energy or enthusiasm, this was an excited and urgent Mortimer, clearly on a mission.

He seemed to be worrying at a whitish root that was buried just under the surface. As I leaned forward to get a better view he jealously clamped his huge jaws around the thing and dragged it up and to the side. It came out from the earth like a dead fish pulled through sludge. Large and shapeless, about the size of a deflated football but soft and spongy with the consistency and colour of decayed flesh. I confess I've not seen anything like it, anywhere. Greyish-white it was, but this was no root. It looked more like a lump of dead meat well past its sell-by date. Whatever he'd found it must have tasted revolting. But Mortimer was very excited now and was chewing at it to try to get it to a size fit for eating. Soon he had it in two parts and the smaller first piece was swallowed down while I was still gathering my wits. Then, sensing I wanted a share in his discovery, he grabbed the remaining chunk and ran off, to polish it off in two or three bites from the safety of about two hundred metres, from where I lost my last chance of ever seeing what it was.

The thing was all gone by the time Syrus and Max realised anything was happening. They sniffed about enthusiastically for a while, but by then it was history.

But what was it? And why was it buried in a shallow grave at the river's edge? It wasn't a recognisable creature. It had no bones, fur or feathers. It was a piece of something, and something large. It seemed to me unlikely that it was a mushroom or any kind of fungus. It was too big. And Mortimer wouldn't eat anything like that.

Any enlightenment on the subject will be most welcome.

A *paysan's* Saturday night

I thank the stars above Kerkelven that for the past fifteen years and more I have had the good fortune to know and be befriended by my neighbour, Mathurin le Belligo, retired farm labourer of this parish. He's at a great age now, is Mathurin and for the last three of these years he's not been well. But if you are to understand our life in Kerkelven, you'll need to get to know

Mathurin a bit better. For Mathurin is unlike anyone else I've ever met.

Mathurin, Angèle's husband, father to Philippe, Pascal and Marie-Laure, is, I think, one of a dying breed, a true man of the soil. He's a manual worker, someone you could easily call a peasant, but it would be a rich compliment, no insult whatsoever. The first time I met Mathurin I noticed how tightly he held my hand in friendship and for a little longer too than was comfortable. But he also held me with his eyes and I couldn't fail to see in these bright blue eyes the warm, impish delight that he was taking, just from meeting me. Mathurin's handshake was firm, sincere, his hands are worn, tough but gentle, his grip was the steady, sure grip of someone who instantly, genuinely, has taken a liking to you, and unassumingly anticipates that you, too, will take to him equally. His time, with which he's generous, he gives to you alone.

From Mathurin I've learned a lot, but most valuably he's taught me to appreciate that there's nothing worth more in this life than an honest and true friend. And there's no one to be envied more than he who is sincerely, simply happy and wants for nothing but that which he has already.

Simple though his life might seem, my neighbour Mathurin is one such man, 'an honest man, the fairest work of God', as the poet Burns put it. And quietly contented too.

Other than a brief sortie to play his part in a foreign war, Mathurin has spent all his life within the boundaries of our Breton commune. He was born a few kilometres from here. Angèle has never travelled further than a day's journey by car. Everything they need or want is close by, within easy reach, including his now extended family, who all live an easily achievable drive away, or less.

Until his retirement 25 years or so ago Mathurin was a tenant farmer, a *locataire*, owning no land himself but working land owned by others, or he worked for others as a daily-rate hired hand. In such spare time as he had he needed to work his small field, his extensive vegetable garden, for to survive and raise his family he had to be self-sufficient in garden produce. He raised his own chickens, ducks, guinea fowl and rabbits too. A heavy manual toil was Mathurin's daily lot, but I never saw him without a smile nor ever heard him utter either complaint, criticism or cross word. His day's work was unremitting and thinly rewarded, yet to all who knew him Mathurin seemed nevertheless to be the picture of happiness, passing each day with his cheery round red face wreathed in smiles of deep contentment.

Mathurin's cheerful hospitality was always infectious and irresistible. Despite his own retired state, he's always been a great respecter of our need to work. Yet almost invariably whenever he saw us he'd invite us round for coffee. We always knew coffee was not uppermost in his mind and most of the time we'd decline, but every now and then it was our great pleasure to accept and pass the afternoon in the genial company of Mathurin and wife. Then we'd wave goodbye to the rest of the day, because an afternoon of coffee with Angèle and Mathurin would lead unfailingly to everything else being put on hold. The eau de vie (his own make, of course) and the robust St Emilion would appear, sometimes accompanied by home-made cider and the local apple wine (*pommeau*). However warm the weather or hot their kitchen was from its wood burner, Mathurin was rarely seen without his cap at a jaunty angle and his shirt buttoned to the neck under a thick woolly jumper. Often the sweat would roll off him as he passed the glass around, but when I'd suggest he try shorts and a T-shirt like me he'd laugh as if it was the finest joke he'd ever heard. Conversation with Mathurin and Angèle was always easy, usually chock-full of intriguing local gossip, or considered analysis of international politics.

I've seldom if ever known a couple happier with each other than Mathurin and Angèle, and this was doubly evident when they were in a group as at the *fête du quartier*, or with their family. We celebrated their golden wedding together and later equally enthusiastically we enjoyed Mathurin's eightieth birthday. These celebratory gatherings were priceless times and it was a privilege indeed for Marie and me to share in them. Outsiders we unquestionably were, but we were never allowed to feel it, even for a moment. To pass a Saturday night with the le Belligo family is to celebrate the past week in a simple, homely way, a tradition that perhaps once would have been found frequently in rural communities across Europe but now is a rare, precious and dying thing. Though to us it seemed they would and should continue forever, we were fortunate indeed to see them as they should be, in their heyday.

We were all then entirely unaware how soon these happy times would be shattered by the insidious condition that was even then creeping unexpected and unseen upon our great friend Mathurin.

Mathurin, my neighbour and the man I most admire, has been diagnosed as having Alzheimer's disease. Unimaginable and unbelievable as it was, this news was easy to deny at first, for it wasn't easy to detect. Then with terrifying speed it became all too unmistakable. Mathurin started to wander away in the evenings and we joined the subsequent searches in cars, on bikes and on foot, across the neighbouring countryside. Thankfully we always found him well and full of purpose, but in his mind on an errand to meet friends long dead, or to find his horse, which he hasn't had for three decades, or to walk into town on a path long disused and dangerous to a man his age.

Steadily, inexorably and much too quickly, Mathurin's condition deteriorated until he became unpredictable and couldn't be left alone. The pain and injustice of this tragic turn of events stung everyone except Mathurin himself. We had already begun to lose him, and there was no going back.

With Angèle's grateful blessing I take my old friend for our last walk together. He knows me still and comes happily with me now, smiling even though with a distant, detached look upon his face. This won't last and I feel we both know it. We start out as usual in easy conversation, but soon it dies and I'm struggling to keep talking, questioning him, pressing for responses, searching to maintain dialogue when it's quickly turned to monologue. The walk, unlike so many previous walks, is not turning out as I had hoped. I have no option but to turn for home. I realise that perhaps in this condition we've come too far, and getting my friend home now will not be easy. Grasping him by the hand, guiding his feet over possible obstacles, gently steering him by the arm, I take my silent troubled friend slowly, painfully home where Angèle greets him at his front gate, her eyes filled with tears. I leave the near empty shell of my good friend with her, she who will never judge or condemn him but will just be there always to do what's needed. Ever so gently and slowly she turns him, centimetre by centimetre, and leads him into the house, to the room, to the fireside chair that will now become his world.

Then I take to the field, to walk a bit more with my dogs and try to make sense of what it is that is stealing my great friend.

I know he's going, that I can't go there with him and that I'll not see his like again. Before long, Mathurin won't know me at all. He won't remember any of the times we've had, but by then he won't recognise anyone, even his closest friend Bertrand, even his sons. The kindly smile is already gone, replaced by a vacant, uncomfortable, worried look. The funny, sharp, attentive mind I loved and admired so much has also gone. The most gentle of men is still gentle, but now he sleeps away most of his days detached from and even oblivious to his surroundings, and of the people and the world he so loved.

Mathurin lives on, but the real Mathurin has gone and I know he'll never, ever come back.

Angèle too knows in her heart that the Mathurin she has lived with and loved these six decades has gone. This may be fact, but it's a fact she'll never accept. While his current mental state may deteriorate even further, Mathurin may be fit enough to live on for a very long time, his physical body still with us while his mind, character and personality have all long gone. To Angèle, that's just confirmation that he still needs her.

Though she can't lift him, she can do everything else for him. Supported by the social services and her ever-constant family, Angèle accepts her new lot without complaint. She wouldn't have it any other way.

Three years have now passed since Mathurin and I took our last walk together. I see him only occasionally these days, but I've stopped worrying about him and I no longer cling to the hope that I'll detect a spark of recognition for me in his vacant gaze, for I've come to accept it isn't there. But Angèle's unfailing courage encourages me and all Kerkelven's people to accept that Mathurin is still with us. We have to be grateful for that.

December

Walking the dogs, December

Oh dear, it hasn't stopped raining for days. I got up this morning and the house was dripping. The insides of the chimneys were dripping, it was dripping round the edges of window frames and even through the hairline cracks between beams. It was dripping under the front door frames and flooding from the sodden thatch down the outside walls. It's been blustery too for ages, with gusty winds adding new groans, rasps, screeches and squeaks to an already unsettlingly creaky, noisy old house. The rain gets driven at odd angles by the wind, blasting in every imaginable direction, plus a few more that seem impossible. Whatever the weather can throw at us mainly just bounces harmlessly off these mighty stones, but when the outside is like the inside of a washing machine there's always some bits of wet that get in, seeping and wriggling among the inevitable cracks. So the house by now needs a good wringing out.

The cement floor of the dogs' niche, never well designed for drainage, is deep in rainwater. The dogs' dishes, all that's left of the night before's dinner, are brim-full with rainwater. Puddles have formed where puddles usually never are. It's welly-boot weather, no mistake.

After the mild autumn there are still plenty of leaves on most of the trees around Kerkelven and all of these are now dripping vigorously, together onto the saturated earth beneath. Still it rains. Max, Syrus and Mortimer are each bedraggled to their bones, but particularly the first two. Mortimer's bulky, solid layers seem impervious to the elements (though, my God, his coat must get heavy) but Max and Syrus have thinner, finer pelts so their fur has gone all sticky-up and spiky. They've become punk dogs. It's like they're covered head to toe in that gel teenagers pay so much for to make themselves look ridiculous. Rarely a pretty sight on humans, it looks even more ludicrous on dogs, but they don't seem bothered.

It's got colder too, which at this time of year is as it should be. But even that isn't reliable these days and sudden relatively warmer spells mean you never know quite what to wear.

Loïc, the farmer, has been ploughing down on his big fields that border ours, so the road round the big pond is like the Somme. Drainage from the pond needs attention, particularly with all these falling leaves, but it would never occur to Loïc to pause from his labours to dig a channel so the accumulated rainfall could find an easier path and run merrily away. Thus a muddy lake has formed across the road, mingling with what's left of Poo Mountain to form a horrid, malodorous stew. If this was human poo we'd be utterly revolted; we'd call in the police and the fire brigade. But because it's pig poo, no worries, we can splash about in it good style as if we were on an outing to Waterworld.

It's more like Soggyworld, to be honest. All round the pond are pools of dubious-looking goo, a mixture of rain, mud and slime with an added dash of pig poo. Fall on your face in this lot and there's no going home.

Back to the field. My feet, already blocks of ice, are telling me that it's actually much colder than I'd first thought, so I feel it's forgivable that we four take a slightly shorter route than usual and progress around it at a slightly quicker than usual rate. The bitter dismal blast didn't arrive overnight, it crept up on us ever so slowly and insidiously. How else would we tolerate its replacement of the balmy air of summer?

When it stops raining – which it doesn't do for long – it gets even colder. On such days stepping outside is like hitting something almost solid, a wall of cold air. The freeze makes breathing hard. Breath hangs in clouds, a moment of warmth then gone forever.

Walking in this freezer is no fun, the wind stabs like a driven nail, hands stick to metal, cold seeps into the bones.

Garb for walking out in

Billy Connolly once said, 'There's no such thing as bad weather, only the wrong clothes.' So it might be useful if I give you some guidance on what to wear when sauntering out into the field in inclement times, particularly when it's very cold. Because if you're inappropriately dressed, the instant you set your welly-booted foot out of our front door, Jack Frost's glacial fingers will be at your throat. But appropriately clad you'll be more than a match for anything the elements can fling at you, though you can be sure they will try their hardest and any omission on your part will lead to a heavy price to pay later.

So, pull hat (woollen bobbly variety) down firmly over ears, turn collar up and tie tightly, thrust both hands in pockets (even with gloves on), hunch shoulders and tread boldly, breathing out the while and marvelling at the billows of steam that rise from your rapidly cooling body into the frozen morning air. You know you should be somewhere else when your teeth feel the cold.

It helps if you are wearing two pairs of woolly socks under your wellies, thermal undies – vest and knickers, or preferably long johns (bought for motorbike but much more effective and useful when walking in the field in winter), warm breeks (trousers) and a thick heavy jacket over several layers of jumper.

Now you're warm, hot even and getting hotter. And you can barely move (note for next time, don't put hat on and seal collar until well outside). The best thing to do is keep moving. Once again, fall over now and you'll never get up.

Flares are back

Yet another fashion item on the Kerkelven catwalk, my old biker's outfit with the flared trousers comes out whenever the weather is so severely inclement that there's unlikely to be any other poor sinner abroad, so my chances of being seen thus attired are slim to nonexistent. If a blackmailer were to get hold of a picture of me wearing this clobber, life as tolerable would come to a sharp end.

The story behind my wearing this outfit for dog-walking is as follows.

In my early days here I was given to regularly crossing back and forth between Kerkelven and London, come rain or shine, on my motorbike. There are specialist retailers who exist solely to provide for bikers' thermal needs and the choice is dazzling, if not often given to reflecting current high fashion. The pinnacle of any bikers' wardrobe is the one-piece outer garment or overall. As a novice biker I had innocently bought one of these affairs but the choice had not proved to be a wise one. I recall that my one-piece had been reduced in price substantially, perhaps because it had flared sides to the legs, so thus attired I resembled, or would have in my more slender days, Rod Stewart, if you remember, from the cover of his album *Atlantic Crossing*. Being even then a bit more substantial than Rod (although perhaps more firm and slim round the bum) I just looked plain ridiculous in this outfit. Anyway, fellow bikers generally being a rough and roisterous lot, I found that my one-piece attracted ridicule, people would point, so I bought another less flamboyant one for motorbiking and took to using the flared version only on very odd occasions.

One such very odd occasion came about when with a team of colleagues I was taking part in a long sponsored bicycle ride for charity. On this particular outing it rained, enough to stop us in our tracks and have everyone scurrying for shelter and unpacking their foldy-up waterproofs, or whatever other protection they had brought. I breezily set to innocently unfolding my one-piece biking waterproofs when my lovely but big-mouthed chum Jane chanced to look up and perceived in a flash the intriguing shape that was unfolding before her on the ground.

'My God,' she screamed, 'Ken's got an inflatable Elvis!'

For the rest of the ride I endured much derision. Despite the fact that I never again wore them in public my overalls were known forever after as 'inflatable Elvis'. It has to be said, however, that these overalls do provide a sensible utilitarian garment for walking the dogs around Kerkelven in cold weather, even though when silhouetted against the Breton skyline I must inevitably look as ridiculous as ever.

I'm distracted from these reflections by a sudden look around me. Shafts of blinding sunshine fill the field with icy light, creating surreal effects on everything around. Everywhere has become very wintry.

Looking up into the clear blue sky above I can see the intriguing shapes of the many vapour trails that streak across our sky, pointing to the passage of Boeings and Airbuses conveying their happy passengers to distant foreign, presumably warmer, climes.

Beautiful though winter surely is, I'm with these good folk above in spirit at least as they head for the sunshine.

Roll on summer.

The sound of leaves falling

Suddenly it's calm, there is no breath of wind. It's the morning after a deep frost, and everywhere is iced with a fine moist white dust. The effect this has on the remaining leaves of the trees is startling. The onslaught of cold, aided perhaps by the extra weight, seems to weaken the leaf stems and speed the process of the fall. Leaves are tumbling all around and, amazingly, the noise is considerable and constant. There seems to be something at work that keeps their fall even; that prevents them all falling at once. It's as if nature has programmed each leaf to wait its turn. Then the wind picks up again and this time it seems to have the biggest influence of all on the rate of falling leaves.

The noise perceptibly increases until it seems all trees are working in unison to shed their clothing and embrace nakedness.

Winter fog and Breton rain

After the long dry summer weeks and the sudden snap of serious cold, we're now firmly back to enjoying the persistent, voluminous Breton rain. Described like this, rain sounds as if it's just one standard, consistent, reliable thing. But rain in Brittany takes many forms, some reasonable and even likeable, some ferocious and utterly horrible. Rain here can come in sheets, in stair rods, in dribbles, in gentle mists, or in lashings. It can come horizontally, vertically, or at any angle in between. As it bounces off the road it can get right up your kilt.

It comes with the full spectrum of accompanying sounds, from gentle pitter-patter to cacophony. Not to be outdone the wind sighs and whispers between and around the trees as the forest joins in with copious moans, murmurs, groans, sighs, creaks and growls. The dogs creak and groan a bit too, for good measure.

October mists have turned to thick fog, a regular and troublesome feature of winter mornings in central Brittany. Here they call it *le brouillard*, which seems accurate as it sounds like a kind of soup, or even stew. The single syllable 'fog' doesn't come close to doing it justice.

Flood

It has now been raining for days so the build-up in streams and gulleys of Kerkelven is beginning to have an effect. The river isn't at all prepared for this sudden surge. Up till now it's been powering along its timeworn track like a racehorse but clearly this can't last. It seems to swell reluctantly as I watch it, as if it were getting ready to spread out.

Suddenly our world transforms as at some time in the night the river breaks its banks, first in one place, then another, and a third, until the whole bank is breached and the still-gathering river flows remorselessly far and wide, soundlessly filling the field with its overflowing excess.

Almost the entire field is overrun. From the ridge above we can only see dottings of higher ground where there should be meadow.

Hundreds of pond-skaters must have been swept away by the rapid rising swell but those that have held on (or maybe these are just some swept down from further upriver – it's really a bit hard to tell one from the other) simply can't believe their luck because now they have three times as much water to play on. They take full advantage of this, showing no outward signs that they've recently survived a disaster of Krakatoan proportions.

I have two big log piles down by the riverbank, both waiting for me to move them to higher ground. Now nature is telling me I'd better move them somewhere safer – and quickly – or they'll be washed away too.

And behold I was too slow, and they were washed away. The swollen river knows no compromise or remorse, it's transformed into a relentless, unforgiving behemoth that will sweep all before it in its rush to the sea.

In a high winter wind

When a storm is brewing the valley of the Sarre acts as a funnel, doubling the speed and force of the wind. For the tall thin trees that crowd the northern slope of our forest, high winds spell danger both from the direct force of the wind itself and from the indirect effect of falling limbs and even trees broken or uprooted. There are quite a few trees that are reasonably likely to fall on the head of an innocent passer-by, but I worry most about the giant pear tree that I told you about in September, which hangs above Bertrand's Descent.

Normal storms are endurable but every so often we get a real corker. Then, and only then, our woods are not a very safe place to be. Well, I suppose it isn't very safe when hunters are about either. Or if you are a rabbit, or a field mouse. Come to think of it, perhaps it's often not very safe in our wood.

The dogs still seem oblivious to the weather, good or bad, except, I've noticed, during the big winter blasts and in the curious calm that occurs an hour or so before a summer storm. (This, I've observed, is to do with changes in air pressure, which I suppose must hurt their little ears. This never seems to bother Mortimer, possibly because his ears are that much bigger.) As winter storms can last for a couple of days or more, the poor dogs sometimes have a dodgy time of it. But they wouldn't miss their walks so we sally forth come what may. I don't think the weather has ever kept us in or sent us back, but at times it's been a close call.

Building a hide down by the river

At least it'll give the neighbours a laugh. And probably the birds too. But how else am I to capture the daily movements of birds as they pursue their business in the woods and down among the undergrowth along the river's margins?

I just have to build myself a covered hide. It's been my secret dream to have one since I was a youngster. A simple wooden frame with canvas covering will do, perhaps with an opening for a window, an old armchair for comfort, several layers of sturdy garments to keep out the chill and a pair of fine binoculars – what more could I need? Well, perhaps a six-pack of lager, a good book and a portable television for when the birds are having their nap. Oh, and a satellite dish to put on top.

I've been meaning to make a start on this for years now, pretty much since I came to Kerkelven. Perhaps I'll begin tomorrow.

For reasons I haven't quite fathomed there's a lot of foamy scum on the river just now and there tends to be more of it when there's not been rain for some time. It must be from the various nefarious chemicals that local farmers use on their fields.

As rain is anything but a rarity now, this problem doesn't persist. Like a flush the flood must have a cleansing effect. It's natural, probably beneficial, but I still worry about the good stuff it washes away, like topsoil, along with this scum and anything not tied down, like my plastic bench.

Mistletoe

To gather this Christmas decoration you need a good pair of clippers, a steady hand and a cool head. And a handy tree whereupon grows the parasite we call mistletoe. And very probably, a ladder, for mistletoe almost never grows anywhere within reach. Proof again if it were needed that nature is indeed wondrous and well prepared against predators. Kissing under the mistletoe is an ancient English custom dating back to pagan (i.e. pre-Christian) times. The juice of the mistletoe fruit is said to resemble semen, which may explain this ritual. Or maybe it's just a bit of fun.

Mistletoe sells for several pounds for even a small bunch in London's Covent Garden around Christmas time. I've often thought of loading the back of a van with it and making a quick seasonal killing up the markets of the old metropolis.

We have rather a lot, to be honest. Though it isn't really a problem because you can just leave it on the tree. In time it goes a bit wrinkly, but that's OK, and by summer it's gone, or at least it seems to be. We collect some of it for our own personal use (don't ask). One Christmas Marie kissed Bertrand when he'd inadvertently come to rest under a bunch. I've no idea what he thought was happening but he had to sit down for a while with a glass of port. French people, he maintained, don't see mistletoe as anything special. According to Bertrand, the kissing thing is a foreign importation and mistletoe is just a rather rampant tree parasite.

But now he always looks for it whenever he visits, for he's never averse to a kiss from Marie.

Le Village de l'an mil

'The village of the year one thousand' is the slogan of Melrand, one of our nearby towns. For a region so steeped in history, it's a good catch-phrase, a reminder of the rich history and traditions of which its inhabitants, even the incomers, are justly proud. For bustling Melrand, despite its high-tech village hall and super-special civic amenities, is the quintessential Breton market town with crumbling old stone buildings, narrow streets, an impressive church with traditional-style tower and market square, and the air and character of all the good things of yesteryear.

Between Kerkelven and Melrand, about five kilometres from us, there are what the good burghers of Melrand claim to be the reconstructed remnants of an actual village from about a thousand years ago, abandoned by its inhabitants some time in the ninth or tenth century and left as ruins and low stone circles. These fragments of early settlement were apparently ignored by generations of Breton farmers, just left where they lay until suddenly, some time in the last century, someone saw their potential and a tourist village was born among the fields. Since we've been here this, the real *Village de l'an Mil*, has been restored and expanded into a charming, substantial and informative window onto the character and characteristics of our antecedents and how they lived here in those distant days.

The site is about the size of Kerkelven and physically similar to it too. But here there were seventeen households, a sizeable community. Though their impact on their surroundings was considerable, it would have been all too easy to eradicate all trace of their presence, so I guess we're lucky that so much survived to give us the insights and impressions we now have of their daily lives. In olden days people were even more scattered than they are today and such habitations were common. Possibly such a community also lived in or by the field by the river at Kerkelven. Perhaps that's the explanation for all the abandoned stones that make up the stone pile we call the Druids' fort. Perhaps people like these ancient villagers fashioned the great stone bench that sits so sedately on our parkland, perhaps their hands carved the hollows in this huge rock that undeniably mark it out as part of some former construction, of some size and importance. Perhaps these same peasant hands also built the mysterious wall in our wood, making it much, much older than we've ever assumed.

Perhaps the river flowed a different course then. Today our morsel of the forest seems a mature, even ancient wood with parts so overgrown that no human can have trod there for years and years. Yet perhaps the wood didn't exist then at all and the field was bigger and maybe divided up differently. That would explain why they built the wall in the wood. I've no idea how old it is, but it must be very old. Initially I'd assumed it must be about 350 years old, to tie it into being built at the

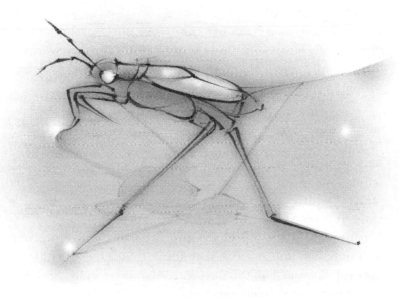

same time as our house. But the forest was surely there by then. So why would anyone build a stone wall in the middle of a wood? And who would build it? Also the stones of the mysterious old wall are crumbled and decayed, whereas our house is solid and almost good as new. No, the wall must indeed be significantly older.

Kerkelven, as I've said, is a remnant of the ancient magical forest of Brocéliande. These woods are the forests of Merlin the magician and the legendary witch Morgane la Fée, that nurtured King Arthur and his followers the knights, who fled to England in the misty early times to found Avalon and create their legendary dynasty around a vast circular counsel place, the round table.

Of course there will be mysteries here.

Walking on water

With Christmas approaching, now seems an appropriate time to be talking about this. Despite the chill air the pond-skaters, bless them, are still about, skipping across the river's surface without a care in the world.

For years I thought these impressive little bugs were called water boatmen. But they are something else, no less impressive in their way but aquatic deep-sea paddlers rather than walkers on water. Another name for the pond-skater is the Jesus bug, for obvious reasons. They're also known as the common water strider, which seems far too modest a moniker for this extraordinary wee fellow.

They are little wonders, for sure. For they can truly walk on water, though unlike some, they think this achievement is no big deal. They do it all the time with ease and facility. And they can perform this wonder because of a little-appreciated physical phenomenon called the surface tension of water, though their four widely-splayed legs may have a little to do with it too. Actually they have six legs but the smaller front two are more like arms, kept for close-up work like eating and squabbling.

When we try walking on water we tend to sink quite quickly, or at least most of us do, so we've come to think that water hasn't really got a surface. But we are wrong, of course, as I learned one day in my physics class back at Nairn Academy, a long, long time ago.

Despite the passage of time and my limited attention span I well remember learning about the phenomenon of surface tension. Ironically this obscure subject is among just a handful of things that I have actually retained from my combined twelve years or so of schooling, each day of which I hated (although I sat in the physics class until I was sixteen I actually gave the subject up when I was eleven, though I didn't tell anyone at the time). I could have learned all of this handful of things back to back in about a half a day and saved everyone a lot of grief and wasted time. Still, you don't expect to learn from an education, or at least, you didn't in my day.

The cohesive forces between liquid molecules are responsible for surface tension. In any body of water, molecules at the surface are the only ones not entirely surrounded by similar molecules so they stick more strongly to those directly associated with them on the surface. This forms a surface film that makes it more difficult to move an object through the surface than to move it when it is completely submerged. Why molecules should decide to do this is something I did not learn. Perhaps I got bored and was looking out the window. Or perhaps we don't really know, it's another of science's mysteries.

Surface tension, however, is typically measured in dynes per centimetre, the force in dynes required to break a film of one centimetre long (a dyne is a unit of force, the force required to move a mass of one gram at a rate of one centimetre per second, squared). Water at 20°C has a surface tension of 72.8 dynes/cm. So it would take a force of 72 dynes to break a surface film of water one centimetre long. And pond-skaters are considerably lighter than that. Apparently because of the polar nature of the water molecule, the surface tension of water decreases significantly with temperature. So when it's hot, pond-skaters move more carefully, one would imagine.

Her name suggests she passes each day like some miniature Torville or Dean, zooming hither and thither having a constant fun time. And this seems to be the long and the short of it. Good for her. But just how does she get a grip on the water's surface, to enable her to move? Scientists at MIT, who spend their lives studying such things, have discovered that, while accepting that I'm right about the surface tension thing and how it keeps pond-skaters from drowning, she achieves forward motion by a very rapid paddling motion of the foot. I wonder how long it took them to work that one out. More interestingly, they've found that pond-skaters can also jump, when necessary (if you think this a dull fact, try it next time you're walking on water), and locate their food (other insects) with the help of minute sensitive hairs on their legs that tell them not only when another insect has landed on nearby water, but also what type of insect it is. Wow! Why can't we have hairy legs that do that?

Une fête 'Tout Per Wahr' and Anne Zummers

Oh, this rural French backwater may seem dull, remote and uneventful but when it comes to partying behind closed doors, there's few can hold a candle to your Breton.

Marie got herself thoroughly confused recently when one of her pals from the village (women of a certain age seem to gravitate together in rural areas) bent her ear in the baker's as she was going about her daily ritual, shopping for bread. Because the French all speak far too fast for our ears Marie, who speaks the language pretty well, nevertheless often has difficulty keeping up with the full content and import in the discourses. So she has the habit of nodding politely as if in full comprehension, hoping no one will notice. This leads to frequent embarrassment. We all do it, we Brits abroad. We've all been caught out at it.

On this occasion her pal Brigitte was gossiping away about various goings-on in the Melrand daily scene. She grabbed Marie's elbow and steered her into the corner of the corner shop where, in hushed tones, she proceeded to invite my susceptible lady wife to an '*Anne Zummers*' evening. Marie flushed and stammered out a quickly fabricated excuse as, thinking on her feet, she tried to work out how their seemingly innocent conversation had taken such a salacious turn.

Then Marie heard her friend mention something she referred to as *une fête 'Tout per Wahr'*. This event, Brigitte confided, had gone down a storm among the local matrons who'd all spent much more money than they should have, while apparently having a thoroughly raucous time.

Would Marie then like to come to this next time?

By now more than a little flushed and discomfited Marie continued blurting out hastily dreamed-up excuses while edging out the door in some disarray and making her escape.

The true nature of what this conversation was about didn't strike Marie until several days later. And when it did, the realisation left her more flustered, not less. As she was relaying her tale of the encounter to some English friends at the weekend, the penny finally dropped.

'*Tout per Wahr*' is Tupperware!

What Brigitte had invited Marie to was a Tupperware party. '*Tout per Wahr*' is French for that rather naff plastic tableware from the 1950s and '60s that people now feel is so retro and collectable.

My God, she thought. An Anne Summers evening of naughty night attire was one thing, but she'd nearly been seduced into a Tupperware party!

Bird, bug and fish migration

Our summer visitors have now long since fled south. Even the small birds fly long distances with unerring accuracy. Perhaps because they seem such fragile, flimsy creatures, this seems to us to be one of the most impressive yet perplexing achievements of the animal kingdom.

Just how do birds find their way from Kerkelven to Africa, or even further? Theories abound around the mysteries of migration, but so it seems do questions that we've yet to answer. Some species may use the sun or the moon, or even star patterns to navigate by, others may have some kind of weird internal compass so are guided by the earth's magnetic field, though I suspect this could just be another instance of scientists searching for an explanation to something they don't fully understand. Birds could in some ways just be cleverer than us. And better travellers too.

Whatever, birds are clearly good at finding their way around. Each year the jays hide hundreds, even thousands of acorns in our field and show an uncanny accuracy in relocating them months later, when they're hungry. Perhaps they use the trees as markers to guide them. Or perhaps they just hide so many and there are so many jays doing it that there's a fair chance some will be found hidden around any tree.

And it's not just birds that can find their way over long distances. Death's-head moths fly all the way from Africa to

Europe guided only by the sun and moon. When they get here they steal honey from native bees (without any evident objection from the bees) before finding a convenient plant on which to lay their eggs. Then back they go unhesitatingly, these tiny globetrotters, undertaking the same seemingly difficult, dangerous and undoubtedly tiring journey without appearing to give it a second thought.

Fish do it too. Not just salmon and tuna, even baby eels will make the immense journey from where they are born in the mid-Atlantic to the sheltered waters of a river by a field just like ours, where the plucky few lucky ones, the tiny percentage of those that make it, will mate, then turn around and the whole perplexing process will be repeated. They too can't see the sun or the sky, so we just don't know how they find their way to us with such unswerving accuracy, to the very same river where their parents mated some years before.

But they do it, each and every year.

The big sleep

As the days get shorter and the nights get longer we stock up on essential food supplies, turn up the recently fixed central heating, make ourselves all snug and cosy round the telly and only venture out when we have to, well wrapped and protected of course.

But what of all the animals, birds and insects that don't fly south? Some birds, animals and insects stay behind and remain active through whatever winter will throw at them. Of the animals, some change their fur to keep their body heat better and a few, like the weasel, even get a winter colour, white, so they can hide in the snow. There wouldn't be many days when that would be a good idea round here.

Food is inevitably harder to find in winter. Animals like

squirrels and some species of mice gather and store food to see them through. Others change their diet, like the fox, who eats berries and insects in the spring and summer but switches to small rodents in wintertime, and birds too if he can catch them. Other species, it seems, just have to work harder to find food in the cold season.

All of which makes hibernation seem like a very good idea. And so it is. Hibernation is a self-induced process of slowing down all of the body's functions and going into a very, very deep sleep. The animal's body temperature drops, its heartbeat and breathing slow to imperceptible levels. Very little energy is needed. Some animals produce a special kind of body fat, brown fat, particularly to help sustain them through the big sleep. Often hibernating animals build themselves a kind of nest, called a hibernacula.

Some creatures are lighter sleepers than others and a few wake often during their big sleep, but just turn around, maybe smooth out the moss and feathers, perhaps get up to go to the toilet, or to grab a few mouthfuls of nourishment, check the weather outside or whatever, before returning to dreamsville.

The process is simpler for cold-blooded mammals like snakes and frogs. They just make a hole, pop themselves in it and become inactive, or dormant. Toads and turtles often find a hidey-hole underwater. Cold water is rich in oxygen and they can absorb this naturally through their skin.

Insects often make galls – artificially induced swellings – in a suitable host tree or leaf and hide inside that. The growing gall then provides them with shelter and a food source through the winter. Many insects spend the winter dormant, in a state known as diapause, literally when all growth and development stops. Some insects pass the winter as larvae or pupae, their transition stage, and when the spring arrives they will cast off their old skin, emerging as something else. Other insects simply die at the onset of cold weather, leaving their eggs to survive and hopefully hatch out in the spring on their own, thus depositing a new batch of orphans upon a hostile but at least less cold world.

As the autumn ends animals like hedgehogs, bats and squirrels eat a lot more, to build body fat that will sustain them through their big sleep. And they might also store up food such as nuts and acorns so that should they wake they can have a few little nibbles before safely drifting off again to their particular land of nod.

I find that rather charming. But hibernation can be a dangerous time too. If disturbed, returning to sleep may not be possible and the consequences of this are often fatal. Sometimes, if the preparations beforehand haven't been right, there will be no reawakening and the long sleep will never end.

I like walking through the woods at this time because I imagine I'm just a few feet away from lots of cosy sleeping animals and insects, all snugly curled up and snoring, awaiting the return of spring. I wish I could do it too.

Torpor

Not quite hibernation, torpor is nevertheless a recognised state on the way to it. It's what we used to refer to as 'chilling out' or 'switching off' in my hippie days, to describe the state of suspended animation or physical inactivity usually lasting for not more than half a day, or until the joints ran out. In certain species, torpor can be induced. It involves the slowing of the metabolism and lowering of body temperature when less active, usually at night. Small birds, rodents and bats use it quite a lot to conserve energy and to survive the cold. Bears do it too, in the woods. Female crocodiles apparently induce a state of torpor during egg-laying time. Lungfish, which famously survive out of water for long periods, do so by inducing a torpid state when their water has dried out, hunkering down in the mud until it returns. I seem to remember, as a schoolchild, that I could induce torpor pretty much at will in the classroom, though actual hibernation eluded me.

Storms and tornadoes

Oooohhh. This is exciting and a bit scary too. What a din! I'm standing by the big old oak in the middle of the wooded garden we call the parkland. Our venerable, ancient tree seems singularly unfazed by the storm and doesn't seem inclined to join in, merely consenting to allow its newer low branches to enjoy some restrained ripples. But everywhere else is in pandemonium.

Trees are bending, branches are swaying wildly around, there's twigs, leaves and light debris blowing about willy-nilly. It's a good time to keep well clear of some of our more fragile trees, which seem likely to uproot at any minute, though the most likely casualty of an impressive, but nevertheless relatively minor, storm such as this is that we might expect a dustbin or two to be overturned and the contents cast to the four winds that, right now, seem to be break-dancing together around my head.

We get a lot of storms around this time of year, so by definition December is frequently an exciting time, particularly if you're planning a cross-channel ferry trip. The dogs are hanging low, stomachs pushed to the ground and ears pressed back. They don't like this one bit.

The Atlantic Ocean is of course synonymous with foul weather and because the rocky coast of Brittany sticks so far out into it, coastal defence systems here are particularly prepared for frequent storms, which can last from twelve to two hundred hours, depending on season and geography. Those from the east and northeast come round most often, especially during winter. Big terrestrial storms, of course, can disrupt transport and other services, interrupt supplies of electricity and other commodities, affect food availability and distribution and so on. They can lead to strong currents, strong tides, increased silting, change in water temperatures and suchlike, all of which combine to make sea and seaside even more dangerous places to be than they are normally. Storms can be really bad news, at times.

But mostly, from the safety of a few kilometres inland, they're rather fun.

The chickens' death factory

'When the skies are dark and murky, thank your stars you're not a turkey', or so the saying goes.

Though perhaps not noticeably better, the average turkey's lot is no worse than that of the ordinary chicken, whose appeal to human palates is year-round and whose brief, troubled life among us leaves a lot to be desired, whatever the weather.

It's a little-known and perhaps not surprising fact that there are three times as many chickens in the world as humans. That doesn't mean though that they are the more successful species, far from it. In fact it's hard to imagine any life less successful, even less appealing than that of today's non-free-range chicken.

Here in Kerkelven the farmer in charge of the fate of all chickens is old Emile. Or at least, he used to be. Now Emile unfortunately is no more. If they could, chickens everywhere would surely rejoice at this news, for the four huge chicken sheds that so recently loomed over the Kerkelven skyline spreading terror and dismay into the hearts of all walking, crawling, flying and burrowing things now lie either dismantled, or in ruins.

The reason for this is sad. On Emile's death one of his sons took over the chicken sheds but soon after, the best of them was gutted in a fire. I was told that there were no chickens inside at the time but even if there had been it may have been a preferable end, for some of the chickens at least. Emile's children couldn't agree on how the remaining sheds should be used, so they lay empty and quickly fell into ruin.

But it wasn't always thus. A few years ago those four iron and steel hangars were a tirelessly efficient production complex working round-the-clock 24/7 to raise, develop and remorselessly deliver chickens by the tens of thousand, mostly in those days destined for the dining tables of the Middle East, particularly Iraq (until the invasion in 2003, Iraq was a good customer for France).

Inside each of these death factories serried ranks of chickens passed their brief, grim, cheerless lives pecking or being pecked until they were judged fat and fit enough to be shipped off to their final destination. There they would be strung up, throttled, plucked, packed and dispatched in oven-ready packaging before they could even ask, 'I wonder if this place'll be any better?'

Not long after we came here Old Emile treated us to a guided tour of his chicken-processing facilities, of which he was very proud.

We were shown the massive gleaming new hangar, the state-of-the-art high-tech lighting and heating system that ensured round-the-clock toasty warmth and brilliant light 24 hours every day. We saw the computer-controlled feeding and watering system designed to deliver nourishment in just the right quantities to ensure that inmates could fatten themselves automatically and without interruption. Though life for your average chicken may be unfair, short, cramped, denied of natural light and any possibility of sleep, at least they didn't go hungry.

We visited on the very day that a new consignment of chickens was being delivered in a huge covered trailer, to replace a hangar-load that had just gone off to market. The contents of this vast vehicle, we discovered as they were poured like liquid onto the huge hangar floor, were entirely newborn chicks, just one day old. There wasn't a scrawny hen in sight, just lovable little yellow, hoppy, chirpy, Easter-type chickies. The truck's back as it rose hydraulically to tip forwards seemed like a huge handleless jug, its contents spilling out to gather in living, flapping, fluttering pools of yellow on the cold concrete floor.

With us that day was Emile's four-year-old grandson, boisterous, hyperactive, unappealing little Ludovic. Like his grandfather he was shod in the fetching white welly boots (only a few sizes smaller) that seem *de rigueur* for all image-conscious employees in the chicken-raising business. And like granddad, little Ludovic was used to the presence of large numbers of chickenkind. As the tiny chirpy chicks fluttered and flapped aimlessly around, young Ludo too ran around, walking upon them as entirely oblivious to their presence as he would had he been wading through so much mud or dross. Within minutes of their arrival the floor was littered with little chick corpses, chickens who never got beyond their first eventful day and so would be denied nearly five full weeks of being force-fed round the clock in a crowded, hostile, artificial environment, before being casually dispatched and eaten.

Maybe young Ludo did them a favour.

On sober reflection later at our own hearthside, Marie gave Emile's place the name by which it was known forever after, the chickens' death factory.

A walk among the stars

It's cold. Night temperatures late in the month have dropped to the edge of freezing and are hovering there, threateningly. The reason is the sudden onset of clear night skies, which on our night walks give us a chance to see in their full splendour the stars above Kerkelven. Perhaps we'll get a white Christmas after all.

To appreciate this particular pleasure you should understand what the Milky Way looks like from above Loïc's big pond. First the whole sky is spread with stars from the brightest magnitudes to the dim orange and twinkly. It's not a stationary picture, for the night sky appears to move constantly as planet earth daily spins around itself and as it annually circles its parent, the sun.

A particularly striking feature of the night sky at this time is what's called the winter triangle, a huge upturned isosceles that appears low in the early evening sky. It's formed by the apparent conjunction of, at top right, the dullish star Betelgeuse, part of the hunter's shoulder in the constellation of Orion, with at the bottom the brightest star in our sky, Sirius, and at top left a distant but quite bright star called Procyon. It's huge. It's spectacular. Once you've seen it, you'll notice it always.

As I walk I like to take a little time to contemplate the scale and nature of the cosmos. The cosmos is all there is and ever will be. We tend to think time started at the big bang but there may well have been other incarnations before then, perhaps quite a few. At Kerkelven, to get a grandstand view of the cosmos you just have to look up. Though the view above may be all that we can see in one go, it remains but the tiniest part of the cosmos, the full extent of which is beyond human comprehension. In his book *Cosmos* the cosmologist Carl Sagan – like Richard Feynman, a rarity in that he's a scientist who writes very well – described the loneliness of space rather neatly. He observed that each star system is an island in space, quarantined from its neighbours by the light years. Of course we share the cosmos with countless stars and each one is a sun to someone. For certain we are not alone and there are others, perhaps not at all like us, also looking out upon their part of the universe and wondering too how to get in touch with us. But the distances in between are so vast, to all intents and purposes we may as well be alone, for our planet and its sun are truly lost in all this. Before we can even begin looking for other lives in other systems we'll have to master the seeming impossibilities of time travel, and that isn't going to happen any time soon. Plus, we'll have to get very good at finding infinitesimally small needles in mega-ginormous haystacks.

In our time, however much we may will ET and his family to drop out of the sky one night and visit us, we know that in reality it's unlikely to happen, to say the least. So nothing's going to change. Contemplating all this under the stars at Kerkelven makes one feel very alone, though surprisingly not lonely. However, if ET calls in on our neighbours instead of us I'll be really pig sick.

Santa wars in the blessed Le Sorce

Le Sorce is one of our most loved and most lovely local villages, not just because it is quaint and ancient with lovely crumbling Breton architecture, but because once some years back, when I was caught short in Pontivy's Intermarché and found their toilets closed for repairs, it was to Le Sorce (a distance of about five kilometres) that I dashed in some distress and urgency, with wife and highly amused children in tow. In this time of great need I aimed for Le Sorce for I knew that they have public toilets in the village that, contrary to normal practice, tend to be properly equipped. And that day, lo and behold, they were. My gratitude to the people of Le Sorce was tangible and touching. From thenceforth the town became known to our entire household as 'the blessed Le Sorce', to be forever held in our hearts with special affection.

However, like many Breton villages, Le Sorce's taste in Christmas decorations is execrable.

There is a rivalry it seems between the town's mayor and the local priest. These two local worthies live at different ends of the village and each strives to outdo the other in the quality, size, lavishness and intricacy of their festive decorations, which they heap unrelentingly on the public buildings within their charge. Each has their local following and each would die rather than be outdone.

The result is that for the six weeks before and after Christmas a visit to Le Sorce is like a trip into an animated electric Christmas cake complete with dotty festive tunes, fire-crackers, carols, swirls, beeps, flashes and festive sound effects.

One is forced to wonder what the little baby Jesus might make of this. Not to mention those wise men. The shepherds, if they're anything like Breton shepherds, would no doubt love it.

The Santa that you'll see climbing up the wall of the town hall on entering Le Sorce completes the impression that you have died and gone to some bizarre kitsch hell.

He is about two metres tall, rather fat and is electrically illuminated from head to toe by a white fluorescent neon border that runs around the ill-fitting red robe that covers his ample, rotund form. His nose too lights up a ghastly green and flashes. The priest's Santa, though, is of even more impressive scale and girth and is stuck slumped forwards on a white metallic ladder attached to the clock tower of the church at the other end of the village.

With this triumph, I think the priest wins the contest, no argument.

The recently acquired Breton tradition of hanging grotesque bloated illuminated effigies of corpulent figures from mythology outside their houses, peering menacingly into children's bedroom windows, is an oddity in a nation that loves children. Imagine the fright of a sensitive seven-year-old waking to see a cherubic rosy-cheeked illuminated Santa leering in on her. It doesn't bear thinking about.

Fin de l'an – the feast of St Sylvester

As elsewhere, the year-end here is a rather special time of jollity and celebration for all.

Traditionally Bretons spend the first day of the coming year with their families around them. The night before is the fabulous feast of St Sylvester and yet another local tradition has restaurants opening their doors to those who can afford it for a once-a-year special celebratory feast in honour of St Sylvester, about whom most French people will know nothing whatsoever. He was one of the very early popes, holding the Catholic Church's highest office for 21 years from 314 AD to 335. He was an Italian, and why the French chose to celebrate him in their end-of-year feast was a mystery to me until Marie explained that for Catholics, every day is a different saint's day and this day just happens to belong to St Sly. (So there must be at least 365 of these saints. Subsequently, I've learned that there are actually over 10,000 saints, real ones too. Not being a

Catholic I was in total ignorance on this subject. I thought there'd maybe be, say, fifty.)

But they do lay on a good nosh in his name, as a glance at a typical multi-course menu for St Sylvester's night will show. It's really more of a gastronomic experience than a mere meal, with a carefully selected array of red, white and pudding wines being served throughout and usually lots of chocolates, sweetmeats and assorted delicacies to finish on. A big appetite is required.

Most New Years we tend to party with friends, dining on simpler fare and seeing in the coming year with people we know. But on occasions, leaving dogs and children behind, we've snuck off, just the two of us, to enjoy some excess by ourselves and see the New Year in with strangers. For the feast of St Sylvester always goes on beyond midnight. It's a strange experience but warm and charming, a symbol of goodwill to all.

Menu de St Sylvester

Royal de foie gras landaise, crème mousseuse aux cèpes chocolat

Bisque de tourteau

****

Fricassée de St Jacques et homard au safran, le cappuccino à la châtaigne légèrement truffe

Vapeur de saumon au caviar
****

Mignon de veau en truffière d'artichauts violets

Caneton challandais grille et glacier d'un mélange d'épices, gnocchi relèves de raifort, sauce au cabernet

****

Le plateau de fromages

****

Le palet chocolat amer et praline croustillant

Souffle chaud aux mirabelles

Le tout accompagne de vins provenant de domaines repûtes comme Pibarnon, terres blanches et Triennes et de champagne Veuve Clicquot millésime 1998

So, enjoy. And a Happy New Year to every one of us.

January

Premier de l'an – a lot of snogging and other festivities

New Year here is and always has been just great. In the not too distant past, when Mathurin was in better health, New Year was a time when all of Kerkelven celebrated collectively, if gently. The year's first day is traditionally a time of quiet hangovers, dry mouths and gentle, slow, considered digestion of the previous night's entirely excessive consumption at the feast of St Sylvester.

Not so many New Years ago, in this delicate state and recently tumbled from our beds, we were disturbed at about 11.30 a.m. by a gentle ping on the doorbell followed by the noisy entry of four of our usually restrained and dignified neighbours Bertrand and Marie-Thérèse plus Bertrand's sister and brother, all hallooing and *meilleurs voeux*ing and generally being badly behaved. As is customary all five of us (as usual our chum Celia was spending New Year with us) dutifully greeted all four of them in the traditional Breton way with two kisses alternately on either cheek. In the middle of this procedure the bell rang again to announce Mathurin, Angèle and their extended family. Only, there are seventeen of them. Celia seemed to light up at the prospect of all this kissing but I got dizzy halfway through and was ever so grateful when the phone rang (it was my mate George) so I could wipe my cheeks off and sit out the remaining slobbers, while Marie, Celia and the boys all swirled and bobbed.

Such fun. Though so much jabbering and gesticulating at such an early hour should surely be banned. We endeavoured to ply our uninvited but heartily welcome guests with wine and victuals but, in similar tribute to the excesses of the night before, they weren't drinking or eating much either. So their visit was brief and, pleasantries exchanged, we ushered them all out into the cold and returned to our warm log fire. They chatted together outside while we collapsed gratefully onto the sofa to watch a video of *White Christmas*, while nature helped us to recover our normal faculties at a reasonable pace.

The gathering described above would have been typical of 1 January at Kerkelven, but now New Year is inevitably a more subdued affair. The le Belligo family still dutifully visit Angèle and Mathurin, but they take it in turns now rather than coming en masse and we see less of them when they're here because now Mathurin is ill the traditional family gatherings don't quite seem right. Bertrand and his family too appear to have less appetite for exuberant celebrations but this may merely be a sign of advancing years. There's no less optimism and enthusiasm for the coming year though, just as heavy hangovers still seem to be the traditional way of starting it.

Back to the all-time favourite British subject

Gales and floods are rocking the British Isles but here winter continues extraordinarily mild and calm. Crisp sunshine mixed with cold winds and surprisingly warm still days, foggy mornings, gloomy afternoons and dark long evenings. It's nice, but I regret the absence of snow. We do sometimes get snow in Kerkelven, and on occasions there's lots of it, a complete white-out, but it rarely lasts for long. Worryingly, it hasn't been seen for some time. I remember just a few years ago, when Joe and Charlie went to the local school, looking enthusiastically out on a world blanketed with snow, knowing the tranquil scene would inevitably and quickly proceed towards complete pandemonium as school buses were cancelled (at the drop of a hat here, or at least, a light smattering of snow). Determined not to be beaten by weather that in my home in the north of Scotland would be considered quite a nice day, we'd then set off confidently in our 4x4 only to realise after about four or five kilometres that the falling snow had gathered speed and weight with each metre and before long we couldn't see the edge of the road. So just before losing all sense of direction we would turn around while we could still follow our own tracks home, all to gleeful whoops from the boys in the back who now faced the prospect of at least one day off school.

These warm memories of cold winter spells do seem to be rather a thing of the past though. It's so mild now that even at this season I can walk around the field without a coat and still get warm from the exercise. Global warming – or climate change as is now the preferred term – is we are told the biggest threat to the continuation of life on earth, yet its effects here, such as can be seen, appear mild and generally beneficial. However, I can't be sure it'll always be that way. As I enjoy the mild start to the year I've a feeling nagging away in the back of my mind that I'll be returning to the theme of climate change quite soon, and probably anxiously too.

But the miracle of Breton weather is how quickly and dramatically it can change. At almost any time it's possible to have every season of the year in one day or at least within the space of a few days. Well, OK, snow in summer is a bit unlikely but calm, wind, rain, sunshine, mist, fog, drizzle, heat and cold can and often do all follow each other in such rapid succession that meteorologists and holiday planners alike are left thoroughly confused and often inappropriately attired.

This winter we've also had our share of gloomy, grey and miserable days. The Scottish word for this kind of weather is 'dreich' (I've no idea how to spell it, but it's pronounced almost as a spit). It means bleak, drizzly, overcast weather, grey and horrible. Dreich is all too often an apt description here.

Life in the dishwasher

Did I say it's calm???

What a difference a day makes. The December storms have snuck back and this time they've brought their big brother. It's still excessively mild, which is a bit weird, and these gales seem to be coming from the south so the wind is warm. But no less fierce.

We awake to a scene of desolation in which every tree is straining and bending. Then suddenly, it's spookily still, the proverbial lull before the actual storm. It's very exciting though, and you can actually watch and listen to the storm as it rushes across the river and through the forest, crashing and roaring as it goes, first in the distance, then alongside you and ahead, then above and all around. What a din. It's like being in the midst of a huge stampede of invisible bellowing dinosaurs, or having some vast celestial hands clashing a pair of giant cymbals at tree height above our heads. In this tempest I worry about the pear tree in particular, but it's no fun for any of the trees. Many lose their branches and a couple have fallen over. I imagine that the goliaths by the river are particularly under pressure, on account of their vast size and inevitably shaky toehold on a steadily crumbling riverbank.

A favourite friend has fallen

One of the casualties is a splendid young, seemingly healthy beech that just toppled, showing that something has rotted its base just where the tree joins the earth. I pray no others are similarly affected and promise to get the tree doctor round to investigate as soon as things quieten down.

This beech that just fell over was one of my favourite trees. It has left a great void in the sky above the steep path at the east end of our field. As I've climbed this path every day for the past however many years this splendid beauty has always been there for me and I loved it. It was upon its branches that I saw my first lesser-spotted woodpecker. It was among and upon its boughs that the flock of rare long-tailed tits perched. Now it's a fallen ruin, a corpse, just firewood, to be cleared.

I feel its loss even more acutely because though seemingly full grown, for a beech tree this one wasn't old at all. I counted 28 rings, which means it had barely lived, for a beech in such an apparently secure position might expect 120 years at least, perhaps much more. And it had positioned itself upon one of the finest spots in Kerkelven.

Pushing up rocks

Something is definitely moving underground. Where recently there was nothing but smooth grassy soil, now there are rocks nudging skywards, and mostly quite big rocks at that. And these rocks can cause me some problems, in that I regularly trim the paths and their edges with my rotary mower and every so often when a new rock pops up from underground in some previously smooth area of soil my mower clatters over it, dulling or even bending the blades until I either work up the energy and strength to remove the offending rock, or I drive round it.

This is no small matter. Something must be slowly pushing up rocks from beneath, through the soil to the surface. Farmers recognise this because they are forever clearing their fields of more and more stones, when logic suggests that after a few ploughings all the rocks should be gone.

They're not. Farmers simply accept this, because that's just the way it is. But I'm looking for answers and I suspect a different explanation altogether.

I'm reminded of HG Wells' brilliant book from a hundred or

so years ago, *The Time Machine*, in which the hero, known to us simply as the Time Traveller, fast forwards into a future inhabited by two distinct races, the Eloi, and the Morlocks.

The Eloi are sweet gentle carefree spirits who live above ground in clearings and secluded spaces deep in the woods and spend their time ooohing and aahhhing and gently singing while dancing among wild flowers. They are small, slight, fine-skinned delicate beings who skip a lot and generally don't do much else.

The Morlocks, are also pale skinned, but there the similarity ends. Morlocks are apelike creatures with squat red ugly faces, their slimy flaky flesh lined with wispy strands of grey hairs. They live deep underground in foul-smelling pits at the end of long dark vertical tunnels, the constant semi to total darkness developing in their subspecies an aversion to light, causing the evolution of the big, blearily bloodshot eyes of the nocturnal predator. They subsist on a diet of almost entirely meat, obtained from the tender bodies of the Eloi who fall victim to nightly raids from these ferocious denizens of darkness, every Eloi's worst nightmare.

Wells idea was that far in its future the human species had split into two parts, basically, the aristocracy and the workers, the rough and the smooth, the light part of our natures and the dark side. The aristos had pursued a life of leisure and beauty on the surface, while the workers had gradually descended both physically and spiritually to become a base, subterranean species of predators. Over time the two races irrevocably split and became implacable, deadly adversaries. But the only weapons of the gentle Eloi were light, fire and the safety of sleeping together in great numbers in the hope that most of them would make it through the long, terrifying night.

I imagine it's them, the Morlocks, who push up these rocks

that arrive so mysteriously at Kerkelven, with me. What other explanation could there be? The Morlocks, HG Wells reasoned, had to get rid of vast quantities of rocks because they too were inundated by a constant supply coming up into their caverns and tunnels by various means, mainly a kind of convection that draws solid matter upward from the earth's bubbling core.

As an exit from their subterranean Hades, at night, the Morlocks use our old hollow oak tree to spill onto the fields of Kerkelven and around.

Perhaps then they glower at us from the darkness, awaiting their moment.

As I step out one winter's morning

Secretly, I like the rain. I've always loved splashing about in puddles. So, I'm going to make the most of it, while I can.

Here I have to pause to describe what it is I am wearing as I go walking of a cold but not too windy January morning. I'm no vision of sartorial elegance or splendour, that's for sure, but as no one sees me bar the dogs (and they think me a vision of loveliness at all times) who gives a poop?

Please, if you will, start with the boots, the bit that's in constant direct contact with mother earth. Here I employ only the best sturdy, reliable, sound, snug, green Wellington boots – my wellies. I love my wellies. As fellow Scot Billy Connolly knew well, whether you're a country boy at heart or even if you were brought up in a tenement, there's nothing like your wellies. Few things are more conducive to misery than wet, cold feet. When it comes to feet there's simply nothing better than welly boots for keeping the outside where it should be. Outside.

Mine are size twelve, a little bigger than I need them, shiny, sleek with firmly rounded toes, ample wiggle room but not too much, deep-ribbed rugged treads for gripping and for squelching through the slipperiest, deepest mud, robust to keep out all kinds of weather and all other threats external. Where indeed would I be without my wellies?

Though nothing else in the outfit comes remotely close to the wellies in importance, the rest is worthwhile nonetheless. Into the wellies are thrust feet clad in warm woolly socks. Covering the rest of the legs from heels to waist are stout trousers of an age and disreputability that dictates they should never be worn anywhere in public. The usual upper garments (T-shirt in summer plus jumper in less clement weathers) are, come rain and cold, sheltered from the elements by a large blue bell-shaped garment that might have been a tent in another life but was originally a skiing jacket. This practical over-garment adapts perfectly to the field-walker's needs because it is unassailably waterproof and weatherproof generally while having the commodious pockets so beloved by skiers everywhere. I particularly treasure this article of clothing because it comes with a handy-snappy inner fleece jacket that can be worn on its own (again, not recommended in refined society or indeed public places of any kind) and a detachable plastic snap-on hood. The whole is utterly un-chic but much more importantly is toasty warm when worn as an ensemble, yet the jacket stays cool when worn on its own, without the fleece.

To complete the outfit, well, anything goes. So I saunter out, a vision in blue, snug, safe and happy, at least as long as I don't meet anyone.

Getting up in the dark

One unchanging feature that characterises this time of year is that while the nights may start drawing out this month, we still have to get up every day in the dark.

It's not just the weather that makes January seem such a

bleak and grim time here, it's because it doesn't get properly light until after nine in the morning. Life must have been so much better in the olden days, when they just went to bed when it got dark (about four o'clock would have been permissible at this time of the year, I reckon) and they didn't have to get up next day until it was light enough to work, which must have meant past nine. Isn't that inspirational? And we thought they were grafters!

Ah, happy days. The solution for us, therefore, is to take a leaf from our ancestors' book and stay longer in bed, which as self-employed people we can do without anyone raising an eyebrow, or even realising. Another plus for our odd lifestyle, I think.

Or we could just switch on the lights . . .

At this time of the year the switch I start to long for is the changeover to summertime, even though that's when the clocks going forward means one less hour in bed. It seems a long way off.

Walking the dogs, January

I can't make up my mind whether dawn is the best time of the day to be out walking, or if the dusk is even better. It's one or the other, for sure. Quite why we should find the transition from dark to light and light to dark so thrilling would be hard to say. Although, maybe not. You just have to look at it.

It's very early in the morning and I'm up and about because I have an early rendezvous in town and want to take the dogs for their walk beforehand. Still and serene, the field lies wrapped beneath a light frosting of creamy white. Blazing orange and red but surprisingly devoid of warmth the sun slowly surfaces above the tree-fringed eastern skyline, bathing our sleepy hollow in amber glow, casting deep and mysterious shadows into every nook and cranny. The sky is the deepest turquoise, a mixture of gold and blue. This is the crisp, clear, misty early morning, the dawn of a winter's day. This is what we miss as we sleep, which is unforgivable really, though tomorrow as I lie snug abed I'll probably opt to miss it again. I know I am a fool to miss out thus, but I'll be a warm fool.

Too quickly the frost melts silently away. The field now is just a great big sponge. The river flows as fast as a racehorse, at least. The dogs bark menacingly at their counterparts that belong to our neighbours across the river, safe in the knowledge that the river is flowing so fiercely there's no way these snarling, rather intimidating pooches can cross. But what will happen when the floods subside?

The noise of chainsaws across the valley encourages me to plod on. It's a regular sound hereabouts, particularly this month. I feel I should mind it, but I don't. Today though we're leaving the sound of chainsaws well behind, deviating from our usual route, going a bit farther out across the prairie then sweeping round across the wide open space to bring us down to the Sarre upstream from our field, to that part of the river that's in Loïc's field.

The reason for the change is lapwings. Hundreds of them, maybe a thousand or more flying in formation, ducking and diving in military precision, wheeling, spinning and dancing across the landscape like a collective Cinderella at the ball. There are numerous flocks of birds around now of all types and sizes but the lapwings are among the most spectacular because of the way the sunshine reflects from their under-bellies, giving these sleek black-and-white plumed birds a sheen of silvery gold as they turn.

Where have they come from, this flock that we're following?

Well, I say we – Max, Syrus and Mortimer are all with me of course but they seem unable or disinclined to even look up. So I doubt if they've noticed anything. They just go where I go, persisting, despite all encouragements, in being the most unobservant of creatures. The lapwings on the other hand seem to know exactly what they are doing. They swoop and soar with extraordinary skill and accuracy. But as we approach to get a better look they wheel off in a different direction as if they're only happy to be wherever we are not.

How I wish I could stand in the middle of them, underneath or even inside their whirling mass, to be for even a second a part of that sea of carefully orchestrated movement and energy. But try as I might, I can't get sufficiently close to them to feel even remotely a part of the flock. I've even tried chasing them in the car, with me standing through the open sunroof with arms outstretched skywards as Marie drives hither and thither like a demented rally driver, but to limited avail.

That their instincts forbid me to get even slightly close to joining with them is yet another indisputable sign of mankind the pariah. Maybe they too have good reason. Apparently lapwings, while not quite endangered, are declining in numbers and I've no doubt that humans will be behind this, probably farmers. Though maybe farmers could be the solution to stemming the lapwing's decline, because lapwings are predominantly farm birds and I suspect that if both farmers and birds are to flourish, ways need to be found for both to benefit from their association. The lapwing does eat the fluke worm, which otherwise would cause disease among sheep. So it's playing its part. In some countries farmers are given incentive payments to keep land fallow for wildlife but I've not heard of this in our part of France.

Lapwings eat fluke worms

According to my dictionary, the fluke worm is a parasitic trematode worm of several species, with a flat, lanceolate body (i.e. long and pointy) and two suckers. The word 'flukes' in Scotland describes a particular flat fish, but flukes in this connection refers not to a kind of flounder, rather it applies to the barbed part of the worm's tongue, which on its bite attaches to the soft flesh of its victim so that the biter can only be removed with the most extreme difficulty. Two species (*Fasciola hepatica* and *Distoma lanceolatum*) are found in the livers of sheep, and produce the disease charmingly known as rot. So anyone who eats those little bleeders deserves to be encouraged, I'd say.

I now look upon our lapwings with an even more kindly eye.

This is a good time for clearing unwanted underbrush from the forest, so often our woods and field resound to the throaty roar of the chainsaw or the repeated snipping of my long-handled clippers. The afternoons are staying lighter longer now. At about five-thirty the sky turns to burnished gold then deep crimson. On a weekend when there's no rush to go anywhere we can stay in the field all afternoon, then doing nothing very much can seem like time really well spent.

As Mortimer, Max, Syrus and I trudge our weary way homeward, puffing and panting, I'm reminded of my age and mortality as I look behind me at the straggling trail of dogs. They're evidently feeling their age too (we're none of us spring chickens) though I think I'm putting a bolder front on it than they are. I wonder which of us will be first to curl up our toes, and in what order the others will follow? The hour approaches, for sure.

We make a silent pact, the four of us. Should any of us peg

out on one of these marathon hikes, whichever of us it is will be buried there on the spot by the remaining three, lest the sheer act of carrying back the corpse finishes off the survivors.

Be nice to farmers

Farmers are custodians of our greatest natural resource, the countryside. Here, their influence and impact are everywhere, because apart from our little patch at Kerkelven they seem to control everything in this vicinity.

It's amazing what farmers do in the interests of all of us, yet so often they get a bum deal from the largely urban rest of the public, who so depend upon them. Farmers usually get little sympathy and understanding and I know they find this hurtful at times. Perhaps it's the green wellies, the Range Rovers and the fact that they own so much lovely land and get to live in it. But farmers have to work hard for often long, antisocial hours while traditionally they earn about 20 per cent less than their counterparts in industry, commerce and the services. They do have something to whinge about.

Farm sizes in Continental Europe are generally smaller than in the UK, where many large conglomerates up the average. France still has mainly small family farms, in vast quantity. In the UK there are over 300,000 farms of an average size of 57 hectares, more than twice the French average acreage. The crops farmers grow are very varied. Around Kerkelven we see mainly barley, wheat and maize, but also some winter greens and oil-seed rape.

We don't see much dairy farming round us, or at least, where we do the herds are small. In Britain there are about 10 million cows, 5 million pigs and 35 million sheep. France has almost twice as many cows and three times as many pigs, but a lot fewer sheep. Exotic livestock like ostriches and llamas are increasingly popular in France, though still numerically insignificant. We do have lots of ostriches near here, and ostrich is now a regular favourite on local menus.

All these cows also produce a lot of cowpats, each one of which is a fertile breeding ground for all sorts of insects. That too is largely beneficial to the great natural scheme of things. Cows also produce a lot of methane gas, for grass combined with the way a cow's stomach works means rather a lot of almost invariably disgusting farts and belches. If all this noxious effluent could be gathered it might provide a useful source of fuel but it mostly escapes into the environment, where it hangs as a nasty greenhouse gas, adding to our already overheating atmosphere. Methane in quantity can be toxic, confirming the homespun old country legend that it's not a good idea to stand too close to the rear end of a cow on days when the wind doesn't blow.

So if we would combat climate change we would do well to focus at least part of our attentions upon farm fodder. As a single cow can produce up to 200 litres of methane each day, grass (i.e. hay) is not the best option. There are potentially readily available alternatives in white clover and bird's-foot trefoil (a leafy legume). These foods could reduce quadruped emissions by as much as 50 per cent, which could do us all a big favour. (Try it on your bedfellow if you like. It could change your life.)

Perhaps though, the future of the meat we will eat lies with kangaroos. They taste nice and are commercially farmed, though not on any scale in France as far as I know. But kangaroo fart contains no methane. Thanks to bacteria in his stomach lining, when Skippy and his friends break wind (which must be a lot, as they bounce along) it's all environmentally friendly. Even as I write, scientists are working on ways of transplanting kangaroo bacteria into the humble cow. Yes, technology at times is indeed spiffing, offering hope to us all.

Collective nouns

Talking of herds and flocks leads me to reflect on the numerous and curious words we English-speakers employ to describe creatures that hang around together. Why is it a herd of cows and pigs and a flock of sheep? It's a flock of seagulls, of course, but why then do we refer to a gaggle of geese and a flight of herons? With birds, is it a flock when they are on the ground and a flight when they're airborne?

Flock is also applied to goats. And even to people (i.e., in church).

Herd is used for animals that are herded (which makes sense) but is also applied to elephants, zebra and wildebeest sweeping majestically across the plains. We wouldn't say a herd of lapwings, but might refer to a herd of accountants, or town councillors. Buffalo and elk apparently travel in gangs, wild dogs and wolves roam in packs (like cigarettes). It's evidently a covey of grouse, a drift of hogs, a school of porpoises (or should that be porpoise, like sheep?), a skulk of vermin, not to mention troops, warrens, watches, wisps and crowds. Apparently a collection of apes is known as a shrewdness, whereas a gang of foxes is also rather unflatteringly known as a skulk. A group of moles is known as a labour (and it is a bloody big labour to remove their wretched molehills from your lawn).

It is a congress of gorillas, though, and not a flange, as was incorrectly reported some years ago in the 'Gerald the Gorilla' sketch on BBC Television's *Not The Nine O'Clock News*. Although apparently, serious scientists have since used this term in some learned books on the subject, making 'flange' the one and only word known to have migrated from a comedy show (the writer just made it up) into serious academia.

Correct collective descriptions include an exaltation of larks, a fall of flying woodcocks, a muster of peacocks and a pod of hippos. How odd the English language is, yet infinitely versatile. And even odder that we should consider this more than faintly reassuring. I've tried to find an appropriate word to describe the experience of seeing my lapwings in flight, and the best I can come up with is a swish. All suggestions welcome.

The funny thing about birds

Their propensity to form into flocks isn't the only distinctive bird behaviour in and around Kerkelven at this time. There are millions of birds around now, they're behind every branch and bough on every tree, in each bush, on our sheds, buildings and telephone wires.

And another thing . . . they're making a lot – but I mean a lot – of noise. Yet it's not unpleasant noise, far from it (though if I catch the blackbird that chirrups loudly outside my bedroom window early each morning I may make a different point). It's far too soon for spring but these little guys don't seem to know that.

It's a recent phenomenon. Kerkelven has always been renowned for the richness of its bird life but from mid-autumn up till just a few days ago they'd been quite restrained, if not all but invisible. Now it's a hive of action and the skies around are just full of them.

Most spectacular of course are the swarms. And what a fantastic, incredible thing a swarm of birds in flight is. You have to use the singular to describe it, because though hundreds of birds take part, in each swarm they move as one entity. Lapwings, starlings, sparrows, herons and others by the skyful. This seems to be the time for flocking, the season of the swarm. The combined force of starlings in swarm is reputedly capable of knocking over a tree and when you see them at it, in full flight, you can believe it. While I'd love them to land on me, I'd probably live to regret it. Or rather, maybe I wouldn't. Starlings filmed in Pennsylvania at the end of 2006 were able to bend two red cedar trees right over till their tops touched the ground again and again, with their combined weight.

Our flocks sweep across the sky as if flowing from an invisible paintbrush held in an invisible hand, swooshing and swirling in perfect, faultless unison. It seems natural and effortless yet if so it's even more incredible. It must be such fun to be a part of this.

Birds don't sing when they're swarming, which seems entirely understandable given what else they must have on their tiny minds.

Try as I might, I can't spot any single bird who is evidently their leader, the one in the swarm upon whose command they make their turns, swings, wheels, dives and swoops. Perhaps it's all done by the miracle of instinct. Perhaps there is no leader and, like ants, the flock only functions as a mass. Maybe the human equivalent is mob instinct, the loss of individual identity as the crowd takes over.

It's quite a scary thought.

As I strain my neck to watch this aerial bird ballet it strikes me that these vast flocks are just a simple step away from the complete domination of us and our species. All that would be required would be for one simple fact to somehow penetrate their consciousness, the realisation that if, instead of all following each other round and around and back and forth rather pointlessly every day, they were to attack us together, in unison, then we'd be at their mercy. There's no tide that, by their sheer numbers, they could not turn.

If you've seen Hitchcock's film *The Birds* I think you'll know what I'm talking about. They could surround us, bomb us, stab us with their beaks, poo on us even. Resistance would be futile. There could be no escape. Well, at least they'd have until we got ourselves together sufficiently to acquire some machine guns. But we humans lack birds' unity and ability to work harmoniously to a common aim. Humans are such a blind destructive lot in a crowd. If these birds were decisive and quick, they could beat us easy.

I think though that birds are generally benign and quite inquisitive too. On our walk this morning I've been treated to some aerial dance routines by a flock of long-tailed tits. There were about twenty of these lovely little chaps in the great oak to the left of the path past the big pond as, dogs in tow, I waltzed by. I could hardly have failed to notice their antics and stood a while watching, just enjoying the unexpected spectacle. As we four progressed round the field I noticed them again, this time occupying a large tree at the foot of the 45-degree path. I had to presume it was the same crowd and delighted in their apparent generosity in flying over to give me a second viewing. Then to my amazement they followed me up the path, flitting from tree to tree in a gang. I couldn't believe my eyes. As we rounded the corner into Bertrand's descent they rounded it too, filling another big oak opposite the Druids' fort. There they proceeded to put on a right pretty routine for my delight as I stood below like one bewitched, entranced by their dance.

Now isn't that the weirdest thing?

View from the top

When the trees have lost their leaves it becomes quite easy to spot where the birds build their nests. Some of the places they choose are simply awesome. To live perched high up in those branches must be thrilling enough, to be born among the treetops, to wake up on the first day of your life in a swaying, insubstantial loose collection of mud and twigs before you've even learned to fly must surely be character-building, quite apart from bloody terrifying. In the corner of our field by the river's edge we have one such tree, a tall poplar, naked now so it's easy to spot the large nest of moss and twigs that was built some time past by some enterprising bird among its topmost branches. This high slender tree sways majestically in the wind so anything up top in the bird's nest would have a high old time, no mistake.

I wonder if birds benefit from this spectacular, if shocking, start in life? I can only imagine what it must be like for a newborn bird to look out for the first time from her fragile perch onto the waiting world beneath. I find it hard not to have the greatest respect for such a creature, though maybe it's meaningless for her, something she can take completely for granted. Either way, it's impressive.

There are in fact two nests almost side by side in this high tree, so close that it must be possible for occupants to watch and wave to each other across the slender branches. I hope the offspring of each get along with those in the next nest across. It would be rather sad to imagine they don't, and it's rather fun to think of them sharing their views of life around and beneath as they grow and get ready for their big leap into space.

Not much grows at this time of year, which in many ways is rather nice, as all of last summer's undergrowth has now died back so we can see our surroundings clearly.

On the road at night

At dusk these days there are hundreds and hundreds of moths on the road; you see them reflected in your headlights as you drive along. Now I don't believe moths are sufficiently disciplined to stick just to the road, particularly at night, so I can assume that these moths are evenly distributed absolutely everywhere at this time. There must be tens of thousands of them, and that's just the ones I can see. Spooky.

Moths mostly fly by night so are best seen then, though more moth species are day flyers than all the butterfly species put together. There are just sixty species of butterfly in Britain, but around 2,500 species of moths and about twice as many in mainland Europe. France boasts over 1,600 different moth species – they call moths simply *papillons de nuit*, which means 'butterflies of the night' and is also the name of one of France's biggest music festivals. The order *Lepidoptera*, to which butterflies and moths both belong, has about 180,000 species worldwide.

Winter really isn't a great time for most moths. Moth eggs or larvae can safely see the cold out as they'll have been stashed away somewhere warm. Other moths may hibernate, while others, perhaps having laid their eggs, just die. But some moth species seem to thrive in winter.

The winter moth is a drab-looking but rather likeable little chap who seems to prefer the cold, appearing only from November to February. After then they die out, leaving behind only the chrysalises of their offspring to hatch out the following winter. The females are all but wingless so have to crawl up tree trunks and wait to be visited by the males, who have fine and fully functional wings.

There's also a good chance in this season of catching a glimpse or maybe more of the elusive roe deer, our largest mammal here and a very, very occasional visitor to our part of the forest. In the cold winter months food for the *chevreuil* is thin on the ground so, singly or in pairs, they will come right down to the road's edge looking for some leaves, grass or berries to help them keep going. They are so shy, often all you'll see is a quick reflection of your headlights, perhaps a pair of bright eyes or the white bob of a tail and the impression of something large moving through the shadows at the edge of the road.

The only time I've ever seen a badger here was late at night when in a moment of magic a large male at the roadside was caught in my headlights. More often I've seen the corpse of one that wasn't so lucky, knocked to the edge of the road like a discarded overcoat. Both badger and deer share a very high flight distance from our species, which generally serves them well for we are their biggest foe.

An ecosystem not quite yet on the edge

Although it has a slightly larger population, France produces carbon emissions just about two-thirds of those of Britain. In part this is due to their nuclear rather than coal-fired electricity industry and their more rural population. Emissions are rising in France though, particularly from its transport industries, so complacency isn't an option. The French, or at least most parts of French society, are also waking up to and accepting the urgent threat of climate change and seem prepared to commit themselves to doing something about it.

Recycling is a new fashion here and even that bastion of *la vie française*, over-excessive product packaging, is under serious threat from a consumer population that knows its power and is quite capable of making a fuss in a good cause. It's as if France, always proud and sensitive, has realised the threat facing the rest of the world and has collectively determined that no fingers of blame will be wagged in its direction (nuclear weapons testing in the sweet South Pacific islands excepted).

But France, particularly rural western France, is unlikely to be among the first to feel the adverse effects of serious climate change. In Kerkelven, at least, the signs seem slight and if anything generally benign. Apart from the flooding that is, and the crops growing too early, and confusion among the bird life, and the absence of traditional signs of winter, and . . .

Am I being foolish, and fiddling while Rome burns? It just seems so sad to me to have found paradise only to watch it slip away in a single generation.

So what can *we* do?

Climate change: what does it mean for Kerkelven?

For some time now we've been hearing about climate change and how it's the biggest threat to life on Earth, bigger than AIDS, poverty, terrorism, or any of the other looming awfulnesses that hang over humanity these days, or any other terror we can think of. So, that's saying something.

However horrific these other things may be, for the purposes of this book they can stay outside the borders and gates of Kerkelven, for we don't welcome their presence.

But climate change is different. It's affecting us here already, visibly and for the worse. It won't go away, even if we close our eyes and pull the pillow down really tight. Of all of life's unpleasantness, this is the one we can't cut ourselves off from.

Climate change is serious stuff and very frightening, yet most people go on with their lives pretty much as they did before it was ever heard of. This I guess is because it's so hard to get our head round such a concept, especially as the signs of climate change's impact on our daily lives can appear few and remote, even positive. Warmer winters have some appeal. Increased summer temperatures here would be warmly welcomed.

So what is climate change and what might it mean for Kerkelven and our field by the river?

Well, the signs that climate change is a reality are many, increasing and much closer to home than most of us might think. They're even noticeable in the field, in the river flowing through it, in the woods that border it and in the sky above it. Here are just those that I've observed:

- Too much rain. An increase in rainfall here is a likely sign of significant warming. At times it seems we have that already, though it's hard to be sure for the rain also seems to be coming at different times and sometimes a lot of it seems to be coming all at once. But there also seems to be more drought. Confusing, perhaps, but sure signs that something is up.

- The early and more frequent overflowing of our riverbanks, leading to erosion, removal of soil and degradation of the riverbanks.
- The frog that popped up in our house in January. We found him last night and were instantly cheered by his energetic hopping around. But of course he should be hibernating now, saving his energy for the spring. That he isn't is as much of a worry for us as for him.
- Mayflies in November.
- The absence of snow.
- Generally it's a lot warmer than it should be, even in the cold snaps. I should be feeling the cold more in my declining years, not less.
- Roses in bloom in January. That's not right. Chives and parsley thriving in the herb garden and signs of confusion among other plants, all blooming too bloomin' early.

I could add lizards breeding into November, and swallows still with us in October. These oddities are rather nice, but it's what they signal that we should be concerned about. What all this means, or will mean for the many inhabitants of Kerkelven and their dependants, we can only guess at. But on balance it's not likely to be good.

Of course there's much we can all do to play our part in reducing carbon emissions, and I don't need to go into that here. But if governments and the people they report to don't take this seriously then it seems from the viewpoint of all those living in Kerkelven that our future is bleak indeed.

Some things a bright boy can do

At this season, the deepest point of a long if not particularly deep winter, a chap's attention frequently from necessity turns to his library. It was on the higher shelves of this that I turned up a marvellous tome that has influenced successive generations of young minds, Harold Armitage's enchanting *300 Things a Bright Boy Can Do*. This well-thumbed treasure house has been my frequent friend and mentor on wet Sundays and from its mildewed pages I have gleaned a lot.

But as he was writing in 1929, Armitage offers little advice that's of much use in combating climate change, though he has some suggestions of relevance for the inhabitants of Kerkelven none the less, such as how to do semaphore, how to escape from inside a tied sack, build an elephant, dig a pit latrine, re-wicker a cane chair and other indispensables.

Goings-on among the moles, ducks and herons

Given that they spend all their time underground, why are moles black, and not white, like maggots? The mole is a curious creature much loved in tales of the riverbank but actually he can be a bit of a nuisance, particularly if he pops up from time to time in the middle of your lawn. Or, to be accurate, the piles of loose earth that he deposits above ground from his subterranean tunnellings are a nuisance.

Moles, not surprisingly, seem to prefer softer ground so we get them down by the river's edge, at the oxbow and in open, not too stony fields. They also like short grass so they can come up more easily, which is bad news for lawns and pathways. I once caught Syrus digging furiously at one of the molehills in our field. At first I thought he was just trying to make a mountain out of it, but as his digging became ever more frantic I realised he was actually chasing the moles which, one presumed, were underneath and which, through some doggy sense denied to humans, he knew full well were there. So, he must have been within sniffing distance of one or more. Imagine what that must be like, for poor Mr Mole . . .

The moles of Kerkelven have been busy. In Bertrand's small field there appeared overnight about a dozen molehills all arranged in a near perfect circle, right in the middle of the field. One imagines them all popping up together, one after the other in the moonlight, the first, evidently the leader, checking round on all the others then saying, 'Right lads, OK, everyone here then? Good. Let's . . .'

But then, what is it that moles do? What are they up to, while the rest of us are sleeping? Maybe they just do nothing, and such tunnellings and circlings are merely formed accidentally, at random.

This doesn't seem likely to me.

I feel the same when I come suddenly upon a gathering of ducks. I happened upon an incredible sight very early one morning, down at the big pond. It was a clear blue dawn, the sky streaked with red and orange, too early for vapour trails, only the birds and me and three sleepy dogs were up and about and us too bleary-eyed to fully enjoy the stunning beauty around us.

As I rounded the corner and the pond came into view I saw a solitary heron standing in the middle of the water, as they do, balanced on just one leg. But gathered around him, apparently listening intently, were about six assorted ducks, mostly mallards, or so it seemed. The heron looked for all the world like an earnest schoolmaster surrounded by eager pupils.

What's that all about?

In the split second before they scattered up and away, ducks squawking and flapping frantically, the languid heron's leisurely pace seeming merely disdainful, I sensed I'd interrupted something important, as if I'd stumbled on a conspiracy, disturbed a trades union meeting, or interrupted a trial.

What were they plotting? And against whom?

I'll never know. I'm sure that nature's ill opinion of me and my ilk sees us excluded from all sorts of interesting goings-on up and down the land, in places like my field. So often I'm reminded that our species, people, in thinking we're so superior to all other species and behaving generally as if the world is ours to play with, probably misses out on such a lot.

Chateaux in the sky
It's been perplexing us for months.

At Kerkelven we could see what appeared to be a particularly enterprising creature that builds her nest in very high places, amidst the topmost branches of pine trees. I had assumed it must be some kind of spider, but could find nothing about it and these nests seemed too large even for the entrepreneurial and ambitious spider. After much researching I've learned that these nests are not the product of spiders, they are the no less wonderful creations of hundreds of caterpillars, who like spiders also spin webs.

I should have known. No small tightly wrapped bits of chewing gum these. The wide cylindrical constructions are usually bright white and as large as a double ice-cream cone but with the appearance and consistency of candyfloss. So they're always quite visible from the ground, yet these superb constructions are nevertheless tantalisingly out of reach.

Inside each nest are hundreds of pine processionary caterpillars, which are the best known of all the processionaries. Not because of the intriguing nests they build but because of the nasty stings they can give. They are also one of the most destructive of forest insects, capable of defoliating vast tracts of pines during their episodic population surges. However, they are among the most social of caterpillars. Brothers and sisters, or more properly 'sibling groups', stay together throughout the larvae stage, often pupating side by side at sites they reach by forming long over-the-ground, head-to-tail processions. Nice to think that they have a sense of family.

Spiders do take over these magnificent nests when their creators the caterpillars have no further use for them, but not in huge numbers it seems, just in twos and threes. To secure their squatter's rights these spiders must have to climb dizzyingly high up into the topmost tips of our huge pine trees. But when they get there it must be like appropriating a vast abandoned chateau. I think of Johnny Depp as *Edward Scissorhands* and Vincent Price as his dad rattling around in their vast and gloomy castle, only this one, despite the security of its anchorage, is swaying alarmingly in the breeze.

Leaves litter the forest floor. Touch any of them at any time and dozens of spiders scamper out, clearly inconvenienced and annoyed. I'm reminded of just how many of them there are in our field.

Spiders and the weather

Is there no end to spider cleverness? According to my *300 Things a Bright Boy Can Do*, you can forecast the weather just by studying spiders. If unpleasant weather of any kind is in the offing – rain, wind, anything but fine – spiders will shorten the filaments that hold their webs in place, so there's less opportunity for the whole structure to sway about. Conversely, if you find that these filaments are long you can be fairly confident we're in for a spell of fine weather. The longer the filaments, the better the weather will be. Spiders apparently are fairly indolent in wet weather, so if it's raining and spiders are running about you can be confident the wet weather will not continue.

Insects

It is said that there are 200 million insects for every person on the planet. That for every pound in weight of human, there are thirteen pounds of insect.

Respect!

That means that if the average human weighs 150 pounds, and there are 6 billion people, there are 900 billion pounds or more than 400 million tons of people and 11,700 billion pounds or 5 billion tons of insect.

That's a lot to clean off your windscreen.

According to *The Pocket Guide to Insects of the Northern Hemisphere* (published by the Royal Society for Nature Conservation) there are 931,966 different species of insect in the world, and 21,709 in the UK alone. That's about twice as many insect species as all other species put together.

Or at least, there were. New species of insect are being found every day, usually several dozen each day, and it's estimated that there may easily be more than a million new species yet to discover. Beetles, with more than 300,000 known species already, are the most numerous of the insect species.

But most illustrated guides to the insect world will feature a tiny part of this huge range of insects – maybe one or two hundred at most. Even if your guide describes more than a thousand insects, it's still quite likely you'll not find the interesting spiky little fellow with the buggy blue eyes and green wings that has just landed on your sandwich. The chances of you spotting something hitherto unknown to science are really quite high.

Because they fear us

Every creature I meet here runs from me, at every encounter. That's the way it is, with all humans. We should be ashamed.

Scotland's farmer-poet Robert Burns put it very well. In the second verse of *Tae a mouse*, his tale of distress on accidentally turning over and destroying a mouse's home with his plough, he wrote:

> *I'm truly sorry Man's dominion*
> *Has broken Nature's social union*
> *And justifies that ill opinion*
> *Which makes thee startle, at me*
> *Thy poor earth-born companion*
> *And fellow mortal.*

We should be ashamed that everything in nature runs from us. Even if we don't need to kill it we'll kill it anyway. That may not be true for all of us, but for sure it's all that other creatures have come to expect of us.

One day, they killed five foxes here

In our woods, right on our doorstep, almost before our eyes, five adult foxes in their prime were driven to earth by dogs and, no doubt terrified beyond reason, were trapped and killed in one afternoon.

The bastards. The thing is, I know the guys that did this. Michael and Jean-Michel for sure, local characters we see invariably at any social occasion round here. Jean-Claude, the local builder, was with them too. You'd be hard put to find a nicer man anywhere, but there he was, killing for no good reason. Etienne, the garage-owner from town, he was there as well, cheerful and affable as ever. Both shook my hand vigorously before the crime. Neither seemed disconcerted, nervous, bashful, even slightly troubled by what they were about to do. For them, killing defenceless small animals is as natural as smoking.

That's why hunting as it is practised here should be stopped and I'm sure, in time, it will be. I don't wish to spoil anyone's favourite pastime one smidge, but when that pastime is barbaric, cruel and desensitising, someone has to stand up to it. In saying this, of course, I'm aware that I've done nothing myself to protest the situation. I feel bad about this. Like most people, it's too easy to accept the status quo when really, metaphorically at least, we should be chaining ourselves to the railings.

Banning the hunt would be an unpopular, even incomprehensible action in this part of the world, for sure. The foxes of Kerkelven haven't many friends hereabouts, far less advocates or even martyrs. But in a world increasingly self-critical and ever more aware of the interconnectedness of all species, surely it can't be long before our society rethinks such issues? This has started to happen in England and Scotland. One day I'm sure hunting will be banned even here, in France, for in time it will be considered as barbaric as bear baiting or witch burning.

Here's mud in your eye

This month we bought a new wooden bridge for crossing the east burn, to replace the slippery old pallet that I'd put into service there a few years back, that had since disintegrated into a positive danger to life and limb, particularly Marie's.

So I loaded the new bridge (it really is a wonderful thing, curved like the Newcastle railway bridge only a bit smaller, made of wooden slats fixed by stainless steel nails all guaranteed for at least ten years, though I'd be surprised if in these conditions it lasts more than three) onto the car and drove it down to its new home. Having previously dug a groove in either bank to receive each end, I then gingerly hoisted it into place only to have all three dogs rush onto it at once, then stand together in a huddle in the middle, unsure of what to do next but looking distinctly pleased with themselves and their new bridge.

About an hour later, after an embarrassing realisation on seeing my reflection in Leclerc's window on leaving their premises in town laden with groceries, I found myself complaining to Marie.

'You might have told me I'd got bits of the field all over my face!'

Trouser stains

I'm not sure if this is a good time to bring up the subject of trouser stains, or not. Is there ever a good time, I wonder? The people hereabouts think Marie and I are odd enough but our reputations are not helped by the frequently dishevelled state of our appearances in public. This is the (I think) deliberate effect of the combined attentions of our three dogs whenever we sit down at one or other of our carefully positioned resting places around the field, when as soon as we've sat down they come and nestle their muddy chops in our groins.

This leads to sizeable and persistent stains that might be of doubtful provenance upon our garments, in places where people really shouldn't be looking. I can find no solution for this problem short of changing my trousers after each walk. Or changing the dogs.

Marie's long fall from the one true path

The nights now are long, dark and cold. Frequently there's not as much as a glimmer of ambient light to guide us on our nightly walks as we unfailingly exercise our three canines, a thrice-daily responsibility as I've explained. So we depend on torches and clutch them closely to us as we brace against the elements to escort the dogs on the day's final promenade. Sometimes in January the cloud cover clears, often just for mere moments, and we are treated to a celestial display that eclipses anything Hollywood or even Bollywood could offer. The stars come out and dance about and we mortals can merely gape upwards in awe.

We'd not seen the stars for quite a while, such was the thickness of the cloud cover that had been enveloping Kerkelven. We were down at the big pond when unexpectedly the skies cleared. Suddenly above us stretched the panorama of the night sky and we craned our necks in wonder, making lots of 'oooing' and 'aaahing' sounds which must have alarmed the owls and other night birds as they perched poised for the night's hunt. Probably we even woke a few robins and others as they slept.

It was a sight, believe me. It fair took one's breath away.

Now if you recall the topography of Kerkelven you'll remember that as old Emile's access road to the fields passes by the big pond to its right, on the left lies the most northerly outcrop of our field, the field by the river. But here the passing years of tumbling water from the big pond have gouged a passage for the western burn out of the living rocks and earth of our field, which lies a good three or four metres lower than the pond. The water draining from the pond flows under the path into a huge and deep (at least in this season) pool where it swirls around before meandering off towards the river, descending gradually all the while. Just east of the swirling pool the undergrowth is particularly thick. The edges of the path too are usually thickly overgrown, but by chance our local council had attacked the hedgerow that very day, so the vegetation by the side of the path was, for a change, completely cleared.

I don't know how long I stood upon this spot, mesmerised in silence, slowly drinking in the scene that was spread in front of us. Time can seem to stop on such occasions and it's easy to shut out everything else around.

But as I gazed thus upon the heavens in wonder, another sound came drifting softly and slowly towards me through the still chilly night. It seemed like a muffled cry or moan, coming from the depths of the earth. I looked around, but all was silence. So I turned to my trusty companion, to see if she'd heard it too.

She was gone!

Marie had vanished. She was nowhere to be seen.

The moaning sound seemed closer and more urgent now. It seemed to be coming almost from my feet, but just behind me and low, low down.

Yet, as moans go these didn't seem at all unhappy. In fact, the spooky thing was I could swear I heard laughter. Muffled it was, but laughter all the same. These laughing, sobbing murmurs seemed to be coming from there, just behind me, just off the road.

But the darkness down there was nigh-on absolute. I peered and peered, but could see nothing.

It took me all of a minute to realise what had happened. Marie hadn't just got bored and wandered off homeward. Minutes earlier she'd been right beside me gazing skywards as I had been, awestruck and starstruck just as I was, when she must have inadvertently stepped backwards a bit too far and plunged at least three metres into the gaping darkness. Miraculously, her fall had been stopped by tangles of brambles. Those same obnoxious growths that cause us so much pain and inconvenience at other times had saved her, if not her life itself then at least from a severe and chilly drenching and probably a serious bang or two on the head.

Or maybe she'd had that anyway, as though I couldn't see her I could still hear her laughing.

I shone my torch down into the murky darkness. Still I could see nothing. Then I detected what looked like a human leg. Then another. It was her, or at least parts of her (I presumed she was attached to them, no other possibility occurred at the time)

I confess though that in that instant, just momentarily it crossed my mind that I could run away and leave her there, then come back in the morning to find the tragedy. Who'd be any the wiser? But I appreciate too much her ability to help me locate lost socks, so I quickly cast that from my mind.

I called down reassuringly (I think in the excitement I said something like 'Is that you?' and 'What are you doing down there?' I may even have asked 'What on earth possessed you to go down there?') though I deny asking if she wanted any help, which is what she says I said.

She did indeed need help, for where she was she could neither see nor move. So, displaying great bravery and disregard for my personal safety and comfort, I urged her to climb up a bit so I could extend my left boot over the abyss for her to clutch and so haul herself to safety. But even that was too much, so after much harrumphing and at dire risk to life and limb I had to hang suspended perilously over the black hole and hoist her bodily out, until she could grasp my sleeve then, hand over hand, haul herself up my clothing. I felt like saying, as in similar circumstances Superman had once said to his Lois, 'I've got you', but I resisted for fear that she'd rejoin with, 'But then who's got you?' which would merely have served to remind me that at that moment, no one had.

But we survived, she completed her climb, I wiggled myself backwards to a state of balance and we were soon back in the house, sipping hot cocoa. Needless to say, throughout this adventure all three dogs were entirely useless.

We can laugh about it now, of course.

February

Walking the dogs, February

I stood a long time silent as stone, scarcely even breathing, waiting to see if I could again catch the vague sense of movement among the distant scrub that had caught my eye through the morning still, causing me to stop in my tracks and watch. It was more a texture change than actual disturbance, a shift rather than a movement, so subtle and understated as to be easy to dismiss as imagination. But it was enough to make me pause and it was worth the wait.

The fox rose up like a vapour exhaled from the earth, then turned and vanished soundlessly within the thicket as if she had never been. She knows her life depends on staying unseen by me and my kind so she's become a genius at blending in. Brief though this sighting was I feel fortunate to see her at all, and worry that such a glimpse, while lucky for me, may well be unlucky for her.

It seems strange to so treasure the sighting of a fox, for they used to be such a regular feature hereabouts. But now they're rare, thanks to over-hunting.

Binoculars are for the birds

Let's see if you can explain this for me, because I'm quite stumped. Since I moved here I've been in possession of a fine stout pair of field glasses. That's binoculars to you. The kind that, in the absence of indiscreet neighbours with open curtains to peer through, are handy for studying nature in all its forms. Or so I thought. But either the winged wildlife of Kerkelven is extremely shy and hyper-observant, or my glasses emit a foul smell only noticeable by birds. Because as soon as I don my bins, all bird life vanishes. The binoculars come out and the birds go in. It's a baffling and to be honest very irritating enigma.

Marie and I contemplate starting the Society of Crap Birdwatchers, so we can mix with similarly useless lovers of nature and swap tales of the exotic bird life that we've failed to see.

The birds of Kerkelven

I noticed a curious thing as early this morning the dogs and I took our usual path through Loïc's field alongside the west burn. We've done this every day for months on end and each day the birds are our constant companions. Hitherto they've not seemed to mind us in the slightest and for sure I've been more than grateful for their company. I've tried bringing my field glasses with me to enjoy their presence the more, though because they fly so fast I'm usually fairly inept at tracking them and, as I've just explained, the mere presence of field glasses seems to drive birds away. So mostly, I leave them behind.

Perhaps we should simply stop trying to spot birds on the wing and concentrate on tracking them when they're at rest, rather than in flight.

But for some reason this morning there seemed to be an unusually large number of birds around, particularly in the trees that grow alongside the burn, but as we walked they seemed to notice our presence, and one after the other all began to fly off towards our wood. All the traffic was eastward, away from us.

What's that about? I'm not talking about a few shy birds here. There were hundreds of them and as we came along they all flew away, all in the same direction.

Birds here seem a distinct and ordered society and they rarely do things without a reason. So I'm sure there is order in this behaviour, which I would love to understand.

The birds wake early. There are countless varieties of bird

species, including some truly odd birds and many exotically named species that I'd struggle to identify and to be honest I can't put hand on heart and say whether they regularly frequent my field or not.

Most of us, even the country-dwellers, tend to take our constant neighbours the birds somewhat for granted and know little or nothing about them beyond the obvious. Among numerous others, the main players here are the perky chaffinches, robins, finches (bull, green), tits (blue, coal, great and long-tailed), blackbirds, thrushes, woodcocks, wood pigeons, jays, woodpeckers, owls (tawny and barn), sparrows and wagtails. Like their close relative the pied and grey wagtails, the charming, delicate yellow wagtails are frequently found dancing around the rocks on our cataracts and along the riverbank. Perversely, the grey wagtail is also yellow, and as yellow wagtails are only summer visitors I guess it's the grey ones that I see by the river now.

I've left out lots and lots of good friends from this quick listing, omitting residents such as herons, ducks, moorhens, fieldfares, rooks, crows and even our regular visitors from the coast such as terns and seagulls. Then, we have the tree creeper, which can only run up trees, and its close relation, the nuthatch, which can run both up and down them. One can only hope, as it is so lucky as to be able to do that, and if it is such a close relation, that the nuthatch will be on hand to help the tree creeper down from all those trees it was foolish enough to creep up.

This reminds me of a pseudo-legend we Scottish people used to relay to incredulous and gullible visitors from south of the border, about that mythical Scottish creature, the haggis. Particularly when I worked as a waiter in a hotel in Nairn we used to regale open-mouthed teenage-girl visitors from

Cheshire about the male haggis's three pair of legs. Females, we'd explain, have only two pairs of legs, one at the front and one at the back. The two in the middle, which grace only the male of the species, are to help him climb over any bumps. The female doesn't need this extra pair of legs though, we'd explain, because the well-brought-up male haggis helps her over the bumps.

We'd usually get away with this perfidy, unless we pushed our luck and were tempted to add that the haggis's left legs are all noticeably shorter than his right legs, so he can run round mountains. But only anticlockwise, of course.

One is forced to wonder, though, how tree creepers do get down trees. Presumably they drop, or fly.

Upwards of 25 menacing big black birds have all taken to gathering together on a single tree in Loïc's field just west of mine. These are rooks, sociable birds, but seemingly only with their own kind. They seem pariahs to all others. I also daily see crows here, either singly or in pairs, sometimes in a small flock. The carrion crow is aptly named. He's a sharp-eyed ruthless scavenging machine. Rooks, ravens and crows, especially rooks, are credited as being particularly clever birds and they are undeniably beautiful and big, but they're also noisy and disagreeable. Hard as I try, I find I can't get excited about them. I don't know why. Haughty and distant, the woods frequently ring to their raucous, unpleasant cries. When I was little I lived near a noisy, messy rookery, which may explain my aversion. I'll have to work at understanding them better.

Pigeons

The position of a pigeon's eyes on either side of its head gives it a field of view approaching 340 degrees. So to fly at speed it has to process visual information three times faster than a human.

Thus, if a pigeon were to watch a feature film at a normal 24 frames per second it would appear to it like a slide presentation. Pigeons need at least 75 frames per second to create the illusion of movement on screen. This is why pigeons seem to wait until the very last second to fly out of the way of an oncoming car, because it appears slower to them. It's not, I expect, why you rarely see pigeons at the Odeon.

Pigeons can navigate with great precision, using a combination of odour trails, the sun's position, the earth's magnetic field and, as they get closer to home, visual landmarks like road systems. Pigeons' eyes have split focus, the bird equivalent of bifocals. The top half sees at great distances, the bottom sees details close-up.

According to the seventeenth-century natural historian John Aubrey, the traditional remedy for the bite of an adder is to apply the fundament (i.e. buttocks) of a pigeon to the wound to suck out the poison.

Shy birds and cheeky birds

As they can all fly away with comparative ease it's hard to understand why some birds are so shy of humans. Several species won't let you even see them at all (which may cause you to believe they aren't there or don't exist – but it doesn't at all follow that just because you can't see something it isn't there).

The chaffinch is one of the most cheeky birds around here. He seems genuinely interested in us. By comparison, the swallow and the swift appear not to mind being seen but are utterly indifferent to their human neighbours, bordering on disdainful.

Disposal of a dead bird

Slumped with wings spread, the wood pigeon looked exactly as if it had died in flight. When I found it, it seemed pristine, unblemished, appearing merely to be sleeping. From above it looked perfect, with no visible sign of what had caused its demise. But underneath it was a mass of ants.

At the time I assumed they were just feeding on it but I've since discovered this may not be the case. One of the strangest of natural phenomena is the cleansing process of some birds known as anting. There are apparently two types, active anting, where a single ant is picked up by the bird and applied to its feathers, presumably so that it can perform certain cleaning activities, and passive anting, which involves the bird sitting on top of a nest of ants and literally bathing itself in hundreds of ants.

Though widely recorded this weird activity of birds is far from fully understood. Jays, starlings and weaverbirds all do it, with some vigour and enthusiasm (though birds tend to be either active or passive anters, not both). Strangest of all is the behaviour of the grey thrush of Japan, which is a passive anter that goes through the actions of an active anter, but without any ants in its bill. One theory is that the birds may just want the ants to discharge their formic acid before eating them. This might explain passive anting, but not active.

According to the charity Earthlife there's a possibly related but even more bizarre bird activity called 'smoke bathing'. Birds such as rooks have been observed standing on smoking chimneys with their wings spread open in a similar posture to some birds when anting. Could be a way of keeping warm, I guess. Birds have also been seen to use smoking cigarette butts for anting, or perhaps more accurately, smoke-bathing. On other occasions both houses and trees have been set alight by birds taking live cigarettes back to their nests. No one has any real idea why they do this. Perhaps they just fancy a fag.

A recipe involving small birds

I came upon the following quite by accident and thought I'd include it merely because it's quaint and it shows how times have changed.

In the mid-1800s Charles Elmé Francatelli was maître d'hôtel and chief cook to Her Majesty Queen Victoria, the British queen at the height of England's empire. In his retirement Francatelli wrote a pompous and patronising but no doubt well-intentioned book called *A Plain Cookery Book for the Working Classes*. I find such titles irresistible. In this slender tome Francatelli sets out a series of economical, nutritious and frequently unlikely recipes that in his view poor people should prepare and eat to keep themselves healthy in mind and body. Among many other recipes he lays out detailed descriptions of the preparations necessary for baked pig's head, stewed eels, boiled tripe, cow-heel broth, giblet pie and how to make gruel. Ah, the good old days . . .

But the recipe that caught my eye was No. 24, a pudding made of small birds.

'Industrious and intelligent boys who live in the country,' explained Francatelli, 'are mostly well up in the cunning art of catching small birds at odd times during the winter months.' He'd obviously not encountered the likes of my boys, Joe and Charlie, who are perhaps products of a later age and would have no more chance of trapping a wild bird than of capturing a reasonable likeness of the sunset here on canvas.

'So, my young friends,' (he goes on to address these small boys directly, though later acknowledges that their mothers must surely be the ones reading his words), 'when you have a good catch of a couple of dozen birds you must first pluck them free from feathers, cut off their heads and claws and pick out their gizzards from their sides with the point of a small knife, then hand them over to your mother who, by following these instructions will prepare a famous pudding for your dinner.'

No, I can't quite see Marie doing this either.

With commendable enthusiasm Charles the chef then goes on to describe his pudding, step by step.

'First fry the birds with a little butter, shallot, parsley, thyme and winter savoury, all chopped small, pepper and salt to season. When the birds are half done shake in a handful of flour, add rather better than a gill of water, stir the whole on the fire while boiling for ten minutes and when the stew of birds is nearly cold (?) pour it all into a good sized pudding basin which has been ready-lined with either a suet and flour crust or else a dripping crust, cover the pudding in with a piece of the paste and either bake or boil it for an hour and a half.'

Interesting and no doubt tasty, but at this point I think I'd make an excuse to leave too. I'd rather watch small birds through binoculars.

Finding the wee Kenny

There it goes again. I've spotted this tiny, tiny bird several times before (see September) but always only for a fraction of an instant and because he's so very small and he flits ere you can point the place, I've never been able to identify him. He's black or very dark brown (the one I saw today looked deepest black), about the size of a butterfly and he hangs tenuously around the roots and branches at the water margins, seeming to inhabit that no-man's land that fills the gap between river and field, a slender territory that's anyway dark, indistinct and over-crowded with moss, ivy and leaf-covered rocks that line higgledy-piggledy the edge of our lovely riverbank. So this quick wee chap is really, really hard to spot. He darts, rather than merely flies.

I've tried to identify him in all the books but so far I've seen nothing like. I'm now sure he isn't Europe's smallest bird so far, the goldcrest, for not surprisingly this little chap is easy to identify because he has a crest that's a kind of golden colour. So it isn't him. It isn't a wren and it's much too small to be just about anything else.

Perhaps it's a species as yet unknown to science. Why ever not? Everything has to be discovered sometime. And this little chappie is quick enough and small enough and dark enough to have stayed hidden for generations.

I was going to give him a name but Marie has beaten me to it. She's called it the 'wee Kenny'. I rather like that.

But now I've discovered him, I wonder, have I really done him any favours?

Back then they didn't think they knew it all

My own encounters with the elusive 'wee Kenny' have convinced me that there remains much still to be discovered about the bird and animal species with which we share the land, sky and waters. This is particularly so with our winged neighbours, our feathered friends, because they are often so shy, so quick and so hard to see clearly.

In Gilbert White's time this was even more true. In his days the study of nature was an emerging and almost entirely amateur science. Discoveries were being made all the time, which must have made it an extremely exciting and rewarding pastime. You can't fault Gilbert and his peers for their choice of gentlemanly pursuit. The routines of a rural parson must have been greatly enhanced by the hobby, elevating Gilbert's chosen lifestyle to one of the most desirable that can be imagined.

Gilbert, however, may have been on to the wee Kenny long before I identified it. In his book he refers to 'three distinct species of the willow-wren' (*motacillae trochili*), but confesses to one of his regular correspondents that he 'knows nothing of your willow-lark'. However, though Gilbert identified what he thought to be three distinct types of wren, now it is accepted that there is only one species of wren in Europe.

As well as sometimes being plain wrong, Gilbert at times is just not helpful, like when he describes the largest species of willow-wren: 'This last haunts only the tops of trees in high beechen woods, and makes a sibilous grasshopper-like noise, now and then.'

Unlike, I suppose, your actual grasshopper, who makes his

sibilous noise continuously. I mean, what kind of a noise is that?

Gilbert regularly trapped and killed specimens of those creatures he wished to study. No criticism intended of the charming Gilbert, of course, but I don't do that.

Goodbye to all that

Some of the wood pigeons around here have invented a great game that they play with gusto and evident enjoyment. They pretend they've been shot.

This is remarkable, and indeed is strange behaviour from a bird. But I've watched them do this on many occasions and can think of no other explanation for their antics than that they must enjoy it.

The game resembles 'best dead', which I used to play at school. It involves soaring upwards to a great height then spectacularly falling forward in mid-flight as if rear-ended by a blast of buckshot or a pellet from a 12-bore. The feint is maintained until plummeting stone dead earthwards seems a virtual certainty then, at the last minute, the wily bird awakes, flaps vigorously and pulls out of the dive, presumably chortling gleefully at the consternation thus caused.

While the wood pigeons of Kerkelven seem to think it a great joke, the other birds hereabouts ignore it, treating these brainless pigeon antics with the contempt they evidently feel they deserve.

But I'd love to have go.

A woodland den

Joe was twelve, a teenager, almost. Charlie was just eight, a cowboy, or a pirate. He wanted to build a den in the woods above the field by the river.

Joe said he would help him. Joe is good like that; he'll do anything for his brother, who he loves to bits and pieces. They set about stripping poles, gathering loose foliage, bending and tying bracken to shape.

'What shall we do now?' asked Joe, when at last the work was completed and they could survey their splendid new abode. It was indeed rickety and hardly deserved the name 'hut', but they could go into it, together.

Charlie hesitated.

'We . . . we can . . .'

'Yes,' said Joe in eager anticipation.

'We can . . .

'. . . just *be*,' he said, with all the emphasis on the last word.

Foxing the hunters

I've found a fox's earth deep in the forest, in a particularly tangled overgrown part of the wood. Or rather I should say Syrus has found it, for it was he, not I, who unearthed the fox family. Curiously, he seems excited by it but not keen to cause it harm or to get too close. Maybe he's remembering a previous experience, where overenthusiasm turned to folly. For foxes are fierce and full of teeth and claws which they'll use unhesitatingly to defend their own.

The animal we know as a fox is really the red fox, one of 27 species of fox found around the world. The red fox is widely distributed across Europe and is considered by many to be a pest. Certainly he isn't endangered but he is one of Europe's few big wild animals. Unlike the badger and the wild boar, who are never seen at Kerkelven, and the roe deer, which is a singular rarity, foxes are seen here from time to time and on occasions hunters will succeed in killing foxes here too. That their smell is powerful and distinctive I have no doubt. But

Syrus still did well to find this den for they are shy, cautious creatures, not easy to spot, far less track.

Attractive and appealing though they undoubtedly are, foxes are not always the cunning and cuddly rascals of children's literature. Frequently they are carriers of the distinctly nasty sarcoptic mange, which can also affect domestic dogs, causing chronic itching and hair loss.

The mange mite usually spends its entire life on a fox. The female mite burrows into the fox's skin and lays eggs several times, continuing to burrow all the while. It literally tunnels into the skin of its host, to a length of several centimetres. After depositing her eggs the female mite then dies, though this signals no relief for her poor victim. Her eggs soon hatch into larvae, which then grow, so the whole process begins again. Meanwhile the unfortunate host has lost all its fur and gone a distinctly funny colour.

So next time someone refers to you as a mangy old git, you'll know what they mean.

It can be a short, bloody and brutal life, the fox's. They can live lives approaching the span of a domestic dog but most foxes are lucky if they survive three years or more. Though they have few predators except men and dogs, they treat everything they meet as their enemy. The exceptions on this occasion are me and, surprisingly, Syrus, though I doubt if any foxes we might encounter will appreciate that.

I have no idea how many foxes there may be in this set, nor of what age or gender. Although I know at least one is in there I can't see the creature itself. I don't need to. I'm just happy it's there and hope it can hang on long enough to see out the hunting season, which ends next month.

Two old and bent hunters pause at the edge of our field where it meets the forest. They ask me if I have seen any foxes.

I try to act nonchalantly and not too friendly. This is always a challenge because they talk too fast for my ears and slur their words too. I remark that there's nothing now left alive in this part of the forest. They think I'm paying them a compliment and seem content. With lots of '*bien, biens*' and '*à tout à l'heures*' they trudge off, while I'm praying that Syrus doesn't get overexcited and rush off to say hello to his new chums.

In a somewhat corrupted form the cheery French farewell of *à tout à l'heure*, meaning 'until later', was possibly brought home by the British Tommy of the Great War, 1914–18, who in those days presumably heard it rather a lot in fields of the Somme valley not unlike ours. This parting duly became the jolly British cheerio, 'Toodle-oo'.

Neither of the hunters as much as glanced back as they left, so I heaved a sigh of relief and our friends the foxes got to live another day at least.

Queer looks from sheep

One of Bertrand's sheep has just given me a real old-fashioned look. What is it with them?

When he retired Bertrand, like many Bretons, continued to keep a generous complement of farm animals. Though he has now moved to town, a few of these are still with us, for a while at least, keeping the grass in the small field neat until, one at a time, he makes space for them in his big chest freezer.

Sheep are every bit as daft as dogs, but we can at least eat sheep, I suppose. When Bertrand was here I quite frequently did, not these sheep of course, but their antecedents. Perhaps I shouldn't grudge them the odd queer look, for they too have little enough reason to like me.

On some days I can be found standing at the edge of the field wherein Bertrand keeps his sheep, making noises at them.

The sheep seem unperturbed, and continue munching at their cud, looking up only occasionally in what appears to be absolute vacant bewilderment at the world around them.

But they're sullen, joyless lumps, sheep. I think long ago they concluded that I am mentally unhinged so decided to ignore me in the hope I'll go away. I won't. I don't hate them, but they annoy me. One day I'll catch them off guard and find out what sheep really get up to when they think no one is watching.

They've had little baby sheep this month too, lambs, a long time behind the sheep belonging to our neighbours, whose sheep were lambing back in December. And when did 'our' sheep have the chance to conceive, I'd like to know? And who with? I've often hung around their field trying to catch them at it, but have never seen any sign of anything remotely like a male sheep within a kilometre of them. Maybe there's something in the cud?

I don't know what it is that's wrong with Bertrand's sheep. They don't seem to enter into the spirit of Kerkelven at all. None of the other animals seem to like them either. Perhaps they're old and should have long since been made into merguez (a north African spicy sausage much loved at Breton barbecues, made from bits of sheep). The little ones are cute though, but they don't stay that way for long at all.

Sentimentality for farmyard animals has no place here. When he lost his mother a bit too early, Bertrand and Marie-Thérèse adopted the cutest little lamb, a wee chap they called Tintin and bottle-fed daily until he grew to be able to fend for himself. He was a jolly, bouncy, cuddly character; I used to enjoy meeting Tintin in his field because he would invariably rush up to me and shower me with rather un-sheeplike enthusiasm.

Then one day I missed Tintin, and on asking Bertrand was

casually told he was heading for, though not yet actually in, the deep freeze. I was rather shaken by his callousness, as I recall. But I didn't refuse Bertrand's supply of merguez, when he offered them.

Extreme cold and deep frost

It's St Valentine's Day, 14 February. So by rights love should be in the air. But today is decidedly too cold for lovemaking and indeed for just about anything. Earth is hard as iron, water like a stone. The air hits you like a hammer blow. It's too cold to stay long outside. (Your feet are always the first bits to go, then your ears, lips, fingers and thumbs, then the naughty bits. At that point you have to scamper indoors sharpish.) But the deep cold can be fun too.

Suddenly there are lots of very fat robin redbreasts around. I counted eight on one morning walk. Where do they go for the rest of the year? And why are they so fat?

I'm told they don't go far afield in summertime, they're here all right, but because there are so many other birds around then the robin is much less noticeable. He also appears slimmer in summer (so is even harder to spot) as in wintertime robins puff up their feathers to keep themselves warm.

Later, in the bitter, bitter cold, I spot a tree creeper shimmying up a silver birch by the river, as easily as a fly would climb a wall. It's unmistakeable, but I've not seen one here before. My bird book describes the tree creeper as quiet and mouselike. Its movements are jerky but very fast and it has a long curved beak for wheeking grubs and insects out of nooks and crannies that he finds in the wood of trees.

Also according to my book (which is obviously potty), the tree creeper has a high note 'treep' uttered when feeding or in flight, and a short song 'tee, tee, tee, sissi-tec'. I heard none of this, and would have worried if I had.

I also saw an amazing pair of bluetits in the same tree (see, I resisted the obvious schoolboy joke). Despite the awesome cold they seemed to be nesting and appeared in high spirits, jumping jubilantly from tree to tree and arguing good-naturedly with each other.

Such fun! Their exuberance transfers itself to me and to Max and Syrus as well, though it doesn't quite infect Mortimer, who is seeming a bit slow and ungainly today.

St Valentine's Day is of course a little early for anything other than the human species to indulge in any serious hanky-panky, and most of the creatures of Kerkelven seem to agree with me. No brass monkeys hereabouts, that's for sure. All the signs are that it has to get a little warmer around the nether regions before the most unstoppable force in nature gets seriously under way here.

The sheep may be an exception of course. The frolicking of so many lambs is a bit of a giveaway for them, they clearly don't mind how cold it is. And the ducks, well there's no stopping them, is there? Nor in fact . . .

What am I talking about? Love is in the air all right and getting pretty much into everywhere else too.

Kerkelven under snow

Our temperate mini-climate and the Gulf Stream make sure that snow is not a common experience at Kerkelven and global warming seems likely to ensure it'll be an even greater rarity in future. But it does come most years, sometimes in quantity, and sometimes it settles.

But when snow does settle here, it's special.

Kerkelven under snow is something to be seen, and best

experienced by the first person to step out into the pristine fields of freshly fallen snow. It helps if whatever wind it was that brought the snow has already faded away. Sunshine is an added bonus for then the world transforms into fairyland. Most of Kerkelven's trees take the snow well. It falls in layers on the upturned branches of the pines so they all look like they've just been cut out of a Christmas card. Snow sticks like a gentle dusting on the bare branches of all the other trees, giving them the appearance of frosted fruits. The effect is a graduated grey and white, like the overnight transformation of our world into the garden of the Snow Queen. Almost always quiet, Kerkelven after a snowfall is utterly silent. Nothing drips, for all is frozen where it sits. Even if a pin dropped you wouldn't hear it, for it would sink slowly and silently into soft snow. Birds don't sing, though not perhaps because they too are made speechless by the sudden change to everything they know, more likely they've buzzed off because they can't find anywhere comfy to perch.

To enter a snow-blanketed field that is perfect and undisturbed is to experience a pure instant in time, something no one else can share, like being the first onto the sand after the tide's gone out.

Your first footsteps can seem like a violation, as if you have no right to be there and your mere presence can only disturb and spoil. Then you recall it'll not last till tomorrow, so you can be as destructive as you like. That's when the fun begins.

After one winter snowfall Charlie and I set off to be the first into the field. We had the best fun possible, tripping and rolling, running around in the field and up and down the paths, throwing snowballs, sledging down the slopes (we have two sledges), building a snowman; all that kind of thing. I persuaded Charlie I should take his photograph, and positioned him under a huge snow-laden fir tree where he stood beaming trustingly at me, looking a perfect picture. Just as I pressed the shutter I pulled the trailing branch that I'd cunningly set up in anticipation of the moment, thus sending cascading down the full accumulation of snow stacked upon that tree, down onto poor Charlie's head.

It made a great photo.

'At first I thought it was kids playing with a chainsaw'

One lunchtime about two years ago the dogs and I had gone for our ritual midday walk when entirely unexpectedly I stumbled across a scene of carnage in the wood, just to the left of Emile's road. Five young trees had been hacked down. The scene was mayhem, as if something huge and powerful had run amuck. The dead trees had just been left where they'd been killed. It seemed senseless, a violation.

All five dead trees were from the same area and had been left where they'd been cut, around the middle of the wood maybe ten metres from the path. At that time, this was one of the easier parts of our wood to get to. The killing seemed completely without point. For the life of me I couldn't work out what had happened there, or why. I presumed some local youngster had been given a new chainsaw and had come to our place to try it out.

This disturbing incident remained a mystery for nearly two years, until Slobodan and Marco came to Kerkelven, bent upon mischief, up to no good.

A visit from the bad guys

They came in the early morning, without warning. There were just the two of them, in a dirty white van with green markings. They had no permission, nor did they show the slightest respect or consideration for whose land they were on, or whose trees they were to kill. They had chainsaws, they were out of earshot of any dwelling and there was nothing to stop them. As they cut, and cut, and cut, they made no effort to clear up behind them. Branches, logs and whole trees fell in their wake. By the time they'd finished they had chopped down 21 mature trees in our forest and had mutilated many others. The path of their destruction was clear. As well as their debris, they left a gaping swathe through our woods that virtually cut our sliver of forest messily and unevenly into two. Three tall trees from the riverbank lay sprawled upon our field where they had fallen across my tractor path, blocking it totally.

The instant I saw this devastation I realised the significance of that much more minor incident the year before. It was the exact same part of the wood. It was directly below where the EDF (Electricité de France) electric overhead cables cross our land, carried by a single three-headed pole, a type known colloquially as the gendarme's hat. The cables pass suspended from a similar pole on Loïc's land, to the pole on our land and from there at a great height across our field and the river to a third pole on the opposite bank of the Sarre.

I knew who had caused this carnage because some days earlier I had been sent a letter asking permission for some workmen to enter my land to make sure no trees or other growths were threatening the overhead cables. I had replied saying fair enough (I knew I couldn't stop them whatever my reservations) but had clearly stipulated that if any trees needed thinning, or had to be cut down, I should be told first, so I could be on hand to see that my field was disrupted no more than was absolutely essential.

Confident that, as my request had been ignored, I was at

least morally in the right, I telephoned the number at the head of this letter, seeking redress.

I was told that the workmen were still in my area and would be sent back round imminently to explain their actions. Fine. I was up for a fight.

To my surprise the dirty white van with green markings did duly return. It was pouring with rain when they came back and they seemed strangely reluctant to get out of their vehicle, but they did roll down the passenger window. Emboldened by this I leant halfway in and gave them an earful (French is a great language if you need to be abusive and I suspect I chucked in a few Anglo-Saxon epithets for good measure too). Then the driver did decide to get out and for the first time I saw the size of my adversary. Seconds later, his even larger colleague joined him.

They were huge and I was immediately prepared to be intimidated. But they seemed strangely subdued.

Stained and dripping, with their long muscular arms and hands like anvils dragging massive knuckles along the ground behind them, Marco and Slobodan looked like two bedraggled escapees from Devil's Island. But instead of devouring me in three quick moves they just stood with shoulders hunched, listening to my tirade and quivering occasionally.

Then it hit me. These guys weren't French, they were from somewhere in Eastern Europe. They couldn't understand a word I was saying, though of the overall gist of it I'm sure they couldn't be in any doubt.

But they could explain or justify nothing. Try as I might, there wasn't anything I could persuade them to do. After standing forlornly together in the rain for a while I bade them good day and went in to the dry and to the phone, determined to contact their superior.

A breakfast visit from M. Guerande (loosely translated, Mr Sea Salt)

I did try first to contact the mega corporation EDF itself but the corporate suits there washed their hands of the affair and referred me to their operative on the ground, their subcontractor. With as much concern as an abattoir boss might have for a trades union rep among the sheep, they sent me on my way.

It transpired that Slobodan and Marco worked freelance for a contractor to EDF and the boss of their enterprise was called M. Guerande. Guerande is the name of a perfectly preserved medieval walled town about a hundred kilometres to the south of here, famous for its salt flats and tangy sea salt.

I knew that nothing I could do would get back my trees. There's nothing a puny little landowner such as I could do to stop these people entering my land and cutting down anything they deem to interfere with their equipment. If it came to open dispute I'd be on my own against the might of an immovable machine. There was little if not nothing I could do. Except perhaps, to appeal to common decency.

In truth, it was now just the mess that bothered me. Twenty-one fallen trees take quite some clearing up. And then there was the indignity of the thing . . .

But when he arrived next day M. Guerande could not have been more charming. He agreed with me unreservedly. They were bears, he said, Marco and Slobodan, absolute bears . . . Ukrainian, you know, not French at all, hard workers but headstrong. He told me he'd had trouble with them before and didn't know what to do.

We consoled each other. He explained the vicissitudes of contract work and the difficulties of finding labourers with brains.

I sympathised some more and gave him more coffee. He

suggested one of his colleagues – a Frenchman, of course – might come round with a chainsaw and cut up the wood, tidying the branches. Would he like some baguette? More coffee? Some orange juice?

'Just a smidge, thank you,' he replied, between chews.

We parted friends, though I've not heard from him since. Marie condemned me as a pushover. His colleague did eventually come round and did a not very good job of tidying up the field. For days we dragged branches to a central spot, then when Joe and Charlie came round with Rozenn and Lucie, their girlfriends, we lit a big fire and had a bit of a party. Though it started low-key, it turned into a great bonfire party. We succeeded in turning an apparent disaster into a fun family reunion.

Revelling and revelations in the stars above

When it comes to what we see above us on a night walk I'm inclined to side with Thomas Carlyle. He said, 'Why did not someone teach me the constellations and make me at home in the starry heavens, which are always overhead and which I don't half know to this day?'

If Carlyle was anything like most of us his ignorance was most probably much more profound. Despite their being so enthralling, most of the rest of us don't even know a speck of what we might or should about the stars. Each night, whether we can see them or not, or choose to watch them or not, the stars above put on a display for us that far exceeds the most brilliant pyrotechnics yet conceived.

Heavens above, we must be mad to show the night sky such neglect.

Here in Kerkelven of course we are especially lucky, for the lack of competitive ambient lighting and the clear, clean air lend to the night skies a sharpness and visibility that I've only ever seen rivalled in darkest Africa.

So assuming we won't all rush out and buy Dorling and Kindersley's definitive visual guide to the heavens, unassumingly called *The Universe*, what should the casual visitor to Kerkelven know about the stars, the constellations and the sky at night?

Since the dawn of time people have seen patterns in the night sky. But this says more about the weirdness of people than about any celestial hand arranging the firmament. There are apparently 88 different constellations and almost all of them look nothing like whatever creature or deity they are meant to represent.

It was the ancient Sumerians who first charted the heavens and created the first constellations. The Greeks and Romans then took the idea and embellished and extended it to fit their own world (or heavens) view. Of course they all could only see their particular parts of the night sky and so the constellations visible from the southern hemisphere tended to be left out, to be charted much later. Nobody sees much of the myths and monsters in the constellations any more but they are still used to help us find our way around the heavens. But it's a sad fact that both the average townie and country dweller alike these days could probably only identify Orion the hunter and perhaps the plough (actually just a part of the much bigger Ursa Major constellation, the big bear) and maybe one or two others at most. A trained eye though can trace the shapes ascribed to many of the other constellations that nightly revolve above Kerkelven, such as those named after the dragon, the small bear, the lynx, the giraffe and those too of the vain Queen Cassiopeia and her husband Cepheus, King of Ethiopia, and also their daughter Andromeda who, in atonement for her mother's vanity, was to be sacrificed to a serpent but instead was saved by Perseus, rescued and whisked off to connubial bliss.

Or so they say. But as I've said, these legends have little to do with the stars above though they're quite fun if you have the patience to tie them in with the stars they were seen to represent. Cassiopeia is the distinctive 'W' shape found in the northwestern part of our sky in wintertime, its centre pointing towards the celestial pole. The stars, or perhaps galaxies, that make up Cassiopeia are called rather unimaginative names like M52 and M103, so sound more like motorways than celestial jewels. Spread above us there's also the lyre (the harp played by Orpheus), Hercules, the swan (of Leda and the swan fame), the lizard, the ram, the bull and many, many others. Plus the lovely mythical Pleiades, the seven sisters that cluster together seeming like a misty window onto another dimension, inexpressibly far, far away. Only six of the seven Pleiades are visible to the naked eye (apparently the one we can't see, the mysterious wandering star, is Merope [Mer-roe-pee], the only one of the sisters to marry a mortal). The Pleiades repay a visit with a telescope but even if you haven't got one and so can't see Merope they're still worth finding and wondering about.

I love the night sky mostly for its sheer scale, intricacy and inexpressible vastness. These stars we and our ancestors have taken for granted since time began, yet what we know of them is still infinitesimally small and the more we find out, the more insignificant we and our knowledge seem.

The night sky can be quite well seen with the naked eye (preferably two) though even binoculars will enhance the experience – however, for this you do need a steady pair of hands. For years at Kerkelven we studied the stars on and off through the multiple lenses of a cheap Russian tripod-mounted telescope. It was a huge, impressive-looking construction but an absolute bugger to find anything with. We have it still, sitting redundantly in our converted barn minus the key lens (long since broken and lost) that would be needed to convert it from so much scrap metal to a precision instrument capable of granting anyone access to the wonder of the stars.

One hundred years or so ago no one imagined that the universe could be any bigger than just our galaxy, the Milky Way (which of course we get a grandstand view of from Kerkelven). Today's astronomers can see, through the huge space telescopes they now have, that there are 100 billion other galaxies, at the very least. Given the size of your average galaxy (big) that's rather obviously far more than we'll ever need. And it seems highly likely that as time passes, as our telescopes improve yet further and as the universe (according to the Big Bang theory) expands even further, we'll probably find quite a few more galaxies even than those we know of already.

Dark eyes

There's something big out there, watching us from the depths of the darkness as we make our night walks. Its eyes fearlessly reflect the light from my torch but it keeps its flight distance and won't let me get anywhere near close. I move, it moves.

It's not likely to be a dog, for it's too consistent and too remote. A dog would run up to ours. This creature stays just outside their range of perception. It's not likely to be a cat because the eyes are too big, too high off the ground. Though I suppose we can't dismiss an escaped big cat, a puma or such like, 'the beast of Bubry' or whatever.

Now that would be exciting. It could be a Morlock, of course, but really I don't think so.

It could be an ostrich, an escapee from the new ostrich farm just up the road from here, towards Bieuzy. But I haven't heard that any of them have got out. It could even be a deer, possibly. Unlikely though, I think.

No, I guess it must be a fox, though it seems too high off the ground for that. Maybe it's the visiting alien that I've so longed for ever since I moved here, the little green man from the planet Tharg who will choose Earth for his holidays and Kerkelven for his ideal resort.

We live in hope. The original little green man from outer space was a concept coined by Cambridge scientists in 1967 when they were looking for the first pulsar. Because they thought its regular oscillations suggested intelligent origins, they bestowed upon it the identification code LGM1, which stands for 'Little Green Man'.

Well, if they are coming, the odds are they'll choose somewhere like Kerkelven. Why not?

The stench of death

As I hunch over my computer there's a horrific bang (more a 'pfouf' mixed with a sizzling sound) and a pall of smoke curls skyward, accompanied by such a smell of burning flesh as would choke Old Nick himself. Something large, juicy and now very dead has flown into one of the halogen uplighter lamps above my head, to be instantly incinerated upon the protective glass. I can't look into the bowl now, not on account of the carnage but because of the brightness of the light. So I switch off at the wall and, having found a torch, balance precariously on a swivel chair to peer into the beam of light. This illuminates the charred wings and carcass of some flying monster that made the mistake of its life when it veered into the furnace, probably just as it was lining up to attack me as I sat innocently at my desk, writing the last of this chapter for you, dear reader.

A sorry end for sure, whatever it was. But I go off for my dinner comforted in the knowledge that it was probably him or me.

Such is life and death in Kerkelven.

March

Walking the dogs, March

I'm sure the largest part of all the rain in all the world has fallen on Kerkelven and its environs these past days. We seem trapped in a permanent wetscape. A walk now is a waddle among puddles, a wade through flooded paths and by broken riverbanks. We wonder if it will ever return to the world we remember from last summer.

This weather seems to bring out the worst in some folks. Notions of politeness and propriety don't really occur to these three hounds that follow me. They're inconsiderate bargers, with no sense whatsoever that their lowly place in the scheme of things means that if there's a wet bridge to traverse or a slippery slope to climb they should patiently wait their turn, or at the very least let me go first. Not them. They just push right past, regardless. Syrus and Max are bad enough in this regard but Mortimer, with the physical characteristics of a sodden overweight grizzly bear, is a menace.

So in this season the morning walk can be a dangerous outing and I've more than once found myself swaying perilously above the abyss that stretches beneath the west bridge, or clinging desperately to outstretched branches as one or other of our ill-bred pooches barges unthinkingly past, monopolising our narrow pathways for his, or her, own selfish ends.

Last night it rained as if it was raining its last. Already overflowing with almost every metre of bank burst, the river has taken over the entire plain and at varying speeds and with seemingly increasing urgency is galloping desperately towards the big river, the Blavet, which surely must be having troubles of its own. At one time an almost invariably single annual event, this is the fourth flood this year. The green banquette (plastic, I know, but it still cost me about ten euros) at the oxbow was swept away last night, never to be seen again. It's the second such bench that I've lost in similar circumstances, proof that learning from experience is unlikely in old people. At some time in the night too the heavy wooden bridge that straddles the east burn was washed from its carefully positioned placement to be deposited a full five metres away in Bertrand's field. I can barely lift that thing, yet still I had to drag it back with no help from the three stooges. But this time I've left the bridge useless but secure on higher ground, for I fear there's worse to come from this river.

Our riverbank seems in serious need of repair now. The erosion that's normal in this season of floods is much more severe this year on account of more persistent rainfall and longer, deeper, faster-flowing floods. What the lasting effects of this damage might be are hard to tell, though I'm already collecting stones, planning to get some trailer-loads down to the riverbank if the ground ever solidifies sufficiently, which in this wet seems unlikely.

Everywhere is bleak and chill and bare. It seems the river is taking advantage of this, flexing its muscle to show who's most powerful hereabouts. All the trees in the woods appear to be leaning forward, all branches pointing downhill accusingly towards the river.

The river is flowing so fast it swirls and gurgles ceaselessly, a picture of bustling feverish turmoil surrounded by a sea of soggy inaction. Max is sloshing along ahead of me, and Syrus and Mortimer are sloshing along in the rear. Today the line between river and field is blurred indeed.

I'm worried about Mortimer. He seems very stiff and slow these mornings. Today, when as usual he followed me as I climbed the steep slope by the east burn, I heard a crashing sound behind me and turned to witness a sight that chilled my heart. Poor Mortimer had stumbled on his first attempt at the very foot of the slope. On the retry he slipped again. Now he was fairly agitated. Not so long ago he'd have bounded up this slope in three. I waited for him, knowing he wouldn't give up. Just as I was thinking we might all have to retrace our steps and go home an easier way, with a huge effort backed more by will-power than actual strength, he made it. But he looked shaken at the top of the climb, not triumphant. In truth, he looked deathly ill. Tomorrow and for the foreseeable future I may have to rethink my route.

Turning the tables

It was in the early days of March that the round stone table arrived, in the company of the three stone benches that fit neatly in a circle around it to form the intimate nest of garden furniture that so appealed when we saw them in our local garden centre but which now seem so, well . . . big. Lifting all the parts onto the trailer was easy enough because three strong men from the garden centre did the humping. Unloading it all down by the river was a lot less easy, with only Marie at hand to take their place. I had to use a whip, but she did it eventually.

Our table now can be seen from almost any part of the field. And how splendid it looks. From afar the cluster of table with chairs around looks like a fairy ring, a little gathering of giant mushrooms tucked away below the big trees in the corner of our field. Charming as it seems from a distance, the stone seats are bloody cold though, another reason to think, roll on summer. Though even in high summer, sitting on this stone can be butt-clenchingly cold.

Trees

Everyone loves trees; they make us all feel good. We depend

upon them and couldn't survive long without them. Yet I know hardly anything about trees. Even after living with the field by the river for some years my ignorance about trees was almost total – their different types, preferences, their seasons, what threatens and what sustains them. Though the tree life that surrounds me looms large, plentiful and varied, what I know about the life challenges of trees could be written on just one leaf.

So I set about learning. But I didn't aspire to know everything about trees, just what would be good to know. And spurred by my memory of that fallen tree from January, I also wanted to find out what, if anything, I could and should be doing to sustain and protect them.

Sixties pop songbird Joni Mitchell prophesied that one day they would take all the trees and 'put 'em in a tree museum', then charge the people quite a lot of money, 'just to see 'em'.

If 'they' did, I think they'd make a mint, because trees are really rather wonderful.

I doubt if at the start of my quest to learn more about this field I could have named more than two or three trees with any accuracy – the oak, of course, the different chestnuts, some of the pines and perhaps one or two of the willows. But the larch, or the ash, or the elder? Sadly, I couldn't. Shameful though this is, I sense that in this educational deficiency I'm far from alone. But how deep is this ignorance? What are we missing, and does it matter anyway?

Trees are usually portrayed as old and wise (remember Treebeard in *Lord of the Rings*). But is there a heart and soul in a tree or are these great towers merely empty? Hippies and soppy people urge us to hug a tree, but will it give anything back?

Let me spread before you some juicy tree facts.

Trees are the oldest living organisms on earth and the longest-living organisms too. So right away, they know something we don't – how to stick around longer. The world's oldest trees are bristlecone pines from northern California, which live up to 4,600 years old. There are trees in Kerkelven that have been growing here many hundreds of years. Our great oak may be more than five hundred years old. And though it's now ridiculously gnarled and decrepit it'll see me out, I'm sure.

Like plants, trees produce their own food through the process we call photosynthesis.

The inside of a tree is composed of cork, phloem, vascular cambium (which together make up the bark) and xylem. Now hold up. Though I wasn't aware all trees have it, I know what cork is, but . . . Well, phloem and xylem are the tree's two internal transport systems, while vascular cambium is a layer of fluid-carrying tissues directly under the bark, where the annual or secondary growth of the tree takes place. Phloem is the living tissue inside a tree that carries nutrients, mainly glucose and starch created during photosynthesis, to whatever parts of the tree need it. Xylem is the other transport system of a tree, it carries water and dissolved mineral nutrients from the tree's roots to the tips of its leaves, no mean task and rather important for the tree. Cork as used to stop bottles comes from the bark of the cork oak tree and not from the cork tree as is commonly supposed. The two are not related at all. It takes up to nine years before the cork oak's bark is ready to be harvested for use in our bottles and apparently the cork of no other tree will do.

The trees of Kerkelven are truly huge and varied and are all incredibly beautiful, though perhaps not always of the storybook beauty that people seem to expect of trees. Many of those you'll find in Kerkelven are quite disabled, with delightfully distorted limbs and bodies, but all the more interesting and beautiful because of it, for it makes them individuals rather than uniform clones.

It may seem soppy but I now feel I should know all our trees by name. I don't, nor do I actually talk to the trees (well, not often). I do know and love quite a few and I may indeed talk to them now I've gained a new respect for them and their kind. Though maybe it would be better if I just learned to listen better to them.

And I'm trying to get to know them better, too. If this seems odd then perhaps you've never walked daily round a place like Kerkelven and had the chance to get to know and appreciate trees. If so, I'm sorry for you. Because like so many of the living inhabitants of Kerkelven, trees repay any attempts to get closer.

But they are perplexing. Trees obviously don't have brains so must be devoid of reason. They can't think. That much, or so you'd think, is obvious. Yet if you look closely at the trees of Kerkelven you'll see that, entirely naturally, they frequently grow quite close to one another. Too close, perhaps, for healthy growth. Yet if you observe how they respond to a too-close neighbour you'll note that trees, particularly the oaks, will make sure that their big branches do not grow into the path of the dominant nearby tree. It's not that they start growing that way and then stop when they touch or sense a neighbour. It's cleverer than that. Many trees that are near another, whether of their own kind or not, will decide after they have started to grow that they will not put out branches in that direction but instead will spread out somewhere else, on another side, where there is room.

Wait a minute, did I say 'decide'? How can a tree decide anything? Yet that's what it appears to do.

The trees of Kerkelven

Many species are found here but we find just six of the main tree families are the most common. These are oak, birch, beech, chestnut, alder and poplar. So, Kerkelven is pretty typical of a north European forest. We have several types of some of these, particularly the oak, which is the dominant tree here for it outnumbers all the other species put together, by about two to one. There are 73 different types of oak tree listed in Collins *Tree Guide*, which will also tell you that there are about six thousand different species of tree in Europe alone and that anyway, the concept of 'tree' is itself a vague one. They also point out that tree watching is an engrossing but under-subscribed hobby and that trees are often overlooked. Having now taken a closer look at trees, I'm inclined to agree. It's a shame.

In addition to the six most common trees, above, we also have several huge maritime pines, some Douglas firs, majestic willows and great Spanish chestnuts. We are lucky.

Apple trees and the water of life

We have a few apple trees in Kerkelven too, about forty or so, and several pear trees, most of these in our small field, just north of the house. As all our fruit trees were planted some years back by either Bertrand or Mathurin, perhaps they don't count, because like us they're introductions to Kerkelven, not natives. They too seem to be thriving, all the same, but their crops, though big on volume, are often not much to write home about quality-wise. The leaves of apple trees are smooth on top but woolly on the underside. Apples here are used widely for home-made cider and for the two other staple drinks of the Breton peasant, *pommeau* and *eau de vie*. *Pommeau* is brewed to about the strength of sherry whereas, despite its optimistic name, *eau de vie* can be lethal, so far above proof spirit that after even a couple of sips you're past caring.

At certain preordained times local growers here still routinely take their fermented apples along in big vats to the village square, where the itinerant local still – a clunky multi-funnelled contraption on big old cartwheels – will have been parked for the purpose. This mobile antique liquor still will be serviced by an equally clunky ancient Breton who will crouch down behind it and, after much puffing and wheezing, will deliver from one or other of the many tubes around a stream of almost pure spirit of a high alcoholic content.

Then, feeling better at having thus relieved himself, at your request he'll draw off your by-now properly distilled liquor from the tap inside his still and in return for a few euros will give it to you, ready for bottling and drinking. This legal still is only for those above a certain age (must be past sixty now), who by law are entitled to make the *eau de vie*, the water of life.

Eau de vie is highly prized in these parts. At the peak of every celebration, fête or any good excuse for a booze-up it is inevitably brought out. And these are many. It is ferocious stuff, a clear, syrupy, innocuous-looking liquid that is really anything but. It's invariably kept in murky bottles of great vintage whose tattered fading labels indicate they once held mystic libations such as Noilly Prat or Isolabella. Much of the eau de vie given me by the kind and generous Bertrand was made by him in his back room back in the 1950s, so has waited half a century or more before inflicting its revenge on this innocent immigrant and his kin. Even a small sip of eau de vie will make your eyes water and your teeth feel funny. After a few glasses you are truly beyond redemption, not least because among its many attributes this infernal liquid has powerful laxative properties, so careless imbibers risk achieving an unspeakable state. The grandparent of all hangovers follows surely and remorselessly on the heels of a night with the eau de vie.

Sex with trees – do trees have feelings?
Or put it another way, how was it for you, tree?

One thing even the most delicate of us can't ignore is that trees ejaculate. As I walk along in this early spring their spores fill the air around me, drifting, gliding, slowly spreading everywhere around. It seems rather unfair if trees can ejaculate so exuberantly yet cannot enjoy the feeling.

Trees stop growing in late autumn, becoming dormant through a process not quite like hibernation but not a lot unlike it either. This is when they start to lose their leaves. As it gets colder the danger for trees isn't so much from freezing as from the lack of moisture getting to the tree, which often happens when the soil is frozen. Because tree growth is competitive, young trees devote all their energies into growing, which is why trees don't seed until they're several years old.

I should have paid more attention to biology lessons at school but, after the human reproduction bits, it all seemed rather dull. How I've come to regret that! Preposterously ignorant though this may make me seem, I've just learned that trees can be either male or female. Not all though. Most trees are monoecious, i.e. they have in themselves all they need to propagate on their own. But some trees, for instance holly and willows, are very definitely either male or female.

Inevitably, this invites me to ask some further questions.

There is indeed, I find, a term for people who like to have physical sexual relations with trees. They're known as arborphiliacs. I suspect they'll also be called some less endearing names in some places, but here in the land of the tolerant, we're cool. There is even a support group (which encourages rather than commiserates). I doubt though if arborphilia is ever legal as anything other than wishful thinking, as almost invariably any actual union would have to take place in public. Anyone seen making improper advances towards Kerkelven's trees will be shot.

Gruesome growths

Not all of the plant life around Kerkelven is benign. Holly, though revered for centuries as a symbol of resurrection and eternal life, produces violent bouts of vomiting if eaten. In the past its sick-inducing qualities have led to it being used as a purgative, to help poor unfortunates who've eaten something even more toxic than holly to get the poison out of their system. Holly is also reputed to act as a lightning conductor, so while lucky to carry, maybe is less lucky in bad weather.

Wolfsbane is handy to have in a crisis for it can prevent the change from human to werewolf, in the event of an unexpected bite of the wrong kind (I'm not sure if there is a right kind of bite, but some are worse than others). Its bell-shaped purple flower can still be seen throughout Europe, though it was much more common in the Middle Ages when it was used as a powerful poison. Wolfsbane gets its name from when, mixed with a concoction of powdered glass, caustic lime and honey (the sweetener), it was smeared on rotting meat and used to poison wolves and foxes. Wolfsbane attacks the nervous system, disrupting the heart rate and breathing. Death is evidently quick. The Chinese used wolfsbane back in the fifth century as the world's earliest recorded chemical weapon.

Belladonna, also known as deadly nightshade, has dull green leaves and bell-shaped flowers with black shiny berries and is found in dark moist corners of the forest. Laden with toxic and hallucinogenic chemicals, belladonna was the poison of choice in Renaissance Italy because back then it was cheap, effective and readily available. It still is. The root of the plant is the most toxic, though its star-shaped berries can also be fatal. However, deer and other forest animals seem able to eat its leaves with impunity. These leaves have a coarse texture and can cause pustular eruptions in sensitive skin. In fact you might wish to give belladonna a wide berth. Symptoms of belladonna poisoning include dilated pupils, rapid heartbeat, hallucinations, blurred vision, loss of balance, a feeling of flight, staggering, a sense of suffocation, paleness followed by a red rash, flushing, husky voice, extremely dry throat, constipation, urinary retention, and confusion. The skin can completely dry out and fall off. Fatal cases have a rapid pulse that turns feeble. There are chemical antidotes, though these may not always be easy to find in the depths of the countryside. So should you think you've spotted it, best to walk quickly round it.

Unfortunately there are a large number of plants and even a few trees that are poisonous to the human species and I've only listed a few of the most deadly. The berries of the yew tree produce taxin, a toxic alkaloid which has featured in Agatha Christie's murder stories and for which there is no known antidote. But rhubarb can kill too, if you eat the leaves, as can hyacinth, narcissus and daffodil bulbs, oleander, rosary peas, castor beans, rhododendrons, laurels, jasmine berries, red sage, wild cherries and even mistletoe (so no open-mouthed kissing under it, or you'll only have yourself to blame). Elephant's ear can also prove fatal, but I'd have thought that obvious, particularly if you eat both ears at once. We have rhubarb growing wild here and daffodils and quite a few of the others too.

Spring in the air and all around

Spring starts here, now! How quickly things can change, and how totally. The transformation happened literally overnight. This is a different world, as far from the grey, chilly gloom of winter as could be. The sun has got his hat on, the birds are riz and spring, it seems, is sprung.

Of course spring is the season of love. At this time of our year we four – Mortimer, the other two and me – should be walking with heads held high and eyes skywards for fear of being distracted and even depraved by all the procreational activities that will inevitably be going on all around us. For this is the season for mating, of planning for birth and rebirth. Having each been 'treated' by the vet, Mortimer, Syrus and even Max are of course naive and innocent of such goings-on, so I try to keep their minds on higher things, with the risk that in this month they'll observe even less than usual from their surroundings.

I've just heard the first cuckoo. The blackthorns are all in bloom, spreading brilliant white across the greening valley as the browns and greys of winter give way to the bright new colour scheme that comes with spring.

To be truthful, spring has been in the air since January, thanks to the generally mild weather, but this year nature has really seemed to be having difficulty making her mind up. I can't recall a time when cold and warm interchanged so rapidly or so often. It's not unpleasant, but may be a bad sign for at least some of the creatures of Kerkelven.

But now spring is fairly exploding all over. The saying 'spring is in the air' of course means this is the mating season. It isn't the work of many seconds to establish that this applies in spades to almost all the natives of Kerkelven (at least, those that inhabit the field by the river).

Gone are the winter winds, the gloomy storms and wild wet days of winter. Spring is here. Look around and love is everywhere. Or if not love, procreation and pairing, an animal version of love and marriage. The instinct to spread the genes may be universal and irresistible, but for sure it's also undeniably enjoyable. On every branch in every tree by every brook and path and hill, they're all at it. Butterflies are at it. Birds and bees are at it. Frogs are spawning and newts are doing what newts do (not just getting drunk, I assure you). Insects until recently unseen now are everywhere and though it's hard to be sure quite what they're up to, you can bet your last penny that for much of the time they too are at it like knives.

There's no better vision of the joys of spring than in the pairings of butterflies dancing in the spring sunshine or in the aerial acrobatics of a pair of nesting tits or finches. And Kerkelven on a sunny March day is the place to come to see them.

There's a pair of grey wagtails bouncing along the riverbank just now, seemingly very much in love. Their exuberant pirouettings would be hard to top, I'm sure.

The plain fact is, at this time of year Mother Nature is at it, morning noon and night.

Love at first and every sight

This is the season of first sights, when we begin to see clear signs that winter is over and summer's on the way. Having spotted the first butterfly earlier in the month, now we're awash with them, shimmering through the trees in white, grey, blue-black and red. The pond-skaters are suddenly busy skating hither and thither across the water or, heads down, facing upstream, struggling to stand still and not slide backwards.

The delicate wild flowers begin to burst out and soon there are little bloomers all over the place. Frogspawn begins to bob up in corners of ponds. And the buzzards appear in the sky once more, a sure sign of better weather on the way.

We've also discovered that thousands upon thousands of tiny little fishes have invaded the newly dug trenches of our drainage canals. These of course are full to their tops with water and weeds that clearly provide an ideal environment within which little tiddlers can flourish. Perhaps we'll see the renaissance of our fish populations yet.

As I sat down one sunny, soft spring morning

Brooks really do babble. For a complete change I've decided mid-walk to sit down on the bridge over the west burn, somewhere I've never thought to sit before. But it just happens to be in the full sun now (itself a welcome rarity) and I can dangle my welly-booted legs above the flowing stream, not in it but nearly, which is fun. It's rather comfortable, truth be told. Now I can't think why I've never thought to do this before.

As I sit the sheer pleasure of what I'm doing grows on me. The burn really does make the most soporific sound. Mortimer nosed about me irritatingly for a while but encouraged by a few none too gentle shoves he's taken the hint and wandered off. The other two are blissfully rooting around for field mice, oblivious of anything else. It's quiet and peaceful save for the buzz of the fast-flowing waters and the songs of rather a large number of exuberant birds. The Champs Élyseés might have less traffic at this hour, though it would be nowhere near so pleasant.

Gradually the banks of the burn seem to come alive. Little beetles start to grub about and some not usually welcome flies put in an appearance. A pair of bright-red butterflies flutter by in a dance of thrilling complexity, if seemingly aimless in direction. A gang of hoverflies pause in midair before shooting off in different directions. The day is heating up and the field is buzzing now, winter a distant memory. To be honest I'm struggling to resist the somnolent effects of the stream's lullaby and the surprising warmth in the early morning sunshine. I could just stretch out here and grab a few minutes of grateful slumber.

Then a little red and black beetle alights on my arm. He's a real stunner with lively, waggly antennae, a cute pointy snout and a really interested air about him. His body is shaped like an upturned boat, his back is the deepest blood red and flat, lozenge-like of shape with a single white spot in the centre, two-thirds down. Above it are two black blotches that look a bit like eyes and with the white dot of a mouth the whole of the animal seems from above like some grotesque mask. I've heard that some insects and moths can adopt a pattern on their bodies that resembles a horrific creature and thus scare off predators. Surely this is just evolution's wise precaution. But in this instance, the face is quite human in aspect, not insect-like at all. How can a little chap like this, a beetle known as a firebug (though I don't know how he got that name, for he doesn't glow in the dark like his cousin the firefly), know to fashion such a scarecrow? And what's more, this particular face looks uncannily like Philip Schofield, the television presenter. How spooky is that?

The firebug is a pretty little bug also known as a cotton stainer, apparently because he loves cotton and when the harvester comes along he and thousands of his little buddies get caught up and crushed, leaving unappealing stains on the newly threshed cotton. Sad though this sounds it probably delighted cotton growers in America's Deep South as these little blighters damage the cotton when they eat it. But as we have no cotton here, this one's safe for the time being at least.

I stretch out a bit, more than happy. A big, busy bumblebee tumbles by on some serious errand, or so her demeanour suggests. A huge buzzard swoops low enough for me to see the gleam in his eye but he's not interested in us so grabs the first upwards eddy and swirls off skywards. Some ducks fly up from the river in the distance and I regret that I need to get going.

But what the hell? Another ten minutes won't hurt. What could be more important?

Eventually as I get up to go I find an empty plastic Canada Dry bottle in the underbrush; goodness knows how it got there, but there it is.

Momentarily I imagine what a pleasure it would be to sail this bottle downstream and watch it bob and spin and weave its way to the river, then to wave it off as it gathers momentum, racing towards its presumably uninterrupted but eventful

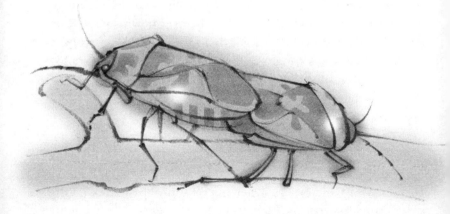

passage to the sea. But I know how naughty that pleasure would be, so I take it home for the recycling bin.

Birdsong and dance

Birds seem to live life with great enthusiasm. They rise early, well before dawn, and seem to be feverishly on the go for most of the morning. There's a curious lull starting around lunchtime and into late afternoon – siesta perhaps – then they're off again, perhaps less of them and with less vigour, until dusk when presumably they go to bed promptly so as to be ready for the next day's early start.

Unsurprisingly it's only the songbirds – wrens, robins, tits, finches, thrushes, blackbirds and the like – that sing to any great degree. Birds sing to communicate and, beautiful though their warbles may be to us, to other birds their songs contain just two main messages. 'Come here', as in their mating calls, which in effect are just their way of saying, 'Hello, dearie, want to be a naughty boy then?' – and 'Go away', as in 'This is my territory and any other bird who fancies it can just sod off'.

It's early morning here and, oh boy, the birds are up and at it now, darting hither and thither in pairs, in fours, sometimes in larger groups and occasionally as solitary singletons. The mating preamble is now in full swing and the bluetits particularly are a delight to watch. Today one female seems to be putting three suitors through their paces. They have to keep up as she exuberantly flits from tree to tree, twisting and dancing and backtracking at breakneck speed. I'm not sure how the winner is decided, but judging by the energy they put into it, the prize must be worthy of effort.

Birdsong and bird calls are quite different. Chaffinches and great tits have a wide repertoire of calls to convince other birds that there are lots of them so their territory is particularly well defended. Some birds (well, the grasshopper warbler, particularly) can even throw their voice, to give other birds the impression that they're mob-handed.

Spring is the season for the dawn chorus, the birds' battle of the songs. Longer, brighter days trigger a chemical reaction in these wee songsters that gets their testosterone rising and their melatonin falling, setting off the surge of sexual activity in birds that mankind has remarked upon since way back.

I suppose this is a good enough reason to sing, if anything is. Though I wasn't aware that there needs to be one, dawn is apparently the best time for mating because, for birds, it's not the best time for feeding or doing anything else, except singing.

We have hundreds upon hundreds of birds in our wood and in the trees and fields around. I've tried to count them but it's hopeless. Best guess would be, oh, zillions. I estimate two or three hundred are in the woods at any time, mostly staying fairly still and singing. But there are some constantly on the move. Every so often I find a convenient spot in the forest or by the river just to sit and watch and listen. Though I may not always advance my knowledge of these tiny timid neighbours it's always time well spent. To be honest I look up my bevy of bird books and they tell me things like, 'Birds are warm-blooded egg-laying vertebrates characterised by feathers and forelimbs modified as wings.' Better to watch and learn for myself, I feel.

It is also the season for scuttling in the eaves. This is not, as it might sound, a sexual peccadillo. (I well remember Rambling Sid from the classic Sunday afternoon radio show *Round the Horn* luridly describing some doubtful goings-on as 'back scuttling in the cabbages'. This conjured up vivid adolescent images for me, helping not at all my early appreciation of matters of a sexual nature.) But this scuttling is the distinctive sound, rather unsettling to townies, that's made by birds flitting in and out of the thatch in our barn by way of the tiny holes and entry points they have picked out of the eaves. Marie thinks it's rats or bats, but I'm sure she's wrong. At least, I hope she is. The noise though is amplified by the confined spaces in the thatch, so whatever they are, they sound more like sheep.

There's a pair of mallard ducks getting ready to nest upon the big pond we know as the *étang*. In their perfect harmony and devotion one to the other they're very endearing. Though I now realise their nervousness, so tiptoe by each morning hoping not to disturb them, I have, I confess, startled them more than once and always their quirky performance is the same. They sense something isn't right and look each to the other for guidance. It's almost as if they're saying, 'After you, sweetness.' 'No, after you, *cherie*.' 'No, no, dear heart, after . . . ' and they paddle gently in circles looking searchingly at each other, emphasising their togetherness, that they're not individuals but each just one half of a perfectly united pair. Then, as if on a signal (I think this comes first from the female, presumably well irritated by the male's deferential nonsense), they shoot off at a low angle with much splashing and squawking, then they wheel round like two lumbering bombers and corkscrew slowly off towards the river, not quite arm in arm, but as close to flying united as ducks can get.

Anyone coming along with a gun could shoot them rather easily. But it would be a dastardly, diabolical crime.

Knock on wood

Today I saw my first ever live woodpecker. I found a green woodpecker dead in a ditch once, in England. I vividly remember this dark discovery as he was so perfect, not a mark on him, with no visible sign of whatever it was that caused his death. But I've often heard these characters over by Bertrand's wood, tap-tap-tapping away on whichever tree they've secreted themselves in, staying mysteriously out of sight whenever I went looking for them. They seem to like the pine trees and if their tapping is to be interpreted as an accurate sign of where they are, they've made their home in Bertrand's biggest, which is found at the far side of his sheep pen.

The one I saw, I'm pretty sure, was a great-spotted woodpecker also known as the pied woodpecker. Although, irritatingly, I didn't see the telltale red marks on his head and underbelly. It might have been a female, of course. She has no red nape patch.

He, or she, is a strikingly handsome bird. And since that sighting I've spotted his smaller cousin, the aptly named lesser-spotted woodpecker who is not much bigger than a sparrow. As so often in nature, the male is more handsomely adorned than the female, with a bright-red crest where she just has a dull old ordinary bird head. Apparently these little chipper chaps creep along branches and scuttle up tree trunks. They fly with an undulating motion and their call is a sort of 'pee pee pee' sound.

Woodpeckers are distinctive birds quite different from other species, not just in their capacity to drill into solid wood so they can wheek out grubs and insects, but also because of the bizarre and frankly rather unsettling nature of their tongues. These birds are apparently very good listeners, so they can detect the minute sounds of grubs scurrying away when they've begun their tap-tap-tapping. Because of its function as a living hammer the woodpecker's skull is so constructed that its brain can't move as it hammers (makes sense – could otherwise be harmful, I guess).

Remarkable, yes. But the tongue thing is really seriously weird, apparently so weird that creationists have cited the woodpecker as a creature that could not have evolved, because its tongue is so complex. I'm not sure what this is evidence of, except that there are few things more weird than a creationist.

A woodpecker's tongue may be one of these. It is barbed for snapping up little insects and has to be quite long so that it can poke into the narrow but long tracks and tunnels that wood-boring insects make in tree bark. In some species, this tongue is more than three times longer than the bird's beak.

So given the tightly packed head thing, where does this long barbed tongue go, when Woody the woodpecker isn't using it?

Simple. He coils it round his head and sticks the end up one of his nostrils. What else? The tongue leaves the skull from the woodpecker's right nostril, passes between his eyes on the outside of his skull and continues over the top of his head. This amazing and clearly very flexible tongue then goes behind the skull where it splits into two halves passing on opposite sides of the neck. The halves rejoin beneath the jaw where both tongue and bone enter the bill through the soft tissue of the lower jaw.

So there you have it. Isn't nature wonderful? I thought you'd like that.

Bird eats tree

I've been watching closely a pair of bluetits as they flit about in one of our oak trees in the late afternoon. The thing is they don't just perch in trees and flutter about their branches, they don't just sleep in them, or make nests therein to raise their clutches. Amazingly, they actually eat the trees on which they sit. These two that I've been watching certainly seem to and it isn't just a sudden binge snacking or occasional bite in passing. As far as I can see they've been nibbling at it most of the afternoon and on and off for some days now. Surprisingly the tree seems none the worse for wear. These are, I suppose, quite small birds, but had they been wood pigeons I reckon the little oak tree might have been eaten up all together.

I'm guessing this is a seasonal thing, that as spring is here there's some tasty sap about or as leaves begin to bud there's something around the places they spring from that makes a tasty snack for tiny tits. Perhaps there's some insect there that's so tiny I can't see it.

Birds' nests

An enterprising bird that I've often spotted here is the long-tailed tit. This little beauty each year builds intricate domed nests using copious quantities of spiders' webs, mosses and feathers.

These bird nests must be beautifully warm, lined as they are with so much webbing and often many hundreds of feathers in a single nest. As well as twigs, debris and feathers many species of bird use spiders' webs in a variety of fascinating ways when building their nests. It is of course a very versatile material, surprisingly strong, pliable and warm.

Despite their prevalence, habitats for bird species are disappearing and there are fewer places where birds can nest safely. I see no evidence of this in Kerkelven but realise I have a duty to understand their needs and could possibly do more to encourage nesting here.

Birds have many predators, so nest siting and construction is crucial to survival. Most birds don't nest in colonies but in pairs, so they'll hope to find a spot that's secure, well protected and not easy to reach. Given the unstoppable encroachment of civilisation upon bird habitats everywhere, perhaps the most important event ever for garden birds was back in the nineteenth century when a German, Baron von Berlepsh (no, I'm not making this up) invented his nest box, a small wooden box with a simple entrance hole. To my mind, inventions don't get much more brilliant than that.

Each year our letterbox is neatly fitted out with mosses and grasses by a pair of kindly but forgetful robins who start to build their nest in the box then, evidently realising it's in daily use by various people, decide to move elsewhere. Still, it keeps our correspondence warm and is nice in another way too. It shows that even when there are naturally plenty of options for safe nesting, some species are still not averse to choosing a site built by humans.

Frostie's back

Once again the whole aspect of spring changes as a sudden frost blankets Kerkelven. I can't help but worry about the lizards, so freshly appeared from their winter sleep, particularly the green speckled ones which are so much more delicate than their hardy brown but much smaller cousins. Until today they've been basking happily in the morning sun on our garden walls. It must be hard for them to know quite what to do.

It may be little compensation for lizards but the sky is particularly wonderful just now on account, I'm sure, of the unexpected cold. Despite the chill there's sun all day and the graduation of blues from palest almost grey to deep sky-blue has to be seen. As night falls the edges of the sky become ice-blue with grey and red streaks turning to sapphire at the centre. Until the sky darkens and stars start to come out, the planet Saturn is the only visible object in the western sky, shining brightly and rising a little higher each night.

It's March and love is in the air

There's no getting away from it. Love is all around now and discreet it isn't. We can't ignore it, for it's everywhere.

When do they start? I mean, at what time in their lives do the creatures of field and forest become sexually active? I suspect it's indecently early. Stripped of all pretensions of modesty and reserve, I suspect everything in nature, when it's not about eating or being eaten, is all about shagging with abandon. But disappointingly I find most references on animal behaviour suggest this isn't so. For most creatures, it seems, the sexual act is purely functional, a commandment from the genes, an instinct to be obeyed rather than enjoyed. But as I look around me at the mating frenzy that's engulfing Kerkelven right now, I find that rather hard to swallow.

Butterflies, apparently, look to mate within seconds of their creation. Female snakes, on the other hand, make love but once every two years. Many creatures pair for life and can be easily seen enjoying enthusiastic pairing rituals. But others go through elaborate courtships even when no actual copulation needs to take place. Yet others do their fertilising when their partner is no longer around. Even in lovemaking, things at Kerkelven are seldom as straightforward as they seem.

The birds and the bees

That the sex act is important to our kind can be measured by the huge number of words in our language that graphically describe it. Making love, shagging, tupping, screwing, rogering, fucking, nobbing, having it off . . . These merely caress the tip of a proverbial iceberg. Whatever it's called, it's universal and pretty damned important. So we're not likely to ignore it in any half-decent account of the goings-on at Kerkelven.

However, this isn't really the place for a detailed account of all the procreational activities going on now in our field simply because we haven't got time. If I were to even attempt to describe the hotbed of activity that's all around we'd be here for a month of Sundays.

So, enough said. It's the time when they're all at it and, though not all may be enjoying it, as far as I can see, most are. About 99.8 per cent, I'd say.

Death floats downstream

I have another cold. Cold germs seem to like me, so linger longer than is decent. Mid-March, and the weather is just delightful. Misty early mornings quickly give way to crisp, clear, sun-bathed days. It's perfection, except for a mini-iceberg that's just floated serenely past. About three foot long and just as wide, it's composed of foamy scum, evidence of run-off from some chemical dumped on the soil by an upstream neighbour without a care or even a thought for the consequences he inflicts upon a downstream fellow landowner whom he (most likely a he) almost certainly has never seen. That's our world today.

Corralled by a long, semi-submerged log, the accumulations of slimy scum can be substantial and at times it takes on frightening forms. There's a vast pool of it now at the river's edge below the last cataract that looks like nothing so much as a white shroud cast carelessly over a floating corpse. As I watch it shimmers, as if there's something restless underneath.

River pollution is endemic in this season. Mostly its only visible sign is that the river looks as if someone's dumped washing-up water in it. Except, there's rather a lot of it. Then it gathers and grows, accumulating in the eddies and snag-spots into great floating islands of suds and scum until fresh rain or even flood flushes it through. Perhaps the river can cope with this, perhaps in the long run it can't. The effects may be more insidious and long term than they seem. For the moment, I just don't know.

Turd golf

As we walk, the dogs scamper ahead until after only a few moments their natural functions kick in and they stop for a poo. Usually, we haven't got further than the big pond, down the shared road. If I'm honest I secretly hope they'll go to the right of the path and poo on Emile's side, though I've never given in to the temptation to actually train them to poo on my neighbour's land. I am civilised, after all.

Well, most of the time. However much I try to encourage them to do their natural business in discreet places they seem to delight in making their defecations as public as possible, usually depositing their disgusting emissions in the middle of one or other of my carefully trimmed footpaths.

In the mornings I take along a stick to help me deal with this problem. To be quite honest I have to confess that I've gotten rather good at disposing of their more solid deliveries with a carefully developed golf swing. If my swing is true and the solidity and consistency of 'the ball' are right I can sometimes whack the little blighters without slicing or hooking, straight down three or four metres into the woods, which might play havoc with the sparrows and chaffinches perched on the lower branches but is very satisfying indeed for me.

And it keeps the pathways of Kerkelven pure and sweet for small children to play upon in total safety.

I think I'll have to work on my handicap though.

Perhaps the solution to this small but practical problem is for me to carry a plastic bag and a pooper-scooper on our walks.

But the thought of me running in three directions with weighty bags of foul excrement flapping at my side has limited appeal, I have to say. If I were, say, to meet a French neighbour on my path, how would I explain what I was carrying?

Late outing

Like his kennel-mates, Mortimer loves being driven around in the car. So, troubled by his seemingly sudden onset of frailty, this late March afternoon I did something unexpected. Leaving his two buddies looking rather forlorn I took Mortimer alone into the back of the car and drove him down to the riverbank so we could spend a little quality time together, just the two of us.

The novelty and excitement of the moment seemed to give my big hairy friend a new spring in his step. The sun was low across the tree line in front of us but very bright as we walked slowly over to the stone seat, intending just to have a quiet sit and a think. We sat together thus, silent but content, like lovers on a park bench, for quite some minutes. Time slowed. It may have been wishful thinking but Mortimer seemed to be loving this. As the sun sank slowly the long shadows of the forest seeped gently down the slope to surround us. It was a perfect moment in a glorious day, but as Mort rested his head trustingly in my lap, obviously as content as content could be, I shivered as an involuntary anxiety for the future spread through me. Mortimer looked up, his eyes wet and bright. Only the present touches him, I thought, but though for sure I don't know what's coming, I can guess. And fear.

April

An astronomer's delight

As these early spring evenings fade into night they produce the kind of sky that compels painters to come from afar to Brittany in the hope of capturing on canvas the intensity of light, shade and colour that is a Breton end of day. It's the unique clarity of the air that does it, that and the splendour of the sunsets, plus the spectacular cloud formations, the seeming absence of air pollution and of course, some special magical ingredient known only to the Bretons, if known at all. Star-watchers too must find this a great place to be, particularly at this time of year. Parents worried about the cost of games systems for their little darlings might be advised to buy them a decent telescope instead and to point their interest outwards, to the stars.

For after evening has fallen, when the sun has set so splendidly and easels, palettes and brushes have been packed away for the night, there remains something else that's worth pausing a while for and gazing upwards to see. It's the starry night sky, of course, but in particular at this time the planets above Brittany can be seen spectacularly well from Kerkelven's prairie.

Saturn at nine o'clock

Clear bright nights bring with them better opportunities for stargazing and planet-watching. This month the planet Saturn, sixth rock from the sun, has been clearly visible in the western evening sky over Kerkelven. To the naked eye it looks insignificant, a shiny dot reflecting sunlight. But through even a simple telescope the amateur astronomer can see it in detail. And it's absurdly thrilling, even though you'll not see it in quite the splendour of its reproduction in the books.

Because this is the real thing, that's what thrills. Try it if you don't believe me. Jupiter, Mars, Venus . . . they're all equally exciting when seen for the first time, for real. I'm sure the others I haven't mentioned are too – Neptune, Mercury and Uranus – so I'll keep looking because these have eluded me so far.

All the planets are very different, as well as being hugely fascinating and startling. Of course this isn't a book about planets, but the skies over Kerkelven do figure because, undeniably, the way to the planets and the stars starts just above your head.

Enthusiastic amateurs have to start somewhere. So some years back we acquired a big white Russian telescope to encourage a love of sky-watching in our sons. It was never terribly effective and was hugely difficult to manoeuvre but it was way, way cheaper than other similar gadgets and it really looked the business. It was big and heavy with a white–barrelled scope mounted on clumsy tripod feet, and the kind of sighting apparatus you might find on a high-powered sniper's rifle. By fiddling with the two hand-wheels mounted at right angles to each other you might, given time and luck, find the right part of the sky to look at.

Though it never quite became the gateway to the stars that I'd dreamed of it was still worth having, because through its lenses we gained a smashing view of the surface of the moon and, if we were very skilled, or very lucky, from time to time we'd catch a reasonable, if brief, view of the major planets.

I say brief because the sky is always moving and finding a planet for long enough to look at it took much skill and perseverance for us. Tracking distant objects smaller than these proved rather disappointing because they all look depressingly the same. Stars magnified however many times just look like stars do without the aid of a telescope, only a bit bigger.

As our Russian telescope no longer works we now rely on

binoculars, which require patience and perserverance. But stargazing is such fun even for grown-ups, I've no doubt that a new telescope will be on one or other of our shopping lists, come Christmas.

Blossom and petals

Wow! We're only a few days into April and already it's that blossom time again. If we held a competition for the best season to visit Kerkelven, the brief appearance of the blossom would be right up there.

Aside from terms of endearment that I bestow regularly on Marie and occasionally upon the dogs, 'blossom' and 'petal' have their own distinct meaning and attraction now. But like so many of the things around me, though I know what they are I really know next to nothing about them.

Blossom is the flower or mass of flowers, especially of fruit trees. These flower profusely but for a really short time. Mostly it's trees that produce fruit with stones in it that blossom – the peach, nectarine, apple and of course the lovely cherry. Blossoms are either pink or white, but all are gorgeous and if you are lucky enough to have several different types of tree all blossoming together the effect can be spectacular.

Petals are parts of the flower, as I suspect we all know. I started to look into these and found that petals are just one part of the corolla, or sterile parts of a flower, and that these divide into the tepals, which are in two parts, the sepals and the petals. At about this point I lost the will to live and decided to leave it there. This isn't at all because I don't believe that such things as perianths, merosity, calyx tubes, eudicots and dicots have the potential to be hugely fascinating, even for the amateur. It's just that with all the variety of great stuff that's around in Kerkelven I think I'll have to leave such detail to works other than mine. We all know what petals are and the other parts of flowers, the bits we can't see, are best left to the serious enthusiast.

But petals are lovely, particularly when cast upon your pillow.

Things from the black stuff

Our pond now is a thick black soup, with the consistency of liquid mud and the appearance of sump oil. In its depths lurk many of the strange, wonderful things that habitually thrive at the bottom of ponds. Though I've yet to find any politicians.

One day I will get round to properly aerating the pond and ensuring it is kept clear as a good pond should be. Until then I'm reluctant to rummage in the bottom of it for fear of disturbing what's down there. One November some years back, while trying to clear fallen leaves, I inadvertently upset what I took to be at least a queen newt, if not a king. It was huge! At first I thought it must be a Spanish ribbed, Europe's largest newt, but they don't come this far north. So I reckon it must have been a great crested newt. These dark-brown almost black reptiles have yellow or orange underbellies with black and white blotches and a silvery strip along their tail. The males have a jagged crest on their backs so I reckon the one I found was a big old boy.

I dredged him up from the depths wrapped in a ball of fetid decaying matter. He was about five inches long and twice as thick as my thumb with big, watery, baleful eyes that fixed on me accusingly as if to say, 'Who are you, who dares to disturb my slumber, in the depths?'

I promptly returned him, after just a cursory examination, as close as I could to his muddy abode and haven't seen him or another like him since.

But that doesn't mean he isn't still down there, lurking.

We also have lots of other, much smaller common newts, called variously, smooth, spotted, warty and palmate, so named because apparently it has webbed feet (don't ask me). They sound more like four of the seven dwarfs.

Newts have four finger-like toes on their front legs and five on their back legs, which sounds ordinary enough, but in other ways newts are the stuff of wildest science fiction. They're amazing particularly because they can regrow most of their body parts at will. They're the only animal that can grow a new eye lens if one is injured or detached. At will, they can grow new legs, tails, jaws and even, apparently, sections of their heart. No other creature can do this half as well. So why and how did they learn such a bizarre ability?

What really bothers me though, is how did they get here? We only dug this pond a few years back, filled it with tap water and left it be. Now it's positively heaving with strange life forms. Where do they come from?

Newts share our pond with a variety of equally weird aquatic characters, particularly the larvae of dragonflies, which pound for pound must be the most fearsome-looking creatures in Kerkelven, resembling nothing so much as the gruesome gargoyles from the nearby church of Saint Nicodème, come to life.

Nightlife for pondlife

You'd be forgiven for thinking that few environments could be less stimulating for rampant libidos than the sludgy morass that is in our pond, but oh no, you've underestimated the passionate party spirit of frog and his friends. As evening falls, from the soupy depths there vibrates a throaty, pulse-like beat. At dusk and into the night they make all sorts of wicked noises too, masking some pretty steamy goings-on. Crickets provide the backing long into the night, supported by the buzzings of various night creatures coming and going, up, down and sideways. Before long frogspawn and toadspawn are floating around all over the place, being fertilised left and right by the males of the species. The newts, dragonfly larvae, grubs and other creatures of the black lagoon that lurk below, all sway to the same jungle music.

Ponds as nature intends them are nothing if not throbbing. If you're in search of a swinging nightspot where anything goes, this is it.

The published works for budding naturalists tend generally to be pretty coy about the business of reproduction, in terms of their detailed descriptions of what field creatures actually do when they get down and dirty. Or are there unexpurgated under-the-counter editions of *Country Walks* or *Hedgerows* that I just haven't been offered as yet?

There are three groups of amphibians: frogs and toads, newts and salamanders, and a third much less well-known group called caecilians, legless burrowing types that live perpetually underground and are rarely seen. They look like snakes or worms, but aren't.

The big hop

Who'd be a frog in the land where frogs' legs is a much-sought-after delicacy? Life is tough enough on frogs, particularly in France. They have many predators and few friends. If that were not bad enough, each year the amorous frog has a further ordeal to undergo, purely caused by his animal urges, the irresistible call that must be answered by all frogs and similar amphibians, to go a-wooing in the season of love.

Each year, every year, on a warm damp night in early

spring – usually a rainy, stormy, unsettled night – the frogs and toads in Kerkelven and presumably across Brittany and the whole of France all set off on a long and dangerous march back to where they were born. This is the annual phenomenon known as frog and toad migration, the long hike of the frogs and the toads, an odyssey to rival the long march of the Chinese people led by Mao Tse Tung, or even the night of the living dead. The frogs set off first, sometimes as early as February, and usually they have less far to go, simply because their range is shorter. Toads, with further to go, take longer to get there but may have more fun when they arrive.

The true explanation for this incredible journey is charming. Frogs and toads are homers and as their mating season begins the randy sods hop it back to the pond or lake where they themselves were spawned in the hope of getting a bit of frog's leg-over and starting the old re-creation process themselves. Somehow, whatever signal sets off the start of their happy season reaches all the frogs or toads at the same time and it's a call they can't help but obey. So, negotiating gates, climbing walls and swimming ditches, they all set off on their march home, usually in the early morning or through the night. As roads crisscross their ancient routes it isn't long before they're all on one or other of the many tarmac-covered highways we've so conveniently provided across their countryside.

Sadly many if not most of these amorous amphibians don't make it and end up squished flat on the road.

But they are a stirring sight to see as in a body they stride forward boldly to fulfil their sexual destiny or die in the attempt. Amid the rain and the wind and the storm, broken branches strewn across the winding rural roads, these plucky lovers strike out for home in a spectacle that would move the hardest of hearts. I've seen them from my motorbike as I've set off early to catch a ferry home myself. Despite their optimistic aspirations as they set off predawn, by the time I get past Pontivy it's just roadkill all over the place with flattened bodies every fifty metres or so. Our amphibian friends pay a heavy price for sharing this place with us.

God of the frogs and toads

It's mid-April and today I had my first swim of the season in our swimming pool. As I was cleaning it yesterday I was upset to find two frogs in the underground box which holds the mechanisms – filter, pump and so on – that keep my pool fresh and functioning. It's about five feet deep and packed with crisscrossing pipes, wires and other pool-type paraphernalia all kept securely under a plastic lid about a metre square, at ground level. As the pool was still covered, quite how these two little chaps got in there I've no idea. But as soon as I lifted the lid, there they were, looking up rather longingly. They couldn't have been there long I'm sure, for what would they eat?

I feel badly about the pool's unintended toll on the wildlife of Kerkelven so do all I can to rectify matters. I had a brainwave. Taking the head off one of the long-handled pool-cleaning brushes I attached to its pole (by whipping, a technique learned from *300 Things a Bright Boy Can Do*) the handle of a silver gravy ladle borrowed from our kitchen. With this I had a very effective ladle on the end of a nearly two metres long handle.

In the last three days, with this device, I've saved three toads and one frog (all different individuals, it's not hard to tell them apart) from a fate worse than death, at the bottom of this pit.

Each time their plight has been the same. Now that it's open they've fallen or jumped into our swimming pool and so have been swept via the circulating water system into the skimmer, which deposits them onto a ledge above the filter. There they can chose a quick and watery end by plunging into the filter or they can cling to life a bit longer and take their chances at the bottom of the box, from which there is no escape, at least, not if you're a frog or toad. The convex floor means they can swim around a bit at the bottom then climb up onto higher, dryer ground, where their only option is to await a slow lingering death from starvation.

But the ultimate power on high has other plans.

Preceded by scraping, clanking and the dramatic lifting of the lid far, far above them, a huge friendly face appears, looming large in the blinding light, with a long white pool pole, which has fixed securely to it a gravy ladle.

They must think me a divine saviour, God-on-high. I imagine they see me as an all-powerful deity who cares for small creatures so rescues his pitiful subjects from the hellish pit into which they've fallen.

What other explanation could they conceive?

However saviour-like I might be feeling it's still difficult to manoeuvre the pole with ladle attached amid all the pipes and wires that combine to block easy access from above to the floor below, where sits the wretched sullen toad or hapless frog, awaiting the fickle hand of fate.

The first time I tried this device it was near the end of the day. Getting the pole into position to catch a wriggly form initially proved beyond my ability. The light was failing fast so I borrowed one of our sheets and draped it down into the hole, hoping the frogs would be smart enough to use it to climb out. I might as well have hoped they'd also bring the sheet up with them when they'd finished, make the beds and tidy the spare room.

Next morning the sheet was still there and so were the frogs, at least one of them was, sitting looking forlorn on the raised bit in the middle around which flowed the waters of a fairly effective moat. In slightly better light I set about trying again with the long-handled ladle. With much difficulty I eventually succeeded in getting him into the ladle and somehow not jumping out. Ever so slowly I hauled him blinking and looking sheepish into the sunlight. I carried him to the well then set him free to rejoin his loved ones.

Buoyed by this success I returned to rescue his smaller buddy, but all I could find was his corpse, floating belly up. I should have persisted yesterday. Half a result, I suppose, but not a happy ending. The cost to small lives does tinge a bit the great pleasure my swimming pool gives me.

But now I'd begun to appreciate the singular skill demanded by this life-saving technique so when others got into similar difficulties, I persevered. Before long I became quite adept and could cajole, nudge, nip and tip even quite large victims into the gravy-ladle cradle. Then, with infinite caution lest my precious burden jump out again (rescuees can be such fools) I'd slowly and gingerly raise him or her to the surface, to freedom and life.

They don't show much appreciation, these saved lives, as they lope away feigning uninterest, but I guess they just must be overwhelmed. I suspect they feel not a little like Adam did when God, sitting on his cloud above, reached down and handed him the spark of life.

I take no glee from my saving act, however. Swimming pools show no respect for insect or animal life and each year exact a heavy toll. Saving toads, frogs and similar unfortunates is the very least I can do. I also dutifully fish out all flying insects and any other beasts unfortunate enough to have an encounter with what must seem to them a great ocean but is in reality just our pool.

Walking the dogs, mid-April

A stroll along the riverbank never ceases to amaze and delight. Trees that just a day or two ago were leafless are now dressed again in leaves. It must happen so quickly – perhaps overnight they transform themselves from naked to clothed top to trunk in millions of tiny perfect leaves. The trees of the forest lag behind a good few days, particularly the oaks; last to lose their leaves but last to regrow them too.

We have about a dozen young heifers in the field across the river. Each day when they see us coming they rush in a gang to greet us. But they never quite get there. Instead they stop hesitantly, each determined not to be in front, as if they seem uncertain of their place and their right to be inquisitive. But their curiosity is unmistakable, it's more like wide-eyed wonder, the kind of enthusiasm you see in the faces of rural East African school kids when a *muzungu* (strange white person) comes to visit. It's a warm, friendly openness that belies the reality of our relationship. I and others like me will one day eat them (the cows, not the school kids). Given that we've consistently let them down, I'm not sure foreign visitors deserve the wonder and enthusiasm of African school kids any more than I deserve the perpetual genuine interest of these docile beasts, the cows.

Just yesterday I cut the grass around the field. As I walk on it now, slightly to the right of the path, tiny black spiders scuttle off just ahead of me into the undergrowth. I don't know the name of this species but it might possibly be *halorates ksenius*, the little black spider with no common name other than LBJ (for little black job), who with some of his friends and family created almost overnight the world's largest recorded web in a field near McBride, British Columbia. It covered sixty acres, about eight times the size of Kerkelven, and was thought to have been made by around fifty billion spiders.

Perhaps the worldwide web could become a reality. One of the puzzled scientists called in to study this phenomenon scratched his head and said, 'Perhaps they were trying to catch a sheep.'

The instant these little dark furry spiders sense my approach they always shoot off in the same direction, north, into the deep vegetation where presumably they'll feel safe from my big feet. But if I walk on the other side of the path, slightly to the left, all the spiders instantly dart southwards towards the river, to where the cover of long grass is nearest. If I walk in the middle, these canny chaps dart left or right precisely depending on their location. Yet from their position it must be impossible to tell where the nearest safety might be. It's uncanny, another instance of the remarkable powers of tiny spiders, reasoned or not.

I feel like being nice to my three canine companions because they didn't really get a good walk yesterday. Max had to go to the vet – she has some kind of allergy and is scratching like a mad thing, which is very distressing to passers-by and makes me want to scratch too. I had to walk them before we went and we were late so I frogmarched all three around the field at top speed, so none of us had any chance to do other than keep eyes front, shoulders back and try to keep up, even Mortimer, who for now at least seems on top form. Today they sense my softer mood and all gather round to give me their equivalent of a supportive hug. Syrus climbs up on the bench and walks all over me. Max rubs her itchy, dripping, grubby body against my legs and looks hugely pleased with herself.

Mortimer plonks his slobbering wet chops in my groin, fills my lap with dribble and looks up at me beseechingly. I know he means well, but I've no idea what he's beseeching me about so give him nothing. He seems quite happy to settle for that, but goes on beseeching.

Night walks are a treat just now. Invariably at this time we're escorted by our guardians, those swooping, spectral almost invisible flying gargoyles, Jonathan and Eric, the bats, our self-appointed night watchmen who, it seems to me, await our departure, come with us all the way then equally eagerly follow us home. But it's hard to tell one bat from another in the rising gloom and it's more likely, though less romantic, that what we're seeing is a succession of individual bats feeding in the dusk above and around our heads. As our caravan approaches the riverbank in the gathering gloom three ducks take flight noisily, sweeping off to the south and east amid a chorus of accusatory squawks.

As a break from the unseasonal warmth, on some days we're treated to a cold, cold April wind. Bracing at first, it's attraction soon wanes and we're delighted when it goes away and the warm weather returns. One of our riverbank trees is now wholly in the water, surrounded by it, though it's still growing strong. I really can't think when this happened or how I haven't noticed it before. It seems as if the tree, a big sturdy alder, has stumbled forward from the bank to stop a good foot or more from the field's edge. There's no going back now. But I wonder what caused it?

The tiny field spiders have come out again in their millions. Every time my foot falls a dozen scrabble excitedly out of its way. Then the next foot lands and a different dozen follow suit. Looking around at the rest of the field these little chaps are hard to spot, but every time I take a step, there they are, scurrying to escape my falling foot. It's weird. For a while I fancied it was the same group of spiders that for some reason of their own followed me around. Now I don't think so. There are a lot of them, they occupy every square inch of the field and they are light on their toes, believe me.

This is also the season when the teeming hordes of fleas that inhabit our canine buddies, Max, Syrus and Mortimer, seem to become particularly active. Mortimer, of course, is a blanket on legs and fleas seem to just be part and parcel of the dust, grime, crumbs and other infestations that he perpetually lugs around with himself. I suspect that other than the insidious ticks (see August) that affix themselves to his skin then hang there like permanent growths, most other parasites can't get through the rat's maze that is his coat. Syrus, I think, moves too fast for fleas so they all settle on poor Max, who despite having no hands manages to develop such dexterity with her feet that you have to admire the fleas' persistence and tenacity.

Truth is though I do give all the dogs a good brushing on occasions and have even been known to bath them (one at a time, of course). This activity is somewhat chaotic to put it mildly and usually ends up with the dog washing me. Except with Mortimer. His coat suffused with soapsuds would be so heavy that the poor chap would never get up, so I confine myself to giving him a vigorous combing with a wire brush, which I have to say I think he enjoys rather too much to be decent. In spring when he's moulting this produces more than enough hair to make a reasonable mattress. The rest I leave to his infrequent and seldom total immersions in the river, which as usual bears all such insults with stoical good grace, washing away whatever grease and grime must billow from him at each entry.

This is also the season of the fly. Big, ugly, long-legged buggers. Fruit-fly types, I should think. We share this field with so many varieties of fly I determine to learn more about them. Not because I think I might come to like them, of course. But it pays to know your enemy.

And finally, if finality is possible in this place, this is also the season when birds gang up and take it in turns to crap on our car, day and night.

But finality evidently isn't an option here, for even that insult is not the last word on the subject.

For April is the season for shit of another kind too. This is the time when piles of poop – and I mean, mountains of poop – sit for weeks on end in our fields and neighbours' fields, only to be spread, one fine April morning, onto the new-ploughed land. Thereafter, of course, the morning is anything but fine. As is the afternoon and evening and into the night. The smell – and it's a very particular smell, the one some people refer to simply as 'country' – gets in everywhere, pervades even the most inner recesses of our houses, fills our nostrils and ensures that the only escapes possible are flight or sleep. And sleep in these circumstances isn't easy. But it only lasts for a few days, once it's been spread.

After the muck-spreading, birds come in from all around for the easy pickings. No more discerning than our dogs, it seems almost all species of birds indulge in this presumably annual poo-fest. I don't know if they actually eat the stuff (though it seems they do) or if perhaps they're finding little grubs and suchlike within it, but the attraction is undoubted.

There is some kind of pecking order here though, with the bigger birds such as seagulls and crows getting first dibs (presumably creaming off the tasty bits) and the smaller lapwings, chaffinches, blackbirds and the rest getting what they can wheek out before serious ploughing begins.

Early in the morning you can see all kinds of birds here. To be honest I'm not sure what many of them are, mostly because I can't get close enough to see them properly and because whenever I really need the field glasses you can be sure I've left them behind, and when I do remember them, there's nothing to see. So I've been consulting various references and there's more than enough variety here to keep me busy for some time.

One I've identified is the dunnock. I've probably seen him hundreds of times but have dismissed him as yet another sparrow. There's more to him, and her, than at first might seem. Dunnocks enjoy a varied and active sex life, both males and females taking several partners with apparent abandon. They look a bit like large wrens, with spots that appear as broken stripes along their undersides.

At sunset the birds seem to settle, though they still make a fair bit of noise, twittering and whispering from every branch. They're like spirits in the air. You can hear them, but you can't see them. As we wander through the gloaming they're all around.

Rabbit, rabbit, rabbit

We have a lot of rabbits here, much to the delight of our hunters and foxes and to the despair of local farmers.

The European rabbit, or true rabbit, originally hails from the southern parts of Europe but he and his family have spread far and wide across almost all continents, sometimes travelling under his own devices and at other times with a bit of help from humans. The rabbit's status as immigrant has often been unwelcome and his settling in parts foreign has frequently spelled disaster for local wildlife. In some places, such as

Australia, this has tended to work out rather badly for the rabbit too. Now rabbits are settled permanent residents throughout Europe, and Kerkelven is no exception.

As any reader of *Watership Down* knows, rabbits are gentle, highly social animals that live in large networks of underground tunnels called warrens. They come out each morning and evening for 'silflay', a kind of extended outdoor virtually all-day breakfast in which all rabbits partake, ruminating dreamily back and forth among the grassy bits around their warren, slowly and gently munching for most of the morning or early evening in an almost torpid state of deep bliss, always under the watchful gaze of a few of their number detailed as guards. Actually I suspect this twice-daily event may be entirely the fanciful invention of Richard Adams, the author of *Watership Down*, but if it isn't true it ought to be, because silflay sounds just like the perfect way with which we should all start and end each and every day.

I can't remember much else about the Adams' book except that the rabbits onomatopoeically called cars 'hrududu' and whenever they inadvertently found themselves in the path of one of these appalling monsters their instinctive defence was to induce a terrified state of frozen suspended animation which they called 'tharn'. Then, rather immediately, they would get run over. Marie and I still use the word tharn to describe the attitude that rabbits adopt when they get caught in our headlights. It happens quite frequently. I suspect rabbits are a bit dim even by small furry animal standards.

We, of course, stop the car, step out and move the silly blighter, or more likely, drive round him. Sometimes I think it must be preferable to be a redneck.

In praise of onomatopoeia

It's not just rabbits. I love words that sound like what they mean. All over Kerkelven there's lots of onomatopoeic sounds all plopping, pinging, slurping and going boing. There's also quite a number of clicks, caaws, buzzes, oinks, baas, twit-twoos and miaows, as well as a few motorised vehicles that probably do sound a bit like hrududus. Apparently every language has onomatopoeic words. The Dutch for a rooster crowing is *kukeleku* and in Turkish the word that describes a sneeze is *hapshoo*. The word onomatopoeia comes from the Greek and really isn't helpful as it sounds nothing like anything.

Rabbit poo

I'm sorry to keep going on about what at even the best of times is a fairly disgusting subject, but I feel you should know that rabbits are odd in that they do two kinds of poo, not just one like the rest of creation. The first of these is the dry round pellets that you see piled or scattered around wherever rabbits have been. These are normal poo, for rabbits. The second kind that they do is called caecal pellets and these the rabbit re-eats. In fact, rabbits depend on these pellets for a variety of nutrients and vitamins. The gut of a rabbit includes a large digestive tract called the caecum, which is where these pellets are produced. Bacteria and fungi live happily inside this second stomach, where they must have great fun because every so often they are pooped out in one of these pellets, get to see a bit of the great outdoors before being eaten and digested again by their bunny host. It sounds a kind of perpetual motion but somehow in the process the nutrients and vitamins that the rabbit needs are not only produced but are also ingested.

So, good luck to them. I don't have any objection to anyone doing two kinds of poo, though normal poo is disgusting enough even when we don't eat it. Though on reflection, it could obviate the necessity of septic tanks and their attendant palaver.

On further reflection, presumably having eaten a caecal pellet this must after digestion emerge as a normal poo, number two. Or is it number three with rabbits?

Sometimes, one can have just too much information.

A blackbird loses her chicks

She's a good mother. She's been nesting by the garden wall across from our house and each day since the babies were born I've watched her urgent comings and goings, marvelling at the attention she lavishes on her new clutch. The father does his duty too but not with the consistent devotion that's evident from the mother. I can actually tell these two apart. The female blackbird is dark brown (what else) whereas the male is, not surprisingly, black.

But Lazarus, Angèle's cat, had noticed her devotions too.

Given where the blackbirds have chosen to make their nest it's just a matter of time before this scene of domestic tranquillity is transformed to disaster.

Her cries of despair are prolonged and pitiful. There's nothing anyone can do that will be of any help.

Despite the tragedy, she'll be back next year all the same. Same couple, same tree, and probably same end result.

Plain cuckoo

I hear a cuckoo regularly these mornings by the river's edge, but spotting her is far from easy. Unlike most forest birds, cuckoos love to eat hairy caterpillars. But that's not their only oddity. As everyone knows, cuckoos are what ornithologists call 'brood parasites' – they lay their eggs in another bird's nest, with fatal consequences for the offspring of the host bird. Instinct compels the cuckoo chick to kill his nursery chums by hoisting them over the edge of the nest to fall and perish on the ground beneath. Now you might think that the mother bird would notice this behaviour but evidently she too is programmed by instinct to recognise only the open mouth of her new foster child. So she proceeds to feed that as if nothing has happened.

Curiously though, she might recognise the foreign egg if it looks too unlike her own. So, the interloping cuckoo has a way of mimicking her host's eggs by producing eggs that look exactly the same, to get round this problem.

In time the young adolescent bird, now sole recipient of the mother's love, will leave the nest to make his way in the world. For the disconsolate mother, that's it. Typically, he'll never write, never call. But, what's a mother to do? That's the thanks you get.

Little, large and absent

Birds are truly remarkable. The little ones can fly straight through chicken wire without appearing to slow, swerve or to even think about it. How cool is that? And how clever? I've watched sparrows take off in flocks of five or six from inside the dog's niche. They just zoom through it, in the blink of an eye. Maybe when they're round the corner they spin off into sliced bits, like they'd been through a chip machine.

But I've not seen that.

Not all of our birds could do it. We have the fattest wood pigeons here. In fact all the bird life of Kerkelven has a well-fed, well-groomed look. We have the fattest bluetits too. Apart from occasional predators, life here for a bird is pretty good, particularly in this season.

But despite occasional false sightings our moorhens have not returned from their wintering in the south. I'm wondering what can have happened to them, for they've never missed a season to my knowledge and they should by now be well on with building their mid-lake retreat, the nest of twigs and leaves upon which they'll rear their annual brood.

It'll be a tragedy if they don't come. It'll cast a shadow over the summer.

Every swallow makes a summer

As with our moorhen, the non-arrival of our favourite summer visitor, the swallow, would be too hard to contemplate, far less bear. Yet it's not impossible, for there have been summers without any swallows here and not so long ago at that.

If the Sahara Desert keeps expanding at its current rate then soon the swallows that visit us each summer from southern Africa will not be able to fly across it, so very likely far fewer swallows will come our way. How sad would that be?

Gilbert has doubts . . . and a weird way of speaking

Swallows particularly fascinated the Reverend Gilbert White. Usually quite unsentimental about the small objects of his study, he was uncharacteristically concerned for the comfort and welfare of swallows and similar species, fearing that 'the poor little birds' must get mightily tired on their long winter journey to the south. So although along with most of his peers, Gilbert accepted that migration was the most likely answer to that perennial question 'where do swallows go in winter', he retained some scepticism because he couldn't quite believe that such fragile creatures would be up to the rigours of such a journey. So he devised some alternative theories to explain the winter habits of the swallow breed, including appearing to subscribe for a while at least to the harebrained ideas of a nutty Swedish naturalist of his time who believed they all hid under water for the winter months. 'Subsist they cannot openly among us and yet elude the eyes of the inquisitive,' wrote Gilbert, in what I suppose must have been the way everyone spoke, back then. 'And as to their hiding,' he went on, 'no man pretends to have found any of them in a torpid state in the winter. But with regard to their migration, what difficulties attend that supposition! That such feeble bad fliers (who the summer long never flit but from hedge to hedge) should be able to traverse vast seas and continents, in order to enjoy milder seasons amidst the regions of *Africa*.'

Gilbert could, I suppose, have simply said, 'I suppose they must go somewhere but who would believe such puny creatures could fly all that way', but he didn't and his prose is the more charming because of it. In fact I like his style and may betimes even try to model my own circumlocution upon it, as the spirit moves me.

Of course he was wildly wrong and vastly underestimated the capacities of the slender swallow. I've never seen them in the hedges. Here instead you will find them in their hundreds and thousands, budged up shoulder to shoulder, hung like festive decorations upon the telephone wires that bedeck Kerkelven.

At last, late but unflustered, the moorhens are back

At least the male is. I'm sure it's him because he has a look about him of a lad enjoying some final days of freedom. He's skulking around the margins of Loïc's big pond, which now as for most of its year is covered in a horrid slimy layer of green stuff, trying to look industrious but actually, I suspect, lying in late and enjoying sedate afternoon swims while he can. Hopefully soon enough his mate will be along and the serious business of nest-building will begin. No more sedate swims then for this lad, for sure.

Two hares

Two hares come down to the river to drink where, to the shock of all, they meet two ageing would-be guard dogs, Syrus and Mortimer. Max has sauntered off elsewhere, so misses the fun. The hares have wandered by mistake almost into the very jaws of their most mortal enemies and my heart races as for a

moment they seem to be at real risk. But the ensuing scene quickly becomes comic as all strive to recover their composure but the hares react first and best, and then the dogs dutifully begin their hopeless chase, the hares with quicker reactions and faster legs already irretrievably in the lead before the dogs have even realised what is happening.

But encounters with hares are not always so happy.

When he was young Mortimer caught and killed a hare down by the big pond. I remember it vividly for in its distress the hare screamed like a small child. It made the hairs on my arms stand up and chilled me to my core.

There does seem to be a surfeit of hares this year and I now see them frequently in the mornings. Yesterday I bumped into one jogging around the path I cut on my tractor. He was doing the jogging of course – I was at the usual amble. He hared off, as hares are wont to do, but sticking all the while to my carefully cut path. This confirms my long-standing conviction that the creatures of Kerkelven make good use of my paths on a fairly regular basis. I like to think of them silently acknowledging, at least to themselves, that I do have a use after all.

Nettles and the nettle weevil

At first encounter stinging nettles seem to be irritating and pointless, the mosquito of the plant world. Why is it that however much you try to avoid them, they always get you? At least, they do when you're in short trousers. Nettles' persistent stinging just annoys people and must over the centuries have led to so many determined attempts to eradicate the noxious plant that it's a wonder they survive. But nettles thrive. Perhaps they have much to teach us.

I've always considered that the best thing one could add to nettles would be a scythe, but it's a mistake to imagine nettles are entirely useless. Indeed, far from it. You can make shampoo out of them, and even use their fibres to make cloth. Nettles are used as ingredients in a range of foodstuffs and are even used to wrap cheese. When boiled they lose their sting so they can be made into a variety of nutritious if arguably not hugely tasty grub, including soups and stews. And there is of course nettle tea. But you have to be quite desperate for a cuppa, in my view, as nettle tea tastes foul. More importantly, nettles are rumoured to be worthwhile natural treatments for a variety of ailments including eczema, arthritis, a range of allergies and more.

Maybe I should rethink my approach to the humble nettle. Many people love the taste of nettle products, considering them the epitome of what good food should be – free, nutritious, tasty and something we might all enjoy with a clear conscience.

Quite a population lives on or among the nettles – flies, spiders, caterpillars, damselflies and other bugs. Presumably, they don't get stung, which is in itself rather remarkable. Butterflies truly love nettles and thrive among them. But for some days now I've been searching for a special little chap who loves nettles more than anyone: the nettle weevil. We have so many nettles, which they live upon and eat, that surely, one would imagine, in a field this size we must have an active population of this charming, attractive and idiosyncratic little bug. He's a little fellow about the size of a ladybird but nettle-green (proof that you are what you eat) from head to toe with a shiny, almost metallic-looking armour. He looks like a tiny six-legged elephant. He eats nothing but nettles, though it's how he cuts up his dinner that most interests me.

The nettle weevil has a femoral tooth, i.e. a tooth on its elbow. He uses it like a saw, to cut holes in the nettle leaves. Now isn't that something?

As I knew it would, my search paid off, and I found one. He was busy eating. I'm sure there will be more around, but given how many nettles we have they're not very plentiful. Perhaps they'd rather eat than mate.

I found myself wondering what I could do to encourage them. I reminded him, if he needed the prompt, that he had rather a large field to finish.

Britain even has a 'be nice to nettles' week, which aims to promote and rehabilitate this much-maligned plant. It's in mid-May and features lots of events and activities to do with nettles. Take the family. Make a day of it, why don't you?

First picnic by the river

It's warm enough now to plan our first picnic of the year. Over-provisioned with goodies and weighed down with food, drink, plates, cutlery and an assortments of glasses we head off to decamp by the stone table and enjoy an open-air feast in privileged surroundings.

It all seems a far cry from earlier picnics in France, when as mere tourists Marie and I would hastily shop at a roadside supermarket stocking up on pork sausage, cheap paté, baguette and a plastic bottle or two of Père Benoit's disgusting but very cheap red wine, to be consumed wherever we could find somewhere to park. In those days our resources were slender and strictly rationed so we had to make sure they went as far as possible. Even if it made your teeth pink and took forever to scrub the colour from the cup top of our thermos flask, the plastic bottles of Père Benoit wine were at least very, very cheap.

Though times have changed and picnics now are in a different league, it remains true that food and wine always taste vastly better in the open air.

When cultures collide

Reptiles need to know their place. Smooth snakes live in the long grass. Grass snakes, curiously, live in the woods. Adders live all around the woodland paths and edges. We have a lot of snakes here at Kerkelven.

There are plenty of lizards too. Common house or sand lizards live all around the houses of Kerkelven and their associated stonework, where they seem to thrive unmolested. Green lizards live on the long dry-stone wall in the parklands, a new and not too large colony. We know they're new because the wall itself was built just a few years ago when the parklands were reclaimed from the wilds and turned into a more accessible garden. These beautiful, really rather exotic large lizards are hard to spot though, for they are much more nervous than their house-trained cousins, perhaps for good reasons, because whatever lurks in our house, it isn't as scary as what lurks in our woods.

A smooth snake has taken to hanging around by the stone wall in the parklands. It's obviously lurking there to trap passing lizards and something tells me it's been successful, probably more than once. That's only natural, though I'm very fond of these shy green lizards and love to see them lounging on the warm rocks soaking up the sunshine.

Out of a morbid sense of curiosity I hang around hoping to see what happens when snake and lizard meet. This requires devoted patience. Both beasts can move quickly when they want to but both seem to spend most of their time stock-still. If I'm very, very patient I can see both snake and lizard, sometimes at the same time, though it's hard to deduce that either is aware of the other.

I wait. And wait. Nothing happens. Eventually the sun goes

in and soon after, so do they. I give up and head home. But it's a temporary truce, I know.

The battle for the new stone wall

There are two sides to this struggle to the death but it is soon clear that they are not equally matched. The defenders are the green lizards, plump, haughty, quick . . . but not quick enough it seems. They're slower than the snake and here that means they're fatally slow. The attackers are smooth snakes, particularly one fine large specimen who obviously ate well here once and hasn't forgotten.

The conflict as we see it, though, isn't quick and isn't dramatic. The fight takes place over several weeks, during which period we barely glimpse proceedings and have to deduce what's happening from sporadic sightings. But the outcome was never in doubt and it's confirmed not just by the fact that soon we see more snakes than lizards, but also by the fact that now, in the late afternoons, the leader of the Enemy, the big smooth snake, can bask in solitary splendour on the rock that recently used to boast a family of green lizards. Now he, big smoothie that he is, is master of all he surveys. And that doesn't include lizards because they, sadly, have gone.

Marie and I are spending a lot of our time looking at this wall. Each afternoon on the return from our walk we approach it gingerly and slowly. Silently, cautiously, we glide along it looking for signs of struggle, a glimpse of lizard, or the sighting of a snake.

Watching us from across the valley our new neighbours inevitably see us at this pursuit, most days. Not for the first time does a simple, sensible pursuit of ours seem inexplicably odd to them, from their perspective. I've no idea what they think we are doing, but suspect that from our actions they must infer that we are slowly assessing the work that would be involved in clearing the weeds and other unsightly accumulated debris from this wall, then deciding whether or not we can be arsed to take the necessary action. Given the absence of any progress in that direction, they must assume that each time we conclude, 'No, it can wait.'

Our dogs are anyone's

Three fierce guard dogs is the impression they give the world. Caged beasts, wild and vociferous, unpredictable, to be avoided. Fear is the emotion we wish to instil in the breasts of any burglars casting covetous eyes upon Kerkelven.

The truth is embarrassingly different.

When it comes to humans, there isn't a ferocious bone in the body of any of our three. Max, Syrus and Mortimer really wouldn't want to hurt anyone; they want to be everyone's friend. Even Syrus' snapping is not done from any sense of aggression.

No, they're utterly pathologically unsuited to their calling as guard dogs because, despite their sometimes gruff appearance, they are really just pussycats who will promenade with anyone, no questions asked.

So burglars in the know would just dispatch one of their number to take the dogs for a walk and our three would happily go along, tails wagging.

But burglars may not always realise what walking the dogs here involves . . .

How come Kerkelven is always so lush?

The following section of essential detail on Kerkelven daily life is described a bit tongue in cheek, but only half so. Quirky and even unsavoury though this subject might be, there's more than a smidge of social utility here. The core issue – and I choose my words with care – may not even occur to the casual passer-by, thanks perhaps to nature's constant efficiency at cleaning and refreshing itself. Almost invariably visitors will be unaware of it. The local council will never even have considered it. It may not seem a concern, far less a priority, even to my neighbours. But it's hard not to notice this problem if you live in Kerkelven, difficult not to get tangled up in it if you walk around the place on a regular basis, as do Marie, Joe, Charlie and I. This, in fact, is a problem that's right in front of the country dweller, one that often literally stares you in the face. If you're not careful, it's one you can easily step in.

You'll note that in my list of affected inhabitants I don't include the dogs, Max, Syrus and Mortimer. For you see, they are the source of this issue, not the victims of it.

I'm talking here about dog turd.

Poop.

Poo, shit, doo-doo, *merde*!

I think you take my meaning.

Just imagine. Here there are three big, or at least biggish, dogs. They eat a healthy, balanced meal, once each, each day. Ergo, they must evacuate. Like bears, they do it in the woods. But being dogs, they lack discipline and method. So they also do it in the grass, on the verges, by the riverbank, on the roads, on the pathways. In fact, wherever and whenever the mood takes them.

They do it every day, each of them, several times a day. They never seem to tire of doing it. They see no shame in it and have no inhibitions about it. Like members of the British Parliament, to Syrus, Max and most of all to Mortimer the notion of concern about when and where to pass a motion just never occurs. Mortimer snaps them out like he was on a production line – it's a joy to watch.

Without going into an unseemly level of detail here, all sorts of factors seem to influence the size, shape, colour and consistency of these emissions. On the highways and byways around Kerkelven – if you are quick and can get in before nature's cleaners, the insects – you will find the entire gamut of turds: large and small, brown, yellow, grey, black and even pure white turds; long and thin, small, stubby and fat, mushy turds and poops hard as bullets with the full range of solidity between. The variety is striking and worthy, I suspect, of further study. Though I'm sure generations to come will think nothing of students undertaking turd-monitoring projects in places such as Kerkelven for their PhDs I accept that this idea might not quite yet be one whose time has come, so I won't pursue the notion, for now.

Nature of course has no such sensitivities and is wonderful about all this. What is horrid poo to us is food and even drink to many of the other inhabitants of Kerkelven. Bugs and weather together in time consume all traces of every turd whatever its consistency, colour or durability, leaving our field crisp, pure and pristine. This is just as well, for I'm sure deer, foxes and badgers do it in the woods too. As do birds, from on high, all over the place.

The richness and diversity of life in Kerkelven owe much to its constant and quite evenly distributed supply of nature's most recyclable and biodegradable organic matter. Our species has surrounded the stuff with all kinds of taboos and aversions, but perhaps we'd be better to see it as nature does, a source of something useful.

Dragonflies and damselflies

We get such a lot of these at Kerkelven, they are so charming, colourful, interesting and uplifting, that I thought I'd invite you to spend a minute or two in their company.

Though often considered the same, dragonflies and damselflies come from two different suborders of the order *Odonata*, which means serrated or toothed jaw. That much they have in common. But worry not, for though the much bigger dragonflies might try to bite, their fierce-looking jaws are not strong enough to break human skin (insects, however, are another matter – they're a fearsome predator with those). The two subspecies differ mainly because damselflies are smaller and not strong fliers, so they tend to hang about the water margins flapping daintily, while the more powerful dragonflies can range far and wide. The damselfly's double pair of wings are the same size whereas the lower wings of the dragonfly are smaller than his upper wings.

Perhaps on account of its fearsome appearance the dragonfly has a range of ominous-sounding and largely undeserved folk-names including horse stinger, adder bolt and devil's darning needle. In 1626 Francis Bacon apparently gave it the name by which we now know it.

Most of a dragonfly's life is spent as a larva, living underwater where it will hunt almost anything else that similarly swims or crawls along the bottom of rivers or ponds (which includes the larval precursors of many if not most of the insects we see). These larvae really are rather ugly creatures, ferocious-looking too but without the charm and elegance in flight of their subsequent personae. Larger dragonflies live for a few months in their flying stage whereas the delicate little damselfly lives just a couple of weeks or so, at best.

Dragonflies and damselflies eat other flying insects,

particularly midges and mosquitoes. That alone is enough for me to put them on my Christmas card list. Though, sadly, they won't be around then to receive it. Birds in turn catch both dragonflies and damselflies, presumably the former at least providing a fairly substantial family meal. Kingfishers particularly enjoy a dragonfly, whether takeaway or home delivery. Spiders too can be a threat, particularly to the smaller ones. But in northern climes most dragonflies and damselflies eventually die of starvation, for in poor weather neither they nor their prey can fly. And they only eat on the wing.

The heat is on

This has been the warmest April in northern Europe since records began, three hundred years ago. The global warming doom-spreaders are at high doh about this and they may well be right. But it has made for a lovely spring here.

May

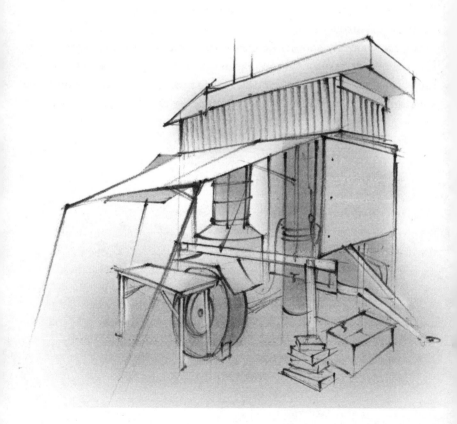

A bug's life

It may be short, a bug's life, but I suspect that it isn't too bad, focusing as it does mostly on sex and eating. In the field by the river the sky is thronged with busy insects seemingly having a high old time. The weather couldn't be finer, the field is looking at its best and nature is taking full advantage of it. After just a few days away I return to find explosive growth everywhere. It's so lush! The river has slowed almost to a standstill. And the bugs are out, in force and staggering variety.

There's an amazing bungee-jumping caterpillar active at the moment. She leaps from the highest branches of the trees by the river, throwing herself out into the void of space attached only by a silken thread that's almost invisible to my eye. I've yet to see her do it, though do it she must for I find her and a few of her similarly kamikaze brothers and sisters after their spectacular dive, seemingly suspended in midair, perhaps bobbing around a bit though mostly hanging motionless maybe five feet from the ground and wondering how to get down. She may of course fall accidentally, but if so there's a lot of careless caterpillars around.

Getting dressed in the summertime

If March is the season for casting off the winter woollies, May is the season for digging out the selection of shorts, each of which seems just slightly to have shrunk over the winter. It's a pleasure to get dressed in summertime, I just fall out of bed and after a quick shower pull on T-shirt, undies (of course) and shorts, slip on a pair of waterproof shoes for river walking and I'm off.

But is it too early for shorts? Briefly I suffer cold knees as well as freezing feet and other extremities for a few painful days until either I become acclimatised or the weather does indeed get just sufficiently warm to venture outside without thermals.

An epic walking the dogs

In the first few hundred metres there's been a close encounter, a life saving, a major confrontation, a near fatality, two surprise discoveries and an urge to fall about laughing.

It's been such a corker of a morning as would make the darkest, bleakest heart to soar. We had a charming chance meeting first thing this morning down by the big pond, though once again I'm the only one who noticed it. The dogs were snuffling around in the mud and mire as I was standing on the narrow path between field and pond, just idly allowing them time in which to do this, when lolloping along towards us there came a great big hare. He didn't spot any of us until he was right on top of us. He saw the dogs first just as I saw him, then his eyes met mine and he slowed to a deliberate, measured walk. For a couple of seconds he held me with a piercing glare. I looked at him and he at me and I realised that in that look he was assessing me, deciding whether or not I would give his game away. I felt then that in that look he had sussed me to the very core of my being. He saw I was a bystander, that I didn't present any danger. And I saw that he wasn't going to turn and go back whence he'd come which, had he concluded that I was a danger, he would surely have done. But no. He'd realised that the dogs all had their backs to him, so were ignorant of his presence. Continuing to study me closely he then, incredibly, accelerated past almost on tiptoe. He made absolutely no noise, just shot by me, so close I could have touched him.

All three dogs remained in blissful ignorance as we set off into the wood, me feeling very bucked by my meeting with a hare with such attitude, style and, apparently, intentional assessment ability.

We hadn't progressed more than a hundred metres when Mortimer's sudden veer to the left and increased acceleration from his normal stagger to an almost trot warned me that something was up, so I got to the fallen baby just half a second before his dribbling maw could fasten around it. It was tiny, naked and wrinkled, a baby bird fallen from its nest, a shivering piece of skin, bone and hairy feather-ends squirming among the debris on the forest floor. My impulse was to do everything I could to save it, though from the depths of my memory I seemed to recall that actually the best thing I could do would be as little as possible, in fact to leave it alone.

But left alone the chick would surely die.

Though it may have jumped, judging by the state of it I presume this scruffy little bag of bones and flesh must have fallen from its nest or been tossed out by stronger siblings. Its pathetic, exhausted strugglings were quite ineffective, taking it nowhere, so I guessed the nest had to be nearby. Holding Mortimer off by his collar (the other two were snuffling in the long grass, oblivious) I found a bit of bark and with the help of some paper in my pocket shuffled the chick onto it, without touching him. For him a touch from me could be a fatal infection, or so I thought. Actually, birds have a poor sense of smell, so his parents would be unlikely to detect me. But I was sure I had to find his nest and return him to it quickly or he'd starve to death. Baby chicks have to be fed every few minutes. If the parents are alarmed and keep their distance the chick can quickly and terminally suffer, so I had to think fast and choose wisely.

My God, but this little chap was ugly. I didn't pause then to reflect much on this, though, for looking around, there was no nest to be seen. The only possible hiding place was a holly bush about a metre away. Within its folds, sure enough I found an empty nest. But it struck me as odd that it was empty. And it looked old. I had expected to find eager siblings all hungrily mistaking me for mama and urging to be fed.

The Field by the River

But I reckoned the empty nest was better than nothing so I tipped the still-struggling naked baby in and turned to continue on my way.

Though the weather was fine I could see from the heavy clouds gathering in the west that a storm was coming. Even before I could see this I'd been expecting it, for while the sky was still clear the two smaller dogs had sensed the pressure change and were running about excitedly. Syrus was plainly terrified and while I turned to comfort him, Max ran off (I find her later under my desk in the barn, which serves now as my quaint but functional office).

The riverbanks are hard to get to these days so I've been cutting passages through the overgrowth for easier access. Big juicy colourful caterpillars are draped over the leaves of the trees and on their branches, looking like enticing fare for passing birds but no one seems specially interested. Perhaps they look nicer than they taste, but I've not been tempted to find out for myself.

As we pass by, a clamour from the treetops escalates to epic proportions as a gang of jays erupt into ferocious squabbling. First they leap around each other for about thirty seconds then, as if on a signal, all tear across the field scattering twigs and leaves in their wake to alight, still fighting, in the tops of the trees above the river. All the other bird life seems discomforted by this sudden, unexplained outbreak so now the jays have gone everyone else rearranges themselves with excited jabbering as if the episode just past had been the most thrilling experience imaginable.

Climbing up Bertrand's descent in the last stages of this epic walk I nearly stand upon a baby thrush, fully fledged though, sitting looking rather bereft at the side of the path. Perhaps he was taking a rest after his first flight. He allows me right up close to him, then with an anxious squawk he careens off at about eighteen inches off the ground, into the thick bushes where though I never saw him land I'm absolutely sure he was quite all right.

Mortimer, the great hairy galoot, has clearly loved every step of this walk and doesn't want to go back. Once again I marvel at his tenacity, his zest for life and his capacity to bounce back just when I'm worrying that it's all up with him. Just as I'm kneeling down to give him an approving look-over he unexpectedly licks me full in the face with such sudden affection that I fall over backwards onto Syrus, who unobserved has crept up behind. For some reason this morning, this seems very much funnier than it really is.

On the far side of the prairie Loïc is ploughing. Hordes of seagulls dominate the air around him, keeping the local birds at bay. Despite his tendency to untidiness he's a precision plougher, Loïc, and his fields look neat and smart when he's done.

When two days later I come back to look at the place where I'd left the baby bird (I thought I should leave it a respectful time) the nest was empty again, and of the chick there was no sign. Despite my best of intentions I doubt I was of little service to the poor chap, if any.

Flying united

I'm pausing for a rest at the circular stone table where two brightly coloured flies have landed on my left wrist. They appear to be mating back to back and on the wing. These are not your fat ugly black houseflies, they're slim, colourful creatures of the woods. And they are having sex, joined together at their back ends in what looks like a fairly convenient but not terribly comfortable nor intimate form of congress that would challenge even those practised at everything the Kama Sutra can offer. More interestingly, they flew here thus conjoined, which I marvel at, imagining the flight must be quite painful or perhaps adds a most exhilarating dimension to the usual connubial bliss. Presumably it's quite normal for them.

The smaller of the pair, I suspect the male, has his wings outspread while his better half, who's twice his size, has hers clasped firmly at her side. I surmise that this means the male is the driver, if not consistently then in this coupling at least. Unless, perhaps, he takes her to somewhere she doesn't wish to go (I mean literally, not metaphorically) in which case an interesting situation could arise. An interesting variation on Dr Dolittle's pushmi-pullyu springs to mind.

The mating of the long spiky flies is rather a dramatic aerial occurrence, one I see a lot of these days. I think some of these that I'm seeing conjoined in this way are horntails, part of the sawfly family. The females have cruel-looking ovipositors, the egg-laying device that sticks out several centimetres from the end of their abdomen, so it must be difficult for them to make love gently. They do seem keen though, proving that even for sawflies, love conquers all.

All around us these days, lots of insects are at it in this fashion. Marie is rather thrilled by their aerial sexual athleticism and reckons it must be a lot of fun. I'm not sure I disagree, though we haven't yet found a way to prove it. We laugh at this, though secretly I worry at her new enthusiasm for all this.

The 200-Foot High Club

The birds too are at it on the wing. Swifts, with kingfishers, have the shortest legs of all European birds. The kingfisher only uses its legs to perch whereas swifts can use them at times to grab onto walls and the sides of buildings, but mostly they seem intent on evolving to a point where they'll not need legs at all. Swifts do everything in flight, from eating to mating – yes, they too have sex in flight, which given how quickly they swoop and dart must be quite an accomplishment and, quite possibly, rather a turn-on too. Swifts even sleep on the wing, though I confess I find that prospect a lot less appealing. It suggests at least an untroubled conscience, though I think I would worry about potential shock awakenings. But they must be used to it, for they only come to land for nesting.

An afternoon in the amphitheatre – even Monet and Millais would struggle with this

In the forest this is the time for wild flowers. Such is the range and depth of their colours that it's a challenge to do justice to wild flowers. Though their time is short, they are gentle, fragile, radiant and splendid. Even the wise and well-dressed King Solomon, or so the Bible says, knew he couldn't compete sartorially with wild flowers. They render adjectives superfluous. All you can do is give whole-hearted thanks to whoever you think is responsible for such things. So hail God, Jesus, Mary, Joseph, Mohammed, blessings be upon his name, Shiva, the great Buddha and all the saints, gurus and angels in all the heavens for the exquisite gift of wild flowers. Hallelujah, inshallah.

I quite often come to the amphitheatre for a short sit during a long walk, or just to pass a few tranquil minutes lost in the depths of the forest. The amphitheatre is a natural three-sided bowl carved out of the hillside, probably aeons ago. Looking up from the river, it's to the right of our main path into the field, screened by trees and quite invisible from anywhere, almost until you're in it.

And when you are in it, boy, you can understand what living in the depths of the countryside is really all about. The bowl itself is not a large area, perhaps ten metres across. It reminds me of the corries of Scotland that were scooped out of the mountains by passing glaciers long, long ago, though on a smaller scale of course. Their open side always looks downhill and that's how it is with our amphitheatre too. It's like a giant armchair in the hillside and is indeed a lovely place to sit.

In the amphitheatre now and all around Kerkelven the forest floor is a carpet of colour. The first yellow and blue blooms of spring flowers are shyly emerging, peeping slowly but determinedly from the river's edges and positively bursting from around the bases of trees and in the nooks and corners of the riverbank. There are daisies, buttercups, corn marigolds, violas, forget-me-nots, periwinkles, dandelions and that curious cross between the dandelion and the buttercup that I've observed here, which we can only assume would be called the dandecup, or perhaps the butterlion. It may be a distinct species on its own, but if so I can't find it.

Dance of death

True to their name, the mayflies are swarming. For just a few days, as they do every year, they rise from the riverbank in beautiful clouds of green, black and gold, their torsos curved like scimitars held aloft by gossamer-thin deep-green wings flapping in a blur. As if in slow motion they soar up into the rich-blue evening sky trailing their elegant three-pronged tails to greet the swarms of grateful predators who come from far and wide for this annual orgy of glorious excess. If you eat flying insects, this is the place to be.

Swifts and swallows have been practising for this moment for weeks. They swoop in waves at first but the prey is so easy, the binge-eating such fun, that soon all sense of formation disappears and an orgiastic airborne free-for-all begins that makes the Red Devils seem like old ladies in wheelchairs.

Other birds are around to feast on the swarming mayflies but the sleek swifts and swallows own the skies now, without a shadow of a doubt. Their aerial dining continues for some days, until only a few stragglers, the lucky ones, are left. Then, presumably quite a bit fatter now than their normal waiflike selves, both swifts and swallows either move on to other pastures, or go somewhere for a quiet lie down for a couple of weeks.

The gruesome, grisly life of the ichneumon wasp

Get your head round this. You (or your wife) have six babies all at the same time. While you pop out one evening leaving your

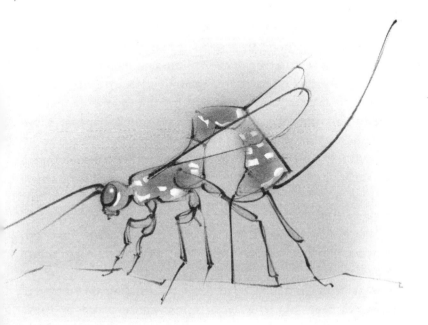

partner in charge of the brood, in pops a seemingly innocuous and inoffensive neighbour, let's call her Mrs Ichneumon. While the babysitter's attention is momentarily distracted the visitor injects some of her own fertilised eggs into the bodies of your darling little sweethearts while they sleep. Immediately these injected eggs hatch and begin to feast on your defenceless offspring, slowly eating them up from the inside.

OK, this seems an unlikely scenario. But it's precisely what happens to caterpillar babies and to the offspring of certain types of fly, when their parents are down the pub and the ichneumon wasp comes around. The little babies may live thus impregnated for quite a while but only one end, a horrible end, is possible. They get eaten up from the inside, by their new foster-brother.

Frightening indeed.

These creatures are so horrible that Charles Darwin, no less (he of *Voyage of the Beagle* and *Origin of the Species*), once wrote to a friend in America to point out that 'I cannot persuade myself that a beneficent and omnipotent God would have designedly created the *Ichneumonidae* with the express intention of their feeding within the living bodies of caterpillars'. But then he was a sensitive soul, Darwin, and was also put out that a cat should play with mice.

With this remark Darwin, an avowed agnostic, does seem to be dismissing God as the creator of all things. It's hard to imagine why anything would evolve to be so horrible, but perhaps that's just the way things are.

These ichneumon wasps are indeed beyond gruesome. The slow, horrific, living death they inflict upon their hosts would challenge even the sickest of imaginations. And they are far from alone, these fiends. In the insect world they have a host of imitators and, like the ichneumon wasp, many of these parasites live and thrive in the flora of Kerkelven. Not all though, are equally selfish and insensitive.

Oak apples and the gall wasp

Not apples at all, oak apples are the galls, or swellings, that form on the oak tree as it protects itself when a gall wasp has laid its larvae upon one of its leaves. An oak apple is a mutation of an oak leaf caused by chemicals injected by the larvae of certain types of gall wasp. They are so called because the gall, which can measure up to five centimetres in diameter but is normally only around two centimetres, looks a bit like an apple, though not much given the size difference, except I suppose they are both kind of round and applish-coloured. Oak apples look and feel like soft wood rather than leaves. Cut one open and inside you'll find a tiny wasp, curled up like a foetus.

Biorhiza pallida is one species of gall wasp that causes oak apples to form. There are different gall stages and these can lead to a phenomenon that's known as alternation of generations. This happens when an organism changes into different forms for alternate generations. One generation often behaves and physically appears different from its following generation. The third generation may then behave like the first generation, the fourth like the second, and so on. Gall wasps may be very much like their granny and not at all like their mum. It happens like this:

- In May, a wingless *Biorhiza pallida* female inserts her egg into the base of a vegetative bud. This activates the oak into the process of forming a protective structure, the gall, around the egg. She may lay several eggs in this way, each forming a separate gall.
- She will lay a single egg, which will contain lots of babies

all of the same sex. The oak apple gall grows and matures through June and July.

- By late July the full-winged male and female wasps that have developed in separate galls leave the structures through exit holes.
- The emerging wasps mate, while the deserted galls shrink and blacken.
- The now-fertilised females burrow into the soil and insert their eggs into the oak tree's roots.
- Root galls then form. These are spherical, brown, single eggs containing just one larva.
- These root galls mature in approximately sixteen months.
- Wingless females then emerge, climb up the oak tree's trunks and lay their eggs in the leaf buds (just like the first female, remember?). Whether they are first fertilised by males or are able to give birth without insemination, I wasn't able to establish.
- The cycle continues, with each alternate generation being different from the last but like the one before.

Scary stuff, huh? There are all kinds of galls commonly found at this time in our woods and not just on oaks. There are leaflet-roll galls, midrib galls, key galls, button-top galls and even a range called, unappealingly, pustule galls. Some people make a special study of galls and the insects that create them, which I can understand for they are indeed fascinating, if a bit morbid.

What about the workers?

Social organisation isn't hot in Kerkelven, except among a bunch of its inhabitants that you'll find to the right of Emile's path, just opposite the Druids' fort. These are ants, the busiest creatures in all the world, the species that many believe will in the fullness of time inherit the earth from us puny humans. Maybe not soon, but then who knows?

In high summer Kerkelven teems with ants. Lines of them head off foraging in all directions and come back the same way laden with microscopic goodies, bits of mould, undergrowth, minute morsels of something edible, buildable, or usable in some way or another.

Ants are stupefyingly incredible. There are as many as 14,000 different species of ants, which really are a kind of wingless wasp. Most amazingly, when on their own ants are clueless. As individuals they show no propensity whatever for organisation, planning or direction. But when they are in a colony it's an entirely different matter. On their own ants are not clever little builders, engineers and architects. But when they are together in a colony, ants become very, very clever indeed.

Apparently the world's largest colony of ants contains uncountable billions of the creatures and stretches nearly 6,000 km from the Italian Riviera to northwest Spain. That's a lot of insects. Even as I write, a breakaway group of them may be building a supercolony right beneath my forest, right next to my field. Or under your house, too.

Wood ants emerge from hibernation in the spring and set off on long trails into the surrounding forest to search for food. Anything they find they carry back themselves or, if it's too big, they'll enlist the help of other ants to share the burden. They never leave anything behind and seem to work all the time, which I suppose may be evidence that as individuals they are not very bright, or at least not as organised as I'd first assumed. No trades union here.

Where women head the family

Bees, wasps, termites and ants are all related, belonging as they do to the order *Hymenoptera*. This insect grouping encompasses 280,000 species worldwide, so it's pretty significant. In a given area of rainforest just the ants and termites alone will weigh more than all other animals together, humans included.

Curiously, almost all the ants, honeybees, bumblebees and wasps that we see around us are female. In the order *Hymenoptera*, males exist solely to inseminate the females, then they die. A brief life perhaps but, it would seem, a happy one.

Bumblebees appear early in spring before most other insects. They differ from bees in being generally bigger, slower, more gentle and they don't produce enough honey to be commercially viable. There are two hundred different types of bumblebee and their lives are very similar to wasps in that the queen hibernates then starts a colony the following year, building a nest much smaller than the wasp's for the small number of workers she'll raise prior to giving birth to next year's queens. Then, she herself will die, along with all the drones and workers. Only the new queens survive, to ensure continuance of the species. It's rather a moving scenario, but quite effective.

All bees eat pollen and because they are messy eaters and gatherers they perform an invaluable service for the rest of us because as they munch and collect pollen for their hives they obligingly pollinate our flowers. Unlike the veggie bees, wasps are omnivores, so they eat things gardeners don't like, such as aphids or greenflies. Therefore wasps too are useful (unless you are an aphid or a greenfly).

Bees come to our well by the house to drink in the hot days and they're also frequently found on the roller for our swimming pool cover, a source of easy moisture for them. Our neighbour Raymonde used to keep four beehives and occasionally swarms from these would be seen alighting on a nearby tree, but he gave those up long ago so I've no idea where the bees in Kerkelven come from now. Mathurin in his day also kept several hives of bees, but his too have all long gone.

Honeybees are apparently the highest form of insect life. They don't have to hibernate over the winter, or at least the females don't. The male drones start dying off in late summer, once there's no more use for them. Instead of hibernating the surviving bees stay semi-active, a state that's perhaps a bit like torpidity. They keep warm by storing up in their hive about thirty kilos of honey. Heat is produced by the oxidisation of the honey and circulated by the fanning of thousands of little wings. All bees take their turn in being at the outside of the colony, where it is colder. If thirty kilos seems like a lot of honey for one hive be aware that beehives in the wild are about the size of a football and on average will contain 35,000 to 50,000 bees. Bees will use the same hive year after year.

Bumblebees, or at least their newly mated queens, do hibernate and you might sometimes find them in tree bark, on woodpiles and in sheds. They crouch over, as if praying, often on top of whatever food they've gathered for the duration. If you disturb them you'll probably kill them, so if you find one in the wintertime, leave it be.

Dumb mutts and birdbrains: the relative intelligence of different species

A theme, or at least a question, is clearly emerging from my observations in the field by the river: are the animals, birds and insects of Kerkelven clever, or are they merely the slaves of instinct and learned behaviour? It seems plain to me that the issue is not whether or not they are smart, but how smart? And is their version of clever the same as ours?

Some weeks after the chance encounter with a hare that I describe in the epic walk, I happened to be staying with my friend Michael Devitt, distinguished professor of philosophy at the City University of New York Graduate Center, with whom I share not only a passion for fine wines and prolonged argument but also, I discovered, an emerging interest in animal intelligence. Michael is now teaching a new course at his university on animal cognition. His analysis of the meaning of my meeting with the hare seemed both profound and insightful. 'The key thing, Ken,' he pronounced in his cultured Australian lilt, 'is this. Had the hare merely learned, as he is clearly able to do, that in the presence of both dogs and humans he should be more afraid of the dogs? Or was he really sussing you out, figuring that you were not going to draw the dogs' attention?

'Sussing your intention,' he opined, 'would take a lot of intelligence because it requires insight into another's mind. A test for this is, what difference to the hare's behaviour would it make whether he had sussed you or not? Suppose it hadn't, would it have behaved differently?'

'How would I know?' I queried. This response seemed to please the learned professor, as apparently it illustrates precisely the kind of dilemma that cognitive ethologists – the people who study such things – find most thrilling.

'Fear of the dogs rather than the human,' he went on, 'could just be learned behaviour and the ability – which hares clearly have – to make a simple judgement and a choice. But sussing your intention would almost certainly imply a process of rational inference; that the hare has an ability to appreciate not just that a third party – i.e. you – has a reasoning process, but what's more, that he the hare can attempt to predict what the outcome of that process might be.'

To answer this, of course, we'd really need to find some way of interrogating the hare or at least of observing him in controlled or contrived situations either in the wild or in the laboratory. As none of this is likely, all information on the incident has to come from me, for other than the hare, I was the only one to see what happened. Though my memory of the encounter is clear, I can't say for sure that I know what was in the hare's mind. But at the time I thought I did. Michael also relayed a lovely story from an article by a guy called Alex Kacelnik about what a crow called Betty did when faced with an out-of-reach morsel in a small basket at the bottom of a vertical plastic well. On previous occasions Betty had been provided with two wires, one straight and the other hooked, and had been able to lift the basket with the hooked wire. On a crucial trial, however, she only had available a straight wire. After failing to lift the basket with the straight wire, she took it to a fracture in a nearby plastic tray, wedged the tip there and pulled perpendicularly from the side, bending the wire until it formed a hook. She then returned to the well, retrieved the basket and ate the food. Further observation showed that she could bend wires using several different techniques to achieve functional tools. 'This,' exclaimed my academic friend, 'is bloody impressive because it involves not just tool *use* but tool *making*.'

Animal intelligence is a big subject, one that, rather obviously, will repay further study. Though I suspect that whatever we learn will itself be flawed, because it will be subject to the Heisenberg uncertainty principle – whatever you study, you also change. This phenomenon is similar to the observer effect, which dictates that whoever or whatever you are watching will change behaviour because you are watching him, or it. Try filming in a crowd and you'll see what I mean. Gary Larsen had this phenomenon sussed in his cartoon of cows standing upright on their hind legs drinking, smoking and having a chat. When the lookout signals that humans are coming, all the cows instantly drop on all fours and commence nonchalantly chewing the cud.

I suspect this happens far more than we realise.

Back at Kerkelven, Mortimer shows just how bright he really is

Today Mortimer found the remains of a largish furry animal down by the banks of the river. I think it was a small fox, or a polecat, or similar, but it was hard to tell because only about one third of it remained and that was in an advanced state of decay, with maggot infestation easily visible. None of this deterred Mortimer from giving it a good licking inside and out. He was loving it.

The other two weren't interested, so grateful for small mercies I set about removing the disgusting object from Mort's slavering jaws and chucked what was left of the carcass into the river where, very gently, it began to float downstream.

Mortimer was inconsolable, of course, for at least 35 seconds. Then it dawned on me that it might dawn on him to just nip downstream a bit to below the last one and a half cataracts, where even his lumbering frame could easily enter the river; with a few swift paddles he'd be in midstream where he could comfortably nab it as it passed.

But obvious though this manoeuvre was to me and would be to any sentient being of even modest intelligence, it didn't even come close to occurring to the mighty Mortimer. He seemed in fact to have held the event in his mind no longer than would, say, Ebb the fish up at our house. Within seconds he had forgotten his near miss of a disgusting meal and had moved on to weightier things. Like, trying to give a good licking inside and out to me instead.

Max and the rubbish bin

Some years ago Max was selected, I think because she's a girl, for grooming as a house dog. So she was allowed to sleep inside. It didn't last, mainly because she turned out to be completely slovenly by nature and was forever making a mess around the place, particularly if she could get hold of the pedal bin in the kitchen and spread its usually quite revolting contents far and wide. However, Marie observed something curious about her behaviour every time she did this.

There was never any doubt that if we were foolish enough to allow Max to get access to the bin (i.e. if we forgot to put it safely out of her reach) then with evident glee and abandon she would invariably treat bin and contents to the same rigorous dismemberment. But each time we'd come down in the morning to discover the mess, Max was obviously contrite, ashamed and very solicitous of our forgiveness. That she knew she'd done wrong there was no doubt.

But given that this is the kind of things that dogs, being dogs, will do, why did she feel bad about it? Was it just that she knew she was about to be sternly told off? Maybe. Nothing would deter her from giving in to the compulsion to be a mucky pup, but she had learned this was wrong and even if her sense of guilt didn't deter her, after the crime she at least had the decency to show regret.

Max may not be one of the most intelligent of beings, but are we humans any better? For the sixth time this week I've stubbed my toe on the same stubby root that's sticking up from the floor of the path we cleared a year ago last October. If the animals of the field and forest can learn from experience, what's my problem?

Showers of spit

I remember as a child finding branches laced with cuckoo spit and searching gleefully for the tiny little insect that is always found inside, the froghopper, or spittlebug. He makes the spit himself, of course, it's nothing at all to do with cuckoos. Froghoppers are a sap-sucking insect and the spit is produced by the creature in its nymph (i.e. immature) phase. The voluminous dribblings these little chaps produce may merely indicate that they are messy eaters but their shrouds of gob also have the handy dual function of hiding them from predatory birds, who consider the froghopper a much-coveted delicacy. But tasty though its inhabitant may be, the spit on the other hand is absolutely horrible (try some if you don't believe me) which also may put off predators.

This spring we are having a veritable plague of froghoppers in the field, we're literally drowning in cuckoo spit. Along the banks of the west burn there are whole trees full of it.

The froghopper seems to prefer certain bushes and trees such as willow in which to spread out his secretions. These they simply swarm over, affixing their little bodies to every available centimetre then surrounding themselves in their cloaks of opaque spit. What they do then is a bit of a mystery. To walk under these trees, or, worse, to brush against them with a tractor is to be deluged in gob from head to foot. Very like a conversation with Albert Steptoe, I suppose, or Roy Hattersley.

The froghopper gets his name because he looks like a frog and can hop when disturbed – simple.

Macbeth's witches used cuckoo spit in their witches' brew

and legend says it's a pretty indispensable ingredient for all sorts of diabolical recipes. But I can't say for sure whether you discard the froghopper first or bung it in your pot for good measure, to add a tad of flavour.

Dilemma of a duck alone

I've seen him several times now, always solitary, always looking a little forlorn, seeming hopeful but still on his tod. He's been solo for some time. Other ducks have paired up a long time ago and most are busy in nest-building and family-raising, but he remains alone. The longer this goes on the less likely his chances are and he may pass the season without a mate, without a function. He's a fine-looking chap too (though I'm no expert, he sure looks all right to me), a male mallard in his prime with gleaming feathers of black, grey and green. He's not distracted by a partner so it's quite hard to get close to him. Maybe that's the problem for the lady ducks too.

How to uncurl a hedgehog

I worry about hedgehogs, partly because they're not very plentiful hereabouts and partly because when Mortimer sees them he tends to shower them with over-affection, which usually kills them on the spot. Also, reports have been reaching me indicating that the recent mild winters in northern Europe have been playing havoc with hedgehog reproduction. They're being born later so don't have time to put on enough weight before hibernation, thus don't see out the severity of winter.

I think that's very sad, because they're lovely animals. Not surprisingly though, they don't make good pets. Apart from their seemingly unfriendly spines, hedgehogs are infested with fleas, which can be seen living comfortably like remora fish on sharks amid the spines on their host's prickly back. Fleas (wingless insects of the order *Siphonaptera*) are amazing if somewhat horrid animals renowned for their extraordinary strength, virility and tendency to bite.

Their hedgehog hosts are timid and delicate creatures so should be handled with care, if at all. Uncurling a hedgehog is not something you need to do for the curl itself is a defensive action and a sign that the beast is agitated. But if you place the curled hedgehog on the palm of your hand (gloves help, but be careful not to drop him) and gently wiggle your hand he'll stick his legs out to steady himself. Then you can study him at close quarters before hopefully returning him to liberty under a nearby hedge, which of course he loves and will presumably now hog.

Gilbert White relays an intriguing observation about hedgehogs. He's handling a clutch of five newborn hedgehog babies when he points out, 'No doubt their spikes are soft and flexible at birth or else the poor dam would have but a bad time of it in the critical moment of parturition (he was mad as a hatter, old Gilbert, though not inconsiderate) but,' he goes on, 'it is plain that they soon harden, for these little pigs had such stiff prickles on their backs as would easily have fetched blood . . .'

I do like his turn of phrase.

Seeing a salamander

As I come back from feeding the dogs one dark night I bump into a determined and grumpy-seeming old black and orange salamander making his way from the corner of our house to the gulley that comes out from under the road to flow into Fox Creek. It's somewhere down here that he and his family spend their days. He's fairly indifferent to me but I rather like him.

The gorgeously attired fire salamander, a close relative of

the newt, lurks in pipes, drains and gulleys, coming out only at night to undertake long obscure voyages to who knows where and for purposes we can only guess at. All over shiny black, but with broad lines in streaks of bright orange the length of his body, the salamander glows as he goes. Why not? He is a creature of legend, a mysterious beast reputed to thrive in the heart of a fire. He gets his name and exotic reputation because a favourite hidey-place of his is inside old logs. When in the fullness of time these are thrown on the fire, out he pops, astonishing folk at their firesides and giving them the impression that he can live in fire. Sadly I suspect he'll have been thrown back more than once, which you'd think in time would quell the legend, but still it persists.

Mild and docile for much of the time, salamanders can suddenly bite and when he does, boy you'll know about it, as I can relate from experience. But he only bites when irritated, not from spite. For defence salamanders rely mostly on poison glands on their backs. If attacked they can secrete toxic liquids that taste horrible and sting the eyes. They can even squirt this foul fluid in the face of a would-be assailant. Obviously it's better for him and you not to pick him up, but if you do you'll find him rubbery rather than slimy, and quite solid. He can live a long time, fourteen years or more in the wild, up to thirty years in captivity.

Salamanders mate in the autumn and give birth, sometimes just every second year, in the spring, usually in water. Their style of lovemaking is interesting. The male salamander carries his ladylove on his back, then deposits his sperm in a kind of package on the ground and lowers her onto it. Isn't that considerate? No sweating and heaving for them. Salamanders are lecitotrophically viviparous, i.e. the young salamanders hatch from the egg immediately, at the moment of birth.

You won't often see a salamander because they hide pretty thoroughly, particularly during the day. Favourite places are anywhere moist, including drains and sewers where they survive by ambushing all the other denizens of dark places that feast on what's left over from our meals, the waste we so casually flush down our sink. We have a biggie who regularly hangs around the sump outlet from our kitchen. On reflection though, he probably eats quite a few of the helpful grubs that digest and break up lots of our greasy, solid kitchen waste, so maybe we shouldn't like him and look out for his wellbeing as we do.

When we go to bed

When we go to bed, the forest comes awake. Not wishing to miss this, Marie and I decided to camp out one night, to find out what really goes on while the rest of the world sleeps. In fact we do this every year, and always regret it. Then, on reflection some weeks after the event, it becomes an adventure.

Camping out is one of memory's tricks, a seemingly delightful series of false rememberings from our childhood which, when relived, in reality turn out to be quite false, not at all like what we recall, being infinitely more uncomfortable, cold, dull and tiresome than the rose-tinted reminiscences of our distant youth. You have to be in bed by about nine o'clock to avoid undressing in the dark, reading by lamplight is both uncomfortable and barely viable, and invariably just as you snuggle down in your sleeping bag you remember you've forgotten something vital, like to clean your teeth.

In fact, camping sucks. I realise this afresh every year, but like memories of pregnancy and dinner with Marie's friends the Johnstons, on every occasion the brain tricks us into imagining it wasn't so bad last time.

Of course I'm just being a grumpy old cynic here. I well remember the last time we camped out, Marie and I stayed up for many happy hours in the glow of our old Chinese hurricane lamp, chatting and laughing the night away as nature buzzed around us and strange noises from the dark depths of the forest reminded us that we should stay up just a little bit longer to enjoy just one more glass of the chilled Sauternes that we'd brought so carefully from the house, with the foie gras. What could be finer?

Taking it all back to the house, perhaps . . .

Clouds

Having rummaged around among the creepy-crawlies of Kerkelven it seems appropriate to look up for a while, to the sky above. There are many types of sky passing over Kerkelven. Frequent and not always welcome visitors here, clouds, according to those that study and love them, are much underestimated and underappreciated. Clouds are usually given little consideration by the rest of us unless we find ourselves obliged to fly through them, when they can repay us for our indifference by delivering a bumpy ride. Or when they pass above and deposit upon us their burden of rain. On investigation I find that clouds are varied and interesting though, to be honest, in my view not hugely so. I may not be unbiased here however, for I bear a grudge against clouds on account of their propensity to blot out the sun every so often. But what can you do?

Apparently, nothing. Despite all our obvious technical and social advances, our ability to influence the course of the weather remains as limited as it was when our ancestors worshipped the sun, back in the dawn of time. Though various attempts have been made at 'seeding' clouds (i.e. lacing them with chemicals to make them behave differently) these have generally been pretty ineffective. Yet rather obviously, all that would be needed is something like a very big hairdryer, to blow the buggers on to somewhere else. You wouldn't think that beyond the wit of our species, would you?

We are lucky to have lots of sky here so have endless opportunities for watching clouds get up to all the things that clouds do. If you are patient, before long every kind, shape, height, colour, shade and depth of cloud will dutifully come along, to be observed and, on occasion, to be cursed.

Weather-watchers divide our sky into layers. Some types of cloud obligingly stick within these layers, while others will cross between them regardless of how inconvenient that is for weathermen and women everywhere. The highest clouds are called cirrus, cirrostratus and cirrocumulus, and are mostly little more than ice particles, which gives them their streaked, rather fetching appearance. Usually, these clouds just look pretty for a while then melt away.

The middle clouds are called altocumulus and altostratus. This latter is known as the 'boring cloud' to meteorologists. Altocumulus looks like a layered quilt or, alternatively and rather unhelpfully, can look like a flying saucer.

Low cloud is known as stratus, cumulus, or strato-cumulus. Climb a high mountain and you can find yourself above the stratus. Cumulus is the cotton-wool cloud that is scattered around on a bright summer's day and stratocumulus looks like the output of a huge candyfloss machine.

It's the cumulonimbus, the big nasty cloud that straddles more than one meteorologists' layer, that brings us most of the foul weather we associate with clouds – rain, hail, thunder and lightning. The word 'nimbus' is Latin and means rain. But it's that other layer-straddler, the nimbostratus, that is apparently the least popular cloud of all time (though such a contest seems in itself rather odd, a bit like having a 'my favourite Nazi' competition). Whenever nimbostratus is about, apparently, it just rains and rains and rains.

So though I may know a bit more about them now I'm still not hugely enamoured with clouds. None of those that I can see appear to have even the least hint of a silver lining.

French lessons (honest)

Marie's been trying to improve her command of the local tongue. To help her, a bloke called Romuald has been calling upon her of a Thursday afternoon for some months now. He comes from the nearby village of Pontguern and has a reputation hereabouts as a bit of a well-do, though that doesn't necessarily mean he's not a good teacher.

Romuald looks odd. He's a big man with a bald head and a big bushy Alexander Solzhenitsyn beard. He has no moustache and, with no other hair on it, his head looks upside down.

Romuald rides a tiny 50cc moped scooter, and dresses as if he's a contender for the 500cc race at the Isle of Man TT. When he takes off his helmet (usually inside our house, just before he shakes you formally by the hand) he has to unfold several dozen matted strands of straggly beard from where he's tucked it neatly inside and where its fronds have subsequently wrapped themselves around his glasses.

Bits of pizza and breadcrumbs fall from his beard as he talks. It wouldn't surprise me if the odd water vole or small bird didn't do likewise.

I'm not sure what Marie sees in him. Oddly his grasp of our language, like hers of his, has barely improved. But Romuald seems an unlikely gigolo to me, not much money changes hands and I suppose it keeps them both off the streets.

A vanishing way of life

Each time I see our postlady, Postwoman Pat (which is almost every day, mid-morning), I'm reminded of distant, bygone days for she so looks like she's just stepped out of the 1950s. She's one of those curious people who seems to have drifted off the set of *Z Cars* or *Softly Softly*. She lives her life in black-and-white, rather than in colour, her hairdo is early *Coronation Street* and even the little yellow van she drives seems a relic of a bygone era. But it's more her apparently endless freedom to stop for a cup of tea and a chat each morning with Bertrand and Marie-Thérèse that seems reminiscent to me of a past age. I can't imagine that she does this in every hamlet she visits, but maybe she does. Time and motion, it seems, matters little here except that some folk seem to have lots of time and little motion.

The impression that the hamlet of Kerkelven is in a fifty-year time warp is no exaggeration. We still have visits on a Friday from the travelling fish shop, and the butcher from Melrand still guides his van our way from time to time, to sell pork and tripe across the garden wall. And we get periodic visits from the travelling clothes shop too – knickers and socks at twice shop prices but delivered to your door. Such scenes, I imagine, have rarely been seen in rural England since the days of rationing, though it would be nice to be proved wrong on this.

For love of ivy

Many of our trees seem as if they're being slowly strangled by sinewy fronds of ivy that grow from their roots to the topmost branches, daily thickening and tightening the grip in which they hold their hosts. This ivy is everywhere; the great chestnuts are swathed in it and it particularly takes to oaks. If left unchallenged strands of ivy can grow as thick as a man's arm and because it attacks in a mob it's really quite difficult to remove. These ivy strands may not be all bad though, for I'm sure the ancient oak would fall down entirely without them.

Having checked up on ivy I find that while few find it useful, opinions as to the harm it does are mixed. Some view ivy as a dangerous parasite, others as relatively harmless because though it can cling on tight it can't penetrate deep into hard wood, so it's dependant on nourishment from its roots rather than through the body of its host.

The clinging of ivy has long been used as a simile for faithfulness. Thomas Gray wrote affectionately about ivy in his *Elegy Written in a Country Churchyard* and Lord Byron in *Childe Harold's Pilgrimage* described it as 'the garland of eternity'. Owls live in structures swathed in ivy and many insects, spiders and others delight in making their homes in it, but humans habitually tear it down and root it out for they feel it damages their precious homes. Which, in truth, it does, though usually slowly and not very substantially.

Under the flags

It's hot, perhaps our first blazing summer's day. A tiny lizard has just scuttled from under my bed (yes, I'm out there already, creamed-up and horizontal, gathering a few rays), ruffling the pages of my book in seeming indignation at my being there, like a German tourist in the early morning, occupying his place. He's a lovely perky little fellow though and seems about as happy as I am at the onset of fine weather.

With a surprising array of other wildlife he lives amid the flowerpots and underneath the massive flagstones that completely cover our front garden. But one of his own kind is perhaps the strangest creature I've seen in some time.

This lizard that I spot by our pool has two perfectly formed tails coming out from the base of his back, where by rights only one should be. I take some photos to use as evidence, for I've not seen anything quite like this before. I look this up and find that it's a rare genetic defect but the lizard will be none the worse for it, though equally, there's not too much benefit to be had from having a second tail either. He's certainly a good-looking fellow and in my view the additional tail adds a certain *je ne sais quoi*. So I hope the naturalists may be wrong, as I imagine that with his extra appendage he must be a hit with the lady lizards.

Of all the creatures living beneath these stones the lizards would probably be my favourites, though beetles, ants, mites and other assorted insects all live here too, as does the occasional salamander and even the odd toad. Flies of course pursue their irritating peregrinations and butterflies swarm around our buddleia in seeming perfect contentment. In fact the buddleia is a bit of a beacon hereabouts, attracting every moth and butterfly that's around, particularly the intriguing and exotic hummingbird hawk moth.

Inevitably, as I contemplate the variety and colour of this underworld within our garden, it's not long before I drift off in the sunshine into blissful, untroubled sleep.

The miracle of Lazarus

It's hard to think of a more difficult start to life than that experienced by young Lazarus, the kitten. His mother, one of Angèle's multitude of mangy semi-feral cats, some years back decided to deliver one of her frequent litters in the presumed warmth and safety of the Kerkelven village bread oven, which at the time had a cosy interior heaped with kindling wood prior to one of our infrequent village pig roasts. Not wanting any more cats, Angèle asked various friends and neighbours to dispose of them. One – and I mention no names – agreed. With typical thoughtlessness he disposed of the kittens in the simplest way he could think of, by lighting the furnace and blocking the sole way in and out with the oven's heavy guard stone.

If he gave it any thought at all, our neighbour may have assumed this was as quick and as sure a way as any. For him, it was simply a job that needed doing. What seems an inexplicable indifference to the suffering of animals isn't even an issue for some people here.

We were away when this happened and only found out about it on the evening of our return, when the plaintive, pitiful caterwauling of the distraught mother cat interrupted our dining under the stars. She kept this wailing up night and day for nearly a week, with no sign of diminishing in either pitch or intensity, by the end of which time we had long realised what had happened, though of course we assumed there was nothing much we could do and that, please God, in time she'd forget what had so distressed her and stop.

Eventually it was me that gave in. Helped by son Joe I lifted aside the huge stone door of the bread oven to let the poor mother satisfy herself that her little babies were indeed no more.

And then out popped Lazarus (at least, the kitten that was, for obvious reasons, to be later named as such), hungry of course but seemingly none the worse for being smoked, burned and starved for his first seven days.

Lazarus has remained hungry ever since. He grew quickly into a mangy, bad-tempered, marauding, flat-faced Tom intent on wreaking revenge on all of the inhabitants of Kerkelven for his shaky start in life by pestering them all into feeding him at least once each day.

Lazarus hangs around in the shadows to remind us each

night of our neighbour's shortcomings and our silent complicity in an act he'll inevitably never forgive until perhaps, if we're lucky, he expires from overeating.

I do hope so.

Of course I'm just kidding. If any creature has just cause to be antisocial, it's Lazarus.

A *mechui* – mixing with the neighbours; and what's French for cliché?

We socialise a lot with our neighbours but never more than on those occasional treasured moments when one or other of them throws a *mechui*. This name derives originally from the Moroccan term for cooking lamb, but here, where big parties are pretty much the norm, a *mechui* is also synonymous with major celebration.

Two years ago Marie-Thérèse held a *mechui* in Bertrand's field for her sixtieth birthday. A huge marquee was put up in the top corner of the field and the party went on for several days.

The morning after the actual birthday, as my old friend Hubert and new-found best buddies, Antoine and Julien, were plying me with leftover wine as we were clearing up for the next round, I casually remarked that in England we call this 'a hair of the dog that bit you', (in my pidgin French, *de la poil d'un chien qui t'a mordu*).

I instantly regretted sharing this intelligence for, not surprisingly, the French language doesn't have a similar phrase and as several hangovers were struggling to comprehend my meaning I made matters far, far worse by chucking in a few more English clichés and idioms to illustrate my point. I spent the next hours trying vainly to explain to a succession of semipissed party stragglers the meanings of phrases including 'six of one and half a dozen of the other' (*six de l'un et un demi douzaine de l'autre*), 'many a slip twixt cup and lip' – I had extra fun with this in trying to get French friends to pronounce 'twixt', because they can't lisp – 'every cloud has a silver lining', 'it's an ill wind that blows no one some good', and 'don't count your chickens', which they got rather more easily than the rest. In truth my cliché lesson was going swimmingly until I threw in a Scottish favourite, 'mony a mickle maks a muckle', at which they drew the line.

I told them their blood was worth bottling, then left for a lie down.

June

Slow walking the dogs on a fine morning in early June

Today could possibly be the nicest day there has ever been. Of course there have been other days in history that came really, really close, but today the sky is just a bit bluer and the air a fraction clearer than ever before, the birds are singing just that tiny smidge sweeter. The nicest thing about it, though, is that quite possibly tomorrow will be even better.

Mortimer isn't a young dog. The chart on our vet's wall tells me that he's the equivalent of 120 years old, in human terms. It doesn't tell me how ancient he'd be if he were a gerbil or a natterer bat but I guess it does mean he's an undeniably old dog, so could be considered as on borrowed time. Really I think he must be doing pretty well, because mostly he's quite frisky or, at least, he makes an effort to show that the spirit is willing even if the flesh is giving up. But on some days I can see that these walks have become an effort of concentration and will for him – his age appears to have caught up with him quite suddenly.

Yet however bad he's feeling inside, Mortimer dutifully lugs his bulk around the field day in day out, just ten paces behind me. When he's looking a bit peaky I want to say to him, 'Take it easy, old pal, have a rest, give it a miss just for today.' But there's no way of communicating with him. He's on autopilot. I don't know if he wants to come or thinks it's his duty to come or if he feels obliged to come, to look after me. But there's no way he won't come.

So we pause for longer rests on the seats by the river, which isn't a hardship for me or for the other dogs. They use the time to snuffle around a bit more and to run up and down chasing real or imagined enemies or intruders.

They're happy, but Mortimer seems to be struggling. He's

feeling the heat now, not surprisingly in his great woolly overcoat at the height of a hot and humid June.

Still, he manages what passes for a smile and so do I. But this really is a worry.

Growth is massively spurting all over the field just now. The riverbank particularly is a cornucopia of unstoppable, uncontrollable abundance. In the field the long grass is at least as high as your average elephant's eye and the banks are not just invisible they're unapproachable with nettles, umbellifers, dock plants and other big riverside weeds that in this season run riot. I could cut grass round the clock but I'd never win. The insects, though, clearly love it and respond by bursting out all over the place. June is the time for bug-watching.

I think in April I spoke too soon about the missing moorhens. What I saw may have been a solitary stray rather than one of our regular pair. They should have been back with us weeks ago, maybe even back in February. And since then, as they've done each year without fail in my memory, they should have built their sturdy nest and delivered unto the waiting world their four to six cute and cuddly fat chicks, which as in past years they should have fussed and fretted over to the daily enjoyment of the human residents of Kerkelven. But this year they haven't come.

I still look out for them and with each passing day we've worried about them more and more. We can see no explanation. But it's undeniable now. This year, the moorhens are not coming.

With the hot dry weather the maize has really started to grow. So too have the ferns, which shoot up so fast you can almost see them growing. But the grass slows down, maybe because it's so dry. I'm left wondering why the hot and dry weather favours some plants and not others?

I'm dispatched to pick up milk from the village so drive past the field of our friend Marc-Henri le Floic, where his horse lies, apparently dead, overcome by fumes from the muck-spreading old Marc-Henri's been doing. Or maybe it just died from old age, or the mange, or the heat. Most likely, it's just grabbing a bit of shuteye. Sure enough, when I drive back twenty minutes later the flea-bitten old nag has hauled itself up and stumbled off to play dead again in another corner of Marc-Henri's field. One day, and it can't be far off, the bell will really toll for this bad-tempered old bag of bones, but then no one will believe it.

The camp

Life continues to erupt all over the field but an invasion of a different sort has taken place at Kerkelven, quite without my realising it. The takeover is pretty entrenched and seems set on occupation for at least a few days, maybe even a week.

While I was out yesterday at our nearby town, Pontivy, a troop of 'Scoots de France' (French Boy Scouts), uninvited, have colonised the top part of the field by the river, without so much as a 'may I?' or 'by your leave'. Now I'm not averse to offering a bit of hospitality and I was in days of yore a 'scoot' myself, though I was of a much tougher breed, the Sea Scout, in Scotland. We were so tough we would eat second helpings of porridge and stuff like that, whereas these wee French scoots seemed likely to blanch at anything not hand-prepared and brought round personally by *maman*.

To be honest, though you might never have guessed it, I wasn't that unhappy to see them settling in on my land, pegging out their little tents and making themselves so at home. But I do like to be asked and, as a responsible landowner, I need to be sure that all decencies and proprieties will be followed, such as taking care not to frighten the wildlife, no loose women after 5 p.m., tidying up after themselves and so on. Plus, I'm open to being invited round the campfire at night with my good lady wife to share their baked beans and partake of discreet slurps from the troop leader's hipflask.

But none of these niceties had been observed. They'd just arrived, sectioned off a bit of my best land and began erecting. So adopting the frontal assault mode, I went to see them, to sort them out.

'*Bonjour m'sieur*,' I said in the best, most confident French I could muster, '*J'espère que tous va bien chez vous. Vous êtes bien installé? Content? Vous avez tous vos besoins? Très bien, très bien*,' I said – loosely translated, this is general stuff to make them welcome, thereby inducing a state of false security.

'*Je suis le propriétaire*,' I continued, '*Monsieur Boornett–tih*.' (You have to say it like that, with the emphasis on the final syllable and the over-stressed ending, or they'll think you're called something else entirely. It doesn't help that bourne-ette in French loosely translates as 'small balls'.)

We both shrugged at each other for while. I shrugged at him and he shrugged back at me. Then we shrugged in unison.

'*Oh, désolé m'sieur*,' replied *le chef* (the troop leader, not their chef, though from time to time he might well have been that also). I always think the French word for an apology, *desolé*, sounds so much more sincere and contrite, implying nigh-inconsolable regret much more emphatically than a mere 'sorry'. But he didn't look desolated, I have to admit. Sensing my disquiet *le chef* tried to make up to me by lavishly praising his surroundings with lots of '*Que c'est beau ici*' and suchlike. I responded with the meaningless '*Oui, bien sur*,' only somehow it came out as 'Whee, byung sewer.' I switched to saying 'yes', often, the cool Parisian way, '*ouais*', which sounds like 'weigh'.

As we chatted thus, seemingly bonding by the minute but inwardly loathing each other, a team of the little troopers was busy lighting a fire presumably to cook their dinner, right there in the long (and very flammable) grass, in the middle of my field. I swear their heads were bobbing as they worked, seamlessly in unison in the way that scouts' heads seem to do whenever they do anything. Impressive though this display of teamwork was, I doubt if any had yet passed their fire-lighting badge, at least not with two stars, for they weren't getting very far.

In the interests of reader comprehension I will now switch to reporting what remains of this encounter in franglais, the language of translated dialogue that both French and English understand, by instinct.

What I really said was something more like, 'Zees ere feeld eez not a camping ground, matey. Eez mine. Pleeze to go away the lotofyou. Immediatement!'

After a few dangerous minutes of potential international incident it all calmed down and I pieced together from the jumbled high-pitched responses of this rather dim-witted *chef* that the day before he had in fact gained permission to pitch camp from my neighbour Loïc but had mistaken which fields Loïc had meant (a likely story, I thought, but I said nothing).

His name, I later discovered, is Le Plaute, or something similar-sounding. I never heard his first name and anyway he wasn't the kind of person that you'd want to be on first-name terms with. But I called him Toulouse (as in Lautrec, but behind his back, of course). It wasn't a term of endearment.

I issued some warnings about the dangers of fire, the need to keep the place tidy and clean up afterwards and decided to leave them to it. He assured me that they'd be gone in a few days and did I have any milk? I pretended not to understand this, and left.

When they did eventually leave, after five days, they left behind them a truly horrible mess of flattened grass, scorched circles of earth, half-filled-in latrines and the wrappings of various sweets. But I'm sure they loved the field. And it recovered, with ease. Ere long, you wouldn't have known they'd been.

Bug wars

Much as I love nature and much as that love grows the more I learn of it, there is no way that I could harbour an even slightly benign thought about one of the winged residents of our field. To be honest, it's not just him, it's his entire family, including even distant relations. For there exists in Kerkelven a creature more horrible than the trouser-gnat, more determined than the vampire bat, more reviled than a roomful of houseflies, more persistent than a chainsaw and more vicious than a swarm of particularly antisocial mosquitoes. I'm talking about the horsefly (*Tabanus sudeticus*) and its close and disgusting relative, the cleg (*Haematopota pluvialis*).

Interestingly, as with mosquitoes, it's only the females of these demons that bite.

Attack of the clegs

At this time of the year, clegs and horseflies infest the riverbanks in their hordes. Clegs are a kind of horsefly, least pleasant among a large family of endlessly unpleasant creatures. They fly and they bite, big time. Seemingly from nowhere, singly or in pairs, they sweep in to alight on your leg and sink their festering, loathsome teeth into your exposed flesh and tear off a chunk nearly as big as their head.

They really are winged misery, painful flying lice, miniature vultures that feast off living carcasses, demons that look like gargoyles and attack like Valkyries. Faced with such assaults humans have no option but to flee in disarray. Before we knew what we were dealing with we used to call these clegs 'those f***ing biting bastards down by the river'. In reality what we appear to be dealing with here is a particularly good year for clegs. Quite inexplicably, their population has exploded.

They started it

This is the war to end wars, the war of the species, infinite unending malice meets fevered, unbending resistance. In the face of such murderous assaults lesser folks would simply abandon their field to the beasts. But not us. Outnumbered and outgunned, we fight on doggedly, determined to find an economically and environmentally acceptable solution. Otherwise, we would simply napalm the field and start again. Revolting though such a concept is, I keep it in mind, in case all else fails.

Normally I would say live and let live. But they started it. We have nothing against them, but there is a limit and in the face of their unprovoked assaults we must fight back. These creatures are very fiends from hell, all your nightmares come real, in the flesh. And the flesh in question is yours, in small strips.

Luckily they don't seem to like the high ground so Kerkelven itself is safety. We can escape there at will, free from the misery of their predations. But I hate to be hounded from my own riverbank.

Fortuitously for us, clegs rarely hunt in swarms. They attack singly or in small groups and though you may not notice them until their work is nearly done, it is possible to kill them, most effectively by waiting until they alight upon your clothing

– preferably in the chest area rather than, say, the groin – then administering a sharp, sudden blow. If you are walking with a friend it is marginally easier to swipe the blighters on your companion's clothing, if he or she will allow you. The experience, it has to be said, is more than a little satisfying as the stunned little blighter spirals downwards, buzzing its last. But, curiously, when one is killed another, within seconds, takes her place. There's no other answer to it, they must by some means signal to each other. Somewhere in the murky depths of the riverbank there must lurk a controller fly, the fat controller, directing his agents one at a time to assault their innocent neighbour as he passes by.

If only we could find him. Or indeed, her.

As in most things, the dogs are all impervious to these assaults. Perhaps they're too thick-skinned, but I suspect they just taste so bad the clegs reserve their attentions for scrumptious little me.

The case for genocide

They lurk by the second cataract or by the bridge, or even somewhere unexpected in between, selecting from a distance the vulnerable point in your defences then swooping silently to fasten onto it, tearing off a single neat chunk of flesh while injecting their foul saliva into your bloodstream before you can spot their assault and sweep them aside.

As their short season progresses I become more adept at dispatching attacking clegs, mostly because they always attack in the same way. By careful study of their attack patterns I have found an effective way to deal with these horrors. Invariably when they attack they first hover, then alight, then bite. After hovering they seem particularly inclined to choose the broad expanse of my belly to alight upon (I can't imagine why). It's at this point, between alight and bite, that they are most vulnerable to a sharp whack with the flat of the hand. This may cause your belly to sting for a while, but it's not as bad a feeling as that which you've inflicted upon your cleg.

After a few days of accidental and not-so-happy slapping I get better at this and they, it appears, don't. Now I get them more than they get me.

Not for the first time we must look more than a little odd to a passer-by from the road high above our field, looking down and spying Marie and me on one of these occasions as she swats me and I slap her in seeming mutual abandon.

Now this may seem a severe judgement upon the poor cleg, who after all is only doing what she is genetically programmed to do. But what other option do we have? I confess that, in the darkness of defeat from overwhelming numbers of these pests, I have wished myself capable of contemplating the unthinkable, of loading the tractor with heavy-duty insecticides and zapping the lot. But I couldn't, for what would that mean for our friends the frogs, and the delicate damselflies, even the river birds including the lovely kingfisher, the wagtails and the warblers? What would become of wee Kenny? So, tempting though it is, that way out – the final solution – is discarded, however cheap ex-army napalm were to become on eBay.

What will the Scouts have made of them?

Suddenly I'm heartened by the thought that the voracious clegs must have dined right royally on the succulent, tender, youthful flesh of our scoot troop. Maybe it wasn't politeness and social decency that ensured these other uninvited guests didn't overstay their welcome, but rather it was down to the clegs. Well, dyb, dyb, dyb . . .

However bad I smell to these clegs (and given that in their world a pile of shite has considerable appeal, it must be pretty bad) I can seek solace in the knowledge that even in her natural state Marie smells or at least tastes even worse, because they only go for her once they've tried all ways to get at me. Which only proves my theory, Burnett's third law of travel, that particularly in parts tropical you should always travel with someone who from the perspective of an insect palate tastes noticeably better than you. They might take immodest pride in this but that way they get bit, and you don't. Marie definitely tastes worse than me and it's a small miracle and a tribute to my devotion to the woman that after more than thirty years we're still together.

At all times I pay a heavy price for forgetting to bring the insect repellent with me. Just one omission and I'm bitten to begorrah.

In desperation now I'm starting to think up all sorts of weird schemes to get rid of our clegs. Having dispensed with napalm because there'd be too many witnesses, I could try bringing in a wind machine. Or make a very loud and distressing noise pitched at a level that only they can hear. Or I could concoct the most revoltingly foul insect repellent of all time, one that will send them packing overnight.

Insect repelling

What did peasants do in the old days, to ward off biting insects? Keep themselves covered up tight from head to foot, I guess.

I don't know why we call it insect repellent because really it's me that has to become repellent, so as to scare off the worst of these biting bugs. Given that your cleg would find even an elephant's arse alluring, I really do have to put on something ultra-odious to be an effective chemical cleg deterrent. Sod's Law, of course, dictates that such deterrents also smell exceptionally foul for me and anyone else who meets me. It's a troubling thought to realise that as I progress on my daily walks I must smell several orders of magnitude worse than a mobile pile of elephants' arses.

Neighbours and people I meet in the shops give me queer looks these days and keep their distance. So too do all woodland creatures. I fear that the flight distance of each species must have increased threefold thanks to my new *eau de toilette*. Still, I do get fewer bites.

The three dogs though don't notice my new perfume and treat me with just as much love and indifference as they always show. If anything, they seem to like my new aroma. But then, I've absolutely no doubt they would find an elephant's arse irresistible.

How we look at things

As June progresses the ferocity of cleg attacks diminishes and again I can focus on the delights and wonders of our field, rather than its temporary downside. The grass just now is extra lush so I spend much time in trimming it and it was while tractoring up the 45-degree path that I made a small but astonishing observation.

Mindful of the power and intrusiveness of even my tiny tractor on the field's delicate web of life, I can on occasions go to great, perhaps absurd lengths to try to avoid running over wildlife that gets in my way. I'd spotted a small but exquisite butterfly in my path and stopped to make shooing noises to try to encourage her to flutter off. I thought she had, just because I could no longer see her. So I started up again and then spotted the tiny beauty gripping firmly onto the wall of my offside front tyre. By now this small wheel was rotating at quite some speed, but she held on for at least six revolutions, presumably enjoying the ride of her life. Then as I slowed again she spun off and giddily flew on her way, seeming, as I was, more than happy and none the worse for her helter-skelter experience.

It's a strenuous, muscular task to hold the tractor on its path up this incline, partly due to the sheer steepness but also because the road is far from level. The middle of the path is lower than its edges, so in places it's more of a channel than a path. Balance is an issue for tractors, particularly going uphill. Because of the heavy implements they haul behind, they have weights to keep their front end down, so when on an upward incline it's sometimes necessary for the driver to lean forward, on account of the back end's apparently increasing weight. This can be alarming, as it can occur when the edges of the path start to crumble and the tractor, it seems, is in imminent danger of slipping off to the side. It wouldn't go far, on account of the tangled undergrowth, but it might tumble over and getting it back on track wouldn't be easy. Tractoring needs a delicate, yet strong, touch.

At the top of the 45-degree path sits, or rather leans, or hangs, the gigantic pear tree that I introduced you to last September. Itself at 45 degrees to the horizontal, the coincidence of steep path and sloping tree creates a right angle causing optical illusions that can easily lead a passer-by to wonder which way really is up. I have to turn the tractor sharply at the top because I really don't want to hit that tree or the crumbly wall it has buried its roots into.

The secret lives of butterflies

Late in June I often see pairs of butterflies dancing in delicate spirals amongst the ferns and bushes at the margins of our paths. I delight in watching them though I feel shamefully voyeuristic at the same time, for I've always imagined this to be the most intimate of courtship rituals. However, they may not be lovers, but rather both may be males engaged in a serious duel. What I see as gentle caressing for them is serious fisticuffs. My impression of a careless dance of love may actually be the investigation of an interloper that has escalated into conflict. But such battles are rarely to the death. Usually the most serious outcome is that one or other of the parties flounces off in a huff.

Butterflies have names that do justice to their exquisite beauty and delicacy, such as Adonis blue, brimstone, Glanville fritillary and clouded yellow. Some though, like the grizzled skipper and the dingy skipper, sound horrid and nasty while others just sound ordinary and dull, like the small copper and the cabbage white. Like the mazarine blue, the large tortoiseshell is now thought to be extinct so we'll never know if they were as impressive or as beautiful as their names suggest.

There are more than 150,000 different species of butterflies and moths, about one-third of which are found in Europe. About 30,000 of these are species of butterfly. Still, butterflies are so lovely that to lose even one of their species seems a tragedy.

Butterflies, though, are not as different from moths as one might imagine. Some species of moth are more different from other moths than they are from most butterflies. In fact there's no real scientific difference between butterfly and moth species. The distinction, however, is firmly planted in the British psyche, so is unlikely to change. Many people imagine that it's butterflies that are beautiful and colourful while moths are drab and grey. So imagine my delight to discover that one of the most attractive of all *Lepidoptera* is the Burnet moth. This family of course is strikingly colourful and varied and, probably, surprisingly intelligent too.

Female butterflies sip nectar and get fertilised – that's all.

Their lives are short and even brutish, but it seems to me they have a ball while they're here.

What's in the name?

Speculation abounds as to the origins of the name butterfly. The fly bit is easy enough to fathom, but what's with the bit about butter? Butterflies don't even eat butter, though they do eat pollen, tree sap, rotting fruit, dung and even dissolved minerals in wet sand or dirt. But not butter.

It is thought by some that the term butterfly originally referred to the brimstone butterfly (often the first to be seen in spring) because of its butter-like yellow colouring. There is little agreement on this, other theories stating that the name refers to the butter-coloured faeces of butterflies – not so, I think, for the delicate butterfly excretes only water – or to the medieval myth that witches transformed into butterflies to steal butter.

It is rather a nice name though, quite fitting for such a stunning creature.

When butterflies flutter by

The French poet Ecouchard LeBrun said of them, 'The butterfly is a flying flower, the flower a tethered butterfly.' I think he put that rather nicely and he wasn't wrong.

Like other insects, butterflies are invertebrates, so instead of an inner skeleton their soft body parts are held in by a firm outer shell. Their bodies are in three parts, head, thorax (chest) and abdomen (stomach and reproductive parts). Butterflies have a strong sense of smell and complex eyes with up to six thousand lenses, though butterflies will see very differently from us. The butterfly's tongue, the proboscis, is long and flexible. It uncoils to sip food as butterflies can only sip liquids. Most butterflies live on nectar from flowers, some sip up the juices of rotting fruit, while others delight in fluids from decaying meat. The harvester butterfly pierces the bodies of woolly aphids with its specially sharp proboscis and drinks their body fluids (may teach them not to be so woolly, I suppose).

Dangling from the butterfly's body are three pairs of legs, with the tarsi, or feet, at the end. Butterfly feet are like a second tongue, with taste buds on them. When a butterfly lands on a flower, to save energy rolling out its proboscis to check the sweetness of the nectar, it lets its feet do the tasting.

Like most flying insects, the unique, amazing natural designs that are butterfly wings are in four parts. Minute scales – so small they appear like dust to us – are in fact flattened hairs which overlap so finely that they appear as a continuous, diaphanous surface. When male butterflies search for a mate it is the distinctive wing patterns and colouring they look for.

Among the butterfly's many enemies are birds, bats, spiders, lizards, hornets, beetles, wasps, fungi, disease, parasites and, of course, humans. Birds remain the most dangerous though, eating both adult butterflies and caterpillars, though butterflies have developed some cunning ways of avoiding their most common threats, including camouflage, chemical repellants and scary body markings designed to frighten birds or to convince them that their intended victim either tastes bad or is poisonous.

Butterfly types

There are many butterflies and moths that are worth looking at and learning from. I've selected just a few of my favourites from those I might bump into daily around Kerkelven.

The comma butterfly is unusual in several ways in that its numbers are on the increase and it is capable of raising two generations of offspring within a single year (i.e. its children have children). Comma butterflies are a bright orange and their wings are ragged edged, a feature shared with no other European butterfly. Caterpillars of the comma butterfly disguise themselves as bird droppings, so as not to be eaten by passing feathered predators.

Each June and July the nettle banks of Kerkelven are simply awash with nests of what will become peacock butterflies. There are dozens, even hundreds of these and inside each are around two hundred tiny black caterpillars. These quickly grow and spill out onto the surrounding leaves, where they can be seen in their thousands bedecking the nettles like strings of black pearls, getting fatter by the day. Those that survive predation from birds and the egg-laying intentions of parasitic wasps will grow into a star of our field, a lovely creature equipped for its protection with a blotch on each wing that looks like a large eye, so that from above it looks like an angry owl. Peacock butterflies also make a scary noise with their back legs, so all in all are quite good at frightening off birds that would make a meal of them. Peacock butterflies hibernate through the winter and die the following May, after laying.

One of the most beautiful of European butterflies, the red admiral is a migrant to France and Britain from northern Africa or southern Europe. Most of these visitors will breed here and some do settle and overwinter, depending on the weather and relative warmth. In early summer they lay a single egg per leaf on nettles, laying about a dozen in total. The larva lives and feeds within a tent of folded nettle leaves, spun together with silk. Every few days, as the leaf-tent gets devoured, the larva moves house, spinning a new tent nearby. The spiky greenish-brown larva can be seen within these tents, normally curled in a J-shape, head-downwards. Red admirals are well known not just because they are lovely but because they are inquisitive and show less fear of humans than most species.

Two butterflies that I'd particularly love to see here are the purple emperor and the Camberwell beauty. I'm keeping my eye open for these, along with all the Burnet moths, especially the six-spotted variety, because any of them might possibly show up here at any time. Marie has suggested that we could even encourage them, by growing plants here that are specifically butterfly- and moth-friendly.

You may hear this guy before you see him

The hummingbird hawk moth (*Macroglossum stellatarum*) is a species of moth, but with its long curved beak and its ability to hover in flight it looks for all the world like a midget hummingbird. It uses its long proboscis to probe deep into the stems of flowers that hold nectar. The amazingly curved mouthpiece looks exactly like the beak that hummingbirds have evolved for feeding from orchids, which are not dissimilar to the long-stemmed plants such as honeysuckle, petunias and buddleias that the hummingbird hawk moth loves. Perfectly made for its job, his proboscis fits into the stamen of the plant like a sword into its sheath.

But mostly this tiny sensation is seen just as a blur of orangey brown. His wings beat so fast they make an audible hum, which is often the first sign you'll get that you are lucky enough to be visited by one or more of these rare but splendid summer visitors.

They're quite plentiful here when it's warm, particularly around the swimming pool and especially the large buddleia that grows by it and the petunias in the window boxes. These moths return south for the winter, being seldom found north of the Alps in the cold months.

Sadly not all invaders from parts foreign are so benign.

The threat of the harlequin ladybird

Gardeners love ladybirds because they eat perhaps the biggest or at least most numerous of all garden pests, the aphid. But our local ladybirds now face a major threat from a newcomer to these shores, the harlequin ladybird. This Asian visitor is widely regarded as anathema to indigenous ladybirds, the native common-or-garden everyday ordinary spotted ladybird, who's much smaller, less colourful (though not much) and not such an avid muncher on aphids. I may possibly be a little unfair to our indigenous ladybird here, for the common ladybug is no sluggard when it comes to aphid-gobbling, you understand. But compared to the harlequin he or she has pretty much lost her appetite.

And that's the problem. If the harlequins take hold there may not be enough of the normally prolific and plentiful aphids to go round. And according to the charity Buglife, these harlequins are a bit of a niche bully and if they get hold, not only will

Britain's 46 native species of ladybird suffer, but lots of other insects as well. France I'm sure has a similar number under similar threat, but I've not been able to establish this precisely.

While farmers and gardeners may see short-term advantage in the arrival of another aphid predator, an infestation of foreign invaders could be seriously bad news for Europe's ladybirds and other important insects. We have to hope therefore that reports of their potential dominance are exaggerated. And that if aphids do get in short supply the harlequins won't, as is predicted, start feeding on native ladybirds, butterfly eggs, caterpillars and lacewing larvae.

Snails, slugs and worms

A snail has an eye at the end of its tentacle-like feelers that it can contract and extend at will and use as a smell-detector. How useful must that be? Snails, of course, are not insects, they're molluscs. Like insects, they are quite wonderful.

Most species of snails and slugs are hermaphrodite (as are some species of fish and some insects), therefore have both male and female reproductive parts. This does mean that when you say to a snail, 'Go f*** yourself', it has more literal meaning than when a similar sentiment is applied to most mammals, including people. But nevertheless only a few hermaphrodites have the ability to pleasure themselves, though those that have, presumably, are among the highest and happiest orders of life.

Big fat orange slugs abound around Kerkelven, perhaps because they like things to be moist and mouldy. They're found draped across our tracks and pathways after the rain in such quantities that it's quite hard to avoid standing on these slimy characters. This can be a quite distressing experience for both parties, though presumably more so for the slug.

Earthworms are even more extraordinary than snails or

slugs and may, because of their crucial function of aerating soil, be more important for the human condition than almost anything else.

For most of us, cut our head off and that's it. But for your ordinary garden or field worm, your earthworm, chop his head off and he just grows another one. It must be worth learning a little bit about a chap that can do that. Truth is though that only some species of worm can do this and as often as not when you cut a worm you are left with one living bit and a second bit that is either dead or won't survive long.

So, don't do it, OK?

Earthworms have very simple brains and don't use them much. If you were able to remove an earthworm's brain, you'd notice very little change in its behaviour.

We see worms a lot in Kerkelven. Conservatively, we've got millions of them. There are, someone has calculated, around eight million earthworms in a single hectare of soil. That means you might find twenty million of them here in Kerkelven.

There are about 5,500 named species of earthworm worldwide, ranging in length from a few millimetres to over three metres (that's more than ten feet). I think only a few of these species live in our field, mostly those that don't exceed twelve or fifteen centimetres.

They have no legs, of course (you knew that) but they have ten hearts (which, I venture to suggest, is news to you). While most earthworms are hermaphrodites, so they can shag themselves, they can't self-fertilise. Still, must be fun, eh, and would provide quite a solution to wet winter Sundays at Kerkelven . . .

According to Charles Darwin earthworms are deaf. He deduced this after he got his children to play the bassoon to them and they appeared not to notice it. But he thought the earthworm to be intelligent because he observed that when it drags leaves into its burrow it would do so pointy end first, so it could pull it inside more easily.

I call that clever.

Snakes in the sun

There seem to be a lot of snakes about this year. We keep almost stumbling upon them on our walks, particularly in the late afternoon when they are coiled up in slumber, sunning themselves on our paths. They like a bit of open space for this and there isn't much of it around at this time. Obligingly I've heaved the strimmer down to the place where the Ukrainian bears ran riot (remember, the electricity guys who cut down so many trees back in February) and with this I've cleared a few largish patches that are out of the way from any pedestrian passer-by so should provide the snakes of Kerkelven with somewhere safe to bask uninterruptedly whenever there's sufficient sun.

A swallow's tragedy

Having been away from Kerkelven for a few days, returning late last night, we were awoken early this morning by a frantic flapping at our bedroom window. The perpetrator was a swallow, male or female I couldn't detect. Close up, these lovely birds are really tiny and fragile-seeming and this one was clearly in some distress. She – I've simply imagined it's a female because of her tenacity and devoted self-sacrifice, but I could be quite wrong – flew around the house a few times then returned again and again to the same window. Then she'd fly round to the side window and flap at it for a while. Sometimes she'd fly right round to the tiny window above the spiral staircase and sit expectantly on the sill there, before starting the whole agitated process again. She kept this vigil up without a break for four mornings.

The easy conclusion is that she had lost her mate, perhaps he'd flown down the chimney above the fireplace in our bedroom. Though the chimney top is open the fireplace is blocked up so if it got right down then escape wouldn't be easy. Death would follow slowly from dehydration hastened by constant, frenzied flapping. We didn't hear anything, so the ordeal, if indeed this is what occurred, must have been over before we returned.

This is infinitely sad to watch. Such loyalty and dedication from this perfect little creature is surely underestimated by the likes of us. Some say swallows mate for life, though the evidence for this is not conclusive. Yet I can believe it, if one is to judge from the devotion shown by my little friend.

On the fourth morning her agitated flappings had diminished quite a bit. Possibly she'd begun to forget why she was doing this. I opened the window for her and tried to entice her in so she could check around for herself, but she seemed reluctant and a bit confused.

I realised now that I had fallen in love with her completely, but by the next day she was gone.

The *fête du quartier*

It's a 'best bib and tucker' day so we're up early to get ready. Today is the *fête du quartier* day, the annual social gathering exclusively reserved for bonding between residents of our 'quarter', our small sub-region of the local commune. I'm not exactly sure which households this encompasses but it's always well attended and is a high point of our year.

Find three or more Bretons gathered together in one place that isn't a bar and most likely you'll find it's for either a funeral or a fête. Bretons love to party and their calendar is peppered with fêtes for this and that, couscous evenings, *jarré et frites* (ham and chips) events, barbeques and street-dancing events, and this on top of their regular cycle of religious festivals and *pardons*. In fact in this season it's hard to see when your Breton gets a chance for an evening in by the fire.

We are now the only *Anglais* who go to the annual *fête du quartier*, at Kelven le Roux, a neighbouring farm. Most communes hereabouts have a *pardon*, a religious festival open to all, but as our community doesn't have a chapel (no one knows what happened to it, but it is no more) we can only have a *fête du quartier*. For our celebration we join with a couple of hundred or so of our neighbours, everyone chips in about ten euros (it was much cheaper in the days of the franc), in return for which we get a simple but quite substantial country lunch, usually about five courses and including things like sliced head of calf and chicken gizzards in salads. Plus seemingly endless cheap rosé or côtes du Rhone. By the time pudding and the pastis and eau de vie come round everyone is past caring. So midway through the afternoon a short nap among the apple trees is usually unavoidable.

To keep spirits high during this excess, traditional Breton music is played cheerfully if perhaps rather badly by Corentin Peron on his squeezebox, accompanied by an array of other neighbours on an assortment of strange instruments including the bombarde (a kind of clarinet) and the biniou-kozh (Breton bagpipes). Only so much of this can be borne cheerfully so those of the men still standing then repair outside for a game of *palet* in the sunshine (throwing a circular slice of lead – the *palet* – at a distant target and trying to stop it from rolling off to get lost in the long grass) while the women – disgracefully, of course, I agree with Marie, but who are we to challenge tradition? – do the washing up indoors, the children play in the orchard and the rest sleep off their lunch in the sunshine, or under some shady tree. Great fun! It takes about a day or maybe more to recover. There's a striking if rather tacky array of cups or statuettes awaiting the team that does best at *palet* and one of these now resides above our kitchen sink, gathering dust and reminding its not very sporty owner of one of his finest hours.

We've been enthusiasts for the *fête du quartier* ever since we came here and were stunned to find such an open, hospitable welcome from our generous and warm-hearted new neighbours. Those were the years when this great event was held at Cosquer, in Corentin Peron's barn. Corentin was an elderly but utterly charming twinkle-eyed Lothario with an eye for anything in a skirt. Recently Corentin has been very ill – he's no longer young and now seems compelled by his health to feel and accept this. So a neighbour, Guy Evanno, has taken over the annual fête, and a less convivial one at that. He has a smaller barn so inevitably numbers for this much-loved tradition have been steadily declining. Half the usual number would fill the new barn of M. Evanno. Anyway he only inherited from the ever-hospitable Corentin the role of front man for the FdQ, as much of the work and many of the decisions are taken by a committee. We knew change was afoot though, for Guy's first action when thus empowered was to spread the word around that an important decision had been reached. No *Anglais* were to be invited.

There may have been some good reasons for this. Not many English people come. Those that do (Burnetts excepted) tend to stick together for linguistic comfort and eschew mixing with the locals, which not surprisingly the locals don't like. The English tend to get rather pissed quite early on (again Burnetts excepted, though not always). And with the mounting influx of foreigners from various lands all collectively lumped together as *Anglais*, an increasing number of Bretons find their resentment for outsiders growing by the year. We still get included because we've been here a long time and because our immediate neighbours stand up for us and insist we are invited. But I'm not sure it will last.

Bagpipes, whisky . . .

Curiously, Brittany boasts as traditional several activities and artefacts more commonly associated with other cultures. Perhaps it's the Celtic roots, but I was surprised to find that Bretons claim as their own the bagpipes, their biniou-kozh, which of course was originally a Scottish instrument, or so I believed. I wouldn't have thought this something that any nation would claim ownership or provenance of unless it had to. I find upon researching that the bagpipe and similar instruments are found in many cultures from Spain to the Middle East and the earliest known reference to the instrument is in the year 400 BC, in ancient Greece.

Whisky is another matter, of course, but Breton whisky is exceedingly fine and tasty, with the kick of a foul-tempered mule.

. . . and clogging up the works

The term sabotage is thought by some to derive from early in the Industrial Revolution. Powered looms, it is said, could be damaged by angry or disgruntled workers throwing their wooden shoes or clogs (known in French as *sabots*) into the loom, effectively clogging the machinery. This is often referenced as one of the first inklings of the Luddite movement. However, this etymology is highly suspect and no wooden-shoe sabotage is known to have been reported from the time of the word's origin.

We have a *sabot* maker not far from here and I've often been tempted to go round and have a fitting. I'm told that after a while in acclimatisation they become really quite comfortable, but I fear that while they may last many years, sadly they wouldn't go with inflatable Elvis.

Suddenly, it just popped into my head

My ears itch. I don't know why, but this minor irritant seems to occur most frequently while I'm idly ambling along the riverbank, around this time of year. It's my own fault. I have the annoying habit while walking along of picking a stalk of grass, twig or sprig from some plant or other and using it to scratch the inside of my offending ear. This process absolutely appals Marie, who is convinced that some hideous brain-devouring mite has been lurking since primeval times at the end of my twig, awaiting just such an opportunity. Thus it will launch itself gleefully into my inner ear and start gobbling up the good stuff that's sure to be found there. The prospect holds no terrors for me though. Apart from the fact that I simply don't believe it, I'm sure there's enough in there to feed an army of such mites for some time before I'd start to miss any of it.

But what if they breed? And what if their munching in itself starts to itch and in combination they begin to drive me mad? What if one or even several of their number gets bored and decides to nibble its way through to the other ear? What if it lays eggs in there and dies and starts to rot? What if they just have to get out, but can't turn round?

However, scratching my ears in this way is deeply satisfying so I'm unlikely to stop, except for short breaks, to sleep and suchlike.

Dancing in the moonlight

It's a nearly full moon and a clear, cloudless sky. The longest day is coming, and even though it's really late the sky has barely darkened, it's a kind of perma-twilight, what the Scots call 'the gloaming'. It is so warm too. The field has just been cut and the smell is deliciously reminiscent of all the good things of childhood.

We take a later than usual late walk, Marie, dogs and I. Halfway round Marie and I start dancing, spontaneously, inspired perhaps to practise for next month's street dancing, or just intoxicated by the pleasantness of the night air. The dogs gaze on in apparent dismay, shifting nervously and glancing furtively around in case someone they know might come along and catch them in their embarrassment. We ignore them and waltz through the woods, gliding up and along the 45-degree path beneath the spreading branches, spinning dizzily in the moonlight, scattering the forest debris at our feet in every direction. We've no idea what the local nightlife might make of this open-air strictly come dancing, but there's no doubting that they'll all have seen or heard us, laughing and singing all the way home.

Clearing the pond and keeping it proper

The slime on our ponds loves this season and spreads out its suffocating green/yellow fronds until there's no water visible at all and the surface looks deceptively solid and reassuring. I wonder what the birds think of it? It must mess up their feathers something rotten.

This pond really needs a pump to keep it properly aerated. It's the lack of this that explains why the wretched slime so thrives. Of course our pond is just a bit too far from civilisation to benefit from an easy supply of electricity. Yet it needs some power source to move the water around, to give it some flow, keep it healthy and ensure it's a good environment in which its vast range of aquatic life can thrive and grow.

So, naturally, I had the idea of installing a solar pump.

Only it isn't easy to find this product, particularly in French shops. Pumps they have aplenty, aquatic ones too designed for just the function I have in mind. But not solar-powered.

Then I saw one advertised in the *Daily Mirror* or somewhere. It sounded just the job. No batteries, plugs or leads. The only problem is that even in the heat of summer it barely generates enough power to stir a cup of tea. I keep looking for a gadget that's environmentally friendly and effective, but suspect I search in vain. Or, I could get some aerating plants, and do the thing naturally.

Breton names

The Breton's have some truly lovely names for girls: Gwenola, Maïwenn, Gaël, Elodie, Nolwenn, Germolene . . . That last of course is a well-known remedy for cuts and scratches but it has the melodic ring of a Breton girl's name, which are all undeniably enchanting. Their boys' names too are distinctive, equally musical and charming: Maël, Corentin, Loïc, Judicael, Mathurin . . . They have a poetic quality about them, are onomatopaeic even. Names here sound very romantic so seem to me worth preserving, for though some of them have spread afield, many are still more or less unique to this region.

On investigation, however, I find that many if not most are recent inventions, not traditional at all. Ah well . . .

A farewell to Mathurin

My friend and neighbour Mathurin le Belligo has died, after a long illness. He was 88. In all our years here, his is the first death of a neighbour in Kerkelven and he was more than special to me and many others.

In this part of the world you could spend a large part of your life at funerals. I try to avoid them, but Mathurin's is an exception.

His funeral was in Bubry, a small town ten kilometres from us. Despite living almost all of his life in Kerkelven, Mathurin came originally from Bubry, so his family felt that's where he should be buried. This is how things are here. Marie goes to Bubry sometimes for dancing in the street and dances there with a lovely man in his mid-seventies called Eugene. He originally comes from Bieuzy. His family and friends there, he says with a chuckle, think him very odd because he's chosen to live most of his married life a full five kilometres away, in Bubry. After living more than thirty years among them, he avows, his neighbours in Bubry still consider him an outsider.

Angèle looks now as she is, small, fragile, very bowed. She seems dangerously frail and vulnerable as she slowly leads the procession of hundreds who have come here today to mourn the passing of Mathurin. But everyone knows her strength and marvels at it, even now. I doubt if I'll ever meet a braver or more noble character than that housed in this diminutive frame. Given that he'd long since stopped recognising anyone, these past months and years nursing the slowly failing Mathurin can only have been heartbreaking toil. But for Angèle, it's evident that she's just lost her world.

The birds are still singing in Kerkelven, which somehow doesn't seem quite right. Or maybe, for Mathurin, it is.

July

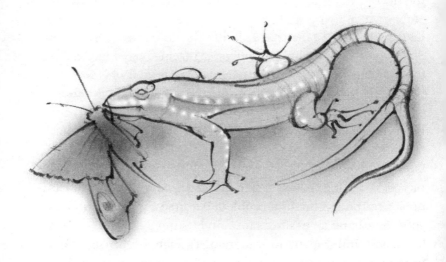

A plan is starting to form

Marie first mentioned it, I think without realising its potential
scale and importance. She said, 'Why don't we plan our field a
bit more and maybe turn at least part of it over to a wild
meadow?'

Why not indeed? What could be better for encouraging
wildlife and adding new depths and dimensions to our already
startlingly diverse and cosmopolitan field? Last month I was
musing on the possible benefits of procuring special plants to
encourage the most spectacular of the moths and butterflies.
I'm sure this'll be a major part of whatever strategy we develop
for the future of the field.

Before we knew it this casual suggestion just grew and
grew, till suddenly a new project is taking shape, for the field by
the river.

Long walking the dogs, July

Sometimes on these fine mornings we're joined by Suki, the dog
that has moved with our new neighbour, Pascal, who's come to
Kerkelven to restore and live in the old ruined stables behind
our house. Like Patrice and Anne-Claire, who acquired
Bertrand's house, Pascal remains something of an unknown
quantity because so far we've seen little of him, but I've got to
know Suki quite well.

Suki's a big, feisty, highly strung golden Labrador. His
presence though is not a problem because the five of us can
get around just as easily as four and I suppose he does add a
bit of youthful vigour to our mob. Though we must look a
formidable posse to anyone we might chance to meet. The
throng gets swollen even further on occasions when Angèle's
yappy little poodle Pilote joins in, though she rarely gets more
than halfway round our circuit before she has to be carried

back, exhausted. One day two other big dogs from across the river joined us, which apart from being seriously crowded dog-wise was also a little tense at times, as each dog established its right to be there by vigorously sniffing the private parts of each of the others while I stood by feeling a bit left out. If it can be completed without scrapping, this 'getting to know you' session seems very effective at reducing tensions all round. Perhaps politicians should try it at their international summit meetings.

I do feel that I'm a bit mob-handed with all these dogs in tow and it does disturb the rural tranquillity a bit, not to mention the more sensitive wildlife such as snakes and lizards, who must resent the disruption to their siestas that only four charging dogs can bring. But then again I've not been set upon by passing ruffians either, so a gang of dogs perhaps has its advantages too.

Today Marie comes with us and because Mortimer seems positively frisky now we decide to take a longer than usual walk so we can visit the special place we call the summer pool. This is our place, a little quiet retreat known only to Mortimer, Max, Syrus, Marie and me. Being at the far side of Loïc's part of the prairie it's a bit off our normal beaten track, but well worth the detour. The summer pool is an area of wild scrubland along the banks of the river, a place where no one else goes because it's in a neglected corner where the fields of three farms meet. Each time I visit I see something interesting because this small area is so packed with nature, probably because it's so secluded. Its pristine peacefulness, I realise, is also helped by the infrequency with which it's turned over by the intrusive presence of our dogs.

As we set off this morning a large adult hare came bounding along our path, stopped and leisurely sat down opposite the second shed. I'm reminded of our meeting with the hare back in May, but this is definitely a different animal. Still entirely unnoticed by all three dogs, of course, he suddenly spots us and slowly turns to lollop leisurely back whence he'd come. There's something strange but very welcome in the apparent abundance and sociability this year of that usually shy and scarce inhabitant of Kerkelven, the hare. As we enter our field a solitary buzzard lifts languidly skywards clutching a fresh kill. I can't quite see what the kill is, though from his position in the centre of the field with its carpet of freshly cut supposedly drying hay, I presume it's a field mouse. Of all their many enemies I expect mice fear the buzzard most, as he circles silently on high until his unerring eye glimpses movement, then he swoops and snatches before anyone can say 'squeak!' As we get nearer the buzzard swings around and so shows off his catch. By the look of it it's a large mouse and it has not yet breathed its last, for we can now see plainly its final struggles. The poor wee chap was minding his own business in the middle of the field, perhaps rounding up his shoals of little children, when out of the morning sun there came a flap of wings followed by a sudden snap of beak and he was gone. It was very quick. Buzzards always are.

The buzzard is by far the dominant bird of prey here and undeniably is at the top of our food chain. The tiny midge is caught and consumed by a damselfly, who later falls foul of a quick-moving frog. Within seconds the frog is caught and devoured by a lizard who, before he can digest his lucky kill is caught and gobbled up by a grass snake. As she sleeps off her heavy lunch in the afternoon sun she, in her turn, is spied and swooped up from on high to be carried off to the buzzard's lair where she makes a delicious family meal. It's a bit like the old lady who swallowed a fly.

But no one eats the buzzard.

I'm really not sure what he'd taste like, but even if delicious, we can't eat him because it's not allowed. Buzzards, even here, are protected birds.

Buzzards follow no rules. While they won't bother with insects, just about everything else is fair game for them. Aristotle, apparently, was convinced that buzzards have three testicles. They fly so fast I suppose it's an easy mistake to make, though why it should have interested him at all is beyond me.

As we set out this morning we're treated to a display of aerial acrobatics from the swallows above the newly cut but not gathered grass. Their high-energy aerobatics would make any heart soar, though Mortimer manages to remain blissfully ignorant of it all, panting open-mouthed in seeming enjoyment of our walk. He may be bravely suffering in silence, of course, but I see no signs now of the slowness, ageing and even distress that dogged these walks on several days last month.

The swallows have returned to perching in numbers on our rooftop, particularly lining up on the television aerial where they make an elegant silhouette against the evening sky. They used to do this years ago but were ousted by a flock of noisy starlings. It's so nice to have the beauties back. Though I've no idea what happened to the starlings, I'm not losing much sleep over them.

Then, suddenly, we see him, clear as day. Wee Kenny. Looking pert and bouncy and just about as small as a bird can be. Marie is sighting him for the first time today and confirms he's about half the size of a wren, as she puts it, 'no bigger than a shilling'. Only we conclude it might be a she, because unlike my other sightings when all I saw was dark black, this little bird is dark green. But green may indeed be his colour, for this time for the first time we've seen the wee Kenny right up close and he's as perfect as can be. And like nothing else we can see in our books of birds.

Though our trip to the summer pool does reveal an array of interesting birds and seemingly even more profuse populations of flying bugs and butterflies, sighting the wee Kenny is undoubtedly the highlight of our outing today. We resolve to visit the summer pool more often while the weather's good, because it is such a treat.

Our little bridge over the west burn is clogged and overgrown with weeds so on the way back I set out to clear it. Mortimer decides to help, only he doesn't get the idea at all and just stuffs his face into mine as I kneel, clippers in hand, wrestling with the undergrowth. Then he bestows upon me a huge slurp. Mort reminds me of those seagulls in the movie *Finding Nemo*, only instead of 'Mine, mine, mine' the word Mortimer has repeating endlessly in his head is 'Ken, Ken, Ken, Ken, Ken . . .' I'm exhausted and haven't been particularly successful. He seems inordinately pleased with himself. And with me.

In the evening I stop to sit on the white slatted bench in the parkland. I'd do this more often because it's really nice here, but as soon as I sit down the three dogs jump all over me, licking and snuffling and generally being smelly and obnoxious. I like it really, but wonder what have I done, to deserve this shower of affection?

The busiest highway

I have seen Oxford Street just before Christmas. I've walked Fifth Avenue in the January sales. I'm familiar with Spaghetti Junction on a bad day. I've even jostled the crowding flood of humanity on Silom Road in Bangkok, Thailand and danced with the throbbing masses at carnival time along the main drag in Port au Prince, Haiti. But the busiest place on earth for me, home to the teemingest of hordes and the most crowded of crowds, has to be the woodland's edge in late July in our field by the river, along the aerial thoroughfare I've rather pretentiously named the Strip.

Talk about diversity, colour and vibrancy! Everything is a battle for space, for growth, for life. Not everyone will survive, there just isn't room, so you have to grab, grab, grab. On the long swaying stalks of nettles I'm finding more and more of the black weblike cocoons that house baby caterpillars of the peacock butterfly. There's thousands and thousands of them, but there seems to be room for more, all the same.

Our field now is a laboratory, a zoo, a museum, a university, an interchange, a refuge, a bordello, a supermarket and an airport.

Harvestmen and women

Harvestmen of all sizes and several different species abound in this season. I love the way they move on their barely visible, seemingly telescopic legs, their tiny bodies in the centre look like miniature controlling Martians directing their eight long limbs to traverse the uneven terrain at breakneck speed. I guess they don't worry as they haven't got necks to break.

Harvestmen look like big spiders but, though closely related, they're not. Spiders have eight eyes where harvestmen have only two, located on the front part of the body. These intriguing creatures got their name because their spherical bodies on long feet look like the carriages used by farmers in the past to bring in hay. Also, they appear mostly around harvest time.

When threatened, harvestmen are able to lose one or more of their long legs and still survive, though the lost legs don't regrow. The leg remains on the floor, jerking about, thus trying to divert the attacker's attention. A harvestman needs only three legs to move about, though these have to be reasonably balanced. Even though some harvestmen are carnivores, most will eat almost anything: from freshly caught prey to the carcasses of dead animals, faeces or plants. Their second pair of legs is slightly longer than the other three pairs. These legs are used as sensory organs to feel their surroundings. When you see them walking these legs are constantly in motion, tapping all around, in a similar fashion to a blind person using a stick.

A menu to suit everyone

There's a species of wild plant called the umbellifer, of which cow parsley, wild angelica, lovage, wild carrot and even fool's parsley are members. These are just great, a grandmother of the plant world, for they support a seemingly infinite variety of wildlife from among the insect nations, who all feed on the pollen and nectar of these profuse blooms with unrestrained enthusiasm. One variety that flowers at this time is wild angelica. Briefly in this season this normally ugly or at least ungainly weed, which grows in quite some profusion along the riverbank, is decked with elegant white flowers. Each plant has several heads and each head further divides into perhaps fifteen or twenty 'nodules' (the term is mine; you won't find it in any scientific books). Every morning now I find upon each one of these nodules a fly, a bee, a beetle, an ant, or even two or three feasting upon the good stuff that they must find within, savouring the supply of, presumably, nectar that they hold. The range of species that come here to dine is staggering, the intensity, serenity and tranquillity of their feeding most impressive. Why can't the human world get on in this way?

But even here on this dreamy pristine angelica, it isn't all peace and love. Danger can lurk everywhere in the insect world and death is seldom far away, though these innocent diners seem all too indifferent to the fact. I've just had the extraordinary sight of a large insect, the curious hybrid known as a bee fly, being jumped by a nightmare beast called the white death spider. Watch it at work and you'll see how aptly is it named. Less than half the size of its victim, this milky white, stealthy predator must be almost invisible against the background of cow parsley and angelica heads. The first – and probably last – thing the bee fly would have known as it too foraged in a field of white flowers was a formless shape leaping at it out of the snow-white background, silently slipping its unseen jaws irrevocably around its victim's neck, gripping it into immobility long enough for the poison which his attacker can now inject at leisure to do its deadly work. The squirming legs of the struggling fly show that death isn't quick but however much the bee-fly might struggle, escape is never an option. On the other nodules, like diners ignoring a rowdy corner table, the other flies, beetles and bugs graze seemingly unconcerned.

Like an actress on the high wire the white death spider then deftly carries its now trussed and bundled lunch over the lip of the plant's head into her improvised lair on the underside, where she fixes it securely before returning topside, unruffled, to again stand motionless and invisible, arms raised outstretched like a supplicant priest, patiently awaiting the arrival of her next unsuspecting meal.

I've watched her now for several days. She is perhaps the perfect predator, one of the scariest of Kerkelven's many scary residents.

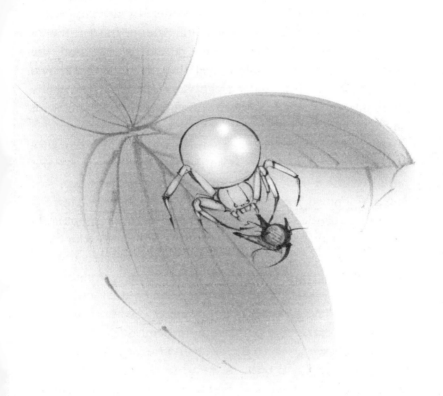

Into the light

Talking of scary beasts brings us inevitably to the king of Kerkelven's flying insects, the dragonfly. His is a world of bright light, for dragonflies have the most amazing eyes in all the world. A dragonfly's eyes surround his head so he's able to see forward, backward and to either side all at the same time. Each eye is made up of literally thousands of small facets called ommatidia, which are double lenses, one flat on the surface and the second a conical lens below. Depending on the arrangement of these dual lenses dragonflies generally see better in front and above, which is why they often approach prey or potential lovers from below and behind. The dragonfly's excellent eyesight is further helped in that they can see ultraviolet light so are able to cope with complex reflections such as shimmering water in bright sunlight. If you are a potential prey, just because you haven't seen him doesn't mean he hasn't clearly seen you.

As I have mentioned, dragonflies belong to the order *Odonata*, which refers not at all to their beauty or grace but means 'toothed jaws'. These are indeed fearsome beasts. But only about half of the 5,300 species of *Odonata* are dragonflies, the rest are species of the more delicate, though not necessarily more genteel, damselfly.

Among the fastest and most manoeuvrable of flying insects, it is estimated that some of the huge dragonflies found in the fossil record from prehistoric times would have had to fly at above 70 kilometres per hour just to keep airborne. Modern-day hawker dragonflies zoom along at about 35km per hour whereas damselflies can only manage a modest 10km per hour. But thanks to their brilliant wing design they can all fly sideways and backwards as well as forward and can change direction in the blink of an eye, even though blinking is something they don't need to do. And they can hover and glide too.

The rape of the banded demoiselle

Early in July I saw this extraordinary encounter and I wrote it down on the spot. Afterwards, as I read about these delicate insects and their habits, I found all other accounts without exception were sterile and restrained by comparison. Perhaps in describing this as rape I'm over-anthropomorphising the actions of the male demoiselles. Such encounters may indeed just be normal. But I merely report what I saw and how it struck me at the time.

Sex in the world of insects is often rough, frequently not consensual. The damselfly is a favourite insect for me, and particularly among that grouping, I like the banded demoiselle. The female of the species is slight, delicate, almost transparent; she has none of the bright, gaudy displays of her larger mate, being coloured a dull green with translucent wings, making her hard to spot. But the male of the species knows what he's looking for and can spot her easily.

He is larger, stronger and much more brightly coloured. The one I observed was a brilliant shimmering blue with darker blue markings across his four splendid wings. His body is thicker than hers and longer too, powerful, pliable and very strong.

Watching insects have sex is a strange pastime. The thing about Peeping Toms is they should aspire not to be seen, but I can hardly avoid it. And Peeping Tom seems a strange name to give a chap when his looming visage must seem to the two sweaty beasts shagging about four inches away to loom like Jupiter seen from its moons, occupying at least a third of their available sky.

There are numerous damselflies and other winged travellers around at the water's edge now. The female I've spotted has also attracted the attentions of a group of idly hovering males. Though all seem interested, one is more attentive and persistent than the rest. Congress can only commence when the male has trapped the female, often after a tiring chase. The chase begins at a dizzying pace with twists, turns and pirouettes up, down and sideways around the plant-strewn riverbank above and across the rocks at the water's edge. But there's only one possible end as the male traps the female on the ground, asserting his mastery by fixing his abdomen firmly around the back of her neck. No female can resist the power of that grip. This is about control, domination and subjugation. The male then grasps and mounts his paramour and there's nothing gentle or discreet about what he does, from here on it's rough full-on sex, no pretence at otherwise. After flying in tandem for a while the pair adopt what's called the wheel position, where he holds her firmly by the neck, forcing her onto his secondary genitals. Dragonflies and damselflies are unique in that males have two sets of genitals. To fertilise his mate the male must first pass a sperm packet from his primary genitals, located at the end of his abdomen, to the secondary genitals at the top of his abdomen, just above the chest. These have hook-like grippers attached, designed for holding her firmly. Here he has to attach her genitals – just one set she has, at the end of her abdomen, which is now curled up and held against his chest, ready for the deed.

Penetration is rough and determined. In some damselfly males the tip of the whiplike penis is equipped with spines for scouring out the genital tract of the female, to remove the sperm of any other males. So, no gentle foreplay here. Of course it occurs to me that despite the apparent brutality the female demoiselle, while not actually enjoying it, might at least be OK. Given her contortions I conclude that this is unlikely. The female is bent over backwards and upside down, pinned down and forced to offer herself to her assailant.

From time to time throughout their vigorous coupling the male appears to pause to mop his brow, brushing his antennae with a loose forearm. The female stays trapped beneath, inverted and held in a vicelike grip while the male thrusts deeply, vigorously, rhythmically, urgently and with scant regard for his subservient partner.

At last the satiated male releases his grip and his victim is set free. It seems to take her some time to recover, while he saunters off to a nearby leaf where he sits, nay reclines, basking in the sunlight, seemingly more than a little pleased with himself – the boy done good.

Having painfully straightened her bruised and sore abdomen, she is having trouble getting her wings to work. The right wings have been bent sideways. For a while it looks like she might be unable to fly. Having forgotten the encounter already the male now moves off, in the insect equivalent of a post-coital fag, to lounge on a nearby leaf. But two more likely lads hove in view and quickly spot the weakened and disabled female, dishevelled but obviously still at least a bit alluring and fair game to her opposite sex. Eagerly they swoop and a second desperate chase begins among the ferns, with again only one possible outcome. A second rape appears inevitable and it's unlikely to be more considerate of the female than was the first. Of course there's nothing to suggest that the apparent abuse I witnessed was her first or even second coupling that morning. The male who inseminates her just before she lays her eggs will be the one who gets to spread his genes. She, poor creature, has no option other than to submit to him and all others before him.

Such is the lot of the female banded demoiselle. Tempting though it is to intervene, I'll resist and leave the banded demoiselles to their own devices, which inevitably means to the less than tender care of their males.

An orgiastic feast of snails

Talk about untidy eaters! The mess on our stone tabletop has to be seen to be believed. It seems that overnight a large number of birds have got together to feast on their collection of snails, which must suddenly have come into season and have paid the ultimate penalty for it.

Boy, those snails must taste good. I don't imagine the feasting birds were many – maybe four at most – but the debris and disorder they've left behind seem more suited to maybe ten times four.

In following days I find that a number of large stones and rocks around the field have been used for a similar purpose. But it's our circular stone table that seems most popular. This is where the birds come with their takeaways to have their own picnics, simply by piling up a collection of snails and bashing them against the tabletop.

But oh, what a mess they make. It's not just that they smash up the shells and leave bits all over the place. No, birds eat and shit, shit and eat, eat and eat and shit and shit.

The curious thing, of course, is how short the snail season is, for these birds. It seems to happen on just a few days of high summer. During this brief season every flat rock, stone and solidish surface around gets covered in snail debris and bird shit. I have to assume that the birds either demolish the entire snail population in one sitting (or perhaps shitting) save for some breeding pairs of snails who, one presumes, must hide out somewhere and save themselves so they can mate and produce next year's bird picnics.

When I found a bunch of snail shells by the stone table, I not unnaturally assumed that the birds had eaten the snail for food and discarded the shell. But perhaps not. If it was in the egg-laying season, it could be the *shells* they were after. The laying female has to eat lots for egg formation – particularly calcium-rich food so as to obtain the calcium she needs to form the shells of her own eggs. Many birds collect and eat snail shells for this purpose.

The presence of broken snail shells could be the work of a song thrush, of which species we have a few and lovely they are. Thrushes are early nesters, choosing a place protected from predators but with a view of what's going on. Their nest, built entirely by the female, is lined with mud, twigs, grass and moss, which she smoothes with her breast to make it comfy for her three or four blue eggs. In the right conditions, she may nest two or three times in a season.

Dancing in the street

National day in France is the fourteenth of July, which Brits refer to as Bastille Day. It's a *jour ferié*, a bank holiday, a day for nationwide celebrating and enjoyment. Curiously in Melrand they celebrate the day before, the thirteenth of July, perhaps because the Melrandais delight in being different. The town really buzzes for the whole of this special day but it's from later in the evening that it becomes truly alive because that's when the band starts up and, slowly, excitedly, the people get ready for the fireworks and the dance.

Fireworks, ever-popular with young and old alike, are also a major feature partly because they're cheap and plentiful here, if perhaps somewhat unstable and unreliable. Each successive summer is marked by different fireworks incidents from the dramatic to the comic, such as the night the church roof caught fire in the midst of an overenthusiastic fireworks finale or the time some local youngsters ran amok with exploding artifices, creating good-natured mayhem among the holiday crowds as they gathered under streetlamps and starlight to dance the night away.

Our Scottish friends Robert and Isobel try to catch this event every year simply because they're addicted to the rare pleasure of dancing in the street. And what a spectacular thing it is, with the peculiarly Breton congas and line dances that make street dancing so distinctive and enjoyable here. Dances in Brittany are usually followed in either a circle or a line that spirals around the room, or, in street dancing, round the entire village square. They range from simple dances, with linked arms and basic footwork, through to dances with more complex arm and foot movements. Both are usually accompanied by lively music on the bombarde and biniou-kozh, and much laughing and clapping of hands.

Street parties are all too rare in most societies now, found in only a few places and mostly at carefully pre-arranged times, which rather defeats the point. While that's generally true also in Brittany, dancing in the street does happen and when it does, locals, newcomers and tourists all seem to love it.

There should be more of it. Why not? Summer's here. The time is right.

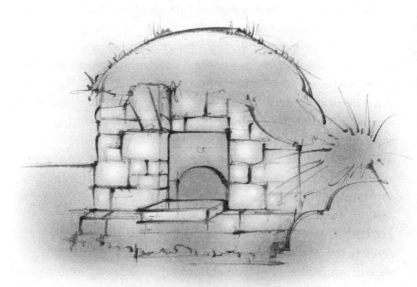

14 July, the fête of Kerkelven

For years, when our friends the Robertson family would visit, we with the enthusiastic support of our neighbours would take advantage of their presence to have our own little village fête just for the four households and their immediate circles. On this occasion the village bread oven would enjoy one of its few productive uses of the year, we would reserve a baby pig for roasting and, hopefully shaded from a warm summer sun, we'd gather around a long table under the trees on Elodie and Raymonde's lawn to enjoy an extended lunchtime feast in the traditional Breton style, finished off for most of us by a little lie-down on the grass, maybe around seven in the evening. One year the local newspaper sent a reporter round to photograph our event because local village fêtes are generally in decline and to see one such as ours, where a village of just three inhabitants had in the space of a few years grown to the point where thirteen residents and their guests could sit down and dine, was news indeed and good news at that. This growth of course came about when we moved here full-time and when, shortly after, Raymonde and Elodie chose to do the same thing and raise a family here. But it was only when we reactivated the bread oven that it became big local news.

The first time we tried this the pig came out raw because we had quite failed to realise that you have to preheat these old stone ovens for a full two days before the event at least, by filling and refilling them with branches for burning, so that the stones inside get close to white hot.

It was a mistake we didn't make again.

Forbidden fruits of the forest

Already the first blackberries have ripened under the summer sun. Chantal, one of our neighbours from across the valley, is up with the lark and on our side of the river collecting *murs*, juicy fat blackberries which are now hanging in shiny black bunches from the brambles all over Kerkelven. Horrible and reviled for most of the year as brambles are, this is the brief window when they justify their existence by producing the most delicious of fruit. Chantal though is clearly determined to enjoy nature's bounty to the full and, bucket under her arm, she's nipped over to collect the entire harvest if she can, oblivious to the needs of us, the proprietors. But all's fair in love and fruit-gathering here; it's survival of the fittest. So I rouse Marie and we rush down to the field to fill a bowl each before there's none left.

Oh, the taste! Our bowls rapidly empty, so we slide back again to thwart Chantal before she's got halfway up the 45-degree path. But nature's bounty can be deceptive and it turns out there's more than enough for all of us and even some for the birds too. So what if we risk a scratch or two to collect them?

Blackberries were once supposed to be the fruit of the devil as brambles evidently are credited with saving Lucifer when he fell from heaven and from grace at the dawn of time, in much the same way that brambles also saved Marie when she fell from the path back in January.

But they taste simply delicious now and would justify any sin if offered as a reward.

Snap, crackle and pop

The black seed pods on the broom bushes (*Apophyllum anomalum*) crack open at this time, sending a delicious breakfast-cereal sound reverberating around the forest. But it's no call to the breakfast table, because these things don't taste of anything much and only a few flies show interest.

If you're not looking, you won't see

This shouldn't surprise us, because it's blindingly obvious. You won't see anything if you don't look. But if you think about it, we so often and so easily miss such a lot simply because we don't look.

Remember Bertrand last September, and the trout in the river. He assumed there were no fish there so he stopped looking. That didn't stop him though, from telling me there were no trout in the river. So, I didn't look either. As a result those fish were swimming around almost at our feet for years, yet we were entirely oblivious of their existence.

I now take a deliberately different approach.

I look, even though there may be nothing there worth seeing. In this way, invariably, I find something that otherwise I would have missed. Not only do I learn a lot from this, I also find life is full of surprises. And I'm more optimistic and perceptive as a result.

It pays to cultivate the art of seeing the invisible.

Syrus and the summer-storm horrors

This is the season of thunderstorms, a physical phenomenon to which this region seems remarkably prone. They invariably occur when heat builds up and are perhaps the price we pay for summer. Animals particularly fear these storms and are particularly attuned to the air-pressure changes that precede them. So the first we humans know that a thunderstorm is coming is usually well before any sign of approaching storm, when the dogs start to go mad. But me, I love these sultry summer storms. It's a time for madness, your hair stands on end, the world goes a shade of green and everything begins to swirl.

Syrus, perhaps because he has the most delicate ears, is always first to feel when a storm is coming, often hours before the event and well before the other two. They will be upset by the storm, but Syrus gets truly terrified and is compelled by an irresistible force inside himself to make a run for it.

Before we detect any other indication Syrus gets hyper-excited and starts, literally, to tear down his surroundings. Max, his sister, then helps as she's only too willing to get up to any mischief if the opportunity presents, though I suspect the storms bother her but little. The lengths Syrus and his twisted sister will go to, to escape from their niche, can be alarming, as there's a real prospect they'll injure themselves. If not let out, they'll bite clean through the wire netting on their door.

Usually by the time the storm actually manifests itself they've calmed down, as if the anticipation is somehow worse than the actual event. Perhaps the air pressure reduces for the storm itself, when slowly the air will change and thicken, the sky will darken and an eerie still descends. Then everything seems to crackle and the air becomes electric. Lightning can flash, although as often as not there'll be no rain. Wind can pick up at this time, even becoming scarily strong, but most of these thunderstorms are short-lived and as soon as you're in them and enjoying yourself, it's over. The world winds down a little and returns to normal, as if it's just recovered from an orgasm.

The only thing I really dislike about these storms is how wound up and upset Syrus gets. The instant he escapes or is released from his pen he'll invariably run into our house – which at other times he avoids, because he clearly doesn't like 'indoors'. But in the storm, this is where he feels at least an acceptable level of safety, hiding under Joe's bed at the top of the house with his paws over his ears to shut out the world.

And when the storm subsides, he's often found sleeping there, as if he hasn't a care in the world.

Max too recovers quickly but Mortimer still seems put out,

though not by the storms. Though mostly pretty good, his off days come round ever more frequently. I fear that this long hot summer may be testing him to his limit.

Beetlemania

We have huge stag beetles around at this time, so large you can hear them crashing through the undergrowth. They can be scary too if they take off and fly towards you, corkscrewing through the air.

In this season I spend a lot of time saving insects that have fallen in the swimming pool, including even whole heaps of beetles who seem determined to commit collective self-destruction. I don't expect their appreciation, though some do seem almost grateful as I lift them out and gently blow on their wings to dry them. Maybe one day some of them will get together, to find a way to thank me.

Suddenly again the swimming pool is full of corpses, not just a few but hundreds, even thousands. It's a mad mass suicide and it lasts just three or four days. These black beetles didn't leave a note so I'm searching for an explanation, as in this short time so many have died. All I can find is the vague suggestion that having successfully mated, now apparently they just allow themselves to die. Why they do this in the company of others of their kind is a mystery. Perhaps it's some sort of collective post-coital blues – life just isn't worth living any more. Or they may be mistaking this artificial body of water for something else. Perhaps more research is needed.

Mass suicide is a curious thing. As insects generally don't live long you'd think they'd cling to life as long as they can.

Last month there were flying ants, who appeared to decide all together to drown themselves in our pool. For two, maybe three days I was fishing them out by the net-full, but I'd save very few and those I did would just head back, like lemmings, to fulfil their suicidal destiny, making whatever grand gesture they thought they were making. These, I discover, are mating swarms, so I can only hope that, having done the business moments before, they choose with a magnificent flourish to end it all in our pool, rather than to live for what would be a rather short time anyway, just with the memory.

A visit to Angèle

Angèle and Mathurin had been married for 64 years. Not surprisingly, in that time you become used to each other. So it's not the funeral or the days immediately afterwards that are hardest to bear, because there's a lot going on then, and there are always lots of people around.

It's the days after the days after the funeral that seem the longest and the hardest to bear. We resolve that we should look in from time to time, to check that our newly widowed neighbour is all right.

Angèle has been crying a lot. But she quickly brightens up when she sees us as she would, I think, for any visitor. We've timed our call to the middle of the afternoon so that with luck she'll not feel obliged to bring out alcohol. But Angèle has assumed Mathurin's mantle of hospitality. She shares his endless generosity and inability to comprehend the meaning of 'No'.

'We won't stay long, Angèle, as Ken has to work,' says Marie as the chairs are brought round, chipping in, 'and so do I,' for good measure. 'We won't have wine now, it's too early in the day,' she repeats as the glasses appear. Really, we *Anglais* do everything later than the French (something that's well known and constantly marvelled at by Breton people: the Brits eat late, stay up late and rise late; it never ceases to amaze).

But it doesn't prevent the production of the wine bottle. 'OK, just half a glass then,' we say as Angèle completely ignores us and fills each glass to the brim. Nor does it prevent the frequent filling of Breton shot glasses (designed to be refilled as soon as they're emptied). We toast Mathurin, the children and grandchildren, our children, the mayor, the President of France and the Prime Minister across the water. And we settle in for the evening.

Three meals a day or what?

As I've observed before, most of the life around us in this land of plenty is forever eating or being eaten.

So at what point in human development did we humans decide on three meals a day and cocoa before bedtime, the norm that has for so long held sway in most of the civilised world?

What, I wonder, is our natural state? Is the human species designed to be a binge eater, or a constant snacker? Or were we meant to eat only when hungry? When and how did we opt for the prevailing paradigm? And is it good for us? What else might we do if we didn't spend so much of our time eating or preparing for food?

I sense this could take me off in all sorts of new research directions.

Perhaps I'll do just that, after lunch.

We don't hear enough about pus

We have heard before, of course, in this tale, about the awful biting of foul insects and how their combined depredations can drive sane folk to distraction. Desperately bad though the likes of your cleg or horsefly are, their attacks are confined to the riverbanks and their season is short. Worst of all is the silent biting mozzie that singly or in pairs descend upon us in our own home in the dead of night, injecting their numbing saliva so they can rip uninterrupted into our flesh and suck out our juices as we sleep. This they do for most of the summer, if we'll allow them. Worse than worst of all are the gangs of malevolent mozzies that surreptitiously attack the ankles of diners out of doors. While we innocently digest, they feast silently upon our feet, choosing the soft, tasty, juicy, blood-laden fleshy parts just above our ankles.

Apart from their impact on sleep for the next few nights (when it's warm anyway there's few things more guaranteed to stave off sleep than bitten ankles), the infections they inflict can turn to wounds that seep an endless supply of pus. I'm sorry if this offends the delicate sensitivities of some readers but pus has for too long been swept under the carpet.

Where does it come from? And what purpose does it have? Does it flow down from the rest of our bodies when we stand, and gather in our ankles? Is it there even when mozzies are not, and are we silently filling up with it? Does it have a purpose? If it's meant to ease our suffering from mozzie bites it doesn't bloody work, that's for sure.

I'm being a bit harsh here. Pus is a combination of dead cells and a thin protein-rich fluid called *liquor puris*, which is part of the body's autoimmune response system. When nasty infections such as those transmitted by the sinister hypodermic jaws of biting mosquitoes invade, this splendid liquid rushes to our defence to neutralise the incoming organisms and so, potentially, save our lives.

It'd be nice if the body could develop something to ease the itching though; however puss-y and snotty it might be I'd welcome that.

The magic of still

Why do I so value this field? Well, one of its less obvious and perhaps surprising attributes is . . . peace. The world outside seems a much less stable place than our field. Of course at times our field is frantic, obsessively busy, everyone on the move. But it's controlled and purposeful. In Kerkelven, each resident seems to appreciate the true value of peace.

In the heavy summer heat at its peak, nothing moves in the middle hours of the day. The stillness of Kerkelven then envelops the entire field and woods. Nothing stirs, not even a mouse. The damselflies and most other insects cease their flying. Dogs lie and pant. Only the flies, those pesky dirty villains who respect nothing, continue to buzz around, but even their drone is lost in the heat of the day. The air has a palpable weight. Breathing is laboured. Shade is obligatory. Words are few and syrupy; thinking is just too tiring to contemplate.

Dirt gets in everywhere

Marie sometimes tells me she imagines that she must get up in the night and go out to dig our neighbours' potatoes, then get back into bed and has no memory of it when she wakes in the morning.

How else can she account for thoroughly washing before going to bed then waking up with dirty fingernails next day? It's the only explanation that adds up.

The mystery of the *chevreuil*

As rare as a ghost and just as thrilling is a glimpse of the shy, fabulous nocturnal *chevreuil,* our local roe deer. Though they are not uncommon either in Brittany or in Britain, these fabulous animals are so timid that it's possible to live a lifetime here and never see them. I've had sightings on just four occasions, though several times my neighbour across the river has told me he'd seen deer in our little bit of forest, I confess I never dared to hope that I'd ever see them here.

I saw one once, just the tiniest glimpse, running along Emile's field to the left of the prairie. Then again I saw two charging through the woods like sprites in a race, in the woods around Angie and Keith's. Then suddenly I saw one standing stock-still in Emile's small field by the river (next-but-one downriver to ours.) It was there just an instant, then gone. Just like a ghost.

The next time I saw this wonder is described below.

Two break out of the forest

Visitors Caroline and Isobel Robertson had just cleaned the table down by the river from its covering of dead snail shells and bird shit. I'd been down inspecting the outcome (it was so tidy I felt tempted to erect a sign saying 'Birds Eff Off!'

The dogs alerted me first. I looked up to see a breathtaking sight. The deer is a regal, noble animal. It moves with superb grace, such effortless and perfect symmetry that despite its fleetness it almost seems in slow motion. This one was full grown, young, slender and athletic with muscles rippling in the afternoon sun. The dogs raced towards it but half-heartedly and curiously; the deer seemed less than concerned. It galloped off just as its mate, a few paces behind so still on the edge of the forest, turned and dove back into the protective cover, so quickly it left me more with an impression of the mate than an actual sighting. Meanwhile all three dogs were in less than hot pursuit of the first, the stag I surmise, though I saw no antlers. I called dementedly at the hounds to try to get them to leave off but with almost no hope of success. Sure enough though, seconds later all three reappeared on the brow of the hillock that the deer had bounded over and excitedly returned to me, their master, panting obediently and looking as if they'd just been very bad. I was thrilled not just by this rare acknowledgement of my senior role, but at last I'd seen roe deer in my forest.

And they were superb beyond my wildest anticipation.

Deer equals queer

In researching this book I uncovered some bizarre things about deer. They have a scent gland between their toes so that other deer can follow them (handy, huh?). And they like to swim in the sea, if they get the chance. Deer have often been spotted frolicking in the waves, though I must say I've never seem them take so much as a wash at Kerkelven.

The gathering gloom

As his health of late has suffered ups and downs I've often wondered what it would be like if I were to lose my close companion Mortimer. He's my daemon, my external soul. We're chalk and cheese, perhaps, but we've also become symbiotic. Though not quite joined at the hip, we've become so noticeably half of a double act that few fail to comment upon it. We're Kerkelven's Laurel and Hardy, Sam and Frodo, or Little and Large. As we've aged the prospect of one or other of us having to go on without the other, while less and less palatable, has become more and more real. I reflect on Ernie without Eric, of Cannon without Ball, and wonder if it's not best to be the first to go. But that's not likely. To be honest I've had to admit that these past few months, for much of the time Mortimer's not been well. This is more than the natural slowing of age, more than just the normal aches and pains as our bodies slowly decline.

These last few years Mortimer has shared the indignity of

ageing with me, as we've both grown older and less agile together. But this is something more: the rheumy eyes, the struggling to keep up, the sudden tendency to swerve and knock people over. The long pauses and the seeming bewilderment. And that's just been me. Mortimer has been much worse, and try to ignore it as I might the realisation's become increasingly unavoidable to me; this time next year it's unlikely that Mortimer will be with me, to take these walks.

Of course I can't be sure I'll be here myself, we none of us can. But I'm likely to outlast Mortimer and that will be hard to bear. To quote my writer friend Indra, in the end we are condemned to lose everything we love. I've always known this, but it doesn't make it easier.

Our project begins to take shape

As yet, we haven't procured so much as a new plant nor initiated any visible change in the field, but the idea that began life as a casual suggestion is already assuming massive significance. We've realised that it's within our power and means to change this field, already a natural treasure, and make it a bit or even a lot better.

For what will be the future of our field, if we just leave it as it is? Perhaps, even probably, it will be fine. But with increasing threats from climate change and the destructive impact of each successive year's hunting, the prospects for decline are real.

Maybe, if we can, we should be doing something to encourage positive change, for the sake of all who live here. Perhaps I can find ways to do something much more constructive for the future of Kerkelven than just the occasional clearing of undergrowth and cutting of paths through the grass, in the belief that creatures of field and forest can move about more easily.

August

Simply, the best

Without a doubt this is my favourite time of year, high summer. But now that I have to write about it, what can I say that can possibly do it justice? Particularly as I'm now edging towards the end of my year-long sally around this field so have to bring the threads of that undertaking together, to try to find some meaning in it all. Sooner or later every writer has to face this sinking sensation: words fail me.

Like all would-be writers I'm also a bit of an idealistic dreamer and I have a secret envy. I'm so, so jealous of the creativity, self-confidence and sheer insanity of the writer of Roy Orbison's classic hit 'Blue Angel' who, presumably, crouching over his typewriter one day, must have announced to whoever else was within earshot, 'I've got it – the chorus! It's "Sha–la-la, doobie-wah, bum, bum, bum, dip, dip, bum". Then you repeat it.'

Oh, how I wish I'd written that. How many people, since Roy himself (for it was he) with his co-writer Joe Melson (it took *two* of them) penned these immortal lines back in 1960, have sung that chorus to themselves in the bath, or with a hairbrush for a microphone in front of the bedroom mirror, perhaps, while combing their hair before stepping out on a Friday or Saturday night?

For me, life need have no more profound meaning than that, to give so many people so much innocent pleasure. If my account of the journey round this field could give just one person even a small part of such undiluted joy then the effort has been repaid.

And it did, I am sure. Even before anyone had read a word of it, the experience was already giving a lot to one rather important individual – me. And it's kept on giving ever since.

So, perhaps that is the meaning of life. If you want to get, you have to give.

I have many happy memories from my schooldays but not much of them are memories of anything useful. All that book learning went in one ear and quickly out the other. Only a very few things my teachers said stuck, and one was a short and not very good poem. It went as follows:

> There goes the happy moron,
> He doesn't give a damn,
> I'm glad I'm not a moron,
> Good God, perhaps I am?

I've no idea why I've never forgotten this. Why, of all things, did this verse of dumb doggerel indelibly print itself on my formative, then fairly empty young brain? Particularly as so much else that was much more learned and much more important simply instantly fell out to be lost forever, or didn't even penetrate at all. It's a mystery.

Bear with me, please, there is a point to this digression, if a somewhat obscure one.

If you are one of those people obsessed by the search for the meaning of life, let me tell you that I think I've found it. This isn't something I've learned from long years and wide experience, it's something I've come to appreciate just recently. You are more likely to find what life means for you right close by you, swimming round your feet, rather than far away up in the stars. Although you might find it is fun to look there too, at times. The answer to the meaning of life is simply in the looking.

The truth is that, never quite satisfied with what I've got and cursed with a restless heart and inquiring mind, I've always been secretly jealous of the happy moron. Now, thanks to my recent encounter with the art of looking, I think I can set that envy, and my envy of the Big O, to rest at last.

Anyway, that's my point. That and shooby-dum, bum, bum, badda-bing, bang, boom, boo.

Ebb and flow

As if an augur of Mortimer's mortality, Ebb the fish died today. He was at least four, maybe five, which is a fine old age for a tropical fish living in captivity.

I hope Ebb had a happy life as well as just a long one. Perhaps you shouldn't expect much interaction or appreciation from a fish but I'm quite prepared to believe that Ebb was aware of us and our comings and goings and knew when, even cared whether, we were there or not. Whenever we would go away for any length of time I was always conscious of closing up the house from Ebb's point of view. I'm sure he realised what was up as soon as the shutters would close and artificial darkness would descend upon his tank, indicating that for a while, we wouldn't be around, that he, Ebb, would be entirely on his own. Ebb always became a bit more than usually animated at this time, swimming back, forth and around while generally looking a bit concerned. As soon as we'd come back Ebb would not perhaps swim about with glee, but he would look pleased and would lurk at the bottom of his watery world with what I could easily imagine was a satisfied smirk across his chops.

Each morning when in residence my looming face would occupy a large part of Ebb's visible sky and I like to think this reassured him in his loneliness. I'm not saying he pined for us when we were absent, but I'm sure he realised something was missing from his world, if only my fat face from behind the glass of his tank, which I suppose must have distorted my features as if it were a giant hall of mirrors. I'm sure he would have missed that.

I liked Ebb. After Charlie left home it fell to me to top up his tank, make an effort to keep it clean, change when necessary the battery on his automatic feeder and make sure it was always full of food and functional. As month followed month it became increasingly clear that Ebb depended totally on me for his very survival. Yet he was never a burden, always a joy. I will miss him.

Herding swine

As I mentioned last October, a few years back when the farm next door was a living, working enterprise we shared Kerkelven with up to three hundred pigs. Old Emile's farm was what's known hereabouts as a 'hotel' for pigs. He took them at two months old – quite fully grown – and kept them for three more, feeding and fattening them the while. Then they went off to the piggy equivalent of the Holiday Home for Pets pie company, to be chopped into chops or whatever. A short but not inevitably unhappy life.

Pigs are not necessarily bad neighbours, though you could be forgiven for thinking otherwise. Pigs treat you as an equal. They don't judge, they're never indifferent and are always touchingly pleased to see you. For most of the time they make little noise and if cleaned regularly they don't smell much. The trouble with our neighbouring pigs was, Emile never cleaned them at all. But this was hardly their fault.

Understandably life in the pigpens wasn't always to their liking and from time to time they would escape. Mainly they could do this when Emile or one of his offspring had failed to properly tie their gate, which happened more than you might expect.

In his declining years Emile the widowed farmer had thrown in his lot with Claudette, a rather nervous but refined, bourgeois widow from the coast, who was, to put it politely, somewhat older even than he. From time to time the good widow would stay over and occasionally Emile would leave her on her own, in charge of house and dependencies, while he went off on business of his own. It was upon such a night that the pigs chose to make their biggest breakout of all time, and when I called to alert the farm of this fact, it was the nervous Claudette who answered.

To her credit she came quickly enough. By the time she got here about sixty rumbling porkers were on the loose and while on their part no clear plan was evident, they were milling about in all directions. I still have a vivid picture in my mind of Claudette, face-pack still drying, curlers at all angles, attempting rather ineffectively to round them up, clad in her silk nightdress with just a skimpy jacket on top, waggling a short stick at them while with forefinger and thumb of her remaining hand, gingerly raising the hem of her nightdress lest it trail in the carpet of sticky mud. To show that chivalry is not dead I rushed to help her, when really I should have shot off to get the camera.

The killing of Mr Pig

Perhaps some things should never be described but as I've committed myself to uncovering the realities of life as it is lived around Kerkelven, I can't leave out some mention of what was once a not infrequent event here – the open-air killing of a pig. If you insist in trying to raise a family next door to a working pig farm I guess this is the kind of thing you have to put up with.

Back in the days when the pigs were in residence, every three or four months or so Sylvan le Gourirrec, the butcher from nearby Locmariaquer, would arrive at the sheds just behind our house. He'd come ready clad in his grimy bloodstained work apron complete with polished knives gleaming, to officiate at the slaughter of an unlucky pig chosen by Emile, presumably at random, to feed his family. Thankfully for Kerkelven and its inhabitants, this event, like the pig farm itself, is now a thing of the past. But when it happened, it was impossible to ignore.

Emile went out of his way to assure me that he only ever killed a pig for his own purposes, to feed his family, which had the effect of causing me to wonder whether much of this meat was not indeed destined to be sold 'on the black', or else he was at the very least up to something questionable. Sometimes he would remember to alert us when he was planning to kill a pig, but other times he'd just forget. I would encourage him to warn us, because such was the distress of the animal and so bloodcurdling the noises it made that we used to try to stay indoors until the sordid business was over.

I'm not suggesting that old Emile really enjoyed killing a pig but there was a time when he seemed to relish it, particularly if he thought he could attract a crowd of squeamish and scandalised foreigners.

One summer, when again our friends the Robertsons from Scotland were with us, the pig-killing ritual intruded more than usual on our happy holiday spirit. All five children were playing innocently outside and we four adults were finishing a slow breakfast in the sun when the noise of a tractor revving at the farm alerted us that something was occurring. The loud squeals from a pig in distress sent me running to round up the children while Marie rather embarrassedly explained to our friends what might be about to happen.

As I rounded the corner I saw immediately that the deed was already far advanced. Emile had moved his tractor with big forked arms into position alongside the pig shed next to where our cars were parked. Here, on the outstretched fork arms of his tractor, he had hoisted the struggling, noisy pig up by its back legs so the slaughterman could more easily get at it to do his bloody deed.

As I took in this scene in horror I saw that all five of our children were sitting on the roof of the Robertsons' Renault Espace, mouths hanging open in spellbound fascination.

At my shout they startled from their dreamlike absorption, tumbling down from their perch as I shooed them indoors where, dutifully, they went. Moments later when I returned to remonstrate with Emile I saw all five hanging out of the upstairs window from where, if anything, their view of the horror was even better.

And what a sight it was. The screaming and squealing of the doomed beast had ceased, soon after its throat was cut. As the carcass swung gently back and forth a syrupy crimson pool had drained from the open neck to gather in a coagulating puddle between the tractor's front wheels. Neither farmer, butcher nor assistant seemed even slightly put out by this, nor were the watching youngsters, though I've no doubt that the 299 other residents of the Kerkelven pig farm were horrified beyond belief, for all were cowering silently in their stalls, keeping their heads down, perhaps thanking their piggy maker that it was this pig that had been chosen and not them.

It was a sorry sight. The kids though seemed fascinated by the whole thing, taking it all in their stride, almost nonchalantly pooh-poohing our outrage and anxieties.

When later we all sat round the dinner table to discuss it, these youngsters pointed out quite forcefully to us grown-ups (having first thoroughly rehearsed their arguments, I surmise) that perhaps our concerns for their distress were unwarranted, for we all ate pork and so should all be prepared ourselves to kill the pig, if needs be. We should just be thankful, said one in vindication, that old Emile was willing to do this kind of thing for us, so that we could consume our pork ready-prepared and shrunk-wrapped from the supermarket rather than sliced still warm from the gore-stained carcass. I refrained from observing that our neighbour seemed to enjoy turning this possibly necessary act into a spectator sport, contenting myself with merely pointing out that it seemed an undignified end for the unlucky animal and plain mean to oblige the other pigs to listen. But it was an argument that we lost to our children, one of an increasing number, it has to be said.

Walking the dogs, August

I first noticed a faltering in Mortimer's step back in March, in the spring. When everything else was waking up, gathering pace and bursting with life, old Mort seemed to be visibly slowing down. It's hardly surprising. Mortimer is a very big dog and he's thirteen years old, a good age for such a big animal. He's had, as they say, a good innings. I try to put a brave face on it and make the appropriate noises, sighing ruefully. But I'm fooling no one, least of all Mortimer.

Now as July turns to August and we're in the midst of the hottest weeks of summer, I can't deny he's having an even harder time.

Today Mortimer fell off the west bridge. I'd stopped on it, for some reason, and he'd brushed past and missed his footing. He landed with his backend dangling over the bank, his feet almost in the stream. In times past he'd have leaped up and brushed the whole thing off. Now his past energy has deserted him so I have to bend down and lift him out. Within a few moments he's his old self again, but we both know this isn't good.

Seeing him like this breaks my heart. I cajole and

encourage him and fuss about him a lot, for though I've often wondered what might happen to him, I find I've really never quite accepted in my heart of hearts that he might actually die. It's only just reached me that this is not just a possibility but an inevitability, the only questions now are when and how will it be? I try to make the walks easier for him. I go slower, and I talk to him more. As usual, he seems much less put out by the prospect of his demise than do I.

I'm in trouble again over the state of my pond in the parklands, which several of my family think is now little more than a breeding ground for mosquitoes and other seasonal winged pond-dwelling pests. I can't deny that this assertion has some merit. I resolve to dig out my pond-owner's guide and search further for aerating plants and solar pumps that might actually work.

There's a small swirling insect around now about the size of a gnat or a midge and the field is full of them. They can only be seen when the sun is behind you, illuminating them in their countless hordes. I presume they're the same species as the midge-like insects that were so evident last November. Several birds seem to be eating them, which I suppose is a benefit, but I've no idea where they've come from.

Suki, our new-found pedigree chum, is now a regular on our summer walks. When it's hot he and the other three like nothing better than splashing about in the river, so all rush along the paths and walkways to get to the riverbank where, for easy access, I've cleared sections of undergrowth so we can all jump in. Well, Mort doesn't rush but he has a game go and manages to tag along. With the river shallow and slow-moving, the banks now are a lush, overflowing paradise, the tree canopy above almost joined to the far side in places, with branches and fronds hanging down to the sun-dappled, mill-pond-smooth surface below. It's extraordinarily good fun to chase the dogs around in this Eden, but because Suki has more energy than all the other four of us put together, he probably has the best of times.

But even he fails to be excited by how the swallows in the field feed as they fly. The most exciting aerial combat from World War aces would be utterly outclassed by these tiny winged wonders as they zoom and dive and pass and roll and eat in flight. The field is suddenly ablaze with their acrobatics in what to them is probably nothing more than a routine hunt, but I could watch it forever, it seems to be the highest level of being to which any creature could aspire. Of all inhabitants of the field the swallow is the one I envy most. What they do on the wing must be like the thrill of high-speed motorcycling only in midair, up, down and sideways all at once and, of course, without the appalling death rate.

Despite the delights above, back on earth Mortimer is struggling. He is very stiff, each step seems awkward and involves effort.

Yet he won't stay behind, nor does he want to turn back.

Spiders that look like wasps and wasps that look that way too

Mortimer has good days and not-so-good days. On the former, at least briefly, we can return to studying life in that great laboratory which our field is now.

At this time down among the ferns, fronds and foliage alongside our favourite walks a curious, rather scary-looking spider is found. She's a big girl, full of figure, she hangs upside down on a vertical orb-shaped web and she looks like a big fat wasp. Or, perhaps, a very small and spidery tiger. That's why, I suppose, this colourful character, *Argiope bruennichi*, is known as the wasp spider, or tiger spider. Better names, it seems to me, than the scientific variety. *Argiope bruennichi* doesn't really trip lightly off the tongue, does it? Nor does it conjure up an image of the sleek, patient, cool killing machine that is the tiger spider.

There's more than a few of these fearsome-looking lassies in our field just now. They're foreign invaders from the south apparently and they're marching in numbers into our countryside, probably catching rather a lot of our good native flies and bitey insects while they're about it. Good for them, say I.

But I wouldn't fancy falling foul of one of these guys myself.

A harvestman with only three of his eight long legs left cuts a pathetic figure as he clings upside down to the top of a tall grass, seemingly unsure of what to do next. Unluckily for him the legs he's lost are four from one side and one from the other, so the best movement he can now make is to spin aimlessly. They lose their legs quite easily these guys, which perhaps isn't surprising, but if I had eight such lovely long legs I'd look after them for sure. Just behind the spinning harvestman is a garden spider hanging (also upside down) in the centre of her smaller but equally intricate web. This specimen is fully fit and alert. A big juicy black-and-red flesh fly has just inadvertently wandered into her orb and trapped itself. Like lightning the spider launches at her prey (which is at least twice as big as her) but the fly isn't securely held and, taking a big chunk of her web with him, he breaks free. If the garden spider is disappointed she doesn't show it, though she'd have every right.

Real wasps are buzzing around here too, in and out of the nest they've made in the willow tree that hangs above the river. Most probably what makes these wasps aggressive at this time is that they are seeking to find a queen to mate with, but their angry buzzing just might be resentment, for soon they are all going to die.

This is a season of overabundance. Swarms of caterpillars drip from the nettle and dock leaves that border our paths at the field's edge. As the wasp spiders set out their sticky stalls along the forest edge to attract the bouncy grasshoppers and endless variety of buzzy flies that form their diet, all around are scenes of comings and goings, massacre and carnage, feasting and hunting, pillage and negotiation. Just a normal summer's day I guess, on this busiest thoroughfare of our field that I call the Strip.

The smooth snake shows off his agility as he hunts, gliding over the rocks and stones, slithering between the nooks, tongue darting all the while. We see a lot of snakes just now and they don't seem to mind us much, even being picked up and played with by the occasional passing small child (OK, me). Sometimes we find the freshly shed skin of a smooth snake draped over some rock or other, but with no sign of the now naked snake. It's as if she's ripped her clothes off in abandon and disappeared dancing into the woods.

There's a small snail whose behaviour amuses me these days. A few days ago I noticed several tiny fragile-looking baby snails each climbing a single stalk of the tall grass. They climbed almost to the top where they now sit firmly fixed, munching happily at the juicy tip for days as they grow and grow. At some point, I imagine, the now quite large snail must look earthward and think, 'Uh-oh, how on earth do I get down?' But here nature plays a remarkable trick. The grass our mollusc friend is perched upon is now somewhat more slender than once it was, thanks to the snail's munching, and it starts ever so slowly to bend. Inevitably in time as the snail grows and the grass bends even more he gets lowered gently to earth, where either he can find larger grasses closer to the ground or someone will come along to catch and eat him.

Snails of the same species climb up and attach themselves to the big umbellifer plants where they grow so large that getting down presents a rather frightening challenge. But these strong plants don't bend, so I guess my neat little theory falls down. As, perhaps eventually, do the snails.

Evidently, some snails are smarter than others.

Big green lizards

If fish forget from one second to the next (apart, of course, from the late lamented Ebb), how good are the remembrances of other small species, lizards, frogs and bats? What about the creatures that lurk at the bottom of our pond?

Our big green lizard here is a truly marvellous species, though it's very shy and hard to spot even when as here they are quite plentiful in number. For some reason I've not yet established this delicate but exotic animal is rare in the UK, only ever found in parts of Dorset, though his smaller, less colourful cousin flourishes throughout the British Isles. Our eighteenth-century friend Gilbert White did once try to introduce a number of green lizards collected from Guernsey in the Channel Islands (so they survived there, at least back then) and proceeded to set these free in the gardens of Pembroke College, Oxford, where they ran about happily enough but did not, for some reason, breed.

The lizards of Kerkelven have no such problem. They appear unfailingly each year on our new stone wall and in various places around and in the forest. They've learned the advantage of staying constantly alert and move with considerable speed.

At this time green lizards take up occupancy on the Strip, where they sit swaying slightly, high off the ground, perched on a tangle of tall grasses and brambles, which presumably lifts them to a good position for seeing and trapping passing prey. You can't get near them without disturbing the undergrowth around them, so they get early warning of whatever's coming.

Toad of Toad Hall and his frogs

Back in the parklands, tucked away in the corner of a deep damp hole in the new wall where the green lizards are found, there sits an old grey patriarch, a senior toad of some proportions. He never moves and seems to be there always. We have called him Gavin after an uncle of mine who lives in the small fishing town in the Scottish Highlands to which I owe my origins. Here Gavin leads a wonderfully complete and happy life, doing not very much at all.

Kerkelven's Gavin is similar in many ways.

Mid-August is lovely because briefly we're treated to a seeming invasion of tiny, tiny frogs, metamorphosed from, surprisingly, much bigger and fatter tadpoles. How does that happen, then, unless the very act of metamorphosis is slimming, in which case someone should bottle it? Up till their change these tadpoles have been swimming around in our ponds and trying to evade the predatory dragonfly larvae.

These cheeky, perky little frogs are not just cute, they're fun and they're everywhere, even all over where Gavin lives. I don't think he eats them, but I'm sure the snakes are having a high old time.

Ticks, and how to get rid of them

The tick is not so much an inhabitant of Kerkelven, more an inhabitant of some of its inhabitants. Mortimer gets at least one fat bloated tick every year without fail. Like attracts like, I suppose.

Your actual tick is a small, innocuous-looking mite but it

feeds by attaching itself to the soft tissue of a larger animal. It hides in the long grass waiting for a suitable host to pass then, silently, it will spring. It will then wriggle into position unseen, seeking out a warm, moist, sweaty part where it will cling on by fixing its powerful jaws into the bloodstream of its benign but innocent benefactor. Behind the ear of a large dog is apparently ideal, as is the armpit or crotch of a human. Once suitably affixed the tick then proceeds to suck the blood from its host, who will most likely be entirely ignorant of its presence until, that is, someone finds it and tries to remove it. Then all hell can break loose.

The only ways to remove a tick are carefully, or very quickly. Otherwise, if you pull or jerk them out, the body or bloodsack will come away leaving the head and legs in the screaming host, attached to the tick's ferocious jaws. This can then go septic, leading not perhaps to a horrid and painful death, but to whatever is the next worst thing.

In days gone by we could have singed it off with a half-smoked cigarette, but we don't smoke now. One folk remedy is to drench a small handkerchief in whisky and apply same to the body and head of the insect, which then supposedly gets addled with the fumes or the surfeit of alcohol and loses its grip, so the whole thing comes away in your hand. Reasonable-sounding though this may be, in my experience it doesn't work near as well as simply taking a firm grip on the fiend and giving it a sudden yank. A sharp single movement will wheek it out. This invariably causes Mortimer to emit a sudden yelp, but it works every time. And saves whisky.

A visit from five white bulls

This was a few years back. The first we heard of it was an urgent ringing of our front doorbell which, when answered, introduced us to a lean, fit, anxious-looking young man unknown to either of us but who turned out to be the son of a local farmer. Quickly, breathlessly, he described how five of his young bulls had escaped that morning. He'd spotted one in Loïc's field behind the old Dutch barn. Could we help?

Such was the agitation of our young visitor, I suspected the losing of his father's prize animals might be down to him. He was in a hurry, so the best intelligence we could get from him was that these were show bulls and that they were white. It sounded interesting.

Explaining that we'd seen nothing and that he needed Loïc's permission rather than ours, nevertheless we – my lifelong pal Robert, who was with us at the time, and me – volunteered to help in the search. Rather than pleasing this young man, though, he tried to dissuade us, explaining with a worried face that young bulls can be dangerous. I think he'd sussed at a glance that two old blokes in our condition wouldn't be of much use when matched against five bulls.

As we set off, his lack of confidence was buzzing in our brains. It seemed just possible that perhaps he knew something we didn't. By the time we'd got to the field where the bull was last sighted, Rob and I had fallen a bit behind the men from the farm – there were four of them – and though we hadn't discussed a plan, I think independently the idea had formed in both of us that maybe it would be best if we could find a safe spot from where to watch proceedings, at a distance.

Gingerly, crouched over like Red Indians in tall grass, Robert and I worked our way down the edge of the field to try to get to a corner of Loïc's field where we'd be closer to the beast at bay, but still on higher ground from where we could safely spy. We were dangerously over-successful at this and soon regretted our curiosity as, impatient and snorting, the bull popped out from behind a clump of trees at least a hundred metres west of where we'd expected him to be and, suddenly, we were the nearest to him, by far, maybe six metres away or even less.

He was indeed pure white. And agitated. I sensed rather than saw the exasperation on the four farmhand's faces as they realised that we were likely to spoil their trap. The huge bull turned to face us, his nearest threat, with what seemed likely to be burning resentment that his new-found liberty might be at risk. It was immediately evident he wasn't going to be taken without a struggle and even with half a dozen humans ranged against him this bull looked well the stronger, from where we stood.

He, meanwhile, appeared to have sussed where the weakest link was in the human chain that had surrounded him. He made to charge.

We could hear him breathing in snorts and pounding the dry earth with his front hoofs. The dry barley rustled as he turned. By God, he was a fearsome, muscular beast, white as snow, gleaming and jittery, prancing, snorting, rippling with sinews that he was ready to put to use at the slightest excuse. Staring death literally in the face, Rob and I did the only thing we could. We turned and legged it.

I knew I couldn't outrun the bull, but I did think that, just possibly, I could outrun Robert. I started to fabricate an acceptable excuse that I could pass to his widow. Neither of us paused for even a second in our headlong dash so we completely failed to see the beast lassoed and corralled by his owners, then being led meekly away. We were almost neck and neck as we rounded the corner of our house and collapsed semiconscious at our front door, much to the amusement of Marie and Isobel and the evident merriment of our children.

We never saw even a sniff of the other four bulls but later learned they were all recaptured without difficulty on the prairie, where white bulls are easy to spot. Their brief bid for freedom ended in failure. Which, we decided, while a shame was just as well.

Buzzards and night owls

It's hot. High above us in the clear summer sky four buzzards circle as the sun beats down. They look superb and clearly are having fun as they scream out their 'key, key' notes. I think they're hunting in the newly cut wheat but Marie reckons they're just doing it because they can.

Why not?

On our night walks we frequently hear through the gloom the throaty, raucous calls of the tawny owls asserting their territorial boundaries. On a clear moonlit night we're sometimes lucky enough to see one silhouetted on a high perch

above the pond or, more likely, at the instant its almost endless patience is rewarded by some small movement in the under-growth when it silently drops down from its tree on massive spread wings and swooping unseen glides in upon and scoops up its scurrying prey, whisking it off to an unspeakable end in the dark recesses of the night.

Moon over Kerkelven

The moon that lights our encounters with owls is the same orb that has been coming and going, month in and month out, over Kerkelven since time began or at least, since the moon was created at the same time as the earth, around four billion years ago.

Theories abound as to how our moon was formed but it's most likely that early in the earth's existence another would-be planet collided with it, forcing out probably several big globules of molten matter. What is now our moon wasn't flung far enough to escape on its own into space, instead it was held by earth's gravity field in more or less the orbit where we find it today. This explains why earth and moon are made of the same stuff. This collision would have been a rather dramatic event had anybody been around then to watch it. But it would have been all over, done and dusted, within about 24 hours.

Between the centre of the moon and the centre of the earth, at a point around 1,740 kilometres below the earth's crust, you'll find the earth/moon combo's centre of gravity. It is this point that moves in elliptical orbit around the sun, in what's called the terrestrial orbit.

The moon is really just a piddley bit of barren rock. But though 400 times smaller than our sun it's only one 400th (or thereabouts) of the distance from us, so the two appear about the same size, a strange cosmological coincidence indeed. Also the moon reflects brightly the sun's rays from the far side of our planet. So ancient races revered the moon as a god just as powerful and important as the sun. As we can easily look upon it and when we do it's not hard to discern something very like a human face within it, this is hardly surprising. What is surprising is that moon worship is now mostly a thing of the past, having been largely superseded by more intangible and less believable gods.

The moon rotates on its axis at roughly the same rate as it takes to revolve round the earth so, from our vantage point, we only ever see one side of it. Its position relative to the sun does change constantly, which enables us to see the dramatic waxing and waning of the moon as the sun illuminates different portions of it. Added to the constant changes of our night sky caused by the earth's slow rotation around the sun, this more rapid change makes the night sky over Kerkelven a constant source of transformation and wonder, seemingly never the same twice, its perpetual transitions really rather hard to anticipate and to follow. The price we pay for the progressively brighter skies that come with each new moon is reduced visibility of the stars. But it's well worth it, we know they'll be back soon enough and meanwhile the moonlight that washes over Kerkelven these warm summer nights converts our little corner of the universe once more into a different, brilliant world, its celestial dome sprinkled with stardust from one horizon to the other.

Charlie's twenty-first birthday party

The normal aftermath of partying: our house and front garden looked like a cyclone had hit. Survivors from the night before were staggering around, heads in hands, the grandmother of all hangovers evident in every step.

Though noon was a fading memory Charlie was still in bed, much the worse for wear. Though we hadn't yet given him his birthday present, for the time being at least he was past caring.

Back in June Charlie's friend FX (pronounced Feex and short for François-Xavier), who raises exotic pets, had been given a python for his twentieth by his friends. Not keen on slithery things, Charlie was hoping for something more practical and less slippery, like a bottle of fine malt, some exotic scent or a year's supply of DVDs. So I couldn't believe my luck on my midday amble to find a very sedate smooth snake coiled on the new wall, presumably digesting an earlier breakfast, or perhaps waiting for his lunch to come by. He made no protest as I scooped him up gently and, followed by an appreciative conga of hung-over party wrecks whom with much 'sshussshing' I gathered in my wake, I tiptoed across the garden, through the front gate and upstairs to enter the birthday boy's bedroom. There, to the accompaniment of strains of '*Joyeaux anniversaire*' sung badly out of tune behind me, I presented the sleepy, grumpy Charlie with a snake which, for at least three minutes, he seriously believed was his parents' twenty-first birthday present to him.

I'm sure both snake and I were still chuckling as I returned him to the wild of the wall, entirely none the worse for his experience. I waved him off promising that, if the opportunity arose, I'd do the same for him one day.

Parties here tend to be drawn out. Most party survivors will stay for lunch the next day – kidneys, muffins and bacon and eggs (Marie is justly popular with Joe and Charlie's friends) – and often a few will still be hanging around that evening, or into the following day.

Sticky gooey stuff on the path in the wood

We've found a curious pile of orange sticky goo in the middle of the 45-degree path. It measures a full five centimetres in diameter and looks like a doughnut. Whatever created it presumably expelled it from a circular orifice of some kind. Marie thinks it is poo. It's clearly not, as it's translucent and much too sticky, almost like the sap of a large and sappy tree.

We photographed it and measured it but can find no mention of it anywhere. I guess it's just another mystery of the field by the river.

It's been raining, three big fat slugs have formed a triangle in the middle of the steep path and are tucking into what looks like another pile of sticky stuff, but this is an obnoxious brown. I count eleven others in their immediate vicinity. I think we've disturbed the slug equivalent of a rave.

Hot August night: the big fire

At the start it seemed to be a night like any other night, but it was to change Kerkelven irrevocably and forever.

Three years ago the pig farm was still in full production, though at the time none of us realised just how severely numbered its days were. On this hot summer night Emile, the farmer, had got drunk and in a moment of madness after an argument with his son Loïc he had deliberately set fire to the hay Loïc had so painstakingly gathered and stacked in his huge Dutch barn. There must have been between 200 and 300 huge bales of hay in there, all neatly piled, above twenty tonnes of it. Even with the constant soakings of five fire engines each taking it in turn to fill their tanks from the nearby river Blavet, the blaze burned brightly all night and into the next day.

In Kerkelven Raymonde and Elodie saw the glow from their window and just for a few minutes assumed that it was us, *les*

Anglais, lighting a bonfire for some satanic celebration or other, and wondered why they hadn't been invited.

Across the valley our neighbours Renaud and Martine saw the blaze and also assumed it was *les Anglais*, celebrating Guy Fawkes' night a bit early.

I was driving back from the local airport after a meeting in Brussels and was late. The first I knew was when I passed the battery factory on the Blavet and saw a fire engine filling up. I knew some of the guys that were there and was surprised when my warm hello was met by stony faces. Then I noticed that the whole sky was on fire. I assumed the worst. I thought our house was going up in flames and raced off into the night, in a panic. When I got to Kerkelven I saw an unforgettable sight. A crowd of maybe 25 or 30 people had gathered. Most were staring in amazement at the furnace that was even then entirely engulfing the huge Dutch barn, while the firemen struggled to soak the nearby outbuildings. The shape of the barn was clearly visible, roof and all, only ablaze from side to side and top to bottom. The flames leaped so high it was a miracle that on this night and this night only there was not so much as a breath of wind, so Elodie and Raymonde's thatched roof, with ours between theirs and the fire, were all spared. Bertrand and Marie-Thérèse were both inconsolable. People I barely knew were standing disconsolate in their night attire, wringing their hands. On every lips was the same question, 'Why did he do it?'

In his stupor Emile must have thought no one would know it was him, but from our top bedroom window Marie and Charlie had seen him light the fire and had shouted in a vain attempt to stop him. Later, as the fire burned, Loïc and his brother-in-law sat round our kitchen table both in floods of tears, seeking solace in my malt collection until their loss seemed at least tolerable. I don't think we'd ever felt so close, before or since.

Next day the farm behind our house seemed a smouldering ruin, though in fact only the Dutch barn and some of the pig sheds (thankfully, on this night, empty of pigs) were destroyed. Most of the other buildings were severely singed, but sound. Of the huge Dutch barn there was nothing but cinders.

For us, this signalled the end of an era. From that moment we stopped living next door to a working farm. Never properly cleaned up, the site became a parking ground for old agricultural implements and a store for pesticides and suchlike until, some years later, Pascal bought it, probably for a song, and somehow managed to wangle planning permission to restore the old stable block into a *maison d'habitation*. A fine home it will make too.

Alien invasion

Late August is the season of especially stunning sunsets. These are the best of the Breton evenings and the slow transition between day and night is the best of times, with the huge slowly sinking sun bathing everywhere around in warm, clear air that's given an ethereal glow by our special star's daily fiery goings-down. Just before night falls the sky becomes almost cloudless and the countless colours become so rich and varied. It would be a great time for an invasion from outer space and Kerkelven, of course, would be a great place from which to begin colonising Mother Earth.

For a start it's quiet, secluded and peaceful. Anyone around would most likely be watching the sunset, so they could slip in unnoticed. They could prepare here for some time without fear of discovery except perhaps by Marie and me, and we wouldn't tell anyone. It's conveniently almost equidistant from London and Paris, two important European capitals that they'd almost certainly wish to capture early on.

He hasn't arrived yet but the Little Green Man and his buddies would be more than welcome here.

Scratching the surface

The more I see in my big field the more I realise that I've opened a very big door and, though I've done my best to record my experiences, only a fraction of its wonders have so far come tumbling out. And most of these I've probably missed or described badly. I'm still not an expert on anything, but I've learned such a lot. I've made lots and lots of mistakes, I'm sure, but putting them right will be half the fun. Most probably, my knowledge will never be complete and that's no bad thing because, for me, the joy of exploring Kerkelven is knowing that I've still got such an enormous amount to learn here.

It's not a bad place to contemplate spending more time in. There are lots of challenges, many things Marie and I could plan to do here to stop, or at least to slow, the process of gentle decline that seems likely to be our lot as the years pass.

Indeed we could get really quite ambitious. For many years I've had a dream of raising shire horses. I know nothing about them, but they've always appealed to me and since I was a boy I've had an idealised view of these great horses, perhaps bred by Disney classics and my natural tendency to wild specu-lation. I see them as huge, endlessly patient and good-natured giants, soppy and uncomplaining gentle beasts of burden.

I won't fulfil that dream, I suspect, but if we set our minds to it, there's much else that really could be possible.

We could plough up our field and plant meadow grasses and wild flowers that would attract all sorts of insects. We could create a nectar garden. We could grow our own rhubarb, gooseberries and other old-fashioned fruits. We could plan an organic herb garden, even raise belladonna and mandrake and other exotic plants. We could even lay down new hedges and surround Kerkelven with blackthorn, honeysuckle and a host of other beneficial plants. We could make a bog garden near the pond to attract more insects and therefore more food for bats and birds.

We could keep bees, who would thrive on the plants in our nectar and herb gardens. We could attract more bumblebees.

We could build bird boxes and bat boxes to further encourage some of the winged denizens of Kerkelven. If we placed them high in a southeast- or southwest-facing position, bat boxes could be used for roosting during the daytime in the summer months.

We could even make more of our log piles. Dead wood is really important to a huge range of invertebrates – including our chum the stag beetle and probably the devil's coach-horse beetle too. Apparently farmland and woodland are much tidier than they used to be, because people tidy away the dead trees and branches, and consequently many creatures are deprived of the decaying wood they depend upon. We could change that.

Many beetle species will lay their eggs in logs that are buried under the soil and the larvae will chew through the decaying wood, breaking it down still further, which provides a home for various insects from woodlice to centipedes, thus contributing to the food chain, because these beasties provide food for other insects as well as many birds and mammals.

Hedgehogs and toads might hibernate in larger woodpiles, which can also become breeding areas for mice and voles. If there are twigs as well, birds that sometimes nest close to the ground, for instance blackbirds and chaffinches, will build their nests there.

Pigs, it seems, could be coming back to Kerkelven. Marie surprised me the other day by suggesting we could keep organic pigs in a pen we'd build deep in the woods. She even claims that she would kill them, when killing has to be done, though even if that anyway were not a job for the professional slaughterman, or slaughterwoman, I rather expect the pigs might be more likely to fly first.

It seems we could even stop the hunters from pursuing their sport on our land. Youngest son Charlie, who's taking his law degree at Rennes University this year, has just confirmed with his professor that even a small landowner can put up an 'interdit à la chasse' sign. Even such as we, it seems, have the power to keep our land free from hunters, if we choose. So I might get the chance to make a tangible protest, after all.

We could also right some other wrongs

Not just compensating for our carbon footprint this, though that has to be a major consideration in any plan for our future. There are other things we could do too.

It seems that if we'd set about ballsing it up deliberately we could hardly have planned our pond in the parklands more badly. Well, planned is a bit of a euphemism, we just dug a hole, lined it with concrete and let it fill up in its own good time with water, debris and wildlife. Of course ere long it choked and now it's a pit of decaying brew with heaven knows what lurking within its recesses.

Our builder friend Kevin, who installed it and probably did have a plan of sorts for it, had hoped that a gravity feed from the pond up at our house would be enough to create a constantly circulating flow of water, but that didn't even work for three minutes – mainly because I scuppered it by removing his hosepipe from our *fontaine*, thinking he'd just idly left it there.

So now we have a unique chance to start again and this time, to get it right. Now we know more we can plan things better. Quite a range of possibilities present, but for sure it's as likely that we'll find as much pleasure in the planning as in the doing.

For that's something we've learned from this field.

Marie's email to Celia

As evidence that our excitement for the way this project is growing, I thought I'd hand over the penultimate paragraphs of this chapter to an email Marie sent at the end of August to her best friend Celia, to explain what we're up to. It went as follows:

I've been wondering what else we could put in the 'bear' garden along with the buddleia, of which there are several varieties, but we should stick with lighter-coloured flowers because they, apparently, attract more butterflies. Ours by the pool seems quite dark to me, yet is always covered in the flappy little blighters. We have to have things that don't need a lot of attention, because it's pretty inaccessible there as you know, i.e. steep and having to undertake a lot of pruning could be hazardous as well as tiring, so I thought, how about hedgerow plants that grow fairly tall, but not so tall that they offend the electricity people?

I'm thinking, things like buckthorn, blackthorn (we can give people sloe gin as Christmas presents and they'll think we really have gone hippy), hawthorn, crab apple, dog roses, sweet briar, all of which provide either berries, fruit, or both, for birds. We could plant lower growing shrubs towards the bottom of the hill. I think the wayfaring tree sounds great, not just because of its name but because it seems so pretty with its dense dome of white flowers in May and June, followed by red oval berries in September, which gradually turn dark to match the purple autumn leaves. It can tolerate dry soils and harsh winters and attracts wildlife all year round. Not sure if that slope is particularly dry, but I should think it's pretty well drained.

Apparently we should also consider planting more fruit trees – what if we cut down the pines in the graveyard and maybe bung in a few damsons, plums, or cherries? And we should scatter some shade-liking wild flower seeds in the woods.

We might have to plant some trees in the meadow – birches, for instance, to aid drainage, which I think is going to be a bit of a problem . . .

Doesn't that sound like fun? I couldn't have put it better.

There are some things more important . . .

Thus concludes my year-long tour around the field by the river. I hope you have enjoyed it as I have. And that while having fun, I hope you've learned some things too, at least that an apparently empty field may not be quite what it seems. According to the admirably informative and entertaining British television programme *QI* (which stands for quite interesting but is really utterly fascinating) the most boring place in Britain is an apparently empty field outside Ousefleet, near Scunthorpe in Lincolnshire, England.

I don't believe it. Much more likely, the people who suggested such a thing just haven't learned how to look at their field properly.

Because at least half the fun of living is in the looking. Half the fun of arriving is in the getting there. If we imagine we already know all we need to know then we'll stop looking and so miss much of what we could know and could enjoy.

I'll be forever grateful to my empty field for teaching me just this. That the best of what we could be, have, or imagine may be just close around us, waiting to be discovered.

While I'm grateful for all I've learned from the many sources that I've turned to in my search for knowledge – and I'm only too happy to acknowledge here my huge debt to them all – I've also learned that we have to take care with how we interpret what we read, for the opinions of experts are often partial and sometimes flawed. Nature continually has a capacity to surprise and we must always resist the temptation to pronounce, 'So-and-so doesn't do that. I know. I read it in a book . . .'

If it is possible to surprise us, for sure nature will find a way.

So, for me, a city dweller turned country bumpkin, I reflect on the changes in my life and think, 'Actually, it didn't turn out so bad.' Though I like to go home and will probably settle back there eventually, living outside Britain has been, I have to say, a fantastic experience and I'm delighted with where I chose to do it. Some may search for a place to lie in the sun. For me, I think it's been more important to find somewhere where I can truly live.

I'm grateful to Max, Syrus and Mortimer in particular for helping me to make this voyage of discovery and I'm grateful too to all the animals, birds and insects of Kerkelven for the fact that by looking closely at their lives I've been able to learn so much about my own and what really matters to me. They may not realise it, but they've been a real force for good with me and that's why they are the heroes of this story and no one else.

And France, my adopted second home, doesn't come too badly out of this history either. I love France. Its people have been so generous and hospitable to Marie, me and our family and friends. I wouldn't say it's the best country in the world, but that's mainly because I don't want to let down my native Scotland and I don't want the French to get even more big-headed. It is indeed a truly splendid place to come to and to live.

I don't think we ever expected our stay here to be anything other than temporary. Indeed both Marie and I often express surprise that we've stayed here so long. We've built a home here that we really love but still, in our hearts, we always think of Britain whenever we talk of home. The language is still an issue, even after all this time. We pine occasionally for the Sunday papers and both seem to miss our London friends and family more than we did.

So it wouldn't surprise me if we don't move back to the UK sometime soon, perhaps when the dogs have gone. But we've got a lot to do before then, so we'd better get on with it, for time is too short.

If we do go home, for sure we'll leave a bit of home behind us here when we go. For this place has become our home too. Of one thing I am sure. Wherever we are, we'll never leave the field.

Thanks

From the opening lines of this book it will have been evident to every reader that, though my name alone appears on the cover, I didn't create it on my own. Far from it.

I've acknowledged already in the final chapter my debt to the creatures of Kerkelven and to the people of France for their very special way of life. This account of a year in the life of a natural treasure is dedicated to them. For the record, I've changed the names of most characters and a few of the places, to protect the peace and privacy of my friends and neighbours in Brittany.

Truly, I couldn't have even attempted this project without Marie, my sounding board, gentle guide, voice of reality, chief researcher and source of strength and encouragement throughout. Other than to acknowledge how much I appreciate her commitment and enthusiastic hard work, I won't embarrass her further.

Not long after the idea had taken shape I had the great good fortune to be accepted as a new author by the literary agency Greene & Heaton and particularly by their director Antony Topping, who took my 'Field' project under his experienced wing, working closely and supportively with me and Marie until our collection of raw, rough scribblings was slowly reshaped into a meaningful, workable book. Though few bar us will appreciate it, his guiding hand is evident on every page except, perhaps, this one.

The people at Portico too have been a great strength and support right from their enthusiastic first response to the project. It was their evident, instant affection for Kerkelven and its characters that convinced me that whoever else might express interest, I should go with them. Publisher Tom Bromley threw his energy, experience and affinity for detail into making this book just as good as it could be. I also must record thanks to editor Malcolm Croft, copy editor Ian Allen and designer Gemma Wilson for their professional care and attention. The wonderful illustrations of Juliet Percival add the final touch.

I want also to record special appreciation for all those who provide information and in one way or another make it freely and easily accessible to the general public, so that writers like me may draw upon and borrow from it so we can seem knowledgeable and smart. For their helpful sharing I should heap praise upon a range of 'good causes' whose published information, websites, helplines and suchlike were well used by Marie and me throughout the writing and editing processes. In particular, thanks to the UK Royal Society for the Protection of Birds (RSPB), to Birdlife International and to Plantlife International in the UK.

Finally, I must say a big 'thanks' to Joe and Charlie for putting up with us for so long and to Celia, Jess, Robert and Isobel with all their children too for coming here often, for giving me so many anecdotes and for helping to make Kerkelven such a great place to be.

I haven't mentioned Mortimer, Max and Syrus not because I'm not extremely grateful to them but simply because they're not likely to be any more interested in this section than they have been in the rest of my account, even though they're the true stars of it. But next dinnertime I will heap their bowls just a bit higher in unspoken appreciation, which for sure will set their tails wagging. As the human equivalent of this is the only reaction I aspire to generate from readers and from the folks listed above, the dogs and I will be more than happy with that.

Ken Burnett
Kerkelven, July 2008

The Field by the River
COMPETITION

WIN a Nikon D80 Digital SLR camera!

Capture stunning wildlife photographs with a fabulous top-of-the-range **Nikon D80 SLR Digital Camera**, courtesy of Portico Books.

There are two prizes available. Winners will be drawn at random on 1st October 2008 and 1st February 2009. All entries must be received before these dates.

To enter this free prize draw, go to www.porticobooks.co.uk

PORTICO

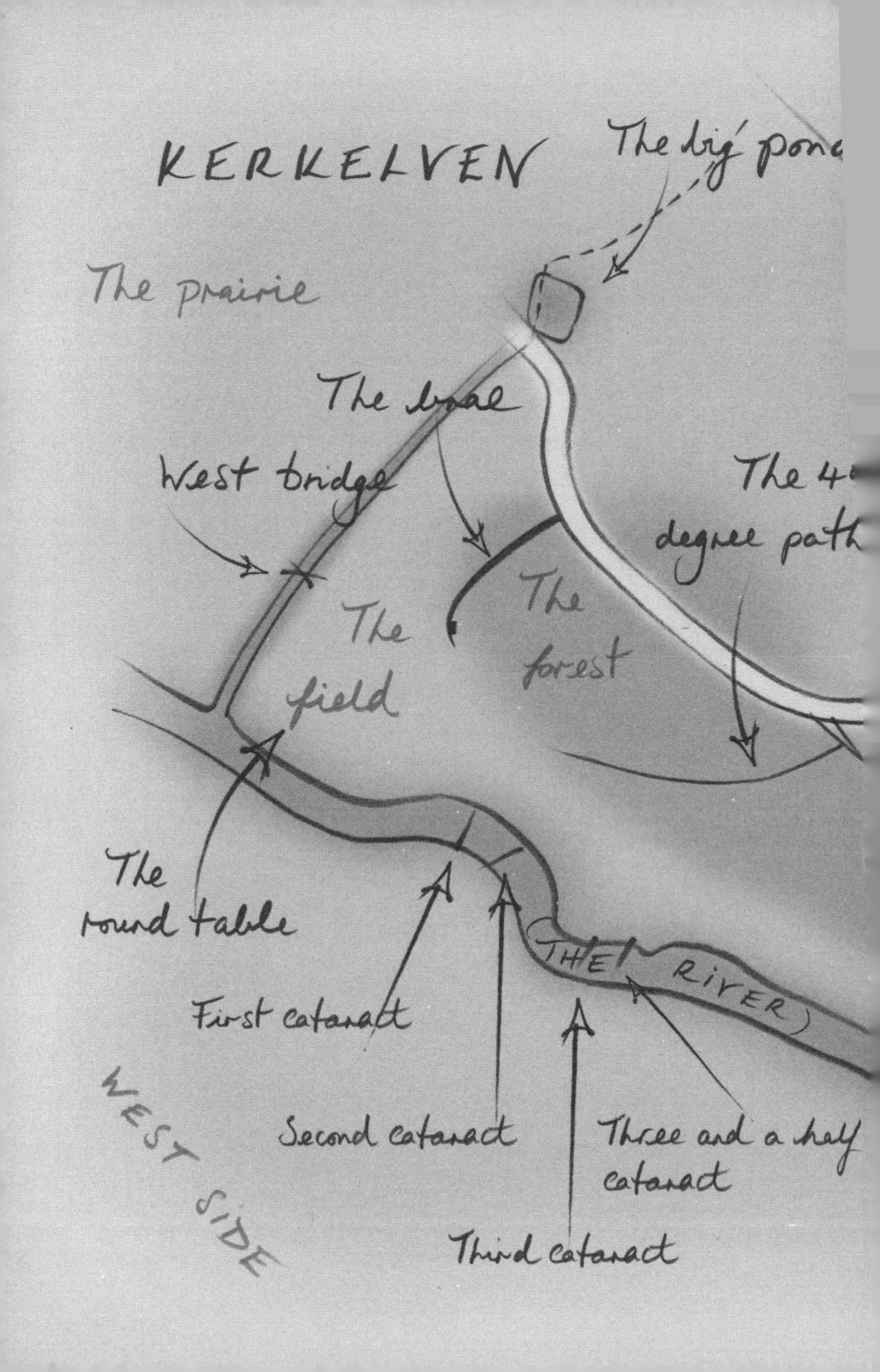

KERKELVEN

The big pond

The prairie

The line

West bridge

The field

The forest

The 45 degree path

The round table

First cataract

Second cataract

Third cataract

Three and a half cataract

THE RIVER

WEST SIDE